T0329748

COMPASSIONATE CAPITALISM

Business and Community in Medieval England

Catherine Casson, Mark Casson,
John S. Lee and Katie Phillips

BRISTOL
UNIVERSITY
PRESS

First published in Great Britain in 2020 by

Bristol University Press
University of Bristol
1-9 Old Park Hill
Bristol
BS2 8BB
UK
t: +44 (0)117 954 5940
www.bristoluniversitypress.co.uk

North America office:
Bristol University Press
c/o The University of Chicago Press
1427 East 60th Street
Chicago, IL 60637, USA
t: +1 773 702 7700
f: +1 773-702-9756
sales@press.uchicago.edu
www.press.uchicago.edu

© Bristol University Press 2020

British Library Cataloguing in Publication Data
A catalogue record for this book is available from the British Library

Library of Congress Cataloging-in-Publication Data
A catalog record for this book has been requested

ISBN 978-1-5292-0925-9 hardcover
ISBN 978-1-5292-0927-3 ePub
ISBN 978-1-5292-0926-6 ePdf

Cover design by blu inc.
Front cover image: extract from John Hamond's map of Cambridge, 1592 (Courtesy of the Cambridgeshire Collection, Cambridge Central Library)
Printed and bound in Great Britain by CPI Group (UK) Ltd, Croydon, CR0 4YY
Bristol University Press uses environmentally responsible print partners

Contents

Figures and Tables

Figures

Tables

Family Trees

Abbreviations

B	Baker, Thomas and John. E. B. Mayor (eds), *History of the College of St. John the Evangelist, Cambridge* (2 vols) (Cambridge, 1869)
BNM	Gray, J. Milner, *Biographical Notes on the Mayors of Cambridge* (Reprinted from *The Cambridge Chronicle*, 1922), pp 1–11
BR	Brundage, James A., 'The Cambridge Faculty of Canon Law and the Ecclesiastical Courts of Ely', *Medieval Cambridge: Essays on the Pre-Reformation University* ed. Patrick Zutshi (Woodbridge, 1993), pp 21–46
BRUC	Emden, A. B., *Biographical Dictionary of the University of Cambridge to 1500* (Cambridge, 1963)
BT	Bateson, Mary (ed.), *Cambridge Guild Records* (London, 1903)
C	Cooper, Charles Henry, *Annals of Cambridge, I* (5 vols) (Cambridge, 1842)
CC	Cazel, Fred A. and Annarie P. Cazel (eds), *Rolls of the Fifteenth of the Ninth Year of the Reign of Henry III for Cambridgeshire, Lincolnshire and Wiltshire and Rolls of the Fortieth of the Seventeenth Year of the Reign of Henry III for Kent* (London, 1983)
CCR	*Calendar of Close Rolls* (London, 1892–1972)
CPR	*Calendar of Patent Rolls* (London, 1835–1986)
EB	Stokes, H. P., *The Esquire Bedells of the University of Cambridge from the Thirteenth Century to the Twentieth Century* (Cambridge, 1911)

EJ I	Rigg, J. M. (ed.), *Calendar of the Plea Rolls of the Exchequer of the Jews, I: Henry III, 1218–1272* (6 vols), (London, 1905)
EJ II	Rigg, J. M. (ed.), *Calendar of the Plea Rolls of the Exchequer of the Jews, II: Edward I, 1273–5* (6 vols) (Edinburgh, 1910)
EJ III	Jenkinson, H. (ed.), *Calendar of the Plea Rolls of the Exchequer of the Jews, III: Edward I, 1275–7* (6 vols) (London, 1925)
EJ IV	Richardson, H. G. (ed.), *Calendar of the Plea Rolls of the Exchequer of the Jews, IV: Henry III, 1272; Edward I, 1275–1277* (6 vols) (London, 1972)
EJ V	Cohen, S. (ed.), *Plea Rolls of the Exchequer of the Jews, V: Edward I, 1277–9* (6 vols) (London, 1992)
EJ VI	Brand, P. (ed.), *Plea Rolls of the Exchequer of the Jews, VI: Edward I, 1279–81* (6 vols) (London, 2005)
F	Faber, T. E., *An Intimate History of the Parish of St Clement* (Cambridge, 2006) *Note*: many of the original documents cited in this study are now in Downing College Library
FC	Farrer, William, *Feudal Cambridgeshire* (Cambridge, 1920)
G	Goddman, A. W., *A Little History of St. Botolph's, Cambridge* (Cambridge, 1922)
J	Stokes, H. P., *Studies in Anglo-Jewish History* (Edinburgh, 1913)
LB	Clark, John Willis (ed.), *Liber Memorandum Ecclesie de Bernewelle* (Cambridge, 1907)
M	Maitland, Frederic William, *Township and Borough* (Cambridge, 1898)
MD	Stevenson, W. H., *Calendar of Merton Deeds for Cambridgeshire* (Merton College Library, n.d.)
MH	Stokes, H. P., *The Medieval Hostels of the University of Cambridge* (Cambridge, 1924)

MR	Miller, Edward, 'Baldwin Blancgernun and His Family: Early Benefactors of the Hospital of St. John the Evangelist in Cambridge', *The Eagle* 53 (234) (1948): 73–9
OBG	Stokes, H. P., *Outside the Barnwell Gate* (Cambridge, 1908)
ODNB	Cannadine, David (ed.), *Oxford Dictionary of National Biography* (Oxford, 2004), available at https://www.oxforddnb.com/ (accessed 1 July 2018)
OED	Oxford English Dictionary Online, available at www.oed.com (accessed 12 August 2019)
OTG	Stokes, H. P., *Outside the Trumpington Gates before Peterhouse Was Founded* (Cambridge, 1915)
PDC	Hunter, Joseph (ed.), *Fines, Sive, Pedes Finium: AD 1195–1214, I: Bedfordshire, Berkshire, Buckinghamshire, Cambridgeshire and Cornwall* (2 vols, 1835–44) (London, 1835)
PDH	Turner, G. J., *A Calendar of the Feet of Fines Relating to the County of Huntingdon Levied in the King's Court from the Fifth Year of Richard I to the End of the Reign of Elizabeth, 1194–1603* (Cambridge, 1913)
PDR	Rye, Walter, *Pedes Finium or Fines Relating to the County of Cambridge, Levied in the King's Court from the Seventh Year of the Reign of Richard I to the End of the Reign of Richard III* (Cambridge, 1891)
PR	*Pipe Rolls*, 98 vols (London, 1884–2016), especially the published rolls for the years 1130–1224, 1230 and 1242, vols 1–9, 11–19, 21–58, 50, 52–8, 60, 62, 64, 66, 68, 73, 75, 77, 80, 85, 86, 89, 91, 93, 94, 95, 98
PRO	Public Record Office, *Lists and Indexes: Lists of Sheriffs for England and Wales from the Earliest Times to AD 1831* (London, 1898)
S	Stevenson, W. H., *Calendar of Merton Deeds for Cambridgeshire* (Merton College Library, n.d.)
SP	Gray, J. M., *The School of Pythagoras (Merton Hall)* (Cambridge, 1932)

StJ	Underwood, Malcolm (ed.), *Cartulary of the Hospital of St. John the Evangelist* (Cambridge, 2008)
StR	Gray, Arthur, *The Priory of St. Radegund* (Cambridge, 1898)
T	Turner, Ralph V., *The English Judiciary in the Age of Glanvill and Bracton, c.1176–1239* (Cambridge, 1985)
TNA	The National Archives, London
VCH 1 Bedford	Doubleday, H. A. (ed.), *The Victoria History of the County of Bedford, I* (3 vols) (London, 1904)
VCH 1 Huntingdon	Page, William (ed.), *The Victoria History of the County of Huntingdon, I* (3 vols) (London, 1926)
VCH 1 Middlesex	Page, William (ed.), *The Victoria History of the County of Middlesex, I* (11 vols) (London, 1911)
VCH 2	Salzman, L. F. (ed.), *A History of the County of Cambridge and the Isle of Ely, II, Victoria History of the Counties of England* (10 vols) (London, 1948)
VCH 2 Essex	Page, William and J. Horace Round (eds), *The Victoria History of the County of Essex, II* (11 vols) (London, 1907)
VCH 2 Huntingdon	Page, William (ed.), *The Victoria History of the County of Huntingdon, II* (3 vols) (London, 1932)
VCH2 Lincs	Page, William (ed.), *A History of the County of Lincoln: II* (1 vol.) (London, 1906)
VCH 2 Oxon	Page, William (eds.), *The Victoria History of the County of Oxfordshire, II* (17 vols) (London, 1907)
VCH 2 Warwick	Page, William (ed.), *The Victoria History of the County of Warwickshire, II* (4 vols) (London, 1908)
VCH 3	Roach, J. P. C. (ed.), *A History of the County of Cambridge and the Isle of Ely, III: The City and University of Cambridge, Victoria History of the Counties of England* (10 vols) (London, 1959)
VCH 4 Bucks	Page, William (ed.), *The Victoria History of the County of Buckinghamshire, IV* (4 vols) (London, 1927)
VCH 4 Cambs	Pugh, R. B. (ed.), *The Victoria History of the County of Cambridgeshire, IV* (4 vols) (London, 1953)

VCH 4 Herts	Page, William (ed.), *The Victoria History of the County of Hertfordshire, IV* (4 vols) (London, 1914)
VCH 5 Cambs	Elrington, C. R. (ed.), *The Victoria History of the County of Cambridgeshire, V* (10 vols) (London, 1973)
VCH 6 Cambs	Wright, A. P. M. (ed.), *The Victoria History of the County of Cambridgeshire, VI* (10 vols) (London, 1978)
VCH 8 Cambs	Wright, A. P. M. (ed.), *The Victoria History of the County of Cambridgeshire, VIII* (10 vols) (London, 1982)
VCH 9 Cambs	Wright, A. P. M. (ed.), *The Victoria History of the County of Cambridgeshire, IX* (10 vols) (London, 1989)
VCH 17 Staffs	Greenslade, M. W. (ed.), *The Victoria History of the County of Staffordshire, XVII* (20 vols) (London, 1989)
VLAE	Feltoe, C. L. and Ellis H. Minns (eds), *Vetus Liber Archdiaconi Eliensis* (Cambridge, 1917)
W	Hall, Catherine P. and J. R. Ravensdale (eds), *The West Fields of Cambridge* (Cambridge, 1976)

Notes on the Authors

Catherine Casson is Lecturer in Enterprise at Alliance Manchester Business School, University of Manchester, and a member of the Centre for Economic Cultures, University of Manchester. Her publications include a co-authored book with Mark Casson, *The Entrepreneur in History: From Medieval Merchant to Modern Business Leader* (Basingstoke, 2013), and articles in *Urban History, Business History Review, Business History* and the *Economic History Review*.

Mark Casson FBA is Professor of Economics at the University of Reading and Director of the Centre for Institutions and Economic History. He has published in *Economic History Review, Explorations in Economic History, Business History Review, Business History, Economic Journal* and other leading journals. He is the co-author (with Catherine Casson) of *The Entrepreneur in History* (Basingstoke, 2013) and co-editor (with Nigar Hashimzade) of *Large Databases in Economic History* (Abingdon, 2013).

John S. Lee is Research Associate at the Centre for Medieval Studies, University of York. He has an MA in Medieval History from the University of Durham and a PhD in History from the University of Cambridge. He teaches for the Centre for Lifelong Learning at the University of York. He has published the monographs *The Medieval Clothier* (Woodbridge, 2018) and *Cambridge and Its Economic Region, 1450–1560* (Hatfield, 2005). He is co-editor, with Christian Steer, of *Commemoration in Medieval Cambridge* (Woodbridge, 2018). Book chapters include 'Crises in the Late Medieval English Cloth Trade', in A. T. Brown, Andy Burn and Rob Doherty, *Crises in Economic and Social History: A Comparative Perspective* (Woodbridge, 2015). He has also published articles in *Urban History, Economic History Review, The Local Historian, Yorkshire Archaeological Journal* and other journals, including 'Decline and Growth in the Late Medieval Fenland: The Examples of Outwell and Upwell', *Proceedings of the Cambridge Antiquarian Society* 104 (2015). He has recently prepared a chapter, 'Trinity in the Town', for a forthcoming multi-volume history of Trinity College, Cambridge.

Katie Phillips completed her PhD, 'The Leper and the King: The Patronage and Perception of Lepers and Leprosy by King Henry III of England and King Louis IX of France', at the University of Reading, funded by the Arts and Humanities Research Council. This work follows on from the dissertation produced for her MA(Res), an edited version of which has been published as 'The Hospital of St Mary Magdalene – The Leper-House at Reading Abbey', *Berkshire Archaeological Journal* 81 (2013). Further publications include 'Saint Louis, Saint Francis and the Leprous Monk at Royaumont', *The Reading Medievalist* 2 (2015), and 'Devotion by Donation: the Alms-Giving and Religious Foundations of Henry III', *Reading Medieval Studies* 43 (2017).

Preface and Acknowledgements

This book is a team effort. One of the authors is interested in the history of English towns; another in the history of the Cambridge region; a third in the history of religious institutions and their royal patrons; and the fourth in the use of statistical methods in economic history. They were colleagues and friends before they began working on this book.

One of the team noticed a pair of handsome leather-bound books on the shelves beside them when studying in the Bodleian Library one day about four years ago. They had found the *Rotuli Hundredorum*: 1,800 pages of statistical information relating to property rents. These rolls, better known as the Hundred Rolls, were prepared c.1279 for King Edward I. A printed edition was published by the Record Commission in 1818, using the original medieval Latin, in a special typeface designed to replicate the abbreviated script of medieval scribes. It is this edition, shelved in the Bodleian, that has formed the basis for most (though not all) subsequent research on property holding at that time.

The Hundred Rolls are well known and often cited. Their place in the development of royal administration has been thoroughly examined. They have been used to analyse manorial organisation, feudal landholding, population and family structure, and to inform local and family histories. But their numerous statistics of property rents have rarely been analysed in a systematic way. The distinguished legal historian Frederic Maitland pioneered statistical analysis of the Hundred Rolls in the appendix to his book *Township and Borough*, published in 1898. This book focused on the early history of towns and the fields that surrounded them. At the time he wrote, however, correlation analysis was in its infancy, and he was therefore unable to discover all the fascinating patterns hidden within this data.

Maitland chose to study Cambridge. The obvious explanation is that he was a Cambridge graduate and a professor there. There is another possible reason for his choice, however. The geographical coverage of the rolls is incomplete, and Cambridge has better coverage than almost all other towns of similar size in England. Good coverage, combined with the opportunity to build on Maitland's work, made Cambridge the obvious choice for this study of medieval property.

Cambridge is, of course, a university town, but the university was in its infancy at the time the Hundred Rolls were compiled. The university had a chancellor and some administrative staff, but the college system was not yet developed. Many students lived in hostels, and those who were members of religious orders often lived in accommodation provided for them by their order. Cambridge was still, first and foremost, an agricultural trading centre and a county town; in this respect, at least, it was similar to many other medium-size towns in England at that time.

Cambridge, however, has been misunderstood. In the early 20th century its history was extensively studied by members of the Cambridge Antiquarian Society and its predecessor organizations, including distinguished scholars such as Gray and Stokes. These scholars, like Maitland, were unaware that the coverage of Cambridge by the Record Commission was incomplete. The first and last rolls were included by the Commission, giving an impression of completeness, but the middle roll was omitted. This additional roll did not come to light until quite recently. As a result, many of the previous judgements made about medieval Cambridge were wrong. It was bigger than previously believed, it extended further east and it contained many more professional people. Activities linked to the nascent university were centred not so much around the present site of Trinity College and King's College as around the present sites of Emmanuel, Christ's and Sidney Sussex.

This book not only reinterprets the history of Cambridge but provides a complete scholarly edition of the Cambridge Rolls on which it is based. The rolls have been transcribed and translated into English from the originals in The National Archives and the transcriptions compared with the Record Commission Latin edition. They provide a complete edition on which future scholarship can build. This new edition of the rolls by the authors has also been published by Bristol University Press. Entitled *Business and Community in Medieval England: The Cambridge Hundred Rolls Source Volume* it is available as a companion volume to this book.

The rolls alone are not sufficient for our purpose, however. Background information on the property owners who appear in the Hundred Rolls is also required. Civic records do not exist for 1279 or earlier; apart from the borough's royal charters, the earliest usable records are the Bede Rolls commencing in 1315. Numerous relevant royal records exist, however, and some episcopal records too. Many of these have been used by earlier writers on Cambridge, who laboriously selected from documents with regional or national coverage items relating to Cambridge. We have followed a similar procedure, but with two important differences. First, thanks to the efforts of many scholars over the past one hundred years, published transcripts of many relevant sources (e.g. Pipe Rolls) have become available. Secondly, modern information technology can be used to organize our information. All the excerpts we have identified were translated into English, entered into one enormous Word folder and then systematically searched, using different variants of family names, to select and collate information at the individual level. A selection of this original material is presented in this book. This provides a richer context for the study of the rolls and leads to a reappraisal of Cambridge society in the 13th century.

We have incurred debts to many people in the writing of this book. Helpful feedback on the book was provided in the course of presentations at the International Medieval Congress, the Economic History Society, Manchester Medieval Society and the Ranulf Higden Society. Colleagues at Alliance Manchester Business School and the Department of History, University of Manchester, have followed the progress of the research, including Georg Christ, Peter Gatrell, Lesley Gilchrist, Elisa Harrocks, Joseph Lampel, Maria Nedeva, Paul Oldfield, Philipp Roëssner, Steve Rigby and Bruce Tether. Adrian Bell, James Davis, Paul Edwards, Richard Goddard, Richard Holt, Rosemary Horrox, Paul Lewis, Mark Ormrod, Nick Mayhew, William Purkis, Sarah Rees Jones and Stan Siebert provided encouragement during the shaping of the project. Dean Irwin and Robert Swanson provided advice on Jewish history and monastic history. Janet Casson performed an invaluable proof-reading service.

We would also like to thank Professor Richard Smith of the University of Cambridge for providing access to the Howell papers, Roger Lovatt, archivist of Peterhouse, the staff of the Bodleian Library reading rooms, Cambridge University Library, the Cambridge Collection in Cambridge Public Library, the Cambridgeshire Archives, the Western Manuscripts reading room at the British Library, The National Archives and the archivist and library staff of Merton College, Oxford.

1

Introduction

1.1 The purpose of this book

The 'future of capitalism' emerged at the beginning of the new millennium as an important topic of political debate – a debate recently intensified by the banking crisis of 2007.[1] Discontent with capitalism has been reinforced by rising income inequalities and job insecurity and has led to increasing populism and political instability reminiscent of the 1930s.[2]

There are, however, different varieties of capitalism.[3] It is generally agreed that modern capitalism emerged from the decline of feudalism.[4] This was a lengthy process, and historians disagree about the most critical stages in the emergence of capitalism and their timing. For many historians the key turning point was the Industrial Revolution, commencing c.1760, or the Agricultural Revolution and the 'Glorious Revolution' of 1689 that preceded it.[5] In England, however, the market system was well established by the Elizabethan period of 1558 to 1603. Weber and Tawney dated the emergence of capitalism even earlier, to the start of the Reformation in c.1520, while Schumpeter dated it to the spread of international merchant banking, c.1400.[6]

Evidence clearly indicates, however, that an international network of market towns had developed throughout much of Western Europe by c.1300. Markets are an indispensable component of the capitalist system, and so the origins of capitalism may be found at about this time. There was undoubtedly a Commercial Revolution in England in the period 1100–1350, which involved the emergence of organized markets for agricultural commodities and artisan production.[7] However, there remain outstanding questions about whether markets in land operated in tandem with markets in manufactured and agricultural goods.

Entrepreneurs and firms have been credited with playing an important role in those markets from 1600 onwards.[8] Medieval businesses were generally structured as a single trader or as a partnership. While some medieval businesspeople did exhibit the entrepreneurial characteristics of risk, innovation and judgement, the terminology of 'entrepreneur' has rarely been used in relation to the medieval period.[9] Those differences in business structures and terminology, coupled with the relevance absence of specific business records, have often resulted in the exclusion of the Middle Ages from studies of the history of capitalism. However, as this book will demonstrate, medieval business activity can be traced through a range of sources, beyond businesses, and the presence of entrepreneurs and family business units discerned.

Recent years have seen an increased scepticism regarding the stability and impacts of capitalism, especially regarding the potential social inequalities that can arise from it.[10] It has been suggested that the medieval period exemplifies a time when the capitalist system demanded greater accountability from entrepreneurs and businesses and achieved greater balance between profit and environmental and social responsibility.[11]

This book investigates the importance of urban business activity during the Commercial Revolution, paying particular attention to the sophistication of the urban property market. It investigates the role played by the family as a business unit in the medieval town, and the extent to which involvement in the property market was connected to other strands of commercial or professional activity. The acquisition of property had the potential to disrupt existing social hierarchies. 'New wealth', represented by families with diverse commercial and business activities, began to invest profits from those activities in property, displacing 'old wealth', namely families for whom ownership and control of land through inheritance had provided social status and influence. Property acquisition also had the potential to lead to wider social tensions, with some becoming rich through capital accumulation while others became poor because they lacked the necessary business skills. The book examines whether successful entrepreneurs and families directed income from property towards local philanthropy in order to maintain local services and enhance existing infrastructure for the wider community.

Cambridge is the focus of this book for three reasons. First, it possesses detailed documentary evidence of the urban property market during the 13th century in the form of the Cambridge Hundred Rolls, described in more detail in section 1.9. Secondly, a new portion of the Cambridge Hundred Roll has been discovered by the authors and is shown here for the first time. Maitland presented material from the Cambridge Hundred Rolls as an appendix to his study of the feudal ownership of land.[12]

However, he did not have access to the recently discovered roll or to the technique of regression analysis to examine rent levels. Thirdly, the urban history of Cambridge during the 13th and 14th centuries has received less attention than subsequent periods. Lee, Zutshi and others have demonstrated how the foundation of colleges impacted on Cambridge's topography from c.1400 onwards.[13] Yet a relative lack of archaeological evidence, coupled with Maitland's focus on agricultural rather than urban areas, has limited our knowledge of the topography of the town before the development of the university. Lee has shown the important trading relationship between Cambridge and its urban hinterland for the period 1450–1560.[14] However, less is known about the connection between the hinterland and Cambridge's prosperity in the 13th and 14th centuries. Rubin examined the activities of the Hospital of St John the Evangelist during the period 1200–1500, but there remains the potential to investigate local philanthropy directed through additional institutions.[15]

1.2 The commercial revolution in medieval England

England in the late 13th century had a dynamic economy, experiencing a period of commercial growth that was as significant as the later Industrial Revolution.[16] Features of this commercial boom included urbanization, the development of new institutions, improvements in transport infrastructure and successful performance in national and international trade. Towns became increasingly important as centralized locations in which merchants could conduct trade in agricultural produce and coordinate the sourcing of exports and the distribution of imports.[17] Central government encouraged consumer confidence through the maintenance of a strong currency, the provision of standard weights and measures and the close regulation of key export commodities such as cloth and wool and the basic necessities of bread and ale. In several locations the Crown delegated many responsibilities for the regulation of trade to local government, in return for an annual payment and the right to resume direct control if the town was poorly governed. Written records were created to document the activities of these institutions and, in some cases, the transactions by the townspeople. Improvements in water management and bridge-building aided transportation, facilitating connections along the inland trade routes of roads and rivers, as well as connections between inland market centres and seaports. The concentration of trade in towns, the effective regulation of markets and improved communications all provided motivations to settle in towns and to invest in property there.

Provision for religion and welfare, as well as trade, was important to townspeople. Local monastic institutions and hospitals provided access to education and charitable support, which improved the productivity of the workforce and supported those unable to earn a living for themselves. The proliferation of parish churches within a town contributed to community cohesion and increased the social capital available to townspeople. Involvement in religious activities also enhanced the reputation of the townspeople for godliness and good behaviour, further enhancing the attractiveness of the town to visiting merchants.

Although the market system penetrated the rural economy, much of the rural population remained under feudal obligations of a customary nature and could not freely dispose of their property without the explicit or tacit consent of their lord. Their urban counterparts, by contrast, owed mainly monetary obligations, often of a fairly nominal size, and as freeholders could buy, sell and bequeath property without the permission of their lords.

While urban and economic historians have explored the development of commodity markets and local trade during this period of commercialization, the role of the property market has been relatively under-researched. This book seeks to increase our understanding of the role of property in medieval towns by examining the operation of the property market in Cambridge during the 13th century, and exploring its resilience to the challenges of the 14th and 15th centuries. The book shows the importance of the property market to both the urban economy and the urban community. 'Property hotspots' in medieval Cambridge are identified from local concentrations of properties paying premium rents. The use of property as an asset by individuals, families and institutions is examined, and property owners' strategies for the acquisition and disposal of their assets is described and evaluated.

Economic expansion during the 13th century was not based on a consumer-driven economy and the concept of individualistic capitalism. The range of consumer goods produced was very limited, with houses being sparsely furnished and the range of 'chattels' handed down comparatively small. Modern individualism would have been considered incompatible with the religious teachings of the time. Family bonds were strong and community loyalty was intense. Economic winners showed compassion for losers, rather than contempt. Successful entrepreneurs used their new-found wealth to support the communities in their place of birth and their place of work. Profits from trade were reinvested in property, and property was then given to charities so that the rental income could fund good works, including infrastructure, healthcare and the spiritual needs of the community. Improved economic performance from these investments boosted the value of property, making gifts of property even more significant in transferring wealth not only in and between families but also between entrepreneurs and the wider community.

1.3 Structure of the book

This chapter sets out the key research questions addressed in the book. These concern the role of English towns in the commercial revolution that was under way in the 13th century. There is a particular focus on the medieval property market and on the citizens who were active in that market. The chapter reviews previous literature and explains the choice of Cambridge as a case study. This choice is largely dictated by a unique source of information, namely the Cambridge Hundred Rolls, which are also described in this chapter. The Hundred Rolls date to 1279, but the origins of the town were much earlier. The early history of the town is set out, so that the context of the Hundred Rolls can be fully understood.

The remaining chapters are structured as follows. Chapters 2–4 present new material on the history of Cambridge, describing both the economy and the social fabric of the town at the time of the Hundred Rolls. There is a lot of important material to present and so these chapters are all very detailed. Chapters 5–7 are more thematic, focusing on the economic environment of the town, the role of its leading families and the long-term legacy of the events recorded in the Hundred Rolls. These chapters place the study of Cambridge within the wider context of the historiography of English towns. Chapter 8 summarizes the conclusions and considers their implications for future research.

Chapter 2 investigates the significance of the property market in medieval Cambridge. It considers how far the property market at this time anticipated the urban property markets of today. Detailed information on the Cambridge property market is provided in the Hundred Rolls. A unique feature of the rolls, compared with other sources such as rentals, is that they record all the rents paid on a property and not just the rent paid to one particular lord, such as the king or local lay lord. The rolls show that many properties paid multiple rents. With full information on each of these rents it possible to analyse separately the total rent paid and the various components of this rent going to individual lords. Chapter 2 introduces the statistical methods required to address these issues and reports the results obtained by applying them.

Chapter 3 analyses the economic topography of the town, building on the results presented in Chapter 2. It investigates how far occupations were specialized in different part of the town. It constructs profiles of all the

Cambridge parishes, showing how many properties were located in each, how much rent those properties paid, to whom they paid it, who held the properties and in some cases their occupation too. It is also possible to chart the spatial distribution of occupational names. Because of the discovery of the missing roll, it is possible for the first time to provide a definitive account of all the parishes. This corrects a bias in previous topographical accounts, which have over-emphasized the north and west of the town at the expense of the south and east.

Chapter 4 exploits another unique feature of the Hundred Rolls, namely that it provides a history of the ownership of each property. Building on this information, and other sources, such as royal records, it presents biographies of leading Cambridge property-owning families. This chapter will be of particular interest to local historians of Cambridge. The unprecedented amount of biographical information now available, and the ability to synthesize it using digital technology, makes this chapter the longest in the book.

Chapter 5 is the first of the three thematic chapters. Using a comparative methodology, it examines the successes and failures of family dynasties using the biographies presented in Chapter 4. It considers the factors that contributed to the survival and success of the leading families and to the decline of others. It identifies the crucial role of entrepreneurs in founding and sustaining the fortunes of leading families. It highlights the importance of the well-known distinction between old aristocratic wealth and new mercantile wealth and refines this approach by showing how the redistribution of income within the family, coupled with a strategic approach to marriage, enabled some families based on old wealth to obtain a new lease of life.

In order to understand the development of the town of Cambridge and its economy it is also necessary to consider its position in the agricultural hinterland and its relation to other local markets. For the discussion of those topics, the source base is extended to include quantitative material relating to those locations. The use of the additional sources in those contexts was also relevant as, while some had been consulted by previous scholars, notably Stokes, they had not had access to econometric techniques with which to analyse them. Chapter 6 therefore examines the economic environment of the town. It considers Cambridge's position relative to other leading towns nearby, such as Ely, Bury St Edmunds, King's Lynn, Huntingdon and St Ives. It examines the road and river infrastructure that connected Cambridge to its hinterland. Once again new information is brought to bear on the subject, in this case the account rolls of the Merton manor in Cambridge, previously owned by one of the leading families mentioned earlier. This information is combined with existing information on local charters for market and fairs to investigate markets in the Cambridge area. The chapter demonstrates the dominance of Cambridge market in the local economy; the strength of this market, combined with the town's control of the export-oriented river trade, assured its leading position in local trade.

Chapter 7 connects the book to work on the subsequent history of Cambridge, including that on the development of the university. It considers to what extent trends identified in the Hundred Rolls continued into the 14th century. Depopulation caused by the Black Death might have been expected to have depressed Cambridge's property market and wider agricultural economy. However, Cambridge remained more buoyant than many other towns and adjusted to the decline in its agricultural trade after the Black Death by developing its service sector, linked to university education. The role of family dynasties remained significant, but the period was characterized by the growth of three key institutions – the borough corporation, the guilds and the colleges. College property holdings increased, driven by increasing student numbers, and the colleges gradually obtained rights to the meadows adjoining the river to the west of the town. The foundation of King's College transformed the street plan in the west of Cambridge, obliterating many ancient streets and buildings, but providing new economic opportunities to supply the academic community.

Chapter 8 summarizes the main findings and considers their implications for future research. The scope for undertaking similar studies of other English towns is constrained by the fact that Cambridge has the most detailed and comprehensive coverage of any town in the Hundred Rolls, so that direct replication of this study may not be possible. There are, however, other towns with excellent records of a different type. While some of these have already been studied in detail, others have not. Furthermore, most of those that have received attention have not been studied using modern databases and statistical techniques.

1.4 Context of the medieval property market

The Crown operated as a landlord in the medieval urban property market, in its role as owner of the land on which property was constructed. The rent on urban property due to the Crown was usually known as landgable, hawgable or some similar name, and was initially collected by a royal official on behalf of the Crown.

The origins of landgable are obscure, but it appears to have represented a payment made by a town resident to the king or a local lord in lieu of labour or military service.[18] In the time of Edward the Confessor and Domesday it was levied on strips of land, but it was later levied on houses too. In some locations the burgess would hold a residential plot within the borough and an agricultural plot outside, making an annual payment to discharge the obligations for both that was collected from the plot within the walls. As time passed the original plots on which landgable was set could be merged or subdivided. In some cases the original owner might retain responsibility for landgable payments even after the property was sold.[19] As a result of mergers, subdivisions and changes in ownership, it could become increasingly difficult for authorities to allocate responsibility for landgable payments. Plots escheated (returned) to the rent-recipient (e.g. the lord) if rent was not paid.

In some towns, such as Hull, the king remained the main landlord.[20] However, in the course of the 13th century many towns, including Cambridge, were granted a degree of autonomy over their affairs and were permitted to have their own local officials, elected and appointed by the townspeople. The conditions of this autonomy were that the town had to be well governed and that an annual payment, known as the fee-farm, was made to the Crown. In such circumstances the collection of landgable was usually transferred from the royal official to the local administrators, such as the mayor and bailiffs, and was integrated into the overall farm payment.

The king was not the only great lord who held large amounts of property in towns. Lay lords held considerable land as well. Following the Norman Conquest, King William allocated large tracts of land to his relatives and to his favourite knights, and their descendants still held considerable property in the 13th century. Each person's portfolio comprised estates distributed across the country, possibly to prevent any one of them from acquiring a regional power base that might constrain the king's authority. This was certainly true in the south and east; in the north and west, and especially on the borders with Scotland and Wales, defensive considerations seem to have favoured a greater concentration of lands. Some local lords had a personal interest in the towns where they held property, and perhaps where they acted as a local earl or sheriff, or as residents of a nearby estate, but others were absentee landlords.

The development of a professional civil service during the late 12th and early 13th centuries created an elite of royal officials. Many were recruited from outside the aristocracy, possibly for their natural abilities but possibly because they had no personal vested interests in aristocratic lands held from the king. Many of these officials were rewarded with grants of land forfeited to the king by rebellious knights, bankrupt crusaders and families with failed lines of succession; they also had the opportunity to acquire wardships of minors and other profitable positions.

The legal reforms of Henry II in the late 12th century clarified the laws of property and their administration. Access to royal courts was improved by itinerant justices in eyre, although the expenses involved still put them beyond the reach of most ordinary people. But for property owners this was a boon. It was easier to buy and sell land, and therefore easier to speculate in property. Property could also be held as a form of disposable wealth that could be sold or mortgaged to finance business ventures. The downside was that it could also be mortgaged to fund an extravagant lifestyle, with the result that many aristocratic properties ultimately found their way into the hands of Jewish moneylenders and their Christian associates. This may have indirectly reinforced the growth of anti-Semitism, which in the late 13th century led to the expulsion of the Jews.

The new opportunities in the land market were almost certainly a factor encouraging enterprising property owners to invest in the development of towns. The 13th century witnessed an urban property boom. This encouraged the redevelopment of older areas of established towns, together with suburban expansion. It also created a wave of smaller 'new towns'. The growth of new towns has received considerable attention from historians, as it was one of the most spectacular aspects of the boom.[21] However, the expansion and redevelopment of existing towns is arguably just as significant.

The urban property boom is sometimes dated to the late 13th century, around the time that Edward I held a council on town plantation in 1296–7. However, signs of urban renaissance can be discerned much earlier in the 13th century, from the accession of the young Henry III in 1216. His predecessor, King John, had heavily taxed existing towns to finance his unpopular wars, and thereby appropriated much of the capital that might otherwise have been invested in them. Although political volatility persisted throughout the reign of Henry III, his reign was a good deal more stable than that of King John and the burden of taxation much lower.

During Henry's reign many local lords paid for charters to establish boroughs and markets on lands in their possession. Burgage plots were laid out systematically within the concept of an urban plan (discussed later). Many of these developments were remarkably spacious; the picture of a medieval town as heavily congested is often the product of later infilling, particularly in market areas, and later building on open spaces within the town. In successful towns burgage plots were quickly occupied by artisans and traders.

The practice of burgage tenure gave townspeople greater autonomy in the property market compared with their rural counterparts, as noted previously.

A burgess acquired a plot by paying a perpetual rent and erecting a building conforming to local plans.[22] By the 12th century charters granted to new and existing towns emphasized the commercial and legal privileges that were conferred on a burgess, but not on outsiders or non-burgesses.[23] The identity of the earliest inhabitants is unclear, but may have included retainers of local ecclesiastical and secular lords or of the king, and craftsmen.[24] While the expectation was that a burgess would be a householder, householders who were ecclesiastics, minors, women and criminals were excluded from being burgesses.[25] As a free man, a burgess was able to bequeath his property to his heirs and successors, or to sell it. The burgess might also choose to give property or income from it to a religious institution, an action that required a royal licence from 1279 onwards.[26]

Religious institutions often became involved in the urban property market as a result of their original foundation endowment and subsequent gifts of property from benefactors.[27] As with the secular nobility, they might be granted land in an established town or make a new foundation. Across the 12th to 15th centuries the monks of Llanthony Priory, Gloucester, for example, developed the land they were granted on the outskirts of an established town and then rented it out to generate an income.[28] The monks of Meaux Abbey, Hull, were more ambitious, and during the late 13th century used their water management techniques to create the new town of Hull, which was then purchased by Edward I.[29] The extent to which religious houses engaged in the property market could vary between towns. In some locations, including Norwich and Bristol, there appears to have been limited engagement by monastic institutions in the urban property market, while in others, such as Cambridge, there was substantial engagement.[30]

Civic authorities performed an administrative function in urban property markets on behalf of the Crown and on behalf of those engaging in property transactions. These functions included organizing the collection of the rents that went towards the annual payment to the Crown and, increasingly, providing a legal framework and dispute resolution process for property transactions. The civic authorities were also occasionally owners of property, often bequeathed by philanthropic townspeople, which generated a rental income for the community. Portfolios for specific purposes were also administered by local government, especially those pertaining to communal infrastructure projects. The construction and maintenance of London Bridge from the late 12th century onwards was funded from urban rents, of which the mayor and aldermen of London were closely involved in the administration.[31]

Mercantile, artisan and religious guilds often became involved in the property market as recipients of bequests of property, income from which went to support the physical and/or spiritual needs of members. They also acted as property developers, especially in the construction of guildhalls and almshouses.[32] Guilds could also be responsible for investing income to purchase property to fund large-scale projects. The Guild of Holy Cross in Abingdon, near Oxford, for example, used rental income to fund the upkeep of the bridge its members constructed across the Thames in 1416.[33] While there were parallels between the activities of guilds and those of monastic institutions and local government, guilds were not involved in the administration of the annual farm payment and did not have the significant endowments of the religious houses.

We can learn about the activities of these different groups from the surviving documentary records that report their activities. As explained, the Crown was the principal source of land in England, but often made grants of land to members of the laity as a reward for military service or contribution to royal administration, or to religious institutions in support of welfare and spiritual contributions. The Crown was interested in keeping track of its landed resources and produced periodic surveys, such as the Hundred Rolls, used here, and also recorded transfers of property to religious houses. The Crown, civic authorities, guilds and religious institutions also recorded information in rentals, which often provide a snapshot of a particular location in a particular year. They have been used, for example, to study the property markets of Gloucester, Hull and London.[34] Deeds and charters were produced when a property was transferred between owners and provide detailed information on individual properties. They often survive in the archives of religious houses and town government and have formed the basis for work on Coventry and York in particular; they survive in the archives of Cambridge colleges too.[35]

The majority of documentary records on the medieval property market were produced from c.1200 onwards. In some locations archaeological work provides additional information on the early topography of a town before the date from which the first written records survive. Rentals and inquiries usually identify the recipient of rent, the location of the property (such as the street, ward or parish), any accompanying buildings, the name of the occupier, the level of the rent and the nature of the rent (e.g. landgable or ordinary rent of assize). Sometimes the use of the building is also indicated (e.g. residential or commercial) or can be inferred from the detail provided on the occupier and location. In some cases, such as Gloucester and Cambridge, the earlier history of the property and its occupiers were also recorded. Deeds and charters usually record the date, the donor, the recipient, the location of the property and whether capital gains on the sale of property are taken as lump sum payments (gersuma, considerations) or as an additional perpetual rent paid to the seller. In the case of donations or bequests, additional obligations from the donor may be mentioned (such as prayers for the soul). If property was being exchanged, then the property offered in exchange was detailed too.

Numerical information on rents was usually expressed in the records as shillings and pence paid per annum, although there were situations in which some rents were paid in kind or waived or not reported because they were in arrears. Many rentals and inquiries were compiled specifically to assess 'ability to pay', for example the ability of the property owners to contribute to the town farm, or the potential for a local landowner to raise rents in order to enhance their income. Numerical information on the rents of individual properties, though widely available, has received less attention than other numerical data from the Middle Ages, such as wages and prices. One reason for this is that it has been suggested that urban rents were often fossilized and did not reflect current conditions but rather long-forgotten circumstances when they were first set. These issues are examined fully in Chapter 2.

1.5 Debates in the literature

The study of the medieval urban property market was initially motivated by a desire to reconstruct urban topography. The absence of surviving contemporary urban maps means that rentals, inquiries and deeds provide important information on the layout of towns, including the location of defences, roads and bridges, marketplaces, religious buildings and residential and commercial properties. The medieval topography of Bristol, Canterbury, Durham, Hull, London, Newcastle upon Tyne, Oxford, Southampton and St Andrews was reconstructed through close analysis of documentary sources, while in Coventry, Gloucester, Winchester, Worcester and York documentary information was combined with archaeological remains and surviving parts of the built environment.[36] This approach had three important legacies. It produced a number of histories of individual towns; it provided a methodology that contributed to the larger-scale British Historic Towns Atlas project;[37] and it resulted in the publication of a number of editions of primary sources, such as the Gloucester rental of 1455 and the London Bridge accounts.[38]

Questions surrounding the process of borough foundation and the function of the earliest boroughs have also been studied through the urban property market. Historians have been particularly interested in urban development and resettlement under the Anglo-Saxons, and in why some towns were resettled and others were not. Fortifications and defence were emphasized by some scholars, notably Maitland and Ballard, as important influences on the resettlement of towns.[39] Other scholars, such as Stephenson and Tait, noted the ability of towns to provide political and economic institutions that could facilitate trade and the maintenance of law and order.[40] Payments for landgable have been used to examine the scale of earlier towns and, more recently, to shed light on their function. They have also informed on the potential remittance of labour services for cash payments. In his examination of new town foundations during the 13th and 14th centuries, Beresford emphasized rental income, as well as market tolls, as an important source of revenue that could attract a lord to found a town in preference to continuing to engage only in agriculture.[41]

Historians have looked to evidence from the property market to provide insights into the economic vitality of towns. While the commercialization process is most commonly associated with the period c.1250 onwards, Langdon and Masschaele used evidence of lay involvement in the property market, the subdivision of properties and the practice of subletting to suggest that the period 1150–1250 was characterized by population growth, which underpinned the subsequent expansion of the English economy.[42] Features that historians have associated with urban vitality during the 13th and 14th centuries include increasing density of occupation, multiple occupation of properties and the construction of new residential and commercial premises. These characteristics were identified in Norwich by Rutledge and in Westminster by Rosser.[43]

The nature of local lordship also potentially impacted on urban prosperity and has been investigated through the records of local landowners. The role of the Church as an urban landlord and property developer has been highlighted in studies of Gloucester, Worcester and York. Differences can be observed between locations and institutions: Worcester Cathedral Priory and Llanthony Priory, Gloucester, were both notable for their creation of suburban developments, while York Minster focused on developing city centre properties in its surrounding streets.[44] In Coventry differences in the nature of lordship between the prior's half and the Earl of Chester's half of the city have been examined.[45] In Hull the town's growth after its foundation by the monks of Meaux Abbey can be attributed to Edward I, and is recorded in the rental of 1347.

The extent to which the 15th to early 16th centuries were characterized by urban decline has been debated by historians, and again evidence from the property market has contributed to the debate. Historians have looked for evidence of empty properties and for declining levels of rent as well as for changes made to the strategies for administering property portfolios. Langton's work on the 1455 Gloucester rental was motivated by that question, and he used evidence from the rental, including the subdivision of properties, to argue that the town's economy was buoyant during that period.[46] Baker and Holt, also studying Gloucester, noted the ability of Llanthony Priory to adapt its portfolio in response to decline by replacing several low-quality houses by a smaller number of high-quality houses and with inns.[47] In his examination of Oxford and Canterbury, Butcher investigated the demand for properties as revealed in the archives of religious houses from the 14th and 15th centuries. His results suggested that, while Oxford faced some challenges during the late 13th century, both towns generally had buoyant and resilient property markets until the mid-15th century.[48] Butcher also examined the state of the property market in 15th-century Newcastle upon Tyne. There he found greater evidence of urban decline, which he attributed to increased competition for international trade and changes in the structure of the agrarian and industrial hinterland that deterred migration to the town.[49] In Westminster, Rosser found indications of recession c.1410–70, but evidence of 'momentum' from the mid-1470s onwards.[50]

The concentration of property in the hands of certain individuals and institutions has led historians to suggest that the operation of the property market may have contributed to inequalities of wealth within towns. Tensions have been noted between the religious houses and the lay population, who were often their tenants, over the rendering of services and tenant liability for upkeep and repairs. The Abbey of Bury St Edmunds, for example, was a major landowner in the town and across West Suffolk. While tensions periodically arose between the townspeople and the abbey over control of the market and other local institutions during the 13th and 14th centuries, Gottfried suggested that 'rent was a widely accepted obligation'.[51] In Durham, meanwhile, Bonney suggested that the priory was relatively ineffective at chasing overdue rent payments during the 13th and 14th centuries, with rents of even the wealthier tenants often being written off 'because there was no effective sanction or machinery for recovering such debts'.[52] Discussion of rural estates, however, has suggested a more complex situation. In the case of Westminster Abbey, for example, Harvey noted that 'the abbot and convent were in a position greatly to influence social conditions' in the West Midlands and Home Counties, where the majority of its holdings were located.[53] She concluded that over time, and especially from c.1390, the monks exerted less control over their tenants, recognizing some of them as free. Management of agricultural land was increasingly structured through fixed-term rental contracts for demesnes, and the abbey became more reliant on its London property as a source of income.[54]

The extent to which inequalities of wealth occurred as a result of lay involvement in the property market is a noticeable gap in the literature.[55] Historians vary in the emphasis that they place on the use of property as a form of investment by individual townspeople.[56] Some historians, such as Rosser, have argued that property was primarily intended to provide business or residential accommodation for its owners, or to provide for the owner's welfare through transfer to a religious institution in exchange for a corrody and the endowment of chantries for the provision of prayers after death.[57] Property could also provide improved access to credit by acting as security for a loan or be sold to raise capital.[58] Taking this view, property owners benefited from greater physical security in sickness and old age, and in greater spiritual security after death.

Other historians have suggested that income from rents made a significant contribution to the material living standards of individual townspeople.[59] Butcher examined the taxable income from rents and property declared by residents in 14th-century Bristol and Oxford and observed that, while only a small group of individuals derived a significant income from property, this income made a 'vital contribution to [their] prosperity and status', especially during economic recessions.[60] A disadvantage for individual owners, however, was that they were potentially more vulnerable than the institutions. Butcher suggested that it was the properties owned by townspeople that first fell empty in periods of economic contraction, as they were 'unable to manipulate cash surpluses to the maintenance of empty properties'.[61]

Historians have sought greater clarification about the identity of these lay owners. Particular interest has been shown in the extent to which merchants engaged in the property market, in addition to inland or overseas trade. Hilton suggested that merchants may have been 'significant property accumulators' in some locations, but that the urban property market was dominated by 'institutional ownership of bigger blocks of urban real property'.[62] Subsequent research on mercantile careers in York, Beverley and Hull has highlighted the use of property as an asset by merchants, and shown how it could be accumulated through direct purchase and from pledges of security for loans. Kermode suggested that merchants were less concerned with using property as a route towards 'gentrification' and more attracted to its potential to provide a secure financial legacy for descendants and its ability to complement their other trading investments.[63]

Research on agricultural property ownership has demonstrated the role of the family as a business unit.[64] Howell pioneered the use of the Hundred Rolls for family reconstruction in her analysis of land ownership in the Leicestershire village of Kibworth Harcourt.[65] Her subsequent work on Cambridgeshire, however, was never completed. For Cambridge's hinterland, Clarke used deeds conveying customary land to analyse family structures in Chesterton, a village adjacent to Cambridge.[66] Outside Cambridgeshire, Razi's examination of Halesowen in the period 1270–1430 found evidence of strong familial connections in the transfer of land.[67] Kowaleski has emphasized the potential benefits that could be derived by applying family reconstruction techniques from agricultural history to urban history.[68] The unusually detailed evidence from the Cambridge Hundred Rolls on the history of urban plots permits this, and enabled Maitland and Miller to identify a number of leading families who created substantial property portfolios.[69] Kowaleski also called for the greater use of fiscal sources in family reconstructions and for closer analysis of the relationship between borough legal structures and the activities of urban families.[70] Rees Jones's study of York in 1086–1350 provided a response to this call, demonstrating the dominance of pre-Conquest and Norman families in some areas of York and new families, whose power derived from civic office holding, in others.[71]

Property transactions and profits from property have been recognized as performing important philanthropic purposes. Property transactions, including gifts, leasing, exchange and purchase, could strengthen social relationships between the lay population and their local religious house; even pawning has been mentioned in this connection.[72] Property transfers could reduce inequalities of wealth and promote community cohesion. Central government rarely provided welfare support during this period, partly because a system of regular taxation was not yet in place to fund it. Local government used taxation income to fund communal infrastructure (including marketplaces, roads, bridges and walls), maintain law and order and support vulnerable groups (including orphans). Individual philanthropists and religious orders have been recognized as playing important roles in supporting healthcare and education for the wider community and in providing accommodation and sustenance for its more vulnerable members. While some individuals established their own foundations or launched their own initiatives, many chose to support local religious orders and houses through bequests of property or income. Such support helped orders with their running costs and allowed them to fulfil their wider welfare functions.[73]

1.6 Cambridge before the 13th century: topography

The physical advantages of the local landscape and the transport links provided by its river network have been credited as key factors that influenced Cambridge's origin and growth. Cambridge is located on a natural fording and bridging point of the navigable River Cam, allowing access to both the coast (via King's Lynn) and the agricultural and natural resources of much of East Anglia (Figure 1.1).[74] Watery fenlands that could

Figure 1.1: River system from Cambridge

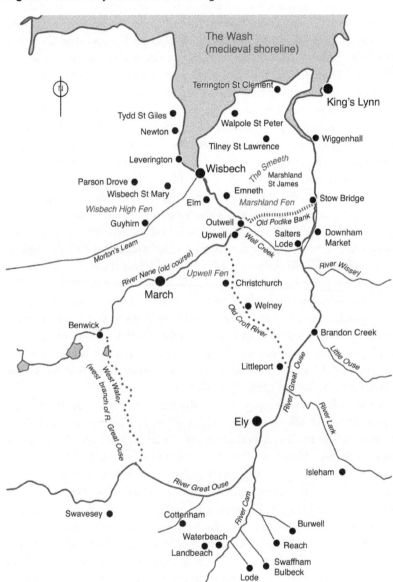

Source: John S. Lee, 'Decline and Growth in the Late Medieval Fenland: The Examples of Outwell and Upwell', *Proceedings of the Cambridge Antiquarian Society* 104 (2015): 137–47 (Reproduced with permission of the Cambridge Antiquarian Society)

provide fish, birds and reeds and, on the edges, grazing for livestock, lay to the north of the town. Crop cultivation and animal grazing were available to the south. Goods could be transported along the River Cam to the seaport of King's Lynn to the north. A junction between the Cam and the Great Ouse provided water transport to Bedford to the west and, via the Little Ouse, to Thetford and via the River Lark to Bury St Edmunds. The River Nene provided access to Peterborough.

It is worth noting that Cambridge was both the first bridging point and the head of navigation for larger craft on the River Cam. As a bridging point it served agricultural estates on either side, to both east and west, while as the head of navigation it served the agricultural lands towards the Suffolk and Hertfordshire borders to the south. Ely, further down the Cam to the north, was in the Fens; potential competition came mainly from places such as Reach, near Burwell, to the east and Swavesey (on the Ouse) to the west.

While water transport was the preferred choice for movement of goods in medieval England, medieval Cambridge also had the legacy of a prehistoric and Roman road network.[75] The Icknield Way was an ancient track that linked the Thames Valley with the Norfolk coast. The Romans subsequently transformed Cambridge into a crossroads in their road system, using the older tracks and new roads to link Cambridge to the Fens to the north via Ely, London to the south, Colchester to the east via Wool Street and Godmanchester to the west. Further afield, medieval travellers could use the network to get to Coventry through St Neots and Northampton, and to Oxford via Bedford.[76]

Cambridge's topography was influenced not only by its natural advantages, but also by the activities of settlers on the site and their investments in trading infrastructure, transport and defence. The history of Cambridge's foundation has been the subject of much debate among historians.[77] It is generally agreed that Cambridge was probably a prehistoric settlement that was then developed by the Romans, who were responsible for bridging the river and improving the existing tracks and developing new roads to create the four-way crossroads. Archaeological evidence suggests that the Roman town was centred on the north side of the river, possibly because this was an area of naturally high chalkland that was appropriate for defensive purposes – it was subsequently to be the site of the castle.[78] Gradually the original settlement seems to have extended across to the south bank, which it appears that the Romans had transformed into a quay. Being on lower ground, this would have been more convenient for the loading and unloading of ships, and indeed some historians have proposed that Cambridge was a Roman entrepôt, with grain brought there from the agricultural hinterland and dispatched to soldiers serving elsewhere in England.[79]

There is little evidence on Cambridge for the period between Roman withdrawal and the 8th century, leading some historians to conclude that the town may have been abandoned during that period in favour of rural settlement.[80] However, the etymology of local place names and archaeological evidence suggest that the town revived again during the reign of the Mercian king Offa (757–96) and under the Danes (c.886–c.921).[81] During these periods the town appears to have served as a port and market centre, and settlement seemed to have continued on both sides of the bridge.

The Anglo-Saxons reconquered the Danish territory of East Anglia in c.921 and Cambridge is known to have served as the administrative centre for Grantabrieshire (the precursor of Cambridgeshire) from that date, and to have had a market and a mint.[82] It has been proposed that the Anglo-Saxons significantly altered Cambridge's topography by constructing the earthworks that became known as the King's Ditch, either for defence or as a trade barrier for the collection of tolls.[83] Subsequently the Normans constructed a motte and bailey castle on the high ground on the north bank of the river.[84]

Cambridgeshire was surveyed as part of the Domesday survey of 1086. For parts of Cambridgeshire two additional versions of the original Domesday returns exist: the *Inquisitio Eliensis* 'gives an account of the estates held, or claimed to be held, by the abbey of Ely in the counties of Cambridge, Hertford, Essex, Norfolk, Suffolk and Huntingdon', while the *Inquisitio Comitatus Cantabrigiensis* surveys 'almost the whole of 13 out of 16 of the Domesday hundreds of the county'.[85] Domesday evidence indicates that hawgable was established prior to the Conquest, but exactly when is unclear. It must have been later than 695, when the monks of Ely found the body of St Etheldreda near the 'desolate city' of Grantaceastir.[86] A Danish army attacked the town in 870, but wintered there in 875, suggesting that the town had survived the attack well enough to supply food and equipment for the troops. By the 970s there is definite evidence of a thriving Anglo-Saxon town. There was a mint (Wilmund was the moneyer in 979), and the monks of Ely held a well-built farm, 100 acres of land and fishing rights. Although further instability ensued, a mint was recorded over the period 1017–42, and a guild of thanes in 1052. This suggests that hawgable was established by the Anglo-Saxons some time around 875–970.

According to Domesday there were 373 messuages in nine wards, together with an unspecified number in a tenth ward. Only the first ward, the Castle ward, is identified in Domesday. There were five personal fees in this ward and one in the third largest ward. These were held by Norman lords as tenants-in-chief, but it is likely that they were previously held by

Anglo-Saxon lords and confiscated from them. Two of these lords, Count Alan of Brittany and Count Robert of Mortain, were close associates of the king and among the richest men in post-Conquest England. Remigius was Bishop of Lincoln and Roger of Childerley, juror of Chesterton hundred, was his man, while Ralph de Baons-le-Comte (known as Ralph de Bans) took his name from a village near Rouen. The final lord was Erchenger, the king's baker, who held land in Comberton and Toft, both near Cambridge, for which he owed the service of delivering a hot loaf every day for the king's dinner.[87]

The *Inquisitio Eliensis* gives additional information, showing that Ely Priory was a significant landholder in Cambridge in 1086. In Castle ward the priory held two messuages, one of which may have been the messuage in St Giles later held by Norman le Cooper.[88] The second ward was known as Bruggewarde (Bridge ward). In the third ward the priory held two messuages and a vacant plot and in the fourth ward a messuage, two vacant houses and a church with inside seating. It held a messuage in the fifth ward and in the tenth ward four *orta* (which may refer to buildings under construction), one of which was vacant. The progression of the list of wards from the Castle to the Bridge suggests that the wards may have been numbered from north to south. The name Bridge ward suggests a ward in the area of St Giles (north of the river) and/or St Clement's (south of the river). It is likely that the third and fourth wards would also encompass the riverbank, and so include the parish of St John, in which Ely Priory held property in 1279. According to this interpretation, the information on the tenth ward suggests new construction on the southern edge of the town.

It can be seen from Table 1.1 that at the time of Domesday only 241 of the 373 messuages paid hawgable. Twenty-seven had been destroyed in order to build the castle and 49 were wasted, but 295 still owed payment to the king or the lords. By 1279 there were 594 messuages and 1,088 separate properties, but only 202 of them paid hawgable. Thus the number of properties that did not pay hawgable was substantial and rising.[89] Vestiges of hawgable are recorded by Cooper as late as the middle of the 19th century, although it seems that no properties pay it today.[90] It appears that the value of hawgable was declining relative to commercial rents, as urban property values increased over time. This may have given the recipients of hawgable (whether king or borough) little incentive to pursue non-payment.

A further change in Cambridge's topography occurred in 1267, just before the Hundred Rolls. Barons revolting against Henry III encamped on the Isle of Ely and began to raid the surrounding countryside. The king, it appears, camped in Cambridge and made defensive improvements

Table 1.1: Basic statistics on Cambridge from the Domesday Book

Wards	Before	Lost	Waste	Render customs	Pay nothing	Comments
1	54	27	2	[10]	15	Personal fees: Count Alan (5*); Count of Mortain (3**); Ralph de Baons-le-Comte (3*); Roger, Bishop Remigius's man (3*), Erchenger (1*)
2	48	[0]	2	32	13	Personal fee: Count Alan (5* + 9 who dwell on the lands of the English)
3	41	[0]	11	30	[0]	
4	45	[0]	24	21	[0]	
5	50	[0]	1	49	[0]	
6						
7	37	[0]	[0]	[34]	3	Frenchmen pay nothing
8	37	[0]	[0]	[36]	1	Priest pays nothing
9	32	[0]	3	[29]	[0]	
10	29	[0]	6	29	0	
Total	373	27	49	241	32	

Notes: Square brackets indicate imputed value; * indicates pays no rent; ** indicates used to pay in the time of King Edward but does not now do so.

Source: Ann Williams and G. H. Martin (eds), *Domesday Book: A Complete Translation* (London, 2002), p 519

to the King's Ditch, including the insertion of two gates – Trumpington Gate to provide access to the town centre from the Trumpington road and Barnwell Gate to provide access from Hadstock Way and Hinton Way.[91] It has been suggested that the final element was to be the construction of a wall, but that Henry III was forced to leave Cambridge early to defend London, leaving the defences unfinished and the town open to attack.[92]

1.7 Cambridge before the 13th century: economy and society

Cambridge's economy was based on the export of corn and other agricultural produce through King's Lynn, with a balancing flow of imports that would have included a range of luxury goods. It was also the general market for the surrounding villages.[93] Henry I gave the town's economy a significant boost when, in an undated writ of 1100–35, he made the town the only place in the county where boats could be charged and discharged and tolls taken.[94] The townspeople also owned the rights to fish in the town and were able to sell licences for fishing.[95] From the early 13th century the town became associated with Sturbridge fair, which was granted by the king to the town's leper hospital of St Mary Magdalene.[96]

The town had a Jewish community from c.1075 until the expulsion in 1275, located within the parish of All Saints in the Jewry.[97] Comparing the Cambridge Jewry with those of Norwich, York and Worcester, Dobson suggested that it was 'at its most substantial and influential in the twelfth century' but 'apparently a good deal less prominent in the thirteenth century'.[98] However the relative absence of surviving documentary evidence for the Jewish community in Cambridge means that there are many unanswered questions about their activities during the 12th and 13th centuries.[99] The earliest conclusive evidence of Jewish settlement, Dobson suggests, is the record of a large sum paid by the Jewish community in the royal levy of 1159 – the fourth largest amount of the ten locations recorded.[100] It seems likely, however, that a community was in place shortly after the Norman Conquest, attracted to Cambridge by the protection provided by the castle, the presence of potential customers for credit in the form of local agricultural landowners and the proximity to the London credit market.[101]

Relations between Jews and their Christian neighbours appear to have been relatively cordial; however, some sources suggest that during the baronial uprising of 1265–7 the barons attacked, and possibly massacred, some members of the Jewish community.[102] The Jews appear to have been expelled from Cambridge in 1275; some apparently relocated to Norwich and others to Huntingdon.[103] From 1236 Cambridge had become a dower town of Queen Eleanor (Henry III's wife and Edward I's mother), and this early date for expulsion may have been the result of her request that all Jews should be expelled from her dower towns.[104]

The opportunity to develop local government and gain some autonomy over their own affairs was very desirable to medieval townspeople. Cambridge first gained a degree of autonomy from the county sheriff and the Crown in 1185 when the burgesses purchased the farm of the town from the Crown. This meant that the burgesses assumed responsibility for the yearly 'rent' payment made by the town of Cambridge to the Crown.[105] Despite costing 330 silver marks and 1 gold mark, this grant of the farm appears to have been temporary and had to be renewed on a number of occasions.[106] There were also subsequent disputes over the extent to which this grant gave the burgesses control over what was to become valuable wasteland in the town.

Two charters of the reign of King John extended Cambridge's privileges and put self-government on a firmer footing. The charter of 1201 granted a guild merchant to Cambridge, provided its members with free trade in the king's lands in England and France and confirmed the town's right to hold the Reach Fair in Rogation week.[107] The contents of this charter suggest that by this date the burgesses had organized three courts: one held five times a year for cases concerning land, one held every week for 'personal action' and a merchant guild court, held daily if required, for cases between merchants.[108] Four bailiffs appear to have been the civic officers at the time of the charter.[109] Shortly afterwards, in 1207, a further charter allowed the burgesses and their heirs to hold the farm in perpetuity and to appoint a mayor.[110] The scope of town governance was further extended in 1256 when the burgesses gained the right for their officials to execute royal writs, extended the scope of actions that they could hear in their town court and received the privilege of electing coroners.[111] Civic government centred on the Guildhall on the marketplace.[112]

The ability to self-govern was always held with the consent of the Crown, however. The citizens of Cambridge were reminded of this in 1235 when, as a result of a riot, the town was taken back under royal control.[113] The riot appears to have been initiated by Alexander de Bancis, his wife Elicia and her sisters Margaret and Cecilia taking possession of a house that they claimed to have inherited and over which there was a dispute of whether the previous owner, Richard of Burghard, died rightfully seized of the messuage. The family accused many men, particularly from the Gogging, Goldsmith and Potekin families, of breaking into the house, attacking them and ringing bells 'to attract others'.[114] The mayor, Harvey son of Eustace (Dunning), and the coroner and provost, Geoffrey Potekin, were accused of failing to use force to stop the riot or catch the rioters and of failing to make a record of the event or to hold an inquiry into it; and as a result the town was taken into the king's hands.[115]

This dispute may reflect some of the problems of succession that bedevilled the medieval property market. At this time freehold properties were still held through subinfeudation, by which each owner held from the previous owner, to whom they normally paid perpetual rent. The previous owner was nominally their lord, to whom they owed the rent as a substitute for service. The owner would normally expect their heir to inherit the property and continue to pay the rent. Failure to pay the rent or prove inheritance could result in the property reverting to the lord. There were, however, many reasons why a rent might not be paid or why a lord might refuse to acknowledge an heir. Disputes could be resolved through the courts, but impatient or indignant disputants might resort to force. It seems that on this occasion many members of the town's merchant elite felt that their interests were being threatened by the actions of an absentee landlord repossessing a property. The rioters were protected by their family connections with the mayor and the coroner, but the de Bancis family trumped this with their royal connections and appealed to the king.

While Cambridge was not a demesne town (under the jurisdiction of a local noble), the Earl of Huntingdon and later the Earl of Cambridge possessed some rights within the borough. From 1050 to 1237, when the earldom of Huntingdon became extinct, the earl received a third of the profits of justice in the shire, including a third of the profits of the town of Cambridge.[116] The earldom transferred by marriage to the kings of Scotland from 1113. In 1207 the earl's rights to the third penny were purchased 'by an annuity of £10' paid to the earl.[117] In 1236, the income from the farm was transferred to Queen Eleanor upon her marriage to Henry III, and she continued to receive it as queen mother under her son Edward I.[118]

The advantages of accessible river systems, accumulated urban wealth and prominent religious houses in the local region drew scholars to Cambridge, including those taking refuge in 1209 from hostile townspeople in Oxford. By 1226 the scholars had organized themselves under a chancellor and appear to have arranged regular courses of study. These students were augmented by the establishment of the houses of Franciscan and Dominican friars in Cambridge.[119] Initially, the university had no premises of its own, but relied on parish churches and religious houses as sites for its public ceremonies. Hostels emerged, which had few endowments and were privately owned, but some survived into the 16th century when they were mainly acquired by colleges.[120] The earliest Cambridge college, Peterhouse, was founded in 1284 by Hugh Balsham, Bishop of Ely.

1.8 Cambridge in c.1279

The culmination of these developments was that by the 13th century Cambridge had what has been described as a north–south orientated topography (see Figure 1.2). The castle was on the north bank of the river, and that area was relatively sparsely settled compared to the south bank. On the south bank the river formed a natural barrier along the west side of the built-up area, while the King's Ditch provided an artificial barrier on the eastern side.[121] The river could be crossed at the Great Bridge (the present Magdalene Bridge) and two smaller branches of the river were crossed at Small Bridges (later replaced by a single bridge at the present Silver Street).[122] Four agricultural fields lay to the east of the

Figure 1.2: Cambridge, c.1500

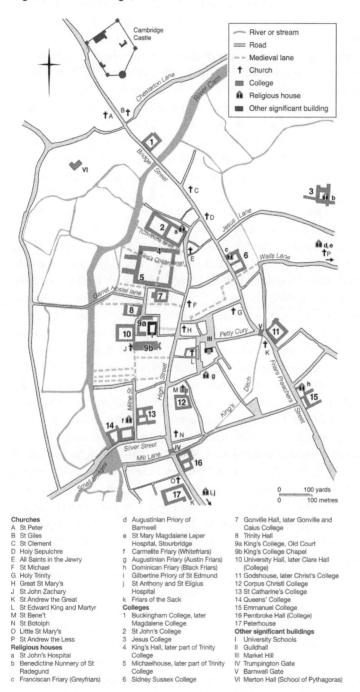

Source: Adapted from a map first published in Mary D. Lobel, *Historic Towns Atlas: Cambridge* (London, 1975) © Historic Towns Trust, 1975 (Reproduced with permission of the Historic Towns Trust)

town (the East fields were also known as Barnwell fields) and four to the west (the West fields).[123] These fields were a large and uninterrupted area of pasture and arable, within which land was held as strips.[124] Suburban development had occurred, particularly to the south, beyond the Trumpington and Barnwell gates, and to the north-east.[125] The suburbs in the vicinity of the Trumpington road was where the Friars of the Sack resided, and later accommodated the Gilbertine canons and St Anthony and St Eloy Hospital. The Carmelites were nearby at Newnham. Beyond Barnwell Gate were the Dominicans, which served as a focal point for urban development. To the north-east of the town lay Barnwell Priory, St Radegund's and the leper hospital of St Mary Magdalene, Sturbridge.[126]

At the time of the Hundred Rolls visitors from London would enter through the Trumpington Gate, with the King's Mill to the left and the King's Ditch on the right. Heading north, the visitor would enter the business district, with the market to the right, just behind Great St Mary's Church – one of 14 churches in the town.[127] On the left would be buildings later demolished to make way for King's College Chapel. Continuing up the High Street past the Jewry would bring the visitor to the Round Church. On the left would be the Hospital of St John the Evangelist, later refounded as St John's College.[128] Continuing to the Great Bridge (now Magdalene Bridge) the visitor would pass St Clement's Church on the right and go through the area where the wealthiest people resided. Passing over the bridge, they could look up the River Cam to the left towards the great stone house (now called the School of Pythagoras) where the influential Dunning family lived. The visitor would then cross the St Neots road by St Giles' Church and ascend the Huntingdon road, with the castle (now a mound near Shire Hall) to the right and views over the grounds of St Radegund's Nunnery (now Jesus College) towards Barnwell Priory. A walk up the Newmarket road, parallel to the river and downstream from the bridge, would lead past Barnwell Priory (where the cellarer's chequer still remains) to the hospital of St Mary Magdalene with its chapel (still standing today) and the site of Sturbridge Fair (now an urban park).

There are few surviving maps of the town. Richard Lyne's map of 1574, produced to illustrate Caius's History of the University (Figure 1.3) contains a brief description of Cambridge and a list of hostels in the town.[129] This map was updated by Cole with recent street names and the colleges built since it was produced.[130] A 15th-century plan of Cambridge marketplace also exists in the Corpus Christi archives (Figure 1.4). More recently, documentary and archaeological evidence has formed the basis for maps of Cambridge provided in the *Historic Towns Atlas*.[131]

Figure 1.3: Richard Lyne's map of Cambridge, 1574

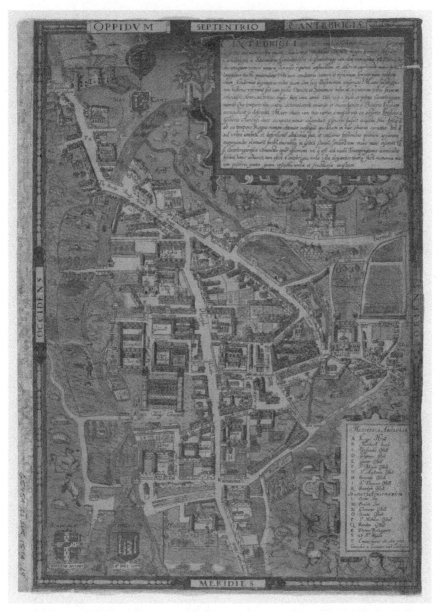

Source: Courtesy of the Harvard Map Collection

Figure 1.4: 15th-century plan of Cambridge marketplace

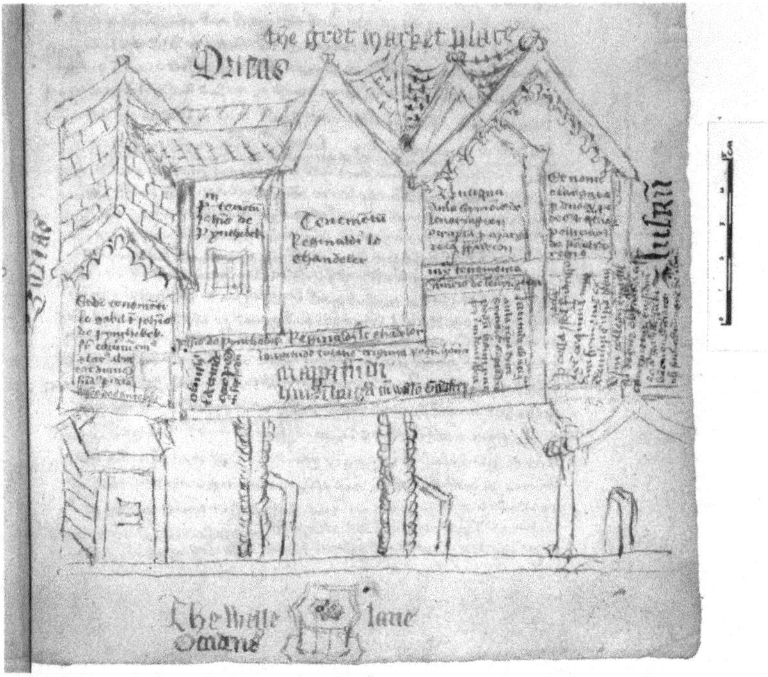

Source: Courtesy of The Parker Library, Corpus Christi College, Cambridge

1.9 The content of the Hundred Rolls

The Hundred Rolls are the records of government enquiries in 1255, 1274–5 and 1279–80 that were conducted across the subdivisions of English counties known as hundreds.[132] The commission of 1255 focused on royal rights, that of 1274–5 on 'liberties and the misdeeds of officials' and that of 1279–80 into liberties and landholding.[133] For each enquiry commissioners were instructed to go in person to their allocated county or counties and to 'take evidence of sworn juries of knights and freeholders in every hundred'.[134] The evidence related to four issues: domains of the king (namely fiefs, escheats, liberties and holdings), who possessed them in and in what form (domain, tenancy, service, cottage, free tenancies, woods, parks, chases, warrens, waters, rivers, freedoms and market days), from whom (tenants or others) and of which fee or other tenures of scutage. The results of these enquiries were recorded and provided to the king, but unfortunately little is known about how the information in the rolls was used.[135] The commissions of 1274–5 were examined by Cam, with a focus on the administrative procedures of the commission and the information they provided on the working of Edward I's government.[136] The report of the commission of 1279–80 was examined by Raban, who presents it as the most ambitious of all the enquiries and suggests that, although unfinished, it may have been intended to be a comprehensive survey of landholding similar to that compiled in the Domesday Book in 1086.[137]

This book is based on material for the enquiries of 1279–80. Twenty-six teams of commissioners for the survey were appointed on 12 March 1279 and were instructed to go in person to their allocated county or counties and to 'take evidence of sworn juries of knights and freeholders in every hundred'.[138] The Cambridge borough and Barnwell suburb Hundred Rolls are the focus of this book, providing a snapshot of the town in 1279 and give its history going back to c.1200.[139]

The articles setting out the scope of the inquiry into Cambridgeshire were distinctive in comparison with other counties; on the one hand they did not require investigation into the conduct of the current sheriff or escheator but on the other they required the history of every property holding.[140]

The immunity of the sheriff suggests that the sheriff may have had exceptional influence over the local inquiry. Sir William le Moyne of Raveley, Sheriff of Cambridgeshire and Huntingdonshire, 1275–8, came from a distinguished Norman family. This family had held the manor of Raveley, Huntingdonshire, since the 11th century and was responsible for the foundation of Ramsey Abbey (the family name translates as 'the Monk'). Sir William had previously been sheriff in 1258, when he had participated in a royal inquiry into grievances in Cambridgeshire.[141] His personal interest may explain some of the distinctive features of the Cambridge Rolls.

The bailiffs of Cambridge, as officials of the borough, may also have had an influence on the scope and scale of the inquiry. They certainly had an incentive to support the inquiry. They had some long-standing grievances against a previous sheriff and they were seeking to confirm two charters of Henry II, in which they were successful. Finally, access to university scholars as well as monks may explain why the rolls were written up in such a professional manner. The choice of Cambridge in this study did not, therefore, derive from its status as a university town, which was largely nascent at this time, but simply from the unprecedented scope of its records. Our interpretation of the contents has been strengthened by the use of additional documents produced by royal officials and religious institutions, and by deeds archived in various colleges.

While comprehensive coverage of England was apparently the intention of the 1279–80 enquiries, in practice the coverage was uneven. Some counties were covered very well, such as Cambridgeshire and

Huntingdonshire, while others were covered only partially or not at all. In 1812–18 the Record Commission printed an edition of the rolls, known at the time as *Rotuli Hundredorum*.[142] The rolls were transcribed but not translated, and printed in archaic script. Since then new rolls have come to light; the definitive list is online in The National Archives Discovery catalogue.[143] The rolls can be inspected at The National Archives in Kew. There are three rolls, but only two were published by the Record Commission because the third had not been discovered at the time. These two rolls were analysed statistically by Maitland in the appendix to *Township and Borough*, and have formed the basis of all Cambridge local history since then.[144] The existence of the third roll was noted by Raban, but it remained neglected.[145] This roll transforms our knowledge of Cambridge because it contains important information on several parishes whose properties were largely omitted from the first two rolls, giving a false impression that their population and density of building was very small.

The numbering of the rolls in the Discovery catalogue reflects the order in which they were identified and not the sequence in which they were prepared in 1279. One reason why the existence of a missing roll was not recognized earlier is that the first roll contains the heading and the second roll has a space at the end, giving the impression that they are complete. It is only when the third roll was examined that it became clear that it is actually second in the sequence. Previous Cambridge antiquarians, such as Gray and Stokes, noted apparent inconsistencies between the rolls and other sources, but did not pursue the issue.[146] For this volume a new edition of the Hundred Rolls has been prepared, with a full translation of all three rolls in their original order, and with additional material on the Barnwell suburb as well.[147]

The county of Cambridge is also covered well by the Hundred Rolls. The county has played a prominent part in large-scale studies of medieval landholding and peasant agriculture.[148] The most ambitious study of peasant landholding in Cambridgeshire based on the Hundred Rolls was undertaken by Cicely A. H. Howell. Howell's study was never completed, but an archive of research materials relating to published and unpublished work on peasant landholding and to unfinished research using the Cambridgeshire Hundred Rolls has survived.[149]

1.10 Additional sources

A range of additional sources were consulted with the aim of obtaining additional information on the families and institutions discussed in

Hundred Rolls.[150] In some cases the text was transcribed and translated from original documents, but in many cases it was translated from a published or unpublished Latin transcript. In a few instances, cases relating to Cambridge have been abstracted from a longer list that has already been translated.

Royal records

Contextual information on Cambridge before the time of the Hundred Rolls is provided in the Domesday Book.[151] The visits of the royal itinerant justices to Cambridge in 1247, 1261, 1268, 1272, 1286 and 1299 provide some additional context to life in the town around the time of the Hundred Rolls.[152] Eyres were usually held at seven-year intervals, and dealt with civil pleas (between individuals on subjects such as recovery of land and debt) and Crown pleas (including deaths caused criminally, felonies and non-violent issues concerning the king's proprietary and prerogative rights).[153]

Financial records of the Pipe Rolls (the Crown's annual income and expenditure records), tallage accounts (inhabitants liable for tax) and subsidy rolls (records of occasional taxes on personal property) provide information on levels of wealth of individuals that is helpful for the composition of the family biographies.[154] The tallage rolls also allow us to directly engage with Maitland's work as he printed the tallage of Cambridge for 1219 as part of his investigation into the presence of a burgess class in Cambridge. We have produced an analysis of payments in the Pipe Rolls of 1211–25 and the tallage of 1225 that corrects Maitland by showing that there was no tallage in 1219. It also analyses the proportion of tallage paid by different individuals.[155]

Members of family dynasties often sought to protect or enhance their holdings through legal process. They may also have been involved in other cases pertaining to their careers and political activities. The activities of some family members appear in the records of the Curia Regis sedentary court (known after c.1250 as the Court of Common Pleas) with a remit ranging from trespass cases involving violence to actions for the recovery of moveable property, the enforcement of contracts and the standard of service provided by professionals and craftspeople.[156] We have translated extracts from the Latin transcription of cases involving individuals from the families in Cambridge at the time of the Hundred Rolls.[157]

Acquisition, transfer and disposal of land are recorded in four royal sources. The Patent Rolls and Close Rolls contain letters and instructions issued by the Crown. They are useful for tracing transfers of land as they record rights or land granted to an individual as well as permission to sell land (sometimes called a 'licence to alienate').[158] The records of the Exchequer of the Jews detailed the civil and criminal jurisdiction of the Justices of the Jews over transactions between Christians and Jews, including loans for which property was security.[159] Feet of fines reveal disputes over property, often stemming from land transfers, held in the king's court.[160]

Civic, religious and educational institutional records

Cambridge has few surviving urban records. The mayors and bailiffs of Cambridge, 1263–1300, were listed by the antiquary the Reverend William Cole (1714–82) and can be supplemented by some information from the Curia Regis Rolls and the Merton College deeds.[161] An edition of the guild records was produced by Bateson.[162] This information was useful for the family biographies in Chapter 4 and for Chapter 7. Additional information on the history and topography of Cambridge was derived from the collections of copies of manuscript documents and observations deposited in Cambridge University Library by the Reverend Thomas Baker (d. 1740) and Cole's additional papers in the British Library.[163]

Records of religious institutions contain information on the operation of the Cambridge property market that can supplement the Hundred Rolls. For Barnwell, *Liber Memorandum Ecclesie de Bernewelle* was probably compiled in the late 13th century and, among other material, contains a rental of 1295.[164] The Prior of Barnwell's register also survives in the Gough manuscripts at the Bodleian and provides panel data of a property portfolio on a yearly basis.[165] Jesus College archives contain the surviving charters and accounts of St Radegund's, many of which were published by Gray.[166] Deeds recording rents and donations of property also survive in the Jesus archives and inform on the support the priory received from many leading families of Cambridge, which was particularly strong during the 12th and 13th centuries. The cartulary of the hospital of St John the Evangelist is incomplete but informs on its urban and rural estate during the period c.1220–c.1280.[167] It survives in the collections of St John's College, University of Cambridge, and was recently edited by Underwood and used by Rubin in her monograph.[168]

Some college archives inform on the acquisition and disposal of property by leading Cambridge families. Merton College archives, University of Oxford, contain information about the Dunning family, whose properties were acquired by the college's founder.[169] Corpus Christi

College, University of Cambridge, acquired many gifts of property from tradesman, each of which came with its record of previous ownership, as recorded in the college deeds.[170] Peterhouse Treasury, Peterhouse College, University of Cambridge, contains deeds of relevance to the family biographies, as it was the first college to be founded.[171]

University archives also provide some information on its interactions with the property market. A compilation of statutes and ordinances dating to c.1250 exists in the Angelica Library in Rome; it was edited by Father M. B. Hackett.[172] It contains a chapter detailing processes by which scholars could find lodgings and masters hire schools in Cambridge at reasonable rents.

Notes

[1] Colin Mayer, *Prosperity: Better Business Makes the Greater Good* (Oxford, 2018), pp 1–22.

[2] Thomas Piketty, *Capital in the Twenty-First Century* (Cambridge, MA, 2014), pp 20–2, 27–30.

[3] For example, Peter A. Hall and David Soskice, 'Introduction', *Varieties of Capitalism: The Institutional Foundations of Comparative Advantage* ed. Peter A. Hall and David Soskice (Oxford, 2001), pp 1–91; Martha C. Howell, *Commerce before Capitalism in Europe, 1300–1600* (Cambridge, 2010), p 13.

[4] Arnold Toynbee, *The Industrial Revolution* (Boston, MA, 1956), p 121; Rodney Hilton, *Medieval Peasant Movements and the English Rising of 1381* (2nd ed., Basingstoke, 2004), p 75.

[5] Joel Mokyr, *A Culture of Growth: The Origins of the Modern Economy* (Princeton, NJ, 2018), p 7; Joel Mokyr, *Economics of the Industrial Revolution* (London, 1985); G. E. Mingay (ed.), *The Agricultural Revolution: Changes in Agriculture, 1650–1880* (London, 1977); D. C. North, *Structure and Change in Economic History* (New York, 1981).

[6] J. A. Schumpeter, trans R. Opie, *The Theory of Economic Development* (Cambridge, MA, 1934); Max Weber, trans Talcott Parsons, *The Protestant Ethic and the Spirit of Capitalism* (London, 1976); R. H. Tawney, *The Agrarian Problem in the Sixteenth Century* (London, 1912), p 177; Amintore Fanfani, *Catholicism, Protestantism and Capitalism* (London, 1935), pp 200–1, 205; Fernand Braudel, *Civilization and Capitalism, 15th–18th Century* (3 vols) 3 (London, 2002), p 31.

[7] R. H. Britnell and B. M. S. Campbell, *A Commercialising Economy: England 1086 to c. 1300* (Manchester, 1995); Cicely A. H. Howell, *Land, Family and Inheritance in Transition; Kibworth Harcourt 1280–1700* (Cambridge, 1983); Chris Briggs, 'Monitoring Demesne Managers through the Manor Court before and after the Black Death', *Survival and Discord in Medieval Society: Essays in Honour of Christopher Dyer* ed. Richard Goddard, John Langdon and Miriam Müller (Turnhout, 2010), pp 179–95; Phillipp R. Schofield, 'Lordship and the Early History of Peasant Land Transfer on the Estates of the Abbey of Bury St Edmunds', *Peasants and Lords in the Medieval English Economy: Essays in Honour of Bruce M. S. Campbell* ed. Maryanne Kowaleski, John Langdon and Phillipp R. Schofield (Turnhout, 2015), pp 201–24; Chris Briggs, 'Peasants, Lords, and Commerce: Market Regulation at Balsham, Cambridgeshire, in the Early Fourteenth Century', *Peasants and Lords*

in the Medieval English Economy: Essays in Honour of Bruce M. S. Campbell ed. Maryanne Kowaleski, John Langdon and Phillipp R. Schofield (Turnhout, 2015), pp 247–96; Alexandra Sapoznik, 'Resource Allocation and Peasant Decision-Making: Oakington, Cambridgeshire, 1361–1393', *Agricultural History Review* 61 (2) (2013): 187–205.

8 For example, T. A. B. Corley, 'Historical Biographies of Entrepreneurs', *Oxford Handbook of Entrepreneurship*, ed. M. Casson, B. Yeung, A. Basu and N. Wadeson (Oxford, 2006), pp 138–60; J. Wilson, *British Business History, 1720–1994* (Manchester, 1995); Koji Yamamoto, *Taming Capitalism Before Its Triumph: Public Service, Distrust, and 'Projecting' in Early Modern England* (Oxford, 2018).

9 Mark Casson and Catherine Casson, *The Entrepreneur in History: From Medieval Merchant to Modern Business Leader* (Basingstoke, 2013).

10 Mayer, *Prosperity*, 46–60; Guido Alfani and Roberta Frigeni, 'Inequality (Un) perceived: The Emergence of a Discourse on Economic Inequality from the Middle Ages to the Age of Revolution', *Journal of European Economic History* 45 (1) (2016): 21–66.

11 The British Academy, *Reforming Business for the Twenty-First Century: A Framework for the Future of the Corporation*, available at https://www.thebritishacademy.ac.uk/sites/default/files/Reforming-Business-for-21st-Century-British-Academy.pdf (accessed 1 March 2019); Davide Cantoni and Noam Yuchtman, 'Medieval Universities, Legal Institutions, and the Commercial Revolution', *Quarterly Journal of Economics* 129 (2) (2014): 879; James M. Murray, 'Entrepreneurs and Entrepreneurship in Medieval Europe', *The Invention of Enterprise: Entrepreneurship from Ancient Mesopotamia to Modern Times* ed. David S. Landes, Joel Mokyr and William J. Baumol (Princeton, NJ, and Oxford, 2010), pp 88–106, pp 103–4; Keith Thomas, *The Ends of Life: Roads to Fulfilment in Early Modern England* (Oxford, 2009), pp 241–3, 254.

12 M. For an evaluation of Maitland's wider contribution to the field of legal history see Alan Macfarlane, *The Making of the Modern World: Visions from the West and East* (Basingstoke, 2002), pp 45–58.

13 John S. Lee, *Cambridge and Its Economic Region* (Hatfield, 2005); P. Zutshi (ed.), *Medieval Cambridge: Essays on the Pre-Reformation University* (Woodbridge, 1993).

14 Lee, *Cambridge*.

15 Miri Rubin, *Charity and Community in Medieval Cambridge* (Cambridge, 1987).

16 R. H. Britnell, *The Commercialisation of English Society 1000–1500* (Cambridge, 1993); Britnell and Campbell, *Commercialising Economy*.

17 R. Britnell and J. Hatcher (eds), *Progress and Problems in Medieval England: Essays in Honour of Edward Miller* (Cambridge, 1996).

18 M, p 180.

19 Subinfeudation, whereby the seller of land retained the right to a token rent, was common prior to *Quia Emptores* of 1290; the resultant complications are reflected in Cole's discussion of the history of individual properties.

20 R. Horrox, *The Changing Plan of Hull, 1290–1650* (Hull, 1978).

21 Maurice Beresford, *New Towns of the Middle Ages: Town Plantation in England, Wales and Gascony* (Stroud, 1988).

22 Mary Bateson (ed.), *Borough Customs* (2 vols) I (1904–6), pp 278–90.

23 Richard Holt, 'Society and Population 600–1300', *The Cambridge Urban History of Britain, I: 600–1540* ed. D. M. Palliser (3 vols) I (Cambridge, 2000), pp 79–104, pp 84–5.

24 Holt, 'Society and Population', pp 79–82.

[25] Henry A. Merewether and Archibald J. Stephens, *The History of the Boroughs and Municipal Corporations of the United Kingdom* (3 vols) I (Brighton, 1835), p vi.

[26] Sandra Raban, *Mortmain Legislation and the English Church 1279–1500* (Cambridge, 1982); Sandra Raban, 'Mortmain in Medieval England', *Past and Present* 62 (1974): 3–26.

[27] Constance Brittain Bouchard, *Holy Entrepreneurs: Cistercians, Knights and Economic Exchange in Twelfth-Century Brittany* (Ithaca, NY, and London, 1991); Barbara H. Rosenwein, *To Be a Neighbour of St Peter: The Social Meaning of Cluny's Property, 909–1049* (Ithaca, NY, and London, 1989).

[28] Nigel Baker and Richard Holt, *Urban Growth and the Medieval Church: Gloucester and Worcester* (Aldershot, 2004); Catherine Casson and Mark Casson, 'Location, Location, Location? Analysing Property Rents in Medieval Gloucester', *Economic History Review* 69 (2) (2016): 575–99.

[29] Catherine Casson and Mark Casson, 'The Economy of Medieval English Towns: Property Values and Rents in Bristol, 1200–1500', working paper; R. Horrox (ed.), *Selected Rentals and Accounts of Medieval Hull, 1293–1528* (York, 1983); Horrox, *Plan*.

[30] Elizabeth Rutledge, 'Landlords and Tenants: Housing and the Rented Property Market in Early Fourteenth-Century Norwich', *Urban History* 22(1) (1995): 7–24, pp 12–13.

[31] Vanessa Harding and Laura Wright, (eds), *London Bridge: Selected Accounts and Rentals, 1381–1538* (London, 1995).

[32] Gervase Rosser, *The Art of Solidarity in the Middle Ages: Guilds in England 1250–1550* (Oxford, 2015); Patricia H. Cullan, '"For Pore People Harberles": What Was the Function of the Maisonsdieu?', *Trade, Devotion and Governance: Papers in Later Medieval History* ed. Dorothy J. Clayton, Richard G. Davies and Peter McNiven (Stroud, 1994), pp 36–52.

[33] Casson and Casson, *Entrepreneur in History*, pp 78–9.

[34] John Langton, 'Late Medieval Gloucester: Some Data from a Rental of 1455', *Transactions of the Institute of British Geographers*, new series, 2 (1977): 259–77; Horrox, *Rentals*; Horrox, *Plan*; Harding and Wright, *London Bridge*.

[35] P. R. Coss, *The Early Records of Medieval Coventry* (London, 1986); Richard Goddard, *Lordship and Medieval Urbanisation: Coventry, 1043–1355* (Woodbridge, 2004); Sarah Rees Jones, *York: The Making of a City 1068–1350* (Oxford, 2013).

[36] Baker and Holt, *Urban Growth*; Margaret Bonney, *Lordship and the Urban Community: Durham and its Overlords, 1250–1540* (Cambridge, 1990); M. Brown and K. Stevenson (eds), *Medieval St Andrews: Church, Cult, City* (Woodbridge, 2017); A. F. Butcher, 'Rent and the Urban Economy: Oxford and Canterbury in the Later Middle Ages', *Southern History* 1 (1979): 11–43, p 13; A. F. Butcher, 'Rent, Population and Economic Change in Late-Medieval Newcastle', *Northern History* 14 (1978): 67–77; Peter Fleming, *Time, Space and Power in Later Medieval Bristol*, available at https://eprints.uwe.ac.uk (2013) (accessed 26 February 2015); C. Platt, *Medieval Southampton: The Port and Trading Community, A. D. 1000–1600* (London and Boston, MA, 1973); Goddard, *Coventry*; Horrox, *Plan*; D. Keene, 'The Property Market in English Towns AD 1100–1600', *D'Une Ville a L'autre: Structures, Materielles et Organisati in de L'espace dans les Villes Europeens, VIIIᵉ–XVIᵉ Siecle* ed. J.-C. Maire Vigeur (Rome, 1989), pp 201–26; Derek Keene, *Survey of Medieval Winchester, II Part I: Winchester in the Later Middle Ages* (2 vols) (Oxford, 1985); Rees Jones, *York*.

[37] Including Mary D. Lobel, *Historic Towns Atlas: Cambridge* (London, 1975).

[38] Harding and Wright, *London Bridge*; D. Ormrod, J. M. Gibson, J. Baker and O. D. Lyne, '*City and Region – Urban and Agricultural Rent in England, 1400–1914*' available at https://kar.kent.ac.uk/29287/ (accessed 12 April 2017); Horrox, *Rentals*; H. E. Salter, *Medieval Oxford* (Oxford, 1936); H. E. Salter, *Oxford City Properties* (Oxford, 1929); W. H. Stevenson (ed.), *Rental of the Houses in Gloucester AD 1455: From a Roll in the Possession of the Corporation of Gloucester* (Gloucester, 1890); Derek Keene and Vanessa Harding, *A Survey of Sources for Property Holding in London before the Great Fire* (London, 1985).

[39] Adolphus Ballard, *The English Borough in the Twelfth Century* (Cambridge, 1914); M.

[40] James Tait, *The Medieval English Borough: Studies on Its Origins and Constitutional History* (Manchester, 1936); Carl Stephenson, *Borough and Town: A Study of Urban Origins in England* (Cambridge, MA, 1933).

[41] Beresford, *New Towns*, pp 65–71.

[42] John Langdon and James Masschaele, 'Commercial Activity and Population Growth in Medieval England', *Past and Present* 190 (2006): 35–81, 40–2.

[43] Gervase Rosser, *Medieval Westminster 1200–1540* (Oxford, 1989) p 45; Rutledge, 'Landlords', pp 11–13;

[44] Baker and Holt, *Urban Growth*, p 275; Rees Jones, *York*, p 151.

[45] Coss (ed.), *Coventry*; R. H. C. Davis, *The Early History of Coventry* (London, 1976); Goddard, *Coventry*; David McGrory, *A History of Coventry* (Chichester, 2003), p 32; J. C. Lancaster and M. Tomlinson, 'Introduction', *The Victoria History of the County of Warwick, VIII: The City of Coventry and Borough of Warwick*, ed. W. B. Stephens (8 vols) (London, 1969), pp 1–23, p 2.

[46] Langton, 'Gloucester'.

[47] Baker and Holt, *Urban Growth*.

[48] Butcher, 'Oxford and Canterbury'.

[49] Butcher, 'Newcastle'.

[50] Rosser, *Westminster*, p 45.

[51] Robert S. Gottfried, *Bury St Edmunds and the Urban Crisis: 1290–1539* (Princeton, NJ, 1982), p 78.

[52] Bonney, *Durham*, p 123.

[53] Barbara Harvey, *Westminster Abbey and Its Estates in the Middle Ages* (Oxford, 1977), p 2.

[54] Harvey, *Westminster Abbey*, pp 1–3, 331–2.

[55] R. H. Hilton, 'Some Problems of Urban Real Property in the Middle Ages', *Socialism, Capitalism and Economic Growth: Essays Presented to Maurice Dobb* ed. C. H. Feinstein (Cambridge, 1967), pp 326–37.

[56] Maryanne Kowaleski, *Local Markets and Regional Trade in Medieval Exeter* (Cambridge, 1995), p 111.

[57] Rosser, *Westminster*, p 95.

[58] Rosser, *Westminster*, p 95.

[59] Butcher, 'Oxford and Canterbury', p 13.

[60] Butcher, 'Oxford and Canterbury', p 18.

[61] Butcher, 'Newcastle', p 43.

[62] Hilton, 'Urban', p 337.

[63] Jennifer Kermode, *Medieval Merchants: York, Beverley and Hull in the Later Middle Ages* (Cambridge, 1998), pp 286–90.

[64] See, for example, J. A. Raftis, *A Small Town in Late Medieval England: Godmanchester, 1278–1400* (Toronto, 1982).

[65] Howell, *Land, Family*.

66 Carolyn A. Clarke, 'Peasant Society and Land Transactions in Chesterton, Cambridgeshire 1277–1325' (DPhil thesis, University of Oxford, 1985).

67 Zvi Razi, 'Family, Land and the Village Community in Later Medieval England', *Past and Present* 93 (1) (1981): 1–36.

68 Maryanne Kowaleski, 'The History of Urban Families in Medieval England', *Journal of Medieval History* 14 (1) (1998): 47–63.

69 M, MR.

70 Kowaleski, 'Urban Families', 51, 59.

71 Rees Jones, *York*, pp 197–5, 315.

72 Brittain Bouchard, *Holy Entrepreneurs*; Carmine Guerriero, 'The Medieval Origins of a Culture of Corporation and Inclusive Political Institutions', Working Paper (ACLE University of Amsterdam, 2013), available at http://EconPapers.repec.org/RePEc:pra:mprapa:70879 (accessed 1 March 2017); Rosenwein, *Neighbour*.

73 Rubin, *Charity*.

74 Lee, *Cambridge*, pp 1–2.

75 F. G. Walker, 'Roman Roads into Cambridge', *Proceedings of the Cambridge Antiquarian Society* 14 (2) (1910): 141–74.

76 Lobel, *Atlas*, pp 1–2.

77 Helen M. Cam, 'The City of Cambridge', VCH 3, pp 1–149; Helen M. Cam, 'The Origin of the Borough of Cambridge: A Consideration of Prof. Carl Stephenson's Theories', *Proceedings of the Cambridge Antiquarian Society* 35 (1935): 33–53; Arthur Gray, *The Dual Origin of the Town of Cambridge* (London, 1908); M.

78 A. Taylor, *Cambridge: The Hidden History* (Stroud, 1999), p 11.

79 Lobel, *Atlas*, p 2.

80 Lobel, *Atlas*, pp 2–3.

81 W. W. Skeat, 'Grantchester and Cambridge', *Proceedings of the Cambridge Antiquarian Society* 14 (1) (1909): 111–22; Walter W. Skeat, *The Place-Names of Cambridgeshire* (Cambridge, 1901); Arthur Gray, 'The Ford and Bridge of Cambridge', *Proceedings of the Cambridge Antiquarian Society* 14 (2) (1910): 126–39; Lobel, *Atlas*, pp 3–5.

82 Lobel, *Atlas*, pp 3–4.

83 Lobel, *Atlas*, p 5.

84 Craig Cessford and Alison Dickens, 'Castle Hill, Cambridge: Excavation of Saxon, Medieval and Post-Medieval Deposits, Saxon Execution Site and a Medieval Coinhoard', *Proceedings of the Cambridge Antiquarian Society* 94 (2005): 73–102; William Mortlock Palmer, *Cambridge Castle* (Cambridge, n.d.), p 6; William Mortlock Palmer, 'Cambridge Castle Building Accounts 1286–1299', *Proceedings of the Cambridge Antiquarian Society* 26 (1925): 66–89; C, p 19.

85 H. C. Darby, *The Domesday Geography of Cambridgeshire* (Cambridge, 1936), pp 264, 313; Ann Williams and G. H. Martin (eds), *Domesday Book: A Complete Translation* (London, 2002).

86 Bede, cited in C, p 13.

87 K. S. B. Keats-Rohan, *Domesday People, Domesday Descendants: A Prosopography of Persons Occurring in English Documents 1066–1166* (2 vols) (Woodbridge, 1999 and 2002); C, p 18.

88 HR 82.

89 One possible reason why the number of properties paying hawgable did not increase as the town expanded is that much of the expansion may have been generated by the subdivision of established messuages. Where a messuage was subdivided, the hawgable could either have been divided between the properties or one part of property could have continued to pay the hawgable while the other

did not. If it were widely applied then the number of properties paying hawgable would have remained static while the number of properties not paying hawgable would have increased. Another possibility is that some of the other wards in the town also had personal fees where properties did not pay hawgable, although there is no direct evidence for this. If it were true then new properties created in these fees would not pay hawgable because the king was not involved. These explanations, however, do not account for the actual decrease in the number of properties paying hawgable. There are three possible explanations for this. The first is simply that poor record-keeping allowed owners to opt out by stopping payment for long enough that no one could remember the reason, and then claim immunity. The second is that immunity was actually given as a reward for some service rendered to the king, or to the civic authorities as holders of the farm. The third is that the property reverted to the king when it was vacated by the owner because they could no longer afford the rent. The king then either gave or sold the property outright to someone else; receiving property in this way was often a perk of royal service. It would then be easier for the king to sell the property outright than simply reimpose hawgable at a higher rate.

90   C, p 18, fn 4.

91   OBG; OTG.

92   C, pp 50–1.

93   Various villages in Cambridgeshire have been studied in detail; for example, John S. Lee, 'Decline and Growth in the Late Medieval Fenland: The Examples of Outwell and Upwell', *Proceedings of the Cambridge Antiquarian Society* 104 (2015): 137–47; W. M. Palmer, 'A History of Clopton, Cambridgeshire', *Proceedings of the Cambridge Antiquarian Society* 33 (1933): 3–60; W. M. Palmer, The Manor House of the Argentines at Melbourn, and their Farm Accounts for 1317–18', *Proceedings of the Cambridge Antiquarian Society* 27 (1926): 16–79. See also H. C. Hughes, 'Windmills in Cambridgeshire and the Isle of Ely', *Proceedings of the Cambridge Antiquarian Society* 31 (1931): 17–29; H. P. Stokes, 'Cambridgeshire "Forests"', *Proceedings of the Cambridge Antiquarian Society* 23 (1922): 63–85.

94   Frederic William Maitland and Mary Bateson (eds), *The Charters of the Borough of Cambridge* (Cambridge, 1901), pp xi–xii, 2–3.

95   Taylor, *Hidden History*, p 81.

96   Lee, *Cambridge*, pp 116–41.

97   For a discussion of debates over the location of the earliest Jewish settlement in Cambridge see Fine Rolls, Henry III, 8/413, 1224, available at https://finerollshenry3.org.uk/home (accessed 17 October 2018); J, pp 113–15; R. B. Dobson, 'The Jews of Medieval Cambridge', *Jewish Historical Studies*, 32 (1990–2): 1–24, pp 10–11; Alison Dickens and Craig Cessford, 'Cambridge Historic City Centre Revealed', *Current Archaeology* 208 (March/April 2007): 22–31; Peter Bryan and Nick Wise, 'A Reconstruction of the Medieval Cambridge Market Place', *Proceedings of the Cambridge Antiquarian Society* 91 (2002): 73–87; J. W. Clark and J. E. Foster, 'History of a Site in Senate House Yard with Some Notes on Occupiers', *Proceedings of the Cambridge Antiquarian Society* 13 (1) (1909): 120–42; Richard Newman and Christopher Evans, 'Archaeological Investigations at the Old Schools, University of Cambridge', *Proceedings of the Cambridge Antiquarian Society* 100 (2011): 185–96. When the Franciscans took over the prison the burgesses were given money to build a new gaol, although the location of this is unknown. It is likely that references to the tolbooth from 1322 refer to the same building. A new guildhall was completed in 1387 and from this point the tolbooth

seems to have been the name applied to the prison only. Cam, 'Cambridge', pp 119–20; J, p 113.

98 Dobson, 'Jews', p 4.

99 Dobson, 'Jews', pp 4–5.

100 Dobson, 'Jews', p 7.

101 Dobson, 'Jews', p 7.

102 Dobson, 'Jews', pp 15–16.

103 J, p 200.

104 Dobson, 'Jews', pp 15–16; VCH 3, pp 2–15.

105 Helen M. Cam, 'Cambridgeshire Sheriffs in the Thirteenth Century', *Proceedings of the Cambridge Antiquarian Society* 25 (1924): 78–102. Maitland and Bateson, *Charters*, pp xiii–xv, 3–4.

106 Maitland and Bateson, *Charters*, pp xiii–xv, 3–4.

107 Maitland and Bateson, *Charters*, pp xv–xvii, 5–6; M, p 75. Maitland and Bateson suggest that the merchant guild probably consisted of 'the general body of burgesses' and say that the origins of the right to hold Reach Fair are unknown.

108 Maitland and Bateson, *Charters*, pp xvi, 5–6.

109 Maitland and Bateson, *Charters*, p xviii.

110 StJ, p xi.

111 Maitland and Bateson, *Charters*, pp xix–xx, 17–19; For detail of individual office holders see British Library Cole Add. MS 5833, Mayors and Bailiffs of Cambridge to 1380 fols 126–35, also partly reproduced by M, pp 134–41; F covers the Badcock, the Bullen, the Dent, Ellis, Harleston, Laurence, Pilate, Purchas, Tabor and Tuylet families; BNM; Cam, 'Cambridge', 36–7, 44–5; J. P. Rushe, 'The Origin of St Mary's Guild', *Proceedings of the Cambridge Antiquarian Society* 16 (1) (1912): 20–52.

112 Alison Dickens and Craig Cessford, 'City Centre Revealed'; Bryan and Wise, 'Reconstruction'; Clark and Foster, 'Senate House Yard'; Newman and Evans, 'Old Schools'.

113 *Rotuli Curiae Regis* XV, pp 358–9 and Catherine Casson, Mark Casson, John S. Lee and Katie Phillips, *Business and Community in Medieval England: The Cambridge Hundred Rolls Source Volume* (Bristol, 2020), Appendix 6.

114 *Rotuli Curiae Regis* XV, pp 358–9 and Casson, Casson, Lee and Phillips, *Business and Community*, Appendix 6.

115 Fine Rolls, Henry III. 19/207, 19/294 available at https://finerollshenry3.org.uk (accessed 11 October 2018); C, pp 42–3.

116 Cam, 'Cambridge', 30–1.

117 In 1340 Edward III created the earldom of Cambridge and allocated it £20 a year from the profits of the county and the earldom was stopped and revived again at various subsequent periods, usually linked to the earldom of York: Maitland and Bateson, *Charters*, pp xviii, 7–8; M, p 75. Cam, 'Cambridge', 30–1; W. M. Palmer (ed.), *Cambridge Borough Documents* (Cambridge, 1931); J. H. Round, 'The Third Penny', *English Historical Review* 34 (1919): 62–4.

118 Dobson, 'Jews', p 16.

119 E. Leedham-Green, *A Concise History of the University of Cambridge* (Cambridge, 1996), pp 3–15.

120 T. H. Aston, G. D. Duncan and T. A. R. Evans, 'The Medieval Alumni of the University of Cambridge', *Past and Present* 86 (1980): 9–86, p 15.

121 Archdeacon Cunningham, 'The Problem as to the Changes in the Course of the Cam since Roman Times', *Proceedings of the Cambridge Antiquarian Society* 14 (1)

(1909): 74–85; Royal Commission on the Historical Monuments of England, *City of Cambridge*, 2 vols (London, 1959), pp xxxiii–lix; Rob Atkins, 'Between River, Priory and Town: Excavations at the Former Cambridge Regional College Site, Brunswick, Cambridge', *Proceedings of the Cambridge Antiquarian Society* 101 (2012): 7–22.

¹²² Cam, 'Cambridge', p 114.

¹²³ Mary Hesse, 'The East Fields of Cambridge', *Proceedings of the Cambridge Antiquarian Society* 96 (2007): 143–60; LB, pp xxxi–xxx; W.

¹²⁴ W, pp 84–5; Taylor, *Hidden History*, p 81.

¹²⁵ OBG; OTG.

¹²⁶ Lobel, *Atlas*, p 10; VCH 3, pp 123–32.

¹²⁷ Roger Lovatt and Marie Lovatt, 'The Religious Life of the Townsmen of Medieval Cambridge', *Catholics in Cambridge* ed. Nicholas Rogers (Leominster, 2003), pp 4–21.

¹²⁸ P. Lineham (ed.), *St John's College Cambridge: A History* (Woodbridge, 2011).

¹²⁹ Harvard Library, Harvard Map Collection, Oppidum Cantebrigiae, Richard Lyne's Map of Cambridge; British Library C.24.A.27(3) Oppidum Cantebrigiae, Richard Lyne's Map of Cambridge.

¹³⁰ Robert Willis and John Willis Clark, *The Architectural History of the University of Cambridge and the Colleges of Cambridge and Eton* (2 vols) I (Cambridge, 1886), p xcvi. For later maps see Herbert George Fordham, 'Cambridgeshire Maps: An Annotated List of the Pre-Survey Maps of the County of Cambridge 1576–1800', *Proceedings of the Cambridge Antiquarian Society* 11 (1) (1905): 101–73.

¹³¹ Lobel, *Atlas*, pp 1–23.

¹³² TNA Special Collections, 'Hundred Rolls and Eyre Veredicta', available at http://discovery.nationalarchives.gov.uk/details/r/C13523 (accessed 30 July 2017). See also Sheffield Hundred Rolls Project, available at http://www.roffe.co.uk/shrp.htm (accessed 2 April 2017).

¹³³ TNA, 'Hundred Rolls and Eyre Veredicta'.

¹³⁴ Diana E. Greenway, 'A Newly Discovered Fragment of the Hundred Rolls of 1279–80', *Journal of Society of Archivists* 7 (2) (1982): 73–77, p 73.

¹³⁵ Sandra Raban, *A Second Domesday: The Hundred Rolls of 1279–80* (Oxford, 2004), p 121.

¹³⁶ Helen M. Cam, *The Hundred and the Hundred Rolls: An Outline of Local Government in Medieval England* (London, 1930).

¹³⁷ Raban, *Second Domesday*.

¹³⁸ Greenway, 'Fragment', p 73.

¹³⁹ TNA SC5/CAMBS/TOWER/2 Barnwell Hundred Roll; TNA SC5/CAMBS/TOWER/1/Parts1–3 Cambridge Borough Hundred Rolls.

¹⁴⁰ Raban, *Second Domesday*, pp 48–50.

¹⁴¹ Helen M. Cam, *Liberties and Communities in Medieval England* (Cambridge, 1944), p 40; VCH 2 Huntingdon, pp 198–9; Sheriff of Cambridgeshire and Huntingdonshire, available at https://en.wikipedia.org/wiki/Sheriff_of_Cambridgeshire_and_Huntingdonshire (accessed 29 October 2018). Sir William was succeeded by Baldwin St George in 1278, who could also have been involved; he too had been sheriff earlier, but little is known about him.

¹⁴² *Rotuli Hundredorum Temp. Henry III and Edward I., in Turr' Lond' et in Curia Receptæ Scaccarij Westm. Asservati* (2 vols) (London, 1812 and 1818).

¹⁴³ TNA, 'Hundred Rolls and Eyre Veredicta'.

¹⁴⁴ M, pp 142–58.

[145] Raban, *Second Domesday*, p 154.

[146] EB; OBG.

[147] TNA SC5/CAMBRIDGE/TOWER/2 Barnwell Hundred Roll; TNA SC5/CAMBS/TOWER/1/Parts1–3 Cambridge Borough Hundred Rolls; Casson, Casson, Lee and Phillips, *Business and Community*.

[148] B. Dodwell, 'The Free Tenantry of the Hundred Rolls', *Economic History Review* 14 (2) (1944): 163–71; Junichi Kanzaka, 'Villein Rents in Thirteenth-Century England: An Analysis of the Hundred Rolls of 1279–1280', *Economic History Review* 55 (4) (2002): 593–619; E. Kosminsky, 'The Hundred Rolls of 1279–80 as a Source for English Agrarian History', *Economic History Review* 3 (1) (1931): 16–44.

[149] Howell's unpublished research particularly focused on East Cambridgeshire settlements about 5–10 miles east of Cambridge and clustered in an arc around Fulbourn Fen, namely Fulbourn, Teversham, Stow-cum-Quy, Little Wilbraham and Great Wilbraham. She examined the relationship between land use, the size of landholdings, the spatial distribution of smallholdings, inheritance strategies and family composition. The paper presented a range of statistical evidence derived from family landholdings recorded in the Hundred Rolls and identified by a shared surname. Howell, *Land, Family*; Cicely A. H. Howell, 'Contrasting Communities: Arable and Marshland' (unpublished draft, 1979); Cicely A. H. Howell, 'Peasant Inheritance Customs in the Midlands, 1280–1700', *Land and Inheritance: Rural Society in Western Europe, 1200–1800* ed. Jack Goody, Joan Thirsk and E. P. Thompson (Cambridge, 1978), pp 112–55; Cicely A. H. Howell, 'Stability and Change 1300–1700: The Socio-Economic Context of the Self-Perpetuating Family Farm in England', *Journal of Peasant Studies* 2 (4) (1975): 468–82; Cicely A. H. Howell, 'The Economic and Social Condition of the Peasantry in South East Leicestershire, A.D. 1300–1700' (DPhil thesis, University of Oxford, 1974).

[150] The survey was a precursor to the mortmain legislation of 1290: Raban, *Mortmain*. The Cambridgeshire Ragman Rolls have also been examined, but they provide little information on the town. Leonard E. Scales, 'The Cambridgeshire Ragman Rolls', *English Historical Review* 113 (452) (1998): 553–7.

[151] Darby, *Domesday Geography*, pp 264, 313; Williams and Martin (eds), *Domesday Book*.

[152] W. M. Palmer (ed.), *The Assizes held at Cambridge 1260: Being a Condensed Translation of Assize Roll 82 in the Public Record Office with an Introduction* (Linton, 1930); TNA JUST 1/81 Cambridgeshire Eyre of 1247 Foreign pleas roll, including essoins, 31 Henry III; TNA JUST 1/82 Cambridgeshire Eyre of 1261, Roll of civil, foreign and crown pleas, jury calendar, essoins and attorneys 45 Henry III; TNA JUST 1/83 Cambridgeshire Eyre of 1268 General oyer and terminer, lands given away as a result of the Barons' War, roll of pleas, presentments, amercements and jury calendar 53 Henry III, TNA JUST 1/84 Cambridgeshire Eyre of 1272 Roll of civil and foreign pleas 56 Henry III; TNA JUST 1/85 Cambridgeshire Eyre of 1272 Roll of crown pleas, 56 Henry III; TNA JUST 1/86 Cambridgeshire Eyre of 1286 Rex roll of civil, foreign and crown pleas, gaol delivery, plaints, amercements and fines, jury calendar, essoins and attorneys, 14 Edward I; TNA JUST 1/96 Cambridgeshire Eyre of 1299 Berwick's roll of civil, foreign, king's and crown pleas, gaol delivery, plaints, jury calendar, essoins and attorneys, 27 Edward I. C. A. F. Meekings, *Crown Pleas of the Wiltshire Eyre, 1249* (Devizes, 1961), p 3; TNA, 'General Eyres', available at http://www.nationalarchives.gov.uk/help-with-your-research/research-guides/general-eyres-1194-1348/#sevenpointthree (accessed 30 July 2017);

[153] C. A. F. Meekings, *Crown Pleas of the Wiltshire Eyre, 1249* (Devizes, 1961), p 3; TNA, 'General Eyres', available at http://www.nationalarchives.gov.uk/help-with-your-research/research-guides/general-eyres-1194-1348/#sevenpointthree (accessed 30 July 2017);

[154] TNA, 'Pipe Rolls'; Eilert Ekwall (ed.) *Two Early London Subsidy Rolls* (London, 1951), pp vii–xiii.; TNA, 'Taxation Before 1689', available at http://www.nationalarchives.gov.uk/help-with-your-research/research-guides/taxation-before-1689/ (accessed 30 July 2017); TNA E179 Database, available at http://www.nationalarchives.gov.uk/e179/default.asp (accessed 30 July 2017); William M. Palmer, *Cambridgeshire Subsidy Rolls 1250–1695* (London, 1912).

[155] PR vols (London, 1884–2016), especially the published rolls for the years 1130–1224, 1230 and 1242, vols 1–9, 11–19, 21–58, 50, 52–8, 60, 62, 64, 66, 68, 73, 75, 77, 80, 85, 86, 89, 91, 93, 94; TNA E 372/70 Tallage of 1225; TNA, 'Pipe Rolls', available at http://www.nationalarchives.gov.uk/help-with-your-research/research-guides/medieval-financial-records-pipe-rolls-1130-1300/ (accessed 30 July 2017).

[156] Anthony Musson and W. M. Ormrod, *The Evolution of English Justice: Law, Politics and Society in the Fourteenth Century* (Basingstoke, 1999), pp 14–15.

[157] C. T. Flower, David Crook and Paul Brand (eds), *Rotuli Curiae Regis/Curia Regis Rolls* (10 vols) I–IX (London and Woodbridge, 1922–2006); Doris Mary Stenton (ed.), *Pleas before the King and His Justices 1198–1202 I: Introduction with Appendix Containing Essoins 1199–1201, A King's Roll of 1200 and Writs 1190–1200* (4 vols) (London, 1952–67); Doris Mary Stenton (ed.), *Pleas before the King and His Justices 1198–1202 II: Fragments of Rolls from the Years 1198, 1201 and 1202* (4 vols) (London, 1952–67); Doris Mary Stenton (ed.), *Pleas before the King and His Justices 1198–1202 III: Rolls or Fragments of Rolls from the Years 1199, 1201 and 1203–6* (4 vols) (London, 1952–67); Doris Mary Stenton (ed.), *Pleas before the King and His Justices 1198–1202 IV: Rolls or Fragments of Rolls from the Years 1207–1212* (4 vols) (London, 1952–67).

[158] CPR; CCR; The Gen Guide, Patent Rolls, available at https://www.genguide.co.uk/source/patent-rolls-medieval-courts/5/ (accessed 9 January 2018); University of Nottingham Manuscripts and Special Collections Guide, 'Letters Patent', available at https://www.nottingham.ac.uk/manuscriptsandspecialcollections/researchguidance/deedsindepth/freehold/letterspatent.aspx (accessed 9 January 2018).

[159] EJ VI; EJ V; EJ III; EJ IV; EJ I; EJ II; TNA, 'Exchequer of the Jews Plea Rolls', available at http://discovery.nationalarchives.gov.uk/details/r/C6509 (accessed 9 January 2017).

[160] PDC; PDH; PDR; TNA, 'Land Conveyances by Feet of Fines 1182–1833', available at http://www.nationalarchives.gov.uk/help-with-your-research/research-guides/land-conveyance-feet-of- s-1182-1833/ (accessed 9 January 2017).

[161] British Library BM Cole Add. MS 5833, pp 112, 127–34.

[162] BT.

[163] British Library MS Harley 5813, Excerpt comprising transcription of Corpus Christi Deeds; Willis and Willis Clark, *Architectural History*; British Library Cole Add. MS 5809, Friars of the Sack, fol. 85; British Library Cole Add. MS 5809, History of Barnwell Priory, fols 87–9; British Library Cole Add. MS 5810, Number of Houses and Inhabitants in Cambridge in 1728, fol. 190; British Library Cole Add. MS 5810, Index to Lyne's Map of Cambridge, 1574, fols 193–5; British Library Cole Add. MS 5813, History of St Clement's Church, fol. 38; British

Library Cole Add. MS 5813, Various Deeds fols 32, 42, 43, 60–2; British Library Cole Add. MS 5813, Benefactors of the Guild of Our Lady (1315) fols 137–42; British Library Cole Add. MS 5821, History of Barton Manor and deeds, fols 229–33; British Library Cole Add. MS 5821, Benjamin's House at the Tolbooth, fols 229–33; British Library Cole Add. MS 5826, Taxation and Advowsons Documents of 1291 from Bishop Grey's Register, fols 171–88; British Library Cole Add. MS 5826, Account of the School of Pythagoras at Cambridge, fols 46–50; British Library Cole Add. MS 5832, Ancient Places in Cambridge, fols 214–15; British Library Cole Add. MS 5833, Mayors and Bailiffs; W. M. Palmer, 'The Stokes and Hailstone MSS.', *Proceedings of the Cambridge Antiquarian Society* 33 (1933): 169–70; Willis and Willis Clark, *Architectural History*, pp xcv–xcvi.

[164] LB. This manuscript was later used by a number of antiquaries and extracts from it were printed in Anon, *The History and Antiquities of Barnwell Abbey and of Sturbridge Fair* (London, 1786).

[165] Bodleian MS Gough Cambridgeshire 1 General collections for the county and University of Cambridge with the Isle and Bishopric of Ely, extracted from the Charters, Registers, etc by Francis Blomefield, Clerk, late of Caius College and afterwards Rector of Fersfield in Norfolk: I Prior of Barnwell's Register (2 vols) I.

[166] StR.

[167] StJ.

[168] StJ; Rubin, *Charity*.

[169] Merton College Archives, University of Oxford, *Liber Ruber*, S.

[170] Online catalogue of Corpus Christi Deeds, available at https://janus.lib.cam.ac.uk/db/node.xsp?id=EAD%2FGBR%2F2938%2FCCCC09 (accessed 1 August 2017); Catherine P. Hall, 'The Gild of Corpus Christi and the Foundation of Corpus Christi College: An Investigation of the Documents', *Medieval Cambridge: Essays on the Pre-Reformation University* ed. Patrick Zutshi (Woodbridge, 1993), pp 65–91.

[171] Peterhouse, St Peter's College A1–3 and the Site of the College A1–29.

[172] M. B. Hackett, *The Original Statutes of Cambridge University: The Text and Its History* (Cambridge, 1970); Leedham-Green, *A Concise History*, p 6.

2

Dynamics of
the Property Market

Introduction

This chapter examines the dynamics of the property market in Cambridge through a comprehensive statistical analysis of the information contained in the Hundred Rolls. It considers how rents varied across the town according to the location of the property, the use of the property, the method by which the property was acquired and a range of other characteristics. As noted in Chapter 1, Frederic Maitland pioneered statistical analysis of the Hundred Rolls in the appendix to his book *Township and Borough*, published in 1898. This analysis significantly expands Maitland's work by including new information that was not available at the time, notably the material from the recently discovered third roll.[1] It employs statistical techniques that were not available when Maitland was writing, but which have recently been employed to analyse medieval urban rents in Gloucester and Hull, and early modern agricultural rents in England.[2] It complements previous medieval scholarship that has used archaeological evidence and geographical mapping to reconstruct the topographies of medieval towns and has drawn upon documentary evidence to identify the individuals and institutions involved in the property market.[3]

Statistical analysis of urban rents requires documentary evidence that both covers a relatively large number of properties and provides detailed information on each property. As discussed earlier, Cambridge is a rare example of a town with such surviving evidence, and an even rarer example of a place where the history of each property is recorded to within living memory. An understanding is also required of the nature of medieval rents, particularly the distinction between hawgable and ordinary rents (sometimes called quit rents or rents of assize). Statistical techniques have been rarely applied to sources on the medieval urban property market because it has often been assumed that all rents in boroughs were set at a uniform level and remained 'fossilized' through subsequent decades or centuries at the level at which they were set when the town was founded.[4] The first section of the chapter therefore explains the nature of rent in medieval towns, and the distinction between hawgable and ordinary rents. Subsequent sections then report the results of the statistical analysis of the Hundred Rolls. The impact of property characteristics, location and tenure on levels of ordinary rent and hawgable is analysed. To further refine that analysis, a statistical analysis of the Barnwell Priory rental of 1295 is presented and the transmission of property between individuals and family dynasties examined. Private individuals and institutional recipients of rents are discussed in detail.

2.1 The nature of rent

To interpret the information from the Hundred Rolls correctly it is important to appreciate the way in which property was traded in the 13th century. Most property in towns was freehold property, which meant that the owner could dispose of their property as they wished. Most freeholders paid rent. This was because they had purchased the property by promising to pay a fixed annual rent in perpetuity. Cash was scarce in the 13th century, because of a limited supply of coins. A purchaser could promise to pay a single lump sum – called gersuma or consideration – but even this might be paid in instalments because of a shortage of cash. It was also possible to combine the two methods of payment, with a modest gersuma up front followed by a modest perpetual rent; the proportions could be negotiated between the buyer and the seller.

Rent was attached to the property rather than the owner. If a property was sold the new owner had to continue paying the rent. The property was therefore burdened with its perpetual rent. The owner could, however, buy back the rent, thereby freeing the property from its burden. That did not give the owner additional rights of any substance, but it did allow their property to be sold for a higher price.

Rent-recipients could sell their rents, even though they no longer owned their property. Both properties and rent could be given, for example, to charitable institutions such as priories. Suppose that A had sold a property to B for a perpetual rent. B could then decide to give the property to a priory. The priory could use the property itself, rent it out on a succession of short-term leases or sell it on to someone else for gersuma or perpetual rent. If the priory held on to the property it would continue paying rent to A. But A could also donate this rent to the priory (or to some other priory for that matter). In this case the priory would no longer pay any rent to A; it would hold the property without any burden attached.

Because both properties and rents could be sold, the system was quite flexible. But because the rents were perpetual the system appears in retrospect to have been rigid too. It seems unfamiliar to modern eyes. But a perpetual rent was really just like a mortgage with an infinite life. The main difference from modern methods of financing property purchase was that the mortgage was supplied by the seller, who effectively provided the buyer with a loan with which to buy the property. In the modern system a mortgage is supplied by a bank (or home loan agency or building society). But because such institutions did not exist in 13th-century England, sellers provided credit instead. In modern economies sellers' credit is often called hire purchase. Effectively, therefore, medieval property was acquired through indefinite hire purchase.

Multiple rents

Many properties in Cambridge carried multiple rents. In most cases this was because they had been bought and sold several times. B may have secured the property from A for only a modest rent. B or their heirs might subsequently wish to sell the property, either to generate cash or to upsize or downsize to another property. At this point they might have been able to realize a capital gain. If the town was booming and property was scarce, then the property might have commanded a rent higher than it did when B first acquired it. B could therefore have increased the rent when selling to C by adding a rent of their own. C would therefore pay two rents: one to A and one to B. The payment to A would be the historic rent and the payment to B the new rent. Comparing the two may indicate to the modern researcher how far the property had appreciated in value. As C sold to D and D to E, so additional rents were added. If any of the parties gave or sold their rent to others that component of rent was diverted accordingly.

It is evident that the payment could be administratively complex. It seems that the holder of the property had sole responsibility for paying the right rent to the right person. This is because only exceptions to this rule seem to be noted. Thus it is sometimes said that B acquits C to A, meaning that C paid the total rent to B and B then passed on their share of the rent to A. This would imply that C normally paid both A and B directly.

Responses to declining property values

Property does not always appreciate in value. Because the rent burden was fixed, depreciation of property could make it unviable to hold, especially in circumstances where the payment of rent exceeded the owner's income. If owner C defaulted on the rent the property reverted to the previous owner B (i.e. the seller). B then had to decide whether they could afford to hold the property too. While reversion eliminated the burden of the rent paid to B, it did not eliminate the rent, if any, that B owed to A. If the fall in value was substantial the property might revert to A. In that situation all the rent burden would be eliminated. The property was valueless and carried zero rent.

In a falling market, rent-recipients might anticipate this problem and allow the owners to build up rent arrears, in the hope of an imminent economic recovery. Conversely owners might revert to moneylenders to maintain their payments. Short-term credit supplied by Jewish moneylenders appears to have played an important role in the Cambridge capital market, as discussed later. When the loans were repaid it could help to stabilize the market, but otherwise recourse to credit could aggravate problems.

Rent as an indicator of economic value

This analysis shows that property rents can both increase and decrease according to economic conditions in a town. The fact that rents are perpetual does not imply that they are rigid, because the total rent can change every time a property changes hands. This suggests that the property rent prevailing at any time can be taken as an indicator of the economic value of a property. This proposition must be qualified, however. If a property was purchased by gersuma then no rent was attached to it as a result of the sale. Payment by gersuma, either wholly or partially, therefore meant that total rent almost certainly understated the value of a property. The value of property was potentially also understated if it never changed hands. In a rising market, properties that change hands frequently tend to carry higher rents than properties that never change hands.[5]

In some cases it is possible to detect this problem. In the 13th century the payment of gersuma was often associated with the payment of a token rent, such as a nominal amount of money (e.g. one penny) or a gift of symbolic value (e.g. rose, clove, gillyflower or pair of white gloves). These symbolic gifts expressed the notion of subinfeudation in the sale of property, namely that the buyer held their property from the seller and therefore owed service and allegiance to them. Yet by the 13th century that allegiance was of purely token value so far as freehold property was concerned, although it continued to be relevant to customary tenants of agricultural land. These token rents should, however, be distinguished from payments of rent in kind, such as consignments of cumin, pepper or candlewax, not to mention extremely valuable items such as goshawks.

A property that paid a token rent may well have been purchased by gersuma, making it likely that the rent alone represented an undervaluation of the property. Evidence that a property had not been traded recently can be more difficult to obtain, but in the Cambridge Hundred Rolls it can be inferred from the history of a property. But because memory can be short, and most transactions are undated, this evidence is not decisive.

The safest conclusion is that total rent indicates the minimum value of a property, provided that the property is occupied. A property where rent is overvalued may be vacant, and so rents on vacant properties could be overstated. There are other reasons why a property may be vacant, however, and so vacancy cannot be taken as a definite indication of overvaluation.

Transmission of property

Property could be transmitted between owners in three main ways, namely transaction, gift and inheritance. These can be further subdivided, giving seven categories in all.

A transaction could involve purchase, exchange or lease. In a typical purchase the buyer committed to a perpetual rent, as discussed earlier, although they could buy outright by paying gersuma instead. With exchange they offered another property in return. Because the details of this property, such as the rent it paid, are not normally given in the records, it is not normally possible to assess the value of an exchange transaction. A lease was typically (though not invariably) a lease for life. Leases were most commonly offered to parents who had given all their property to their children, and who then leased back from their children a property in which they could live.

Gifts also fell into three main categories: a straightforward gift, a disguised transaction and a gift in marriage. A straightforward gift was one in which the donor transferred the property to the beneficiary and received nothing tangible in return. Such gifts could, however, provide intangible returns; they could place the beneficiary under obligation or, in the case of gifts to monasteries, be exchanged for prayers for the souls of the donor and their family. A disguised gift was one in which the donor received a tangible reward, and which looks like a transaction to modern eyes. Charters, deeds and feet of fines often refer to gifts of property, but then state that a lump sum payment (gersuma or consideration) was made in return.[6] In Cambridge several donors received rents or gersuma in return for their gifts, but there are many gifts where it is unclear when a payment was involved or not. A gift in marriage was typically a payment of dowry by the bride's parents. Remarriage also transferred property when property was held by man and wife, which was very common at the time.

The final category was inheritance. This was typically from father to son, but a daughter might inherit if there was no son. In some cases property was simply left to surviving children as co-owners.

Investigation of the proportion of property traded between people compared with that which was gifted or inherited can improve our understanding of the dynamics of the medieval urban property market. The Cambridge Hundred Rolls provide unusually rich information on this topic. This makes it possible to compare, for example, the proportion of properties purchased by the current holder from the previous holder with the proportion of properties purchased by the previous holder from their previous holder. For some properties the trail goes back for seven generations before it goes cold. The number of properties diminishes as the number of generations of owner increases, and for statistical purposes it is only viable to go back six generations.

Hawgable

Hawgable was introduced in Chapter 1. It was a rent (normally on a house or messuage) paid by a tenant-in-chief to the king. When a tenant-in-chief sold a property, the buyer normally became liable for the hawgable, in addition to any rent due to the tenant-in-chief as the seller of the property. In many towns, including Cambridge, the bailiffs collected the hawgable on behalf of the king, and where they held the town at fee farm they retained the hawgable for themselves; it contributed to the annual lump sum they paid to the king. In other towns the rent was known as landgable.

Hawgable and landgable are interesting because they go back to the very beginnings of many market towns in Anglo-Saxon or early Norman times. At that time agricultural land was held from the king by aristocratic tenants-in-chief, who sold land to knights in return for military service. A common unit of land was the knight's fee, which was sufficient to support a knight, together with his men and horses. A knight's fee might in turn be split into manors held by yeomen or minor aristocracy. The lord of the manor would then pay the knight service in proportion to the amount of land they held, allowing the knight to fund his service to the king through the subdivision and sale of his land.

This principle of subdivision could be pushed further. Land at strategic positions, such as bridging points, would naturally attract trade, and the local landowner, in conjunction with his lord, might decide to turn a small local settlement there into a town. They would acquire charters, lay out burgage plots and set a rent for each plot equivalent to the agricultural value of the land involved, or some similar amount. Just as the knight owed service to the king, and the lord to the knight, so the holder of the burgage plot owed service to his lord. This service was hawgable or landgable, and was ultimately due to the king in lieu of military service.[7] A man who came and lived in such a town for a year and a day could acquire a burgage plot in return for a hawgable rent, provided that he erected on his plot a residence in line with the town plan. The town plan also allocated land for a marketplace, and perhaps a mint, together with open spaces for churches and other amenities, as explained in Chapter 1. The people who held burgage plots became the burgesses of the town. By permission of the king the burgesses could become self-governing and collect hawgable on his behalf. By taking on the farm of the town for a fixed payment, the financial risks of collecting hawgable were also transferred to the burgesses, and this gave the burgesses a strong incentive to ensure that their fellow citizens paid the rents that were due.

Not all the properties in a town paid hawgable. Exceptions could be made. Churches were immune. The king could also grant immunity to selected institutions, such as priories, and even to individuals, perhaps as a reward for royal service. These immunities, it seems, related to the properties rather than the owners; thus if the king gave land to a priory it would not pay hawgable, but if a third party gave the priory property liable to hawgable then the priory would have to continue paying it. In Cambridge some properties paid hawgable and some did not, but the records do not go back sufficiently early to determine exactly why this is the case.

2.2. Descriptive statistics

Format

The Cambridge Hundred Rolls begin by examining the portfolios of major landholders and the rental incomes accruing to them.[8] The main part of the rolls itemizes 1,088 individual property holdings. It is this list that makes the rolls such an important document. The list groups holdings by owner and by parish. Some items refer to more than property, but mainly, it seems, where those properties had a common owner and formed an integrated unit. Each entry, with a few exceptions, lists in sequence the holder of the property, the nature of the property and the descent of the property (whether by inheritance, gift, purchase or other means), and concludes with a statement of the rents that are paid. Entries often indicate family relationships, such as father, mother, brother, sister or uncle, and also note cases where the property is only leased (usually for the lessee's life). Two examples will serve to illustrate the information available.

> Thomas Godeman holds one messuage in the parish of St Peter's at the Castle which he acquired by gift of Michael Pilat, which same Michael acquired by purchase from Dennis, son of William Elesheved, and the same Dennis acquired by inheritance through the death of his father William, and the same William acquired by inheritance through the death of Elena Ampe, and in respect thereof he pays per annum to the said Michael and his heirs 1 rose, and to Margaret, widow of Radulph Capmaker, and her heirs ½ mark, and to the heirs of Robert Seman 1 lb of pepper, and to the bailiffs of Cambridge who hold the said town in fee farm etcetera in hawgable 2½d.[9]

The entry relates to a messuage – the most common form of property – and provides a fairly full account of the descent of its ownership. A messuage was basically a plot of land with a residential building on it. Note that four separate rents were paid: one was a substantial money rent of half a mark, one was a small money rent for hawgable, one was a reasonably valuable payment in kind of 1 lb of pepper and one was a token payment in kind of one rose. The payment of a rose to Michael and his heirs corresponds with the description of the transaction as a gift from Michael, although some payment of gersuma may have been involved as well; such payments are never recorded in the rolls, although they regularly appear in deeds. Although the hawgable is low, it was quite large relative to the norm for the town, which was either a penny or halfpenny; neither is the sum a rounded figure, as is often claimed to be the case.

> Richard son of Simon Brenhand of Howes holds one messuage with a certain croft by hereditary right from the succession of the said Simon, his father, which same messuage with croft he bought from Acius, brother of Cambridge and he pays in

respect thereof per annum to the prior of Barnwell 3s 6d by assignment of the said Acius.[10]

This second entry refers to two items of property, a messuage and a croft. The location is not explicit, but adjacent entries place it in the hamlet of Howes, from which the owner took his name, which was on the Huntingdon road just north of the castle. Unlike the previous entry, the descent of the property goes no further than the father's purchase of the property. It is known, however, that Acius, the seller, was a monk of Barnwell Priory, and that he gave Barnwell Priory three messuages in the town, one held by Simon son of Ailede, one by Adam Stars and one that was adjacent to the stone gate.[11] The property described here was probably an additional property, which Acius continued to hold but on which he assigned the rent, so that if Simon defaulted it would revert to him and not the priory. Acius was clearly a wealthy individual before he entered the priory.

Types of property

Eleven main types of property are identified in the rolls, namely messuages, houses, shops, selds, stalls, granges, granaries, curtilages, crofts, vacant urban land and agricultural land.[12] The rolls provide limited information on agricultural land. Occasionally specific fields, such as Binnenbroc, are mentioned, but in most cases land is simply described as being in either the Cambridge fields or Barnwell fields. Agricultural land areas are expressed in acres and roods (a quarter acre), whereas urban land areas are not normally specified. The main focus of this research is urban land; agricultural land is better studied using other sources, such as the Ely Coucher book of the 13th century, and it was indeed on sources from the 13th century onwards that Maitland based the majority of his agricultural analysis.[13]

Table 2.1 shows the breakdown of property recorded in the Hundred Rolls. For statistical analysis it is necessary to have a certain number of properties of each type; a threshold level of six was set. This meant that some categories had to be merged, for example selds and stalls were merged into a composite category, as were granges and granaries. Overall, therefore, seven types of urban property and two types of agricultural land were identified. Some properties could not be classified because of missing information; they were given their own category. It can be seen that messuages were by far the most numerous urban category, while land in Cambridge fields was the predominant form of agricultural land.

Table 2.1: Types of property

Type of property	Number of plots	Percentage
Messuage	594	73.7
House	27	3.3
Shop	91	11.3
Stall or seld	6	0.7
Grange or granary	11	1.3
Curtilage	7	0.9
Croft	9	1.1
Urban land	15	1.9
Vacant urban land	46	5.7
TOTAL URBAN	806	100.0
Agricultural land		
Cambridge fields (total 595.875 acres)	187	51.1
Barnwell fields (total 171.25 acres)	142	38.8
Unspecified location (total 91.5 acres)	37	10.1
TOTAL AGRICULTURAL	366	100
Less multiple uses of same plot	84	
TOTAL	1,088	

Source: TNA SC5/CAMBS/TOWER/2 Barnwell Hundred Roll; TNA SC5/CAMBS/TOWER/1/ Parts1–3 Cambridge Borough Hundred Rolls; Catherine Casson, Mark Casson, John S. Lee and Katie Phillips, *Business and Community in Medieval England: The Cambridge Hundred Rolls Source Volume* (Bristol, 2020)

Location of property

The basic unit of urban location used in the rolls was the parish. The only non-parish locations given are the communities of Barnwell, Newnham and Howes, together with the marketplace. Unfortunately street names were rarely reported. The numbers of entries relating to each parish are given in Table 2.2.

All the parishes have a viable number of entries for statistical analysis. The largest is St Mary's with 76 entries and the smallest is St Peter's at the Castle with 19. St Radegund's was a separate parish in 1279, but was so small that it is merged into All Saints in the Jewry, from which it had earlier been separated, for statistical analysis.

Table 2.2: Location of properties

Parish or area	Number of plots
All Saints at the Castle	34
All Saints in the Jewry (including the parish of St Radegund's)	32
St Andrew	52
St Benedict	56
St Botolph (excluding Newnham)	46
St Clement	48
St Edward (excluding the Market)	44
St Giles	45
Holy Trinity	56
St John	46
St Mary (the Great) (excluding the Market)	76
St Michael	29
St Peter at the Castle	19
St Peter outside the Trumpington Gate (excluding Newnham)	27
St Sepulchre	13
TOTAL PARISHES	625
Marketplace	14
Newnham	20
Barnwell	92
Howes	4
Unspecified urban location	32
TOTAL URBAN	787
Purely agricultural land	301
TOTAL	1,088

Note: Not all entries refer to messuages, while some refer to messuages as well as other properties. As a result, the number of entries generally overstates the number of messuages and understates the total number of properties in each parish.

Some of the properties described as being in Newnham were also in the parish of St Peter outside the Trumpington Gate, and some may also have been in St Botolph's, although this is not explicitly stated in the rolls. Dual attribution complicates the interpretation of the statistical results. Properties with dual attribution were therefore allocated exclusively to Newnham. For similar reasons properties in the market were allocated exclusively to the market even though they may also have been in St Mary's or St Bene't's. Overall 57 per cent of all entries related to specific urban parishes and, if Barnwell and Newnham are included, 72 per cent related to the urban area as a whole.

Source: TNA SC5/CAMBS/TOWER/2 Barnwell Hundred Roll; TNA SC5/CAMBS/TOWER/1/ Parts1–3 Cambridge Borough Hundred Rolls; Catherine Casson, Mark Casson, John S. Lee and Katie Phillips, *Business and Community in Medieval England: The Cambridge Hundred Rolls Source Volume* (Bristol, 2020)

Some locations are defined by settlement rather than parish. Howes has only four entries and is merged into All Saints at the Castle, which it adjoins. Newnham and Barnwell have sufficient entries to be viable.

Type of owner

Table 2.3 shows that although men dominated property ownership, women were well represented too: 74.7 per cent of entries relate to properties held only by men, but 13.6 per cent of properties were held only by women, and 10.5 per cent by men and women jointly, mainly as husbands and wives. Only 1.2 per cent of properties were held by institutions. Most properties that appear in the individual entries were held *from* institutions rather than *by* institutions. In other words, institutions appear mainly not as holders of property paying perpetual rents but as

Table 2.3: Types of owner

Type of owner	Number of plots
Personal	
Male only	812
Female only	148
Male and female	114
Institutional	14
Other	
TOTAL	1,088
Personal titles	
Lord	3
Master	15
TOTAL	18
Religious titles	
Archdeacon	2
Rector	4
Chaplain	21
Cleric/clerk	7
TOTAL	34

Source: TNA SC5/CAMBS/TOWER/2 Barnwell Hundred Roll; TNA SC5/CAMBS/TOWER/1/ Parts1–3 Cambridge Borough Hundred Rolls; Catherine Casson, Mark Casson, John S. Lee and Katie Phillips, *Business and Community in Medieval England: The Cambridge Hundred Rolls Source Volume* (Bristol, 2020)

recipients of rent. Only 14 entries relate to properties held by institutions; these comprise ten properties held by the Hospital of St John, two held by Sir Alan of Little Bradley, Chaplain and Warden of the Hospital of Balsham, and one each by the Abbot of Warden, Bedfordshire, and the Abbot of Tilty, Essex.

2.3 The use of regression analysis

A variety of statistical methods are available for the analysis of rent. Given the nature of the information provided in the Hundred Rolls, regression analysis is the most appropriate technique. Regression analysis is an extension of correlation analysis; correlation developed around the turn of the 20th century and regression some 20 years later. The specific form of regression analysis used in this book is often described as hedonic regression because it analyses the value of an asset in terms of its special characteristics.

Regression analysis distinguishes between the dependent variable, whose variation is to be explained (in this case rent), and a set of explanatory variables representing factors that might explain that variation. In the present case the explanatory variables are the location and use of the property, its previous ownership and additional factors itemized in what follows. By using regression analysis it is possible to estimate the impact of each type of property characteristic on rent while controlling for variations in all the other factors; for example, it measures the impact of type of property while controlling for location and the impact of location while controlling for type of property. The impact of each factor is measured by a separate coefficient.

Several different regressions are estimated in this chapter. They pool all the relevant data from the 1,088 properties listed in the Hundred Rolls. The results are reported in the tables in this chapter. The explanatory variables are listed in the left-hand column of each table. The estimated coefficient for each variable, together with its probability value (p-value), are reported in the second and third columns of the table respectively. Sometimes two sets of results are reported in the same table, using additional columns.

The p-value indicates the probability that the true value of the coefficient is actually zero, even though, owing to random fluctuation, the estimated coefficient is not. The lower the p-value, the greater the 'significance' of the coefficient. By convention, three levels of significance are used to summarize the results: the highest level is 1 per cent, corresponding to a p-value of 0.01, the generally accepted level is 5 per cent (p-value = 0.05) and the lowest acceptable level is 10 per cent (p-value $= 0.1$). Levels of significance are indicated by the number of stars in the relevant cell of the table; more stars means greater significance. The overall significance of the regression is assessed from the goodness of fit, measured by R^2, and the significance of the F-statistic.

A range of diagnostic tests are available to assess whether the underlying assumptions of the regression theory are valid in each case. A heteroskedasticity test examines whether the magnitude of the deviations from the fitted line varies according to the characteristics of the property that have been included in a regression, while a normality test assesses whether the deviations follow a Gaussian 'bell-shaped' distribution.[14]

Dependent variables

Two dependent variables are used: total rent and the logarithm of total rent. It is total rent that governs the opportunity cost of holding property and therefore affects economic decision-making. The separate components of rent, and the people to whom they are paid, are discussed in detail later in the chapter. The regression involving total rent is based on the assumption that rental value is determined additively, as the sum of a location premium and a property characteristics premium, while the logarithmic regression assumes a multiplicative process whereby the location premium scales up the characteristics premium by a suitable proportion. Both assumptions are plausible, and so it is best to 'let the data decide' by running both regressions and comparing the results. In Table 2.4, for example, the dependent variable is total rent and in Table 2.5 the logarithm of total rent.

Finally, it is possible to analyse not only variation in the *level* of rent, but also variation in the *variation* of rent as well; that is, to investigate whether property rents varied more for certain types of property than for others and for certain locations more than others. High variation in rents for a certain type of property, for example, may indicate that the property came in many different shapes and sizes, while low variation might indicate conformity and perhaps even standardization of design (e.g. standard sizes of burgage plots).[15] High variation in rent in a given parish may be an indication that the parish was socially mixed, with rich and poor living side by side, while low variation could point to the uniformly rich or poor. Tables 2.4 and 2.5 therefore each report two regressions, one for level and the other for variance.

Explanatory variables

The explanatory variables are mainly binary dummy variables; this means that each variable is defined so that it takes a value of one if a property possesses a specific characteristic and a value of zero if it does not. For example, the dummy variable 'house' takes a value one if a property is a house and a value zero otherwise. In presenting the results of the regressions it is useful to take one of the explanatory dummy variables as a control. For location, for example, Holy Trinity was selected for this purpose as it is a large parish with roughly average rents. The Holy Trinity dummy is omitted from the regression, and rents at other locations are measured relative to Holy Trinity. This makes it possible to determine whether there are significant differences in rents between locations. This procedure also avoids multicollinearity (excessively high correlations) that would rise if every location dummy were included in the regression.

The explanatory variables for type of property and for location were described in the previous section. Additional variables were constructed to take into account the nature of property tenure. If a property was bought outright rather than held for perpetual rent then only a token rent paid would be paid; either a rent in kind, such as a rose, or a nominal money rent such as one penny. To avoid confusing nominal money rents with market-driven rents, a variable nominal was created. This is a dummy variable that takes a value of one if the reported rent is less than 6d and otherwise takes a value of zero.

Another tenurial factor is leasing. Some properties were leased rather than owned. Leases were mainly for the lessee's life and mostly involved parents leasing from their children or other heirs. Given the fixed term of the lease, the rent could have been higher, especially if the lessor remained responsible for repairs to the property. On the other hand, family connections suggest that the rent may have been lower because of a sense of filial obligation, and perhaps for the more practical reason that the lessee may have been retired and unable to afford a market-based rent. This reflects a more general proposition that family connections influenced rents. Binary variables were constructed to indicate whether a property was leased, whether the current owner purchased it or acquired it by other means (e.g. inheritance) and whether they acquired it from another family member.

2.4 Impact of location and property characteristics on rent

Tables 2.4 and 2.5 examine the relationship between property characteristics, location and levels of rent. A large proportion of variation in rent levels was explained (74.6 per cent when logarithms were used).[16]

Table 2.4: Regression analysis of total property rents in Cambridge, 1279

Variable	Rent (total paid)		Unexplained variance of rent	
	Coefficient	p-value	Coefficient	p-value
Constant	32.291	0.000***	1257.5	0.001***
Type of property				
Messuage	9.819	0.004***	312.5	0.119
House	−0.592	0.910	−367.1	0.432
Shop	6.500	0.077*	375.3	0.171
Stall	−1.600	0.842	−357.0	0.272
Croft	−7.371	0.186	−211.6	0.448
Curtilage	−4.447	0.353	−107.9	0.760
Grange	−8.610	0.309	−324.9	0.658
Land (piece)	5.020	0.532	464.5	0.364
Land (acres)	2.642	0.001***	−9.9	0.828
Vacant land	−0.480	0.932	238.1	0.739
Parish location				
All Saints at the Castle & Howes	−9.901	0.016**	−595.8	0.011**
All Saints in the Jewry	12.403	0.193	997.6	0.415
St Andrew	2.238	0.700	49.4	0.916
St Bene't	1.286	0.848	937.4	0.193
St Botolph	−1.792	0.723	−224.6	0.467
St Clement	24.593	0.002***	1403.6	0.057*
St Edward	9.240	0.168	361.4	0.435
St Giles	−1.319	0.801	−212.5	0.549
St John	6.368	0.362	799.4	0.221
St Mary	12.361	0.028**	538.6	0.230
St Michael	−8.639	0.064*	−673.6	0.010**
St Peter at the Castle	17.092	0.068*	333.9	0.550
St Peter outside the Trumpington Gate	−11.032	0.011**	−763.9	0.002***
St Sepulchre	35.702	0.038**	2326.2	0.285

(continued)

Table 2.4: Regression analysis of total property rents in Cambridge, 1279 (continued)

Variable	Rent (total paid)		Unexplained variance of rent	
	Coefficient	p-value	Coefficient	p-value
Other locations				
Newnham	−13.533	0.005***	−529.4	0.021**
Barnwell	−20.544	0.000***	−941.3	0.000***
Marketplace	4.6780	0.616	−228.2	0.489
Cambridge fields	−0.122	0.708	0.1	0.996
Barnwell fields	0.387	0.748	−36.1	0.566
Location not specified	−6.144	0.113	−514.2	0.016**
Contractual arrangements				
Lease	12.073	0.163	576.6	0.412
Purchase	1.0419	0.750	−259.1	0.504
Family transaction	−2.386	0.450	−356.3	0.351
Feudal rent of 6d or less	−33.615	0.000***	−1032.7	0.000***

	Rent (total paid)	Unexplained variance of rent
R-squared	0.376	0.104
Adjusted R-squared	0.356	0.075
F-statistic	18.696	3.600
p-value (F-statistic)	0.000***	0.000***
Average rent	25.32	
Standard deviation of rent	37.37	
No of observations	1088	1088
Heteroskedasticity test: Breusch-Pagan-Godfrey	3.600	1.504
p-value	0.000***	0.033**
Jarques-Bera normality	4671.7	193656.6
p-value	0.000***	0.000***

Note: White heteroskedasticity robust standard errors. Significance levels are ***1 per cent, **5 per cent and *10 per cent. The location control is Holy Trinity.

Source: TNA SC5/CAMBS/TOWER/2 Barnwell Hundred Roll; TNA SC5/CAMBS/TOWER/1/ Parts1–3 Cambridge Borough Hundred Rolls; Catherine Casson, Mark Casson, John S. Lee and Katie Phillips, *Business and Community in Medieval England: The Cambridge Hundred Rolls Source Volume* (Bristol, 2020)

Table 2.5: Regression analysis of the log of total property rents in Cambridge, 1279

Variable	Log rent (total paid)		Unexplained variance	
	Coefficient	p-value	Coefficient	p-value
Constant	3.004	0.000***	0.714	0.000***
Type of property				
Messuage	0.350	0.000***	0.125	0.170
House	−0.022	0.873	−0.037	0.794
Shop	0.184	0.008***	0.124	0.050**
Stall	−0.052	0.860	0.163	0.354
Croft	−0.245	0.134	−0.231	0.031**
Curtilage	−0.171	0.391	0.061	0.531
Grange	−0.365	0.148	0.092	0.724
Land (piece)	−0.018	0.931	0.184	0.373
Land (acres)	0.040	0.060*	0.018	0.569
Vacant land	−0.029	0.831	0.010	0.498
Parish location				
All Saints at the Castle & Howes	−0.231	0.084*	−0.195	0.077*
All Saints in the Jewry	0.224	0.236	−0.051	0.803
St Andrew	0.119	0.361	−0.250	0.041**
St Bene't	−0.019	0.896	0.120	0.447
St Botolph	0.024	0.852	−0.216	0.056*
St Clement	0.444	0.004***	0.072	0.604
St Edward	0.204	0.178	−0.032	0.823
St Giles	0.032	0.808	−0.209	0.081*
St John	0.106	0.450	−0.145	0.309
St Mary	0.305	0.018**	−0.021	0.850
St Michael	−0.192	0.229	−0.198	0.109
St Peter at the Castle	0.430	0.026**	−0.156	0.346
St Peter outside the Trumpington Gate	−0.234	0.100	−0.307	0.007***
St Sepulchre	0.609	0.037**	0.209	0.563
Other locations				
Newnham	−0.335	0.027**	−0.205	0.136
Barnwell	−0.490	0.000***	−0.325	0.001**
Marketplace	0.194	0.456	0.110	0.520
Cambridge fields	−0.007	0.426	−0.008	0.324
Barnwell fields	0.048	0.096*	−0.010	0.676
Location not specified	0.009	0.942	−0.240	0.026

(continued)

Table 2.5: Regression analysis of the log of total property rents in Cambridge, 1279 (continued)

Variable	Log rent (total paid)		Unexplained variance	
	Coefficient	p-value	Coefficient	p-value
Contractual arrangements				
Lease	0.244	0.137	0.045	0.784
Purchase	0.044	0.509	−0.080	0.202
Family transaction	−0.002	0.977	−0.073	0.222
Feudal rent of 6d or less	−2.279	0.000***	−0.312	0.000***

	Log rent (total paid)	Unexplained variance
R-squared	0.746	0.111
Adjusted *R*-squared	0.738	0.083
F-statistic	90.896	3.881
p-value (*F*-statistic)	0.000***	0.000***
Average log rent	2.345	
Standard deviation of log rent	1.430	
No of observations	1088	1088
Heteroskedasticity test: Breusch-Pagan-Godfrey	3.880	1.504
p-value	0.000***	0.033**
Jarques-Bera normality	8.5	193656.6
p-value	0.014**	0.000***

Note: White heteroskedasticity robust standard errors. Significance levels are ***1 per cent, **5 per cent and *10 per cent. The location control is Holy Trinity. White robust standard errors.

Source: TNA SC5/CAMBS/TOWER/2 Barnwell Hundred Roll; TNA SC5/CAMBS/TOWER/1/ Parts1–3 Cambridge Borough Hundred Rolls; Catherine Casson, Mark Casson, John S. Lee and Katie Phillips, *Business and Community in Medieval England: The Cambridge Hundred Rolls Source Volume* (Bristol, 2020)

Property characteristics had some statistically significant impacts on rent levels. The first column of Table 2.4 shows, on the top line, a constant term of 32.3, which is the imputed value in pence of a vacant property in Holy Trinity parish. Comparison of that figure with the other results in the table reveals the premia attached to other types of property. A messuage had a 9.8d premium (second line in Table 2.4), giving a total imputed value of 32.2 + 9.8 = 42d for a messuage in Holy Trinity. Shops were worth less than a messuage, at 6.5d premium, while stalls did not carry a premium and were worth less than shops or messuages.

The most striking variations in rent, however, were driven by location rather than type of property. St Sepulchre and St Clement's carry large premia of 35.7d and 24.6d respectively. St Sepulchre is a small parish and its coefficient is significant only at the 5 per cent level but St Clement's, being a larger parish, is significant at the 1 per cent level. St Mary's also has a significant premium of 12.4d (5 per cent significance). The marketplace did not carry a significant premium, but this is partly because the shops that dominate the market carry premia in their own right. The only other parish with a significant positive premium was St Peter's at the Castle, which had a premium of 17.1d (10 per cent significance).

The cheapest parishes were St Peter's outside the Trumpington Gate (11d discount at 5 per cent significance), All Saints at the Castle (9.9d discount at 5 per cent significance) and St Michael's (8.6d discount at 10 per cent). The suburban locations of Barnwell and Newnham are particularly cheap; the former has a discount of 20.5d (1 per cent significance) and the latter 13.5d discount (5 per cent significance). This supports the view that peripheral locations were cheaper than central locations. All Saints at the Castle was the most northerly parish, St Michael's was a westerly parish and St Peter's, Barnwell and Newnham all lay on the southern or eastern edges of the town.

So far as the 'centre' is concerned, the area of highest rent was around St Sepulchre and St Clement's; it may be identified with the southern part of Bridge Street near the Hospital, close to the round church of St Sepulchre and by the junction of High Street [St John's Street] and Conduit Street [Sidney Street]. But this was not the only 'centre'; there were also high rents in St Mary's where property carried higher rent than in the market itself. The premium in St Mary's seem to be accounted for by the rents for residential properties that were close to the church but far enough from the market to avoid noise, smell and nuisance. A third, much smaller, centre was the parish of St Peter at the Castle; this may once have been a major centre of trade, but by 1279 had become largely (but not exclusively) a residential area.[17] In contrast, no significant results were obtained for land in the Cambridge and Barnwell fields. Rents seem to have had little relationship to the amount of land involved.

Tenurial factors had little impact on levels of rent. Lessees paid on average higher rents than ordinary holders of property, but not significantly so. Purchasers paid slightly higher rents than those who acquired their properties in other ways, but not significantly so. Properties acquired from family members paid slightly lower rents than others, but again not markedly so. The only noteworthy tenurial variable is the dummy variable for very low rents, which is highly significant. This takes the expected negative sign.

The two final columns of each table indicate whether property rents varied more for certain types of property than others and in certain locations more than in others. Results for unexplained variance reveals that it is highest in parishes where property rents are on average high, and lowest where rents are low. It was significantly high in St Clement's (10 per cent) and significantly low in All Saints at the Castle (5 per cent), St Michael's (5 per cent), St Peter's outside the Trumpington Gate (1 per cent), and in Barnwell (1 per cent) and Newnham (5 per cent). One possible explanation is that high-rent parishes were a mix of valuable properties and poor properties, while low-rent parishes were more uniform, with a predominance of low-value properties. This could have been due to newcomers to high-rent areas acquiring properties for high rents while those who had remained in these areas for several generations continued to pay low rents.[18] Another possibility is that properties with low rents in high-rent parishes had been bought outright by their wealthy owners and therefore no longer paid rent to the sellers. In some parishes both explanations may have some validity.

Comparison with other studies

The results suggest that Cambridge is best viewed as a multi-centred town, with its three centres lying along a north–south axis across the river, and with the major centre in the middle near to the bridge and at a junction of two main roads. To some extent, this situation has parallels with that of Durham and Coventry. However, key differences are that in Durham and Coventry there were two centres, rather than three, and the alternative centres developed as a consequence of control of the town being shared by two lords, a situation that did not occur in Cambridge. The Bishop of Durham and Durham Priory controlled the east and west of Durham respectively. In c.1200–50 the Bishop of Durham developed a suburb to the east of the town, around the Elvet bridge.[19] This gradually developed in importance to the extent that it effectively became an alternative commercial centre to the marketplace on the peninsula. In Coventry two centres emerged as a result of the Earls of Chester and Prior of Coventry Priory both claiming lordship over parts of the town. The prior controlled the marketplace and the north of the town and the earl the castle area and the land to the south, including the main east–west street. When the prior invested in developing a commercial zone at the marketplace in the 12th century, the earls correspondingly developed Earl Street as a commercial centre in their half.[20]

Bristol is another possible potential parallel to Cambridge as it had two locations of high rents, though in Bristol these locations changed over time. In the period 1209–1365 evidence from feet of fines suggest that Bristol's suburbs were reasonably affluent. However evidence from civic rentals from the mid-14th and the 15th century suggests that rents in the suburbs south of the River Avon were in decline and that the property hotspot had returned to the city centre, especially near Bristol Bridge.[21]

The cheapness of the suburbs and rental premium for the centre that appears in Cambridge has been noted in other towns. In Gloucester premium levels of ordinary rent occurred in the main streets around the High Cross in c.1455, while properties inside the walls attracted higher landgable than those outside.[22] In Hull in 1347 and in 13th-century Southampton, meanwhile, properties on the main north–south streets in the town centre attracted higher rents compared to others.[23] In 14th-century York the streets approaching the minster were property hotspots, while in Sandwich during the period 1360–1560 waterfront properties with quays in the centre of Strand Street were particularly desirable.[24]

Overall, therefore, location of property was more important than type of property in determining rents, and both of these were more important than whether the property was acquired from a family member or whether it was purchased or inherited. This does not mean that social factors were unimportant in determining rents; it could mean simply that relevant social factors cannot be captured in terms of recorded and measurable variables.

In Cambridge there is only limited evidence of inequalities of wealth that may have occurred as a result of lay involvement in the property market.[25] Rich and poor seem to have lived alongside each other, as in other medieval towns such as Norwich and Westminster.[26]

2.5 Hawgable

Having examined the dynamics of ordinary rent, the distribution of hawgable is now considered. It is often suggested that burgage rents such as hawgable were set at uniform rates, and were determined by custom rather than by economic value.[27] In Cambridge, however, there was considerable variation in hawgable rents. In St Giles' parish, for example, there were messuages, listed in sequence in the Hundred Rolls and therefore probably closely located, that paid hawgable of 0.5d, 1d, 1.5d and 3d, while two paid no hawgable at all.[28] There were also three houses in the same parish, two of which paid 0.5d and the third 2d.[29] A messuage bought from the nuns of St Radegund's paid no hawgable, which is consistent with their charter of exemption from hawgable; but other messuages held from St Radegund's in neighbouring parishes did pay hawgable.[30] Some shops in the marketplace paid 8d, as did a shop in St Edward's.[31] Margaret of Abington paid 2s for a shop in St Mary's.[32] By contrast three shops in St Michael's paid in total only 0.25d.[33]

Further detail is provided by the frequency distribution of hawgable rents presented in Table 2.6. The table relates exclusively to messuages because confining the analysis to one type of property eliminates variation across different types of property and thereby focuses on variation driven by other factors. Fifty-six per cent of hawgable rents were of 1d or 2d,

Table 2.6: Size distribution of hawgable rents for messuages

Value	Rent	Comment
0.125	2	Half a messuage in St Giles' [HR 137]
0.25	6	Includes half a messuage in St Giles' [HR137], a messuage in St Clement's [HR 176], a messuage in St Benedict's [HR 221] and 2 messuages in St John's [HR 480/2]
0.5	16	Various
0.75	4	Includes a messuage in the market [HR 1022], 2 messuages in St Andrew's [HR 1038/9], a messuage in St Botolph's [HR 256]
1	46	Various
1.25	3	Includes two separate messuages in St Clement's [HR 185/6] and a messuage in Holy Trinity [HR 958]
1.5	8	Includes messuages in St Giles' [HR 38], in Newnham in the parish of St Peter's outside Trumpington Gate [HR 272] and in St Clement's [HR 176], half a messuage in St Botolph's [HR 326], and messuages in St Benedict's [HR 426], St John's [HR 496], St Mary's [HR 644] and All Saints in the Jewry [HR 715]
1.75	1	Messuage in St Andrew's [HR 1057]
2	31	Various. Includes a messuage in St Clement's bought from Queen Eleanor through escheat of the Jews
2.5	4	Includes messuages in St Peter's at the Castle [HR 199], St John's [HR 466], St Clement's [HR 930] and St Andrew's [HR 1049]
3	4	Includes a messuage in St Giles' [HR31], two messuages in St John's [HR 333], and two separate messuages in St Botolph's [HR 313,653]
3.5	2	A messuage in All Saints at the Castle [HR 46]
4	6	Includes a messuage in St John's [HR 351], in St Botolph's [HR 499], two in St Michael's [HR 678,690], in Holy Trinity [HR 998] and in St Andrew's [HR 1018]
4.5	1	
6	2	A messuage with shop in St Edward's [HR 14] and two messuages in St Andrew's [HR 1071]
More than 6	2	Values are 7 and 78 (a messuage in St Sepulchre [HR 307], a messuage in St John's with 26 acres pertaining to it [HR 487]
TOTAL	138	

Note: Total value: 288 75d. Units are in pence.

Source: TNA SC5/CAMBS/TOWER/2 Barnwell Hundred Roll; TNA SC5/CAMBS/TOWER/1/ Parts1–3 Cambridge Borough Hundred Rolls; Catherine Casson, Mark Casson, John S. Lee and Katie Phillips, *Business and Community in Medieval England: The Cambridge Hundred Rolls Source Volume* (Bristol, 2020)

with 1d alone accounting for 33 per cent of cases. Including rents of 3d, 4d and 6d indicates that 64 per cent of rents were expressed in multiples of a penny. Of the remaining rents, 33 per cent were for 0.5d. Some rents were very small indeed: six were for a farthing and two for half a farthing; at the other extreme there was a rent of 7d and another of 78d. Most intriguing are the intermediate rents: four for three farthings; three for a penny farthing and one for a penny three farthings. There were other rents for 2.5d, 3.5d and 4.5d.

The precise causes of individual variations are unclear. One possibility is the redevelopment of plots, in which a plot returned to the king or the bailiffs of the town who initiated redevelopment and set a higher rent. As noted, three shops in St Mary's paid 8d hawgable when others paid only 1d, and it is possible that these shops were created through 13th-century redevelopment of the marketplace. Another possibility is the subdivision of properties, which may account some of the smaller rents, or the consolidation of neighbouring properties, which may account for some of the larger ones. Subdivision could arise where a property-holder needed to generate income by selling off part of their property or where siblings inherited a property but did not wish to live together. Consolidation could occur when wealthy individuals bought out their neighbours, or their neighbour's heir, in order to acquire a larger property without the inconvenience of relocation. Business expansion could also motivate consolidation. Whatever the reasons, it is clear that uniformity of hawgable did not apply to Cambridge; rents were very diverse.

The types of properties that paid hawgable and its distribution by parish can also be considered using evidence from the Hundred Rolls. Table 2.7 has four columns: columns one and two (labelled Hawgable) relate to the type of properties that paid hawgable and their location. Columns three and four (Hawgable rent paid) present the amount paid. The bottom line of Table 2.7 shows that overall just under 20 per cent of all properties paid hawgable and the average rent they paid was just over 2d.

Substantial variation is, however, apparent between properties and locations. Houses (37 per cent) and shops (27 per cent) were more likely to pay hawgable than messuages (23 per cent). Curtilages were likely to pay hawgable (on the basis of a very small sample), while stalls and crofts paid no hawgable at all. Parishes divide naturally into two groups. Four parishes (St Peter's outside the Trumpington Gate, All Saints in the Jewry, St Sepulchre and Holy Trinity), had very few properties paying hawgable (under 10 per cent), while the remainder had a much high proportion (over 20 per cent). These four parishes held a lot of properties paying rent to St Radegund's, and the nunnery's exemption from hawgable may explain the situation.

Table 2.7: Analysis of hawgable rents: whether hawgable was paid and if so how much was paid

Variable	Hawgable		Hawgable rent paid	
	Number	Percentage	Total	Average
Type of property				
Messuage	138	23.1	297.38	2.16
House	10	37.0	11	1.1
Shop	25	27.3	68	2.72
Stall	0	0	0	
Croft	0	0	0	
Curtilage	5	71.4	7	1.4
Grange	1	9.1	6	6
Land (piece)	3	20.0	6.5	2.17
Land (acres)	8	21.6	87.25	10.91
Vacant land	8	17.4	10	1.25
Parish location				
All Saints at the Castle & Howes	11	32.4	25.75	2.34
All Saints in the Jewry	2	6.3	3	1.50
St Andrew	17	32.7	29.75	1.75
St Bene't	16	28.6	16	1.00
St Botolph	19	41.3	31.75	1.67
St Clement	18	37.5	23	1.28
St Edward	13	28.3	41	3.15
St Giles	15	33.3	16.25	1.08
Holy Trinity	10	7.9	15.25	1.53
St John	18	39.1	101.5	5.64
St Mary	16	21.1	28.5	1.78
St Michael	9	31.0	18.75	2.08
St Peter at the Castle	4	21.1	4.5	1.13
St Peter outside the Trumpington Gate	1	3.7	4.5	4.5
St Sepulchre	1	7.7	7	7
Other locations				
Newnham	0	0	0	
Barnwell	2	2.2	5	2.5
Marketplace	3	21.4	16.75	5.58
Cambridge fields	23	2.1	47	2.04
Barnwell fields	3	2.1	2.25	0.75
Location not specified	6	18.2	9.25	1.54
TOTAL	202	18.6	421.5	2.09

Note: This table analyses data from 202 entries in the rolls where hawgable was paid. Units are in pence.

Source: TNA SC5/CAMBS/TOWER/2 Barnwell Hundred Roll; TNA SC5/CAMBS/TOWER/1/ Parts1–3 Cambridge Borough Hundred Rolls; Catherine Casson, Mark Casson, John S. Lee and Katie Phillips, *Business and Community in Medieval England: The Cambridge Hundred Rolls Source Volume* (Bristol, 2020)

The situation appears rather different, however, when the average amount of hawgable is considered. Column three shows that shops (2.7d) paid marginally more than messuages (2.2d), which paid about the same amount as a piece of land. With respect to average rents, the parishes now fall into three main categories. St Sepulchre, St John's and the marketplace all paid on average more than 5d; St Peter's outside the Trumpington Gate, St Edward's, All Saints at the Castle and St Michael's all paid between 2d and 5d, and the other parishes paid less than 2d.

The seven parishes paying the highest hawgable rents do not correspond to the parishes paying the highest ordinary rents. It is possible that they may be the areas of the town that had most recently been developed or redeveloped. This would certainly explain the high level of hawgable in St Peter's outside the Trumpington Gate, and possibly in St Mary's and St John's as well. The other possibility is that they reflect the area of the plots involved. This could explain the high levels of hawgable in the two peripheral parishes of All Saints at the Castle to the north and St Peter's outside the Trumpington Gate to the south, where plots appear to have been large; it could also explain the high rents in St Sepulchre, which bordered on St Radegund's where settlement was light.

Comparison with other studies

The detailed analysis has shown that variation in hawgable was significant; it varied by type of property and by location. Significant variation has also been found in Gloucester in c.1100 and in the new town of New Winchelsea in 1292.[34] This contrasts with towns, such as Grimsby, that show evidence of uniform rents.[35]

The pattern of variation in Cambridge contrasts with that in Gloucester.[36] Both towns reveal significant variation in hawgable, but the pattern is rather different. In Gloucester, shops did not incur a premium over ordinary tenements and landgable was generally similar across properties, with the exception of inns, which carried a higher rent. In Cambridge, however, messuages paid about the same amount as a piece of land, which is consistent with the view that the amount of hawgable paid on a messuage may have reflected the estimated opportunity cost of land that it occupied, a situation that appears to have occurred in New Winchelsea.[37] Another difference between Cambridge and Gloucester is that in Gloucester the spatial variation of rent reflected that in ordinary rent, with a significant centrality premium, whereas in Cambridge it did not.

2.6 Barnwell Priory rental

A rental of Barnwell Priory has survived from c.1295, some 16 years after the Hundred Rolls. It reports the rents due to the abbey on 86 properties in the town (together with other properties in some surrounding parishes, which are not considered here).[38] The properties may well have paid other rents too; the rental notes that hawgable was due on certain properties but is silent concerning other rents. Since there is no definitive information on the total rents it cannot be assumed that the rent reflects market conditions in 1279. If the rental reflects market conditions at all, it reflects conditions at the time at which the properties where sold by the abbey for perpetual rents. In some cases this could be the late 12th century. It is fairly safe to say, however, that these rents mostly reflect the property market earlier than the Hundred Rolls, and not later, as might at first appear.

The priory's attitude to its property portfolio may be inferred from the introduction to the rental written by a monk:

> It is known that the almoner, the head of the infirmary and the head of the refectory have many rents in the town of Cambridge, of which none are mentioned in this volume, because they are levied by themselves or their servants. However, it is certain that all rents pertinent to the community that are not fully recorded here relate to plots that have been vacant, submersed or enclosed and have yielded no rents for many years.
>
> Furthermore Eustace Dunning used to pay 10s. per annum for 20 acres of land and two shops in the market, because we have a good charter.
>
> Similarly Master Philip de Insula used to pay 20d. per annum for the house of Robert Seman. Item: John le Rus 28s.11d. per annum.
>
> Many others used to pay many rents which are no longer paid and so are not recorded here.[39]

With 86 properties and many different parishes represented, some grouping of parishes is required before applying hedonic regression. If the numbers in any location category are too small it becomes almost impossible to achieve statistical significance. For this reason the three ancient parishes north of the river, All Saints at the Castle, St Peter's at the Castle and St Giles' are grouped and, following the rental itself, are titled 'beyond the bridge'; they are used as the location control. The adjacent

St John's and St Michael's parishes are similarly merged, while St Botolph's is merged with 'Lorteburnelane', which borders St Botolph's to the east and is the address of several properties.

A wide variety of different types of property are distinguished in the rental. Messuages and shops predominate, as in the Hundred Rolls, but there are also references to houses, solars, stone buildings, crofts, granges, cemeteries, hythes, fields, vacant plots and vicarages. These have been grouped by similarity of function and level of rent, as indicated in the left-hand column of Table 2.8.

There are three tenurial variables. Some properties paid non-trivial rents in kind as well as in money. For a property of given value, the obligation to pay a significant rent in kind in reduces money value; cumin, pepper and capons are paid on some properties and so variables are introduced to account for them. As before, two variants of the regression are reported. Money rent is the dependent variable in both, but logarithms are taken in the second regression. As before the two regressions provide similar results, but the fit is much better in the case of the logarithmic regression.

Messuages, houses, solars and shops all carry significant premia, with messuages having the highest value. Shops have a lower value, but it is still statistically significant because of the substantial number included. The most valuable properties of all, however, are vicarages, and their statistical significance is highest in the logarithmic regression. Rents are highest in St Botolph's and second highest in St Peter's outside the Trumpington Gate. In the logarithmic regression, however, it is Holy Trinity and St Michael's that have the highest rents. The difference arises because the

Table 2.8: Regression analysis of rents paid to Barnwell Priory in 1295

Variable	Rent		Log rent	
	Coefficient	p-value	Coefficient	p-value
Constant	3.466	0.894	2.895	0.000***
Type of property				
Messuage	65.333	0.016**	0.997	0.000***
House/solar	57.233	0.092*	0.852	0.039**
Stone house	88.885	0.331	0.258	0.732
Shop	23.959	0.084*	0.499	0.009***
Croft/grange/cemetery	23.795	0.452	0.242	0.517
Hythe	42.077	0.302	0.682	0.166
Fields	78.909	0.101	1.010	0.176
Vacant plot	12.6249	0.758	0.363	0.271
Vicarage	248.769	0.076*	2.172	0.002***

(continued)

Table 2.8: Regression analysis of rents paid to Barnwell priory in 1295 (continued)

Variable	Rent		Log rent	
	Coefficient	*p*-value	Coefficient	*p*-value
Parish location				
All Saints in the Jewry	−22.329	0.373	−0.409	0.436
St Andrew	−22.296	0.690	−0.698	0.455
St Bene't	−21.075	0.489	−0.393	0.452
St Botolph/Lorteburnelane	145.671	0.033**	0.776	0.149
St Clement	−29.558	0.335	−0.549	0.212
Holy Trinity	6.056	0.770	0.420	0.065*
St John/St Michael	−43.619	0.047**	−0.793	0.017**
St Mary	32.107	0.222	0.234	0.472
St Edward	−43.165	0.469	−0.390	0.393
St Peter	83.865	0.077*	0.142	0.792
St Sepulchre	20.807	0.609	0.332	0.404
Other locations				
Market	9.042	0.825	0.760	0.029**
Newnham	−55.375	0.175	−0.668	0.360
Rent in kind				
Cumin/pepper	26.051	0.279	0.463	0.123
Capons	−147.995	0.022**	−1.596	0.001***
Feudal	−75.295	0.002***	−2.326	0.000***

	Rent	Log rent
R-squared	0.548	0.647
Adjusted R-squared	0.360	0.500
F-statistic	2.910	4.406
p-value	0.000***	0.000***
Average rent	60.40	3.43
Standard deviation of rent	89.49	1.18
Breusch-Pagan-Godfrey heteroskedasticity F statistic	3.820	1.228
p-value	0.000***	0.254
Jarques-Bera normality test	97.6	1.1
p-value	0.000***	0.578

Notes: White robust standard errors.

The rental gives sub-totals for individual parishes, and also a grand total, but these do not always agree exactly with the figures given for individual plots. This table is based on information for the individual plots. The rent paid by Helewisa lotrix is missing and has been interpolated using the sum of the rents assigned to the parish of St John.

Source: LB

logarithmic regression attaches less weight to very high rents and more weight to lower rents. The existence of a few high rents therefore pulls up St Botolph's and St Peter's in the first regression while a few very low rents pull them down in the second regression. In both regressions rents are significantly low in St John's and St Michael's parishes. Tenure is important; payments in capons and low 'feudal' rents have the expected negative impacts in both regressions and are statistically significant.

2.7 Transmission of property

This section investigates the transmission of property between generations. The Hundred Rolls record all the transfers of each property within living memory, sometimes going back as far as six generations. They describe the nature of the transfer, the names of previous owners and, where applicable, the family relationships between them. Four types of transfer are distinguished: transaction, gift, inheritance and remarriage. Transactions include purchases, exchanges and leases, while gifts include both ordinary gifts and gifts in marriage. Some gifts may have involved an element of undisclosed payment. Gifts in marriage normally relate to sons and daughters while remarriage refers to widows or widowers.

Table 2.9 presents the results for the first three generations and Table 2.10 carries the story back to the sixth generation. Missing information becomes an increasing problem the further back the property is traced. Transactions are classified as market transfers and the other categories as non-market transfers. Two ratios are provided: the first is the ratio of transactions to all transfers and the second is the ratio of purchases to inheritance. The tables show that transactions were equal to almost 70 per cent of transfers for up to three generations back, while the ratio of purchases to inheritance was even higher. The role of transactions increased as property transmission became more recent, indicating a growing role for transactions over time. Gifts increased over time, while inheritance diminished, potentially reflecting a situation in which property was increasingly given way before a person's death.

Further light can be shed on these issues by an analysis of family relationships. Table 2.11 analyses family relations involving current holders of property. Family members figured in just under half of all property transfers (48 per cent). Conversely, non-family members were involved in more than half of transfers. These figures must be treated with caution, however, as the stated relationships concern close family members. The family case studies in Chapter 4 reveal that many transactions took place between more distant relatives. When two people married they connected

Table 2.9: Transmission of property between generations: the latest three generations of owners

Method of transmission	Current holders		Previous holders		Two generations back	
	Number	Percentage	Number	Percentage	Number	Percentage
Purchase	416	38.5	406	37.6	294	27.2
Exchange	3	0.3	3	0.3	1	0.1
Leased	6	0.6	0	0.0	0	0
TOTAL TRANSACTION	425	39.3	409	37.9	295	27.3
Inheritance	357	33.0	444	41.1	406	37.6
Gift (unspecified)	198	18.3	139	12.9	57	5.3
Gift in marriage	66	6.1	26	2.4	0	0
Remarriage	7	0.6	0	0	0	0
TOTAL TRANSFER	628	58.0	609	56.4	463	42.9
'Held'	22	2.0	14	1.3	30	2.8
Unspecified	6	0.6	0	0	0	0
Previous owner not known	0	0	49	4.5	293	27.1
TOTAL	1,081	100	1,081	100	1,081	100
Transaction/Transfer percentage	68		73		64	
Purchase/Inheritance percentage	116		91		72	

Note: Owing to missing information on property transmission, nine records were omitted from this analysis.

Source: TNA SC5/CAMBS/TOWER/2 Barnwell Hundred Roll; TNA SC5/CAMBS/TOWER/1/Parts1–3 Cambridge Borough Hundred Rolls; Chapter 4 in this volume and Catherine Casson, Mark Casson, John S. Lee and Katie Phillips, *Business and Community in Medieval England: The Cambridge Hundred Rolls Source Volume*, Appendix 14 (Bristol, 2020)

Table 2.10: Transmission of property between generations: from third to fifth generation of ownership ancestors

Method of transmission	Three generations back		Four generations back		Five generations back	
	Number	Percentage	Number	Percentage	Number	Percentage
Purchase	143	13.2	32	3.0	13	1.2
Exchange	1	0.1	0	0	0	0
Leased	0	0	0	0	0	0
TOTAL TRANSACTION	144	13.3	32	3.0	13	1.2
Inheritance	186	17.2	75	6.9	22	2.0
Gift (unspecified)	21	1.9	6	0.6	3	0.3
Gift in marriage	3	0.3	1	0.1	0	0
Remarriage	0	0	0	0	0	0
TOTAL TRANSFER	210	19.4	82	7.6	25	2.3
'Held'	14	1.3	3	0.3	1	0.1
Unspecified	0	0	0	0	0	0
Previous owner not known	727	67.3	964	89.2	1,042	96.4
GRAND TOTAL	1,081	100	1,081	100	1,081	100
Transaction/Transfer	69		39		52	
Purchase/Inheritance	77		43		59	

Notes:

The percentage figures relate to the total number of entries in the Hundred Rolls and not to the total number of cases in which each generation appears.

The sixth generation records only one purchase and one inheritance, while the seventh generation records a single purchase. The oldest recoded transmission is often described as 'ancient purchase' or as inheritance from 'ancestors'.

Owing to missing information on property transmission nine records were omitted from this analysis.

Source: TNA SC5/CAMBS/TOWER/2 Barnwell Hundred Roll; TNA SC5/CAMBS/TOWER/1/Parts1–3 Cambridge Borough Hundred Rolls; Chapter 4 in this volume and Catherine Casson, Mark Casson, John S. Lee and Katie Phillips, *Business and Community in Medieval England: The Cambridge Hundred Rolls Source Volume*, Appendix 14 (Bristol, 2020).

Table 2.11: Previous owner of property analysed by relation to the current owners

Previous owners	Number of plots	Percentage of plots
Parents		
Father	260	24.1
Mother	43	4.0
Father & Mother	8	0.7
Parents-in-law		
Wife's Father	59	5.5
Wife's Mother	11	1.0
Siblings		
Brother	79	7.3
Sister	3	0.3
Spouses		
Husband	14	1.3
Wife	6	0.6
Wife's remarriage	7	0.7
Other relatives		
Son	9	0.8
Uncle	12	1.1
Cousin	1	0.1
Nephew	1	0.1
Wife's son by a previous marriage	3	0.3
Same name and probably related	7	0.7
TOTAL: related previous owners	523	48.4
Unrelated or unspecified previous owners	558	51.6
TOTAL: All personal previous owners	1,081	100.0

Note: Owing to missing information on property transmission nine records were omitted from this analysis.

Source: TNA SC5/CAMBS/TOWER/2 Barnwell Hundred Roll; TNA SC5/CAMBS/TOWER/1/ Parts1-3 Cambridge Borough Hundred Rolls; Chapter 4 in this volume and Catherine Casson, Mark Casson, John S. Lee and Katie Phillips, *Business and Community in Medieval England: The Cambridge Hundred Rolls Source Volume*, Appendix 14 (Bristol, 2020)

members of one extended family to another extended family, encouraging transactions, for example, between a husband's brother and their wife's brother, or between a husband's uncle and their wife's nephew. Such a transaction involved nominally unconnected people whose relationship can only be inferred from a family tree.

The table shows that, where relationships are stated, fathers were an important source of property transfers, followed by brothers and a wife's father. In contrast, mothers were less important and transfers of property between spouses were of limited significance. Among the category of 'other relatives', uncles were of some importance, possibly reflecting a situation where a young man's father had died and an uncle had no heir of their own.

Table 2.12 examines the importance of family connections in transmissions by inheritance, gift and purchase.[40] It shows that inheritance almost always involved a family connection but not invariably so, since people were free to make other arrangements. Conversely, purchases did not normally involve close family relationships, although some did so. Eight purchases involved parents, for example, where children wanted to take their inheritance early, and another eight involved siblings, for example, joint inheritance where one sibling elected to buy the other out, or where a sole heir gave their siblings an opportunity to buy in.

Gifts represented an intermediate case, where approximately half (47 per cent) of donor–recipients pairs were related to each other. If gifts within a family did not involve undisclosed payments and gifts between non-family members did, this would mean that roughly half of all gifts were in fact transactions, and this would increase the estimated proportion

Table 2.12: Family relationships involved in different types of property acquisition by current owners

Property acquired from	Inheritance	Gift	Purchase	TOTAL
Parents	237	62	8	311
Wife's parents	26	4	0	70
Siblings	56	14	8	82
Spouse	17	1	0	20
Other relative	4	24	2	23
No relationship indicated	17	93	398	465
TOTAL	357	198	416	971
Percentage of transfers taking place between known relatives	95.2	47.0	4.3	52.1

Notes: Parents = Father, mother or father and mother jointly; Siblings = Brother or sister; Other relative = Son, uncle or other relative, or person with the same name and a probable family connection.

The table shows the number of properties recorded in the Hundred Rolls that were transferred to the current owners in this way. Owing to missing information on property transmission, nine records were omitted from this analysis.

Source: TNA SC5/CAMBS/TOWER/2 Barnwell Hundred Roll; TNA SC5/CAMBS/TOWER/1/ Parts1–3 Cambridge Borough Hundred Rolls; Chapter 4 in this volume and Catherine Casson, Mark Casson, John S. Lee and Katie Phillips, *Business and Community in Medieval England: The Cambridge Hundred Rolls Source Volume*, Appendix 14 (Bristol, 2020)

of transactions in property transfers. This statistic would need to be qualified, however, by the fact that many paid transactions took place within extended family networks mediated by intermarriage.

2.8 Rents paid to institutions

Importance of institutions

The following sections investigate rents paid to institutions and compare the different types of institution to which they were paid. A key finding is the high proportion of all rental income that accrued to charitable institutions (Table 2.13). Fifty per cent of all rental payments recorded in the Hundred Rolls were paid to either abbeys, churches or hospitals. Abbeys received 39.3 per cent of all payments, hospitals 6.4 per cent and churches 3.2 per cent. The scholars of Merton also received rent, together with the sheriff, and the bailiffs who received the hawgable.

The high level of charitable income was not, of course, a direct consequence of the charity of the current property owners. It arose because a high proportion of Cambridge properties had been given to these institutions in the past and they had then sold them back to the private sector for perpetual rents. On some occasions the institutions may have used their own resources to purchase such properties, but those resources would in turn have ultimately been acquired through donations. The fact that many individual owners in Cambridge paid a high proportion of rent to charitable institutions does not therefore

Table 2.13: Rents received by category of recipient

Type of recipient	Income (pence)	Percentage of total
Private individuals	13,335	48.3
Abbeys	10,825	39.3
Hospitals	1,762	6.4
Churches	892	3.2
Hawgable	421	1.5
Scholars	278	1.0
Sheriff	22	0.08
Not specified	12	0.04
TOTAL	27,557	100.0

Source: TNA SC5/CAMBS/TOWER/2 Barnwell Hundred Roll; TNA SC5/CAMBS/TOWER/1/ Parts1–3 Cambridge Borough Hundred Rolls; Catherine Casson, Mark Casson, John S. Lee and Katie Phillips, *Business and Community in Medieval England: The Cambridge Hundred Rolls Source Volume* (Bristol, 2020)

necessarily mean that they themselves were charitable, but rather that previous holders of these properties had been charitable.

Differences in property portfolios between institutions

Table 2.14 shows that the relative amounts of rent accruing to different institutions depended more on the number of properties that owed rent than on the amount of rent per property that was owed. This is what would be expected. The rent that could be charged by an institution offering a property for sale would be dictated by the state of the property market and not by the wealth of the institution. The wealth of the institution would be determined by the number of benefactors that it could attract, and that would in turn determine the number of properties that it could offer for sale.

There was some variation in rents per property, however. The share of rent per property accruing to abbeys and hospitals exceeded the share of rent per property for churches and for scholars. A possible explanation is that abbeys and hospitals attracted wealthier benefactors who donated more valuable properties. Churches may have attracted donations from local people of lesser means. The low value of rents paid on properties held by the scholars of Merton is more difficult to explain because Merton acquired a large part of the Dunning estate, which included some very

Table 2.14: Analysis of rents received by category of recipient

Type of recipient	Number of properties	Average rent per property (pence)
Private individuals	672	19.8
Abbeys	297	36.5
Hospitals	48	36.7
Churches	49	18.2
Hawgable	203	2.1
Scholars	16	17.4
Sheriff	12	1.8
Not specified	6	2.0
TOTAL	1,303	21.1

Note: The total number of properties includes double-counting owing to multiple rents on the same property.

Source: TNA SC5/CAMBS/TOWER/2 Barnwell Hundred Roll; TNA SC5/CAMBS/TOWER/1/ Parts1–3 Cambridge Borough Hundred Rolls; Catherine Casson, Mark Casson, John S. Lee and Katie Phillips, *Business and Community in Medieval England: The Cambridge Hundred Rolls Source Volume* (Bristol, 2020)

prestigious properties. The answer may be that the scholars retained some of the most prestigious properties for their own use and sold off the poorer properties to other people (see Chapter 6).

Variations of rent by location and type of property

Institutional property portfolios can be examined further by comparing the three main types of charitable institution, abbeys, churches and hospitals, and examining the characteristics of the properties that paid rent to them (Tables 2.15 and 2.16).[41] For purposes of comparison, rents accruing to private individuals are examined too; these rents are the other side of the coin; as they represent the component of rent that is not employed directly for charitable purposes.

Results show that the type of property was not a major influence on the destination of rent. The destination of rent from shop owners was broadly

Table 2.15: Regression analysis of whether properties paid rents to abbeys and churches

Variable	Abbey rent		Church rent	
	Coefficient	p-value	Coefficient	p-value
Constant	0.121	0.000***	0.018	0.017**
Type of property				
House	−0.065	0.379	−0.003	0.936
Shop	−0.040	0.168	0.010	0.577
Stall	−0.199	0.001***	−0.109	0.001***
Croft	−0.206	0.101	−0.025	0.097*
Curtilage	−0.255	0.000***	−0.100	0.003***
Grange	−0.164	0.298	−0.008	0.509
Land (piece)	0.125	0.326	−0.057	0.012**
Land (acres)	−0.013	0.262	−0.002	0.518
Vacant land	−0.092	0.191	0.066	0.206
Parish location				
All Saints at the Castle & Howes	0.139	0.074*	0.012	0.692
All Saints in the Jewry	0.393	0.000***	−0.022	0.045**
St Andrew	0.270	0.000***	0.162	0.004***
St Bene't	0.129	0.037**	0.044	0.199
St Botolph	0.088	0.157	0.001	0.952
St Clement	0.302	0.000***	0.001	0.949

(continued)

Table 2.15: Regression analysis of whether properties paid rents to abbeys and churches (continued)

Variable	Abbey rent Coefficient	p-value	Church rent Coefficient	p-value
Parish location (continued)				
St Edward	0.361	0.000***	0.019	0.566
St Giles	0.137	0.044**	−0.020	0.023**
St John	0.187	0.009***	0.071	0.109
St Mary	0.143	0.009***	0.160	0.001***
St Michael	0.351	0.000***	0.009	0.776
St Peter at the Castle	0.292	0.017***	−0.017	0.024**
St Peter outside the Trumpington Gate	0.253	0.009***	0.059	0.252
St Sepulchre	0.582	0.000***	0.060	0.434
Other locations				
Newnham	−0.037	0.505	−0.023	0.028**
Barnwell	0.512	0.000***	0.005	0.777
Marketplace	−0.061	0.4794	0.110	0.278
Cambridge fields	−0.005	0.1215	−0.002	0.033**
Barnwell fields	0.005	0.7055	−0.005	0.071*
Location not specified	0.264	0.0033	0.011	0.720

	Abbey rent	Church rent
R-squared	0.159	0.081
Adjusted *R*-squared	0.136	0.055
F-statistic	6.913	3.197
p-value (F-statistic)	0.000***	0.000***
Proportion paying rent to:	0.274	0.045
Standard deviation of binary variable	0.446	0.207
No of observations	1088	1088
Heteroskedasticity Test: Breusch-Pagan-Godfrey	3.760	3.646
p-value	0.000*	0.000***
Jarques-Bera normality	130.0	12597.4
p-value	0.000***	0.000***

Note: White robust standard errors. The dependent variables are binary variables. The controls are messuages and Holy Trinity. Significance levels are ***1 per cent, **5 per cent and *10 per cent. Probit and logit regression are not reported because the estimations do not converge owing to both dependent and explanatory variables being binary.

Source: TNA SC5/CAMBS/TOWER/2 Barnwell Hundred Roll; TNA SC5/CAMBS/TOWER/1/ Parts1–3 Cambridge Borough Hundred Rolls; Catherine Casson, Mark Casson, John S. Lee and Katie Phillips, *Business and Community in Medieval England: The Cambridge Hundred Rolls Source Volume* (Bristol, 2020)

Table 2.16: Regression analysis of whether properties paid rents to hospitals or private individuals

Variable	Hospital		Private individual	
	Coefficient	Prob.	Coefficient	Prob.
Constant	0.014	0.034**	0.731	0.000***
Type of property				
House	0.008	0.820	−0.160	0.080*
Shop	0.038	0.163	0.050	0.108
Stall	−0.066	0.007***	0.272	0.000***
Croft	−0.083	0.123	0.197	0.186
Curtilage	−0.028	0.193	−0.136	0.255
Grange	−0.102	0.018**	0.275	0.054*
Land (piece)	−0.050	0.003***	−0.052	0.665
Land (acres)	−0.001	0.766	0.004	0.786
Vacant land	−0.029	0.174	−0.006	0.940
Parish location				
All Saints at the Castle & Howes	0.027	0.383	−0.376	0.000***
All Saints in the Jewry	0.129	0.055*	−0.245	0.014**
St Andrew	0.010	0.643	0.268	0.000***
St Bene't	0.026	0.327	0.0791	0.192
St Botolph	0.052	0.168	−0.056	0.449
St Clement	0.084	0.068*	−0.210	0.007***
St Edward	0.077	0.098*	−0.260	0.001***
St Giles	0.013	0.592	−0.099	0.211
St John	−0.010	0.164	−0.102	0.187
St Mary	0.071	0.031**	−0.084	0.180
St Michael	0.064	0.202	−0.373	0.000***
St Peter at the Castle	−0.010	0.214	−0.251	0.039**
St Peter outside the Trumpington Gate	0.028	0.459	−0.255	0.012**
St Sepulchre	−0.015	0.072*	−0.091	0.499
Other locations				
Newnham	0.488	0.000***	−0.250	0.030**
Barnwell	−0.001	0.935	−0.288	0.000***
Marketplace	0.084	0.400	0.034	0.756
Cambridge fields	−0.001	0.054*	−0.005	0.448
Barnwell fields	−0.004	0.090*	0.030	0.039**
Location not specified	−0.016	0.187	−0.107	0.262

(continued)

Table 2.16: Regression analysis of whether properties paid rents to hospitals or private individuals (continued)

	Hospital	Private individual
R-squared	0.094	0.088
Adjusted R-squared	0.069	0.063
F-statistic	3.763	3.514
p-value (F-statistic)	0.000***	0.000***
Proportion paying rent to:	0.036	0.618
Standard deviation of binary variable	0.155517	0.486
No of observations	1088	1088
Heteroskedasticity Test: Breusch-Pagan-Godfrey	3.763	2.190
p-value	0.000***	0.000***
Jarques-Bera normality	14699.6	126.8
p-value	0.000***	0.000**

Note: White robust standard errors. The controls are messuages and Holy Trinity. Significance levels are ***1 per cent, **5 per cent and *10 per cent. Probit and logit regression are not reported because the estimations do not converge owing to both dependent and explanatory variables being binary.

Source: TNA SC5/CAMBS/TOWER/2 Barnwell Hundred Roll; TNA SC5/CAMBS/TOWER/1/ Parts1–3 Cambridge Borough Hundred Rolls; Catherine Casson, Mark Casson, John S. Lee and Katie Phillips, *Business and Community in Medieval England: The Cambridge Hundred Rolls Source Volume* (Bristol, 2020)

similar to that of the control group of messuage owners, although they were slightly less likely to pay to abbeys and slightly more likely to pay to churches, hospitals and private owners. Owners of houses were more likely to pay to abbeys, churches and hospitals than were the owners of shops and messuages. In contrast, the owners of stalls and curtilages were less likely to contribute to institutions overall.

Distribution by parish shows that properties in some parishes were more likely to pay rent to abbeys than others. St Sepulchre, All Saints in the Jewry and St Edward's were most likely to pay to abbeys, while St Benedict's, St Mary's, Holy Trinity and some others were least likely to do so. Properties in the Barnwell fields were more likely to contribute than properties in the Cambridge fields, owing to the link with Barnwell Priory. So far as churches were concerned, St Andrew's and St Mary's parishes both performed strongly in terms of payment, although the payments were not invariably to the parish church. St Giles' and St Peter's at the Castle performed very poorly, for reasons that are not entirely clear. A high proportion of properties in All Saints in the Jewry, St Clement's and St Michael's paid rent to hospitals, which is not surprising given that they occupied lands adjoining properties that were probably owned by benefactors of the Hospital of St John. St Sepulchre, however, is an exception, having little connection to the hospital even though the hospital was just across the road from the church. A high proportion of Newnham properties supported hospitals, but few properties in the Cambridge and the Barnwell fields did so.

Tables 2.17 and 2.18 examine the amounts of rent that were paid in each category, expressed as a proportion of the total amount of rent paid on each property. The variation between parishes was not so systematic as before. St Clement's, St Michael's and St Peter's outside the Trumpington Gate, together with Barnwell, paid high shares of rent to abbeys, while Newnham, and to a lesser extent the Cambridge fields, paid low shares. St Andrew's, St Michael's and Newnham paid relatively high shares to churches, as did Holy Trinity (the control). Newnham and St Botolph's supported hospitals more than other parishes, while St Giles' and St Peter's at the Castle did so less than others.

Table 2.17: Regression analysis of shares of rents paid to abbeys and churches

Variable	Abbey rent		Church rent	
	Coefficient	p-value	Coefficient	p-value
Constant	0.211	0.000***	0.028	0.006***
Type of property				
House	0.031	0.746	0.030	0.443
Shop	−0.028	0.444	−0.006	0.516
Stall	−0.039	0.714	−0.019	0.576
Croft	0.037	0.784	−0.041	0.070*
Curtilage	−0.003	0.984	−0.049	0.038**
Grange	−0.097	0.499	0.089	0.339
Land (piece)	−0.004	0.974	−0.046	0.016**
Land (acres)	−0.014	0.075*	−0.000	0.970
Vacant land	−0.014	0.822	0.016	0.594
Parish location				
All Saints at the Castle & Howes	0.036	0.655	0.019	0.620
All Saints in the Jewry	0.155	0.111	−0.031	0.110
St Andrew	0.105	0.141	0.051	0.159
St Bene't	−0.016	0.793	0.009	0.711
St Botolph	−0.038	0.531	−0.037	0.002***
St Clement	0.188	0.014**	−0.043	0.007***
St Edward	0.092	0.213	0.046	0.263

(continued)

Table 2.17: Regression analysis of shares of rents paid to abbeys and churches (continued)

Variable	Abbey rent		Church rent	
	Coefficient	p-value	Coefficient	p-value
Parish location (continued)				
St Giles	−0.034	0.606	−0.040	0.002***
St John	−0.031	0.626	−0.002	0.936
St Mary	−0.033	0.541	0.044	0.189
St Michael	0.174	0.047**	−0.037	0.007***
St Peter at the Castle	0.176	0.134	0.041	0.596
St Peter outside the Trumpington Gate	0.188	0.050**	−0.031	0.005***
St Sepulchre	0.114	0.456	0.037	0.692
Other locations				
Newnham	−0.207	0.000***	0.063	0.308
Barnwell	0.236	0.000***	−0.022	0.070*
Marketplace	0.020	0.876	−0.045	0.004***
Cambridge fields	−0.007	0.057*	−0.002	0.036**
Barnwell fields	−0.004	0.732	−0.009	0.031**
Location not specified	0.085	0.349	−0.035	0.005***
Rent total	0.000	0.282	0.000	0.152

	Abbey rent	Church rent
R-squared	0.059	0.045
Adjusted *R*-squared	0.031	0.016
F-statistic	2.106	1.565
p-value	0.001***	0.028
Average share	0.262	0.045
Standard deviation of share	0.427	0.166
No of observations	1,036	1,036
Heteroskedasticity Test: Breusch-Pagan-Godfrey	1.655	1.599
p-value	0.015**	0.022**
Jarques-Bera normality	186.4	36074.2
p-value	0.000***	0.000***

Note: White robust standard errors. The controls are messuages and Holy Trinity. Significance levels are ***1 per cent, **5 per cent and *10 per cent.

Source: TNA SC5/CAMBS/TOWER/2 Barnwell Hundred Roll; TNA SC5/CAMBS/TOWER/1/ Parts1–3 Cambridge Borough Hundred Rolls; Catherine Casson, Mark Casson, John S. Lee and Katie Phillips, *Business and Community in Medieval England: The Cambridge Hundred Rolls Source Volume* (Bristol, 2020)

Table 2.18: Regression analysis of shares of rents paid to hospitals and private individuals

Variable	Hospital rent		Private individual rent	
	Coefficient	p-value	Coefficient	p-value
Constant	0.015	0.0886	0.652	0.000***
Type of property				
House	−0.023	0.0121	−0.035	0.713
Shop	0.023	0.2468	0.031	0.415
Stall	0.091	0.4620	−0.058	0.742
Croft	−0.063	0.0378	0.216	0.188
Curtilage	−0.010	0.5900	−0.233	0.039**
Grange	0.005	0.9214	−0.210	0.091*
Land (piece)	−0.010	0.7424	0.069	0.608
Land (acres)	−0.007	0.1172	0.019	0.082*
Vacant land	0.005	0.8692	0.025	0.745
Parish location				
All Saints at the Castle & Howes	0.021	0.5054	−0.264	0.003***
All Saints in the Jewry	0.012	0.7631	−0.147	0.135
St Andrew	−0.000	0.9923	−0.224	0.003***
St Bene't	0.040	0.2237	−0.046	0.528
St Botolph	0.070	0.0814	−0.117	0.123
St Clement	0.010	0.7847	−0.215	0.005***
St Edward	0.029	0.3473	−0.180	0.023**
St Giles	−0.019	0.0319	−0.081	0.315
St John	0.027	0.4304	−0.187	0.015**
St Mary	0.019	0.4994	−0.080	0.227
St Michael	0.052	0.2402	−0.346	0.000***
St Peter at the Castle	−0.024	0.0562	−0.189	0.121
St Peter outside the Trumpington Gate	0.055	0.2706	−0.246	0.009***
St Sepulchre	−0.028	0.0679	−0.059	0.716
Other locations				
Newnham	0.201	0.0317	−0.095	0.413
Barnwell	−0.011	0.2332	−0.133	0.025**
Marketplace	0.017	0.7930	−0.080	0.584
Cambridge fields	0.000	0.9935	0.002	0.838
Barnwell fields	−0.004	0.1489	0.044	0.008***
Location not specified	0.022	0.5479	−0.111	0.252
Rent total	0.000	0.2148	−0.001	0.203

(continued)

Table 2.18: Regression analysis of shares of rents paid to hospitals and private individuals (continued)

	Hospital rent	Private individual rent
R-squared	0.048	0.062
Adjusted R-squared	0.019	0.033
F-statistic	1.673	2.195
p-value	0.013**	0.000***
Average share	0.036	0.545
Standard deviation of share	0.178	0.476
No of observations	1036	1036
Heteroskedasticity Test: Breusch-Pagan-Godfrey	1.319	1.347
p-value	0.118	0.102
Jarques-Bera normality	24111.9	127.5
p-value	0.000***	0.000***

Note: The controls are messuages and Holy Trinity. White robust standard errors. Significance levels are ***1 per cent, **5 per cent and *10 per cent.

Source: TNA SC5/CAMBS/TOWER/2 Barnwell Hundred Roll; TNA SC5/CAMBS/TOWER/1/ Parts1–3 Cambridge Borough Hundred Rolls; Catherine Casson, Mark Casson, John S. Lee and Katie Phillips, *Business and Community in Medieval England: The Cambridge Hundred Rolls Source Volume* (Bristol, 2020)

Comparison with other studies

The high proportion of rents going to charitable institutions compared with private individuals suggests that the profits from property were retained in the town for the support of local institutions. This finding resonates with Brittain Bouchard's conclusion, drawn from 12th-century Brittany, that property transactions provided a mechanism for strengthening social relationships between the lay population and their local religious house.[42]

Religious institutions were involved in the urban property market in Cambridge, largely as a result of their original foundation endowment and subsequent gifts of property from benefactors.[43] However, their involvement seems to have been as largely passive recipients of rental income rather than as active founders or active developers. In this respect their actions differ from those of the monks of Meaux Abbey who founded Hull and then sold it as a going concern to Edward I. They also differ from those of Llanthony Priory, Gloucester, and Coventry Priory, houses that actively developed commercial and residential areas on their land.

The high proportion of rent received by abbeys also suggests that relations between Cambridge's local religious institutions and the local population may have been cordial. This is in contrast to locations such as Bury St Edmunds, where tensions periodically arose between the abbey and the townspeople. The rental of Barnwell Priory suggests that some rents may have lapsed in a manner that parallels the inefficiencies Harvey noted in rent payments to Durham Priory.[44]

The finding that the share of rent per property accruing to abbeys and hospitals exceeded the share of rents per property for churches has some parallels in other studies. Abbey foundation was expensive and therefore usually undertaken by royalty, nobility or people who had acquired substantial land or wealth through military or administrative service or commerce.[45] Abbeys and hospitals attracted wealthier benefactors than churches, and these benefactors donated more valuable properties. More generally, the incentives to support abbeys and hospitals were potentially higher too; both institutions could offer donors prayers for their soul, and some supplemented that by offering physical care for sickness and old age and/or an annual pension.

Initial endowments by wealthy founders could attract additional patrons from a similar social background. St Radegund's, for example, received some of its earliest endowments from the Bishop of Ely.[46] This endowment was then enlarged by King Malcolm of Scotland, who had become the Earl of Huntingdon in 1157. Hospitals also required substantial funds for foundation, which could realistically only be achieved through one wealthy donor (such as Roger Thornton who founded St Katherine's Hospital in Newcastle upon Tyne in the early 14th century) or through the cumulative efforts of several donors.[47]

This interpretation is corroborated by evidence from the port of Sandwich, which suggests that support for local churches during the 13th century frequently comprised small donations from their lay congregation.[48] The importance of the distinctions between different types of donor is corroborated by Rousseau's examination of chantry foundation in St Paul's Cathedral in 1200–1548, in which she distinguished between founders who bequeathed only money to cover the core running expenses of chaplain's wages, the provision of bread, wine and wax, and others who funded additional 'charitable and educational provision', including by the provision of rental income.[49]

2.9 Profile of the charitable institutions

Summaries of institutional property portfolios from which institutional rental income was derived appear at the beginning of the Hundred Rolls before the itemization of individual properties. These portfolios are summarized here, together with brief histories of the institutions themselves. Institutional ownership is described mainly in the introduction to the rolls, where the portfolio of each major institution is described collectively. Some of these properties may have used by the institutions themselves but many had been sold on to others, usually private individuals but sometimes other institutions. Most institutions had sold the properties for a perpetual rent, and the rents paid on donated properties are recorded in the Hundred Rolls under the properties concerned, with the external institution identified as a recipient of rent rather than the holder of the property. Information is provided on institutional property holders both inside and outside Cambridge.

Institutions based in Cambridge

Barnwell Priory was the first religious house to be founded in Cambridge, in 1092. The Augustinian house was founded and endowed by Picot, Sheriff of Cambridgeshire and Lord of Bourn and Madingley, and his wife Hugoline to fulfil a vow made on her sickbed when she called for help from God and St Giles.[50] Table 2.19 summarizes the properties held by Barnwell Priory as documented in the opening section of the Hundred Rolls. It begins by listing the foundation endowments from the king and sheriffs of the county. Next appear endowments from some of the leading aristocratic families resident in the town.

The Priory of St Mary and St Radegund, founded in c.1130, was Cambridge's second monastic foundation and was based just outside the borough, at Grenecroft in the parish of St Andrew, Barnwell.[51] There are few specific details on the house's foundation, but the earliest recorded grants of land came from William le Moyne, the king's moneyer, and from the Bishop of Ely.[52] From 1159 to 1161 further lands next to the present Midsummer Common were provided as a site for the nuns' church by King Malcolm of Scotland, who had become the Earl of Huntingdon in 1157.[53] Table 2.20 summarizes the properties held by St Radegund's, as recorded in the opening section of the Hundred Rolls. Comparing the St Radegund's list with that of Barnwell's shows that St Radegund's had fewer benefactors, and that the properties given tended to be smaller. There were still royal and aristocratic benefactors, however, as well as wealthy local people. Thus the type of people supporting the nunnery was similar to that supporting the priory, but there are fewer such people and their gifts are smaller.

The Hospital of St John the Evangelist appears to have been founded in c.1203.[54] The exact circumstances of its foundation were the subject of

Table 2.19: Properties in Cambridge held by Barnwell Priory

Property	Received from
A messuage once held by Stephen Hauxton, and 6 acres of land. The messuage lies waste, burnt and empty.	John, father of Robert, former Prior of Barnwell
Various properties acquired by Thomas Toylet, mainly lands, plus a croft and some rent income [itemized in HR P8]	Thomas Toylet in consideration for 6 marks per annum paid to his widow Maddi de Ballham for her life. Given to the almoner for a chapel to celebrate mass for his soul and others.
10s annual income	Walter of Wissington, paid through the bailiffs. Richard son of William acquired the income from Count David who held the third penny of Cambridge. It was sold to Robert son of Martin, and then to Thomas of the wardrobe, who sold it to Walter.
Various parcels of land: (1) 6 acres of land in exchange for another 6 acres; (2) 2 acres of land in perpetual alms; (3) 1 acre in perpetual alms; (4) Half an acre of land in perpetual alms.	(1) Master Nigel (2) Roys, son of Reginald de Marshall; acquired as dowry. (3) Isabella de Nedigworye (4) Eustace of Needham
(1) Property in the parish of St Mary previously held from the donor by Reginald of Abingdon; (2) 22s annual income; (3) 1d rent from Robert son of Richard Colt for one messuage before the stone gate; (4) 6 acres of land in Baldwin; Blancgernun's fee yielding 12d rent; (5) A chapel for celebrating mass for the soul of Brother Acius and others.	Brother Acius

(continued)

Table 2.19: Properties in Cambridge held by Barnwell Priory (continued)

Property	Received from
(1) 40 acres in the fields of Cambridge by chirograph in the king's court (2) Services of tenants on lands in Cambridge and Barnwell	John le Kaleys and Basilia, his wife in return for two complex contingent corrodies (described in HR P12) *Comment*: Tenants are Master Henry of Notley, Master Reginald le Blund of Welles, Master Bartholomew son of Radulph of Fordham, brother of the hospital of Stourbridge Common, Osbert King, William Mole, Denis son of William Fabro, John, mason, Walter son of Peter Hunte, Robert Wulward, William of Abingdon, Alicia of Walden, William Prickenie, Simon ad Aquam, Richard Sadelbowe, John Sictus, and Everard of Trumpington, brother of St John's Hospital, Cambridge
A messuage next to Segrimmeslane held by Ethelred Plote for his life for rent of 2s rent. Hawgable 4d.	Thomas Plote *Comment*: Thomas created the messuage through multiple purchases from Robert son of Andrew Buddy, Arnold le Hunte and Richard le Saun' [see HR P13]
5 roods of land	Thomas Plote (1) Half an acre [2 roods] purchased from Eustace Selede for rent of 0.5d. (2) 3 roods purchased from Alexander de Grang', who purchased them from Richard Bateman, son of John Selede, for rent of 0.5d and 1.5d to the heirs of John le Rus
Two fees held by Richard Bateman, son of John Selede, paying 12s annual income and owing 4d hawgable. Also 1 mark of silver given to Richard Bateman for his quitting from Judaism.	
2 acres of land in perpetual alms.	Bartholomew Gogging
Two messuages of the bailiffs held for life by the donor.	William de Piston, chaplain
3 acres by the Barnwell Gate.	Nicholas of Hemmingford

(continued)

Table 2.19: Properties in Cambridge held by Barnwell Priory (continued)

Property	Received from
A messuage and croft in Barnwell, which Robert Cook sometime held from Barnwell; (2) A messuage that Robert de Brunn sometime held from Barnwell yielding 16d and two capons per annum; (3) Half an acre that the same Robert held from Barnwell yielding 5d rent; (4) 1 acre that Andrew son of Hugh Leusene and Alicia, daughter of Richard at the head of the town, held from Barnwell paying 10d and 2 capons per annum.	William, cleric, son of John, mason
(1) A messuage in St Sepulchre's; (2) A messuage opposite St John's Hospital; (3) A croft that lies in the suburbs opposite the nuns of St Radegund's All the properties pay hawgable.	Adam Weriel son of Walter, heir of Agnes, his mother, who inherited from Adam Weriel senior.
A messuage previously held by Oliver the porter for 3s per annum.	Jeremy of Barnwell, son and heir of Hugh de Camera
(1) A messuage in Barnwell and 5 acres of land in Barnwell fields bought from Walter, son of Master Geoffrey of Barnwell, for 8d rent (2) Half an acre bought from Richard son of Ivo for 2d rent (3) Half an acre bought from Alan Godeman for 3d rent (4) A messuage paying 18d rent and 2 acres paying 18d rent bought from William Fabro and Agnes, his wife (5) One acre paying 8d rent bought from Andrew son of Edriz, which was previously sold to William Paie and Isabella by Prior Laurence for 1 mark rent to the almoner of Barnwell.	Geoffrey of Barnwell, chaplain
A messuage in Barnwell previously held by Radulph Cook for 12d rent	Richard of Stansfield, who purchased it from Warin le Mazun, who purchased it from John son of Geoffrey

(continued)

Table 2.19: Properties in Cambridge held by Barnwell Priory (continued)

Property	Received from
Half an acre of land in exchange for two selions that lie next to the land of Walter Potion.	Geoffrey Fabro
8d annual income acquired by the donor from Walter Werret, in respect of his messuage in Cambridge enclosed by the Friars Minor within their walls next to the King's Ditch.	Master Robert Aunger
3 acres of land owing 3d hawgable	Henry Melt
(1) 15 marks given to the donor by Barnwell for his quittance from Judaism; (2) A messuage in Barnwell; (3) 1 acre and 1 rood of land in Barnwell fields; (4) One messuage in Barnwell acquired from the priory, owing 1d hawgable	Geoffrey Melt
Other rights	
Annual fair in Barnwell on the feast of the Nativity of St John the Baptist for four days	Charter of King John, confirmed by Henry III, to preserve the indemnities of Cambridge market; the priory pays the bailiffs half a mark of silver annually for the fair.
Common pasture in Cambridge. Two windmills for grain-milling.	
Advowson of Barnwell church	Lord Gilbert Speche, heir of Pagan Peverel
Advowsons of St Peter's at the Castle, St Giles', St Sepulchre's St Edward's, St John's and St Botolph's	Not known, as beyond living memory

Note: In this and other tables in this chapter the phrase 'in pure and perpetual alms' has been omitted for brevity. A carucate was the measure of land that could be ploughed by one plough team.

Source: TNA SC5/CAMBS/TOWER/1 Barnwell Hundred Roll; TNA SC5/CAMBS/TOWER/1/Parts1–3 Cambridge Borough Hundred Rolls; Catherine Casson, Mark Casson, John S. Lee and Katie Phillips, *Business and Community in Medieval England: The Cambridge Hundred Rolls Source Volume* (Bristol, 2020)

Table 2.20: Properties in Cambridge held by St Radegund's Priory

The prioress and nuns receive £10 and more annually from rents in the town of Cambridge from lands and messuages, many in perpetual alms, and some paying hawgable, as detailed below.

Property	Received from
Church, priory and 10 acres of land in Grenecroft	Malcolm, King of Scotland
4 acres of land nearby	Nigel, Bishop of Ely
5 acres of land nearby	Eustace, Bishop of Ely
2.5 acres of land	Lord Reginald of Argentin, who purchased it from Hugh Spylet, who inherited it. Rent 2s per annum paid to St Giles' church by assignment of the donor.
2.5 acres of land in exchange for an equal area of land.	Richard son of Laurence of Litleber', who inherited the land from his father and ancestors.
3 acres of land and one rood in the Cambridge fields	Philip son of Adam of Girton. Philip held the land from Baldwin son of Acelinus.
15 acres of land	Harvey son of Eustace, who inherited from Dunning and his ancestors.
6 acres of land in the fields of Cambridge	Hugh son of Absolon, who inherited from his father and his ancestors.
1 acre of land in the fields of Cambridge	Philip of Oakington, who inherited from his ancestors.
2.5 acres of land	Margaret Vivien, who bought the land from John, son of Jordan, who inherited it. Rent charge of 3d to donor's heirs.
10 acres of land in the fields of Cambridge	Margaret, widow of Radulph Parson, who inherited the land.
4 acres of land in the fields of Cambridge	Jordan son of Radulph of Brecet', who inherited the land.
5 acres of land and 3 roods	Stephen, son of Alneva. Alneva inherited the land from her mother Athelina.

(continued)

Table 2.20: Properties in Cambridge held by St Radegund's Priory (continued)

Property	Received from
1 acre of land in the fields of Cambridge	Matilda, widow of Simon Bagge. Matilda was given the land by Robert Bagge, who inherited it from William, his father and his ancestors.
1.5 acres of land in the fields of Cambridge owing 1.5d rent to All Saints in the Jewry by assignment of the donor	John son of William, who purchased the land from his brother Robert, who inherited it from his father, William, and his ancestors.
2 acres of land in the fields of Cambridge in perpetual alms	Warin Grim, who inherited from John Grim, his father, and his father's ancestors.
1 acre of land in the fields of Cambridge in perpetual alms	John Grim
One messuage in their parish of St Radegund's owing 3d hawgable	Walter de Noncius, who purchased it from Radulph Bolle, who purchased it from Nicholas Sarand, who inherited it by ancient succession.
Four messuages and a piece of vacant land in St Andrew's. The nuns pay a chaplain to celebrate mass in perpetuity in St Andrew's Church for their souls. Hawgable is paid	Robert Crocheman and Cassandria, his wife
One messuage in St Andrew's for which 1d hawgable is paid	William Sweteye, who purchased it from Radulph Bole, who purchased it from Nicholas Sarand, who inherited it.
Two messuages opposite St Radegund's, now held by Geoffrey of Dunwich who bought them from Agnetha le Veve, who bought them from the nuns. Geoffrey pays 8s rent to the nuns	Nicholas Sarand, who inherited the properties.
Other rights	
Annual fair for two days beginning on the eve of the feast on the Assumption of Blessed Mary	Charter of King Stephen
Ownership and advowson of St Clement's church and All Saints in the Jewry Church	Not known, as beyond living memory

Source: TNA SC5/CAMBS/TOWER/1/Parts1–3 Cambridge Borough Hundred Rolls; Catherine Casson, Mark Casson, John S. Lee and Katie Phillips, *Business and Community in Medieval England: The Cambridge Hundred Rolls Source Volume* (Bristol, 2020)

disagreements during the preparation of the Hundred Rolls of 1279–80 regarding whether it was a joint foundation of the Bishop of Ely and the townspeople or whether the townspeople alone should be given the credit.[55] The townspeople argued that in fact they were the founders of the hospital, crediting Henry Eldcorn for getting the community's approval to build the hospital on a piece of waste ground belonging to the town. Subsequent to this, the jurors stated, permission had been obtained from the Bishop of Ely for an oratory and burial ground on the site, and for the income from the church of Horningsea.[56] In the 1280s attempts were made by the Bishop of Ely, Hugh de Balsham, to extend the role of the hospital to the provision of hostel accommodation for scholars.[57] This was not successful, however, and the scholars were relocated to hostels near St Peter's Church, which were subsequently the basis for the foundation of Peterhouse College.[58] The hospital has been noted by historians for the support it received from the burgesses.[59] Table 2.21 lists the principal benefactions of the Hospital of St John. The interesting feature here is the absence of royal and aristocratic endowments. Many of the benefactors were from leading families resident in the town and there is an absence of royal and aristocratic endowments. Compared with St Radegund's, there is a relative absence of ordinary families outside the local elite.

Table 2.22 summarizes the endowments of various smaller local institutions. The leper hospital of St Mary Magdalene Sturbridge, located on the current Newmarket road in Barnwell, is likely to have been founded in the 12th century.[60] Its foundation and endowment is likely to have been a collaborative effort by the townspeople of Cambridge, but control of the hospital later transferred, for unknown reasons, to the Bishop of Ely. In the late 13th century its role as a hospital ended and it became first a chapel for the local community and then a storage centre for Sturbridge fair.[61] Despite its early foundation date, the hospital has fewer recorded endowments in the Hundred Rolls than the other early foundations.

From the mid–13th century the established contemplative houses already described began to face competition from mendicant orders of friars, whose focus was on active preaching. The arrival of these orders in Cambridge was associated with the growth of town as a centre of scholarship. The Dominicans established themselves in Cambridge in 1238 with a church on the present site of Emmanuel College.[62] In 1225 the Franciscans established a house in Cambridge on the site of the town gaol.[63] In 1238 the king granted them additional land to extend their site, and gave the burgesses money to build a new gaol.[64] Carmelites settled in Chesterton in 1249 and then divided into two.[65] Some of the

Table 2.21: Properties of the Hospital of St John the Evangelist

Property	Received from
Land in fee of the Lord King [opposite St Sepulchre church] on which the hospital and chapel are built	Henry Frost, burgess of Cambridge. *Comment*: Henry acquired it from the burgesses who held it from the King. Hugh of Norwold, Bishop of Ely, is alleged to have appropriated the right of presentation of the master of the hospital, with serious loss to the town.
2 carucates of land in the fields of Cambridge, for which they pay hawgable	
£6 annual income in the town of Cambridge	
One carucate of land in Cambridge for a rent of 20s to the bailiffs in accordance with the donor's charter	Robert de Mortimer, who was given the land by King John.
2 acres of land with appurtenances in the fields of Cambridge	Anthony, chaplain of Stockton, who bought the land from Baldwin son of Baldwin Blancgernun for 2d rent.
A messuage in the parish of St Giles' outside the ditch of Cambridge, lying near the St Neot's road	Geoffrey Blancgernun. Baldwin Blancgernun gave the messuage to Geoffrey for 4d rent.
8 acres of land in the fields of Cambridge and 1 acre in Binnenbroc	Baldwin Blancgernun, for the souls of himself and his ancestors.
1.5 acres of land in the fields of Cambridge	Geoffrey Prat of Ely, who purchased them from Baldwin son of Baldwin Blancgernun for 1.5d rent.
1 acre of land beneath Barnwell	Geoffrey Prat of Ely. Rent to Geoffrey of 2d and one pair of gloves.
2 acres of land in the fields of Cambridge	Nicholas of Hemingford
15 acres of land in the fields of Cambridge	Maurice le Rus
1 acre of land by gift	Harvey son of Eustace. For the maintenance of a lamp by night before the sick.

(continued)

Table 2.21: Properties of the Hospital of St John the Evangelist (continued)

Property	Received from
14 acres of land in the fields of Cambridge	William Toylet
Two houses in the parish of St Sepulchre's, yielding a combined rent income of 6s.	William Toylet
Two houses in the parish of St Botolph's owing 1.5d hawgable.	Deacon of St Bartholomew's
8 acres of land in the fields of Cambridge	Michael, cleric of Huntingdon, who was given the land by his uncle, Master Robert of Huntingdon.
2.5 acres of land in the fields of Cambridge, owing 2d rent	Eustace son of Harvey
3 acres of land in Newnham owing 1d rent	Peter son of Richard of Newnham, chaplain
Half an acre of land in the croft of Newnham	Gilbert Baker, who purchased it from Adam son of Eustace for 2d rent.
Other rights	
Ownership and advowson of the church of St Peter's outside the Trumpington Gate	Henry son of Sigar. For the use of the Hospital for the sustenance of the poor and sick.
Marketplace of Cambridge	Eustace of Wimpole.

Source: TNA SC5/CAMBS/TOWER/1/Parts1–3 Cambridge Borough Hundred Rolls; Catherine Casson, Mark Casson, John S. Lee and Katie Phillips, *Business and Community in Medieval England: The Cambridge Hundred Rolls Source Volume* (Bristol, 2020)

Table 2.22: Properties of other religious and charitable institutions based in Cambridge

Property	Received from and comment
Leper Hospital of St Mary Magdalene Sturbridge at Sturbridge Common	
Advowson and endowment of the hospital	Burgesses of Cambridge, who hold from the king. It is alleged to have been wrongfully alienated by Hugh, Bishop of Ely for the use of chaplains instead of lepers.
24.5 acres of land in the fields of Cambridge	Many donors. Potential liability for hawgable but none paid.
Two-day fair in the hospital enclosure beginning on the eve of the Feast of the Holy Cross	King John
Scholars of Merton	
A messuage with 45 acres of land and 50s income in the town and fields of Cambridge, owing the seller 1d rent and the bailiffs 4s 10d hawgable	Purchased from William of Manefield, who inherited from John of Barnard Castle who inherited from Guy of Barnard Castle, who bought from Eustace Dunning.
15 acres of land and 10s 2d rent, in fief in the county of Leicester, owing 3s 10d and scutage when required.	Purchased from William of Manefield, as above. The rental income was held inherited by Eustace Dunning from his father Harvey son of Eustace who acquired it from the Count of Leicester [as tenant-in-chief] who acquired it from Lord Edmund, brother of the King [Edmund Crouchback]
Hospital of St John of Jerusalem in England	
(1) A messuage in St John's parish (2) A messuage in St Mary's parish	Purchased from Master Bartholomew of the Larder, who inherited from Master Stephen of the larder, his father, and thence through ancient acquisition

(continued)

Table 2.22: Properties of other religious and charitable institutions based in Cambridge (continued)

Property	Received from and comment
Friars Preachers residing in Cambridge (Dominicans)	
Residence and church on an 8-acre site assembled from various separate holdings. These holdings paid geld and feudal aid to the town, but there are no charters and no-one knows how much they owe	Various unnamed individuals
Friars Minor residing in Cambridge (Franciscans)	
Residence and church on an 6-acre site assembled from various separate holdings. These holdings paid geld and feudal aid to the town [as above]	Various unnamed individuals
Friars of the Sack	
Residence and church on 3 acres of land	(1) Richard of Heke Lingham in perpetual alms (2) Acquisitions from many people (3) Gifts from many people. Confirmed by charter of Henry III
Carmelite Friars	
Residence and church in Newnham on 3 acres of land	(1) Michael Malerbe in perpetual alms (2) Acquisitions from many people (3) Gifts from many people. Charter not known
Crutched Friars residing Cambridge	
A messuage where they reside and have their chapel, owing 12d rent and 4d hawgable	Purchased from Henry of Barton

Source: TNA SC5/CAMBS/TOWER/2 Barnwell Hundred Roll; TNA SC5/CAMBS/TOWER/1/Parts1–3 Cambridge Borough Hundred Rolls; Catherine Casson, Mark Casson, John S. Lee and Katie Phillips, *Business and Community in Medieval England: The Cambridge Hundred Rolls Source Volume* (Bristol, 2020).

friars remained in Chesterton but then later moved into the town. It is unclear what happened to those friars after the mid-14th century.[66] Others relocated first to Newnham and then, in the late 13th century, to Milne Street in Cambridge. A number of houses were demolished to provide a site for the Carmelites, and they have therefore been credited with being the first religious group to have made a major impression on the topography of the town. It has been suggested that the relocation was motivated by the order's increasing engagement with the academic life of the town through both teaching and study and their transition from a contemplative order, which welcomed isolation, to a preaching order that desired a closer link to the developing university.[67]

The Friars of the Penance of Jesus Christ, more commonly known as the Friars of the Sack, arrived in Cambridge in c.1258 and initially established themselves in the parish of St Mary, before moving to a site where the Fitzwilliam Museum now stands, where they seem to have accommodated students from their order.[68] This was a large 'stone house' with court and chapel of John le Rus, Mayor of Cambridge in 1258. It was held of the fee of Barnwell Priory, which initially forbade the sale.[69] Despite receiving support from local burgesses the order's time in Cambridge was brief as the Council of Lyon of 1274 prohibited them and other small orders from recruiting more members.[70] In 1307 the friars made over their property to the neighbouring college of Peterhouse. The mendicant orders were characterized by many smaller endowments from individuals. The exception was the Crutched Friars, whose holdings were acquired by purchase from Henry of Barton.

Institutions outside Cambridge that occupied properties in Cambridge

Two institutions appear to have held property in Cambridge to provide temporary accommodation for their members. The Knights Hospitallers held two messuages in Cambridge, one in St John's and the other in St Mary's, both bought from Master Bartholomew of the Larder, son of Master Stephen of the Larder, who first acquired the properties.[71] These properties appear to have been used by the order itself, possibly as hostels for their Cambridgeshire houses at Chippenham (founded in 1118) and Shingay (c.1154–9).[72] The scholars of Merton College in Oxford are recorded as having an operational base in Cambridge in 1279, which may have been for the management of their estates (see Chapter 6), or a hostel for visiting students or both. They had a single powerful patron in Walter of Merton, royal administrator and future Bishop of Rochester.

He acquired much of the Dunning estate through a middleman, Master Guy of Barnard Castle, an official in the service of the Bishop of Ely. Walter's method of acquiring properties for his scholars through buying up bankrupt estates is examined in Chapter 6.

Institutions based outside Cambridge that derived rents from Cambridge properties

Other institutions based outside Cambridge were also given properties in Cambridge to either sell or lease or make use of themselves. This situation was not unique to Cambridge – there is evidence in other English towns of people and institutions residing or headquartered outside a town holding property in the town.[73] Table 2.23 details the institutions outside Cambridge receiving rent from Cambridge in 1279.

Religious institutions receiving rents from Cambridge were widely spread. Although some were quite close, for example, Anglesey Priory, many were quite distant, such as Crowland near Spalding, Hatfield Peverel near Chelmsford, Lavendon near Olney, Buckinghamshire, and Kenilworth in Warwickshire. Nunneries receiving rents were particularly dispersed; locations included Goring-on-Thames, Oxfordshire, Stratford-by-Bow, Middlesex, and Great Gaddesden near St Albans. These rents almost certainly resulted from the granting of property by Cambridge families to external institutions rather than from speculative acquisitions of Cambridge properties by such institutions using funds obtained elsewhere.

One explanation why properties in Cambridge might have been given to institutions further afield, such as St Albans, is that after the Norman Conquest some families were given estates scattered across a number of locations. It is possible that a family based, for example, in St Albans might have decided, when supporting its local religious house, to relinquish a piece of property on one of the family's more distant estates. Occasionally other explanations are hinted at – Sawtry Abbey may have come to the attention of Cambridge residents because its founder Simon de Senitz, Earl of Northampton and grandson of William the Conqueror's niece Judith and her husband Earl Waltheof, was related to the Earls of Huntingdon, who held the third penny of Cambridge, and to Malcolm IV of Scotland, benefactor of St Radegund's.[74] Warden Abbey, near Biggleswade, Bedfordshire, meanwhile, also numbered among its earliest benefactors Malcolm IV of Scotland.[75] Swaffham Priory may have benefited from its geographical vicinity as it was only 7 miles north-east of Cambridge and held 12 properties in the town.

Table 2.23: Institutions outside Cambridge receiving rent from Cambridge in 1279

Name, location and foundation date	Source of rent
Anglesey Priory 6 miles north-east of Cambridge Founded c.1212	Robert son of Robert Huberd was a canon of the priory and a major benefactor. He gave a messuage and some vacant land in St Michael's, a granary and vacant land in St John's, a messuage in St Peter's outside the Trumpington Gate and 8 acres in the Barnwell fields.[i] Robert also gave 15s in rents: 5s from a messuage formerly of Peter son of Ivo, 4s from property held by Richard Bateman, and 6s from property held by Harvey the butcher. Those properties paid in total 11d for hawgable and 2d to St John's Hospital (from which Robert may have bought some of them).[ii] Individual properties paying rent to the priory included three shops in St Michael's and a messuage in St Edward's held by Richard Bateman junior paying respectively 5s and 6d to the priory, and a messuage in St Michael's held by the rector, Master Stephen of Haslingfield, paying 2s to Lord William de la Bruere and 1s to the priory.[iii] A messuage in St Andrew's held by William Astocam paid 1s to the priory. William gave the messuage to Barnwell Priory, leasing it back for his life free of charge. He bought it from Simon Flinston; the priory presumably sold it for a perpetual rent to Simon or a previous owner.[iv] The priory also seems to have sold outright a messuage in All Saints in the Jewry, held by John son of William Waubert, from which they received 1d rent. This property also paid rents to Radulph son of Felici Quoye, John Porthors and Master Robert Aunger, one of whom may have bought the property from the priory.[v]
Berden Priory A village on the border between Essex and Hertfordshire near to Bishop's Stortford Founded pre-1214	A rent of 2s from a messuage in St Botolph's parish held by Thomas of Hogiton (possibly Hauxton).

(continued)

Table 2.23: Institutions outside Cambridge receiving rent from Cambridge in 1279 (continued)

Name, location and foundation date	Source of rent
Bury St Edmunds: The Abbey Founded c.903	The rolls state that the abbot received 21s rent from 'certain houses' in Cambridge by ancient purchase, but by what warranty is unknown.[vi] Seven properties are itemized in the rolls. They all relate to messuages in parishes near the river and the bridge (St Giles', St Clement's and St Peter's at the Castle). This suggests that the houses are in fact messuages and that they may have occupied adjacent plots of land on either side of the river. The itemised rents add up to 19s 2d, leaving 1s 10d of the 21s rent unaccounted for. The list is as follows:
	A half-mesuage in St Giles' paid 15d to the abbey plus hawgable. It was held by Isabella, one of the daughters of Thomas Froyslake, who bought it from her brother John, who may have bought it from the abbey for a perpetual rent.[vii]
	Another half-messuage in St Giles', held by Laurence Seman and Agnes his wife, purchased from Isabella Froyslake, and paying 15d to the abbey plus hawgable.[viii] This is probably the other half of the previous messuage, which suggests that the messuage paid 30d rent before it was divided.
	Another messuage in St Giles' paid 3s 2d rent; it was held by Roger son of Richard Ampe whose great-grandfather Reginald Kankelia bought it from Andrew son of Peter of Cambridge.[ix] It may have been Peter who bought it from the abbey.
	Another messuage in St Giles' paid 12d to the abbey and 5s to St Radegunds. It was held by Geoffrey Spartegrave and Agnes his wife, who bought it from Robert son of Robert Vivien, whose grandfather Henry had bought it previously.[x] In view of the much later foundation of St Radegund's it is possible that the property was given first to Bury and sold by them before it was given to St Radegund's and sold by them to the Vivien family.
	A messuage in St Peter at the Castle paid 3s; it was held by Robert son of Robert Seman, and had been in his family from time immemorial, which suggests that it was sold by the abbey in the 12th century or even earlier.[xi]
	A messuage in St Clement's held by John But paid 3s 6d. This descended from John le Rus to Gilbert le Rus, his nephew, who sold it to Thomas Merwilus, who sold it to John.[xii] The abbey may have sold it John le Rus or his ancestors.
	Another messuage in St Clement's, held by Helewisa Plumbe, paid 6s to the abbey and 3s to Master Robert Aunger.[xiii] Helewise inherited it from Walter her father, who purchased it, probably from Robert Aunger, whose family may have bought it from the abbey.
Caldwell Priory Located on the banks of the River Ouse south of Bedford Founded c.1135	Caldwell Priory is unusual in that it received portions of the 'third penny' of Cambridge rather than property rents. The identity of the donors is therefore explicit. Richard son of William gave 70s of annual income and Roger of Anstey gave 100s. Both incomes originally accrued to Earl David of Huntingdon by gift of the king, and were paid 'through the hands of the bailiffs' of the town. Roger of Anstey bought his income from Simon of St Luke's who presumably acquired it from the earl.[xiv]

(continued)

Table 2.23: Institutions outside Cambridge receiving rent from Cambridge in 1279 (continued)

Name, location and foundation date	Source of rent
Chicksand Priory Chicksand, near Bedford Founded c.1150	A messuage in St Peter's at the Castle, held by Michael Wulward, paid 7s rent to Chicksand, as well as 3s to Lord Peter de Chavent as lord of the fee. The messuage descended in the Wulward family, from Wulward the founder through Robert his son, Peter his grandson to Michael his great grandson. Thus the rent was almost certainly assigned by either Lord Peter or a member of the Wulward family.
Crowland Abbey In the marshes near Spalding, Lincolnshire Founded c. 700	The almoner of Crowland received 4s from a messuage in All Saints in the Jewry held by William of Rudham, cleric.[xv] The rent was probably given by Bartholomew the tanner or, more likely, one of his ancestors.
Ely Priory Founded 673	Both the bishop and the prior were involved with Cambridge. Bishop Nigel gave 4 acres of land to St Radegund's and Bishop Eustace gave them another 5 acres, in a grant later confirmed by Bishop John.[xvi] Barnwell Priory held a messuage with 20 acres of land in fee from Ely Priory, given to Barnwell by Baldwin Blancgernun, paying 20 marks per annum and acquitting the Prior of Ely for hawgable.[xvii] In addition, the priory had 40s of income from the town, on which it paid over 5s hawgable.[xviii] It also held a granary in St Michael's and two messuages in St John's. According to the rolls, it also held the patronage of St Andrew's Church from time immemorial.[xix]
	Individual properties paying rent to the priory may be itemised as follows:
	A messuage in St Giles' held by Norman the cooper paying 12d. It also paid half a mark to John Porthors.[xx]
	A capital messuage held by Richard son of Laurence, inherited from his father, and paying 4s. Laurence or his ancestors presumably bought this messuage from the priory for a perpetual rent.[xxi]
	A messuage in St Mary's paying 16d rent, held by Walter le Hunte, whose paternal grandmother bought it from the priory.[xxii]
	A messuage in St Edward's held by William Astocam, previously held by Juliana Pageles, which had been bought from the priory for 18d rent.[xxiii]
	A messuage in St Andrew's held by Walter of Hauxton, clerk, paying 3s to the Almoner of Ely. The messuage had been bought some time ago from the priory by Geoffrey Prat. His son and heir Simon sold it to William the miller, whose son William sold it to William at Broke, who sold it to Walter.[xxiv]
	In addition, a messuage in St Botolph's held by Master William le Blunt, paying 28d rent to Master Eustace of Shelford, was a 'gift' to Master William from the priory. It was possibly given (by an unknown benefactor) to the priory with the rent attached and then sold on to Master William for gersuma.[xxv]

(continued)

Table 2.23: Institutions outside Cambridge receiving rent from Cambridge in 1279 (continued)

Name, location and foundation date	Source of rent
Fordham Priory 12 miles north-east of Cambridge Founded c.1227	The priory received a rent of 20s from a just single property in Cambridge, namely a messuage in All Saints in the Jewry held by Johanna, widow of William le Mire. The prior purchased the property from Ernisius the merchant, who bought it from John Porthors, who bought it from Agnes of Barton, who bought it from a man called Merndale about whom nothing is known.[xxvi]
Hatfield Peverell Priory Located north-east of Chelmsford, Essex, Founded 1087–1100	The priory held a 10s rent from a messuage in St Mary's where William Tingewick resided and a 6d rent from a grange in St Michael's, which Alice sister of Ernest had inherited from her brother Ernest the merchant. The grange had been bought from the priory by Bartholomew the tailor, who gave it to his daughter Margaret who sold it to Ernest The messuage also passed through Ernest's hands. Ernest bought it from Henry son of Robert Nadon and gave (probably sold) it to William.
Huntingdon Priory Founded c.1100.	The priory held 60 acres of land in Cambridge given by Lord Radulph de Turbevile and Alicia his wife. It had a charter from Lord Reginald de Grey that acquitted it from scutage.[xxvii] The priory was given 2.5 acres in the fields of Cambridge by Geoffrey, chaplain, who bought them from William Fabro, who held them from William Novacurt. The priory sold these to William Paie and Isabella his wife, with a rent burden of 21d payable to the Earl of Huntingdon; the earl acquitted them of service due to William Novacurt as tenant in chief.
Kenilworth Abbey The town of Kenilworth is south of Coventry, Warwickshire Founded 1122	The rolls simply state that the priory received 20s annually from the town 'through the hands of the bailiffs of the town, by which manner and by which warranty they do not know'.[xxviii]
Lavendon Abbey Lavendon is a small settlement near Olney on the border between Buckinghamshire and Bedfordshire Founded c.1155	Little is known about the abbey, but it is clear that property was given to it by Cecilia Godso, a relative of Robert son of Robert Huberd, canon of Anglesey Priory. She gave a messuage in St Peter's outside the Trumpington Gate, which was held by John Perin for 12d rent.[xxix] The messuage also paid 1.5d hawgable. The gift must have been fairly recent because John had purchased the messuage direct from the priory

(continued)

Table 2.23: Institutions outside Cambridge receiving rent from Cambridge in 1279 (continued)

Name, location and foundation date	Source of rent
Ramsey Abbey Located on an island in the Fens, 10 miles north of Huntingdon, near the present market town of Ramsey. Founded c.969	Ramsey received two modest rents from Cambridge. A shop in All Saints in the Jewry, located next to the Hospital of St John, and held by William Seman, paid 6d. It descended to William from Nicholas son of Andrew of Wimpole through Cecilia, William's mother. A messuage in Holy Trinity held by Roger Goldsmith paid 16d rent. It descended to Roger from Harvey son of Eustace through Eustace, Harvey's son, who sold it to William of Thetford. Master William Golde inherited from William, and his son John then sold it to Roger.[xxx] It may well have borne the rent to the abbey when Harvey first acquired it.
Sawtry Abbey Sawtry, between Huntingdon and Peterborough Founded in 1147	In 1279 the abbey received rent from just one property in Cambridge: a messuage in St Botolph's held by Walter son of Henry of Howes. His father, Henry senior, had bought the messuage from Elisius, chaplain, who had inherited it from his grandfather, Nicholas the weaver. It paid 4s rent to the abbey, and 1d hawgable
Spinney Priory Spinney is close to Fordham and Wicken Fen, north-east of Cambridge Founded c.1227	The priory received rent from just one property in Cambridge: a messuage in St Peter's at the Castle, held by Alan of Howes, which paid a substantial rent of half a mark. It was given to the priory by Robert, former vicar of St Edward's Church. He bought it from William Casteleyen, possibly the castellan of the nearby castle, who inherited the property from Geoffrey Godeman his father. The priory sold the messuage to Robert Chaloner, and his daughters and heirs, Katherine and Elena, sold it to Alan.
Thremhall Priory Thremhall, near Stansted Mountfichet in Essex Founded c.1150	The priory received 8s rent from three Cambridge messuages: two in St Michael's, one held by Adam son of William and another by Richard le Der, both paying 2s, and one in All Saints in the Jewry held by Avicia daughter of Simon Godeman paying 2s. The rents on the first two properties were assigned to the priory by John de Engayne, tenant–in–chief of both.[xxxi] The third property paid an additional rent of 1d to Robert de le Bruere. The rent may have been assigned to the priory by Robert, or possibly by the Brampton family who bought it from him and sold it to Simon Godeman.

(continued)

Table 2.23: Institutions outside Cambridge receiving rent from Cambridge in 1279 (continued)

Name, location and foundation date	Source of rent
Thorney Abbey Island in the Fens east of Peterborough, on the northern edge of the Isle of Ely Founded in 972	It held a rent of 8d on a piece of vacant land in St Mary's, held by Walter le Hunte, which also paid a rent of 20d to William Seman. Walter bought it from Walter the Plumber, whose family had held it for several generations. It is possible Walter the Plumber's ancestors purchased the property from William Seman's ancestors, who had purchased the property from the abbey for a perpetual rent of 8d.
Tilty Abbey Tilty, near Great Dunmow Founded c.1153	The abbey was connected with three properties in Cambridge; one was owned by the abbey; one had been given to the abbey but was occupied free of charge by the donors for their lives; and the third paid rent to the abbey. From one it received rent.
	The abbey owned a messuage in St John's that they bought from Philip le Burgelun, cleric. Philip's brother, William, had bought the messuage from William Seman, who had inherited from his father Seman, and Philip had inherited the messuage on William's death. The messuage paid 1d in hawgable. It seems that the messuage was either leased out or employed for the abbey's own use, possibly as a hostel for brothers studying at the university.[xxii]
	The abbey was given a messuage in St Edward's by John le Franceys and Margaret his wife, daughter of Alicia Scolice, which the donors occupied until their deaths. This property too paid 1d hawgable. The gift was effected 'through a deed issued in the court of the lord'.[xxiii] John witnessed a deed of gift to the Gild of St Mary in 1286, but direct connection to Tilty can be established.[xxiv] However, there were other members of the Franceys family in Cambridge. According to a charter of Stephen of Boxworth in the archives of St John's Hospital, William Franceys, who might have been a relative, held land in the fields of Boxworth where a cell (or possibly a grange) of Tiltey Abbey also held land.[xxv]
	The Almoner received 4s rent from two shops in Holy Trinity held by Henry Page. Henry bought them from the widow Matilda Aleyn, who was given them by her father William le Pittere. The shops also paid 3s to St Radegund's and 1d to Isabel widow of Albrin the butcher. It is possible that Albrin bought the shops from St Radegund's for a perpetual rent and then sold them to William, Margaret's father.
Warden Abbey Warden, near Biggleswade, Bedfordshire Founded c.1136	The abbey held a messuage in St John's that they bought from Nicholas of Hitchin, cleric, who was given it by his uncle, Master Nicholas of Hitchin. Master Nicholas bought it from Master Bartholomew of the Larder, who got it from his Master Stephen of the Larder, The messuage was free from rent, apart from 1.5d hawgable.[xxvi]

(continued)

Table 2.23: Institutions outside Cambridge receiving rent from Cambridge in 1279 (continued)

Name, location and foundation date	Source of rent
West Dereham Abbey Dereham is a Norfolk town about 20 miles west of Norwich Founded in 1188	At some stage the priory acquired the patronage of Holy Trinity Church, but by what warranty the prior did not know.[xxxvii]
The anchorite of Trumpington Unknown	They received a rent of 4s 6d from a shop in the marketplace in St Mary's held by William of Norfolk and Margaret his wife. It seems likely that the gift was made by the ancestors of Richard Perles, from whom the property descended by purchase through Richard son of Ivo to Henry Hubert, Margaret's father. The property also paid 2s 6d to Ernest Merchant by assignment of previous owners.[xxxviii]
Nunneries	
Chatteris Abbey Chatteris is a town in the Fens about 15 miles north of Cambridge Founded 1006–16	The nunnery held rent from three messuages in Cambridge: one in St Clement's, held by Geoffrey the cooper, one in St Edward's held by John of Braintree and his wife Mabilia, and one in Holy Trinity held by Geoffrey of Walden.[xxxix] The rent on the first property had been assigned to the nuns by Robert Seman. The second property seems to have been bought outright from Robert Bateman senior, and paid a total of 10s rent, comprising 6s to the nuns and 4s to the Hospital of St John. The third property paid 5s rent to Albatisse of Chatteris, which may signify the abbess; the same record also refers to Albarissa of Madingley, who knows of no other claims on the rent, and could be the same person.
Goring Priory Goring, South Oxfordshire Founded in or before 1181	The Hundred Rolls identify two messuages in St Clement's that paid rent to Goring. One was held by Giles son of John of Barton and the other by Margaret daughter of Edmund de Stewincton; they both paid 3s rent.[xl] Their connection with Goring is difficult to explain. Giles' property descended through Margaret Wulward, while the other descended through Humphrey of Clapton and Geliona his wife, and neither family had any apparent connection to Goring.
Ickleton Priory The small village of Ickleton, near Linton, off the road to Colchester Founded c. 1163	The nuns received rent from only one property in Cambridge: a piece of land next to the court of St Radegund's, held by the prominent burgess Richard Laurence, which he bought from John, clerk, son of John Adelhard. The prestigious location of this property, the wealth of its holder, and the substantial rent of 12s, all point to this being a gift of some significance. However, there is no further reference to John Adelhard in the Hundred Rolls or elsewhere.

(continued)

Table 2.23: Institutions outside Cambridge receiving rent from Cambridge in 1279 (continued)

Name, location and foundation date	Source of rent
St Mary de Pré Priory Great Gaddesden near St Albans Founded in 1194	The charters of the priory indicate that it had a rent of 20s from property in Cambridge, which was used to provide clothing for the sisters. Apparently this land was purchased by Warin through a grant of land to Anketil of Cambridge. Little is known about Anketil; he could be Anketil son of Herbert and Juliana his wife (Appendix 5), and/or Anketil whose son Warin was tallaged £1 in 1211 (Appendix 1).[xii] The rolls list four properties paying rent to St Mary's: two messuages and a shop in St Mary's and a messuage in St Sepulchre.[xiii] Those four properties paid a combined rent of 13s to the nuns. Two of the properties were acquired from the nuns by a member of the Odierne family. Aspelon Odierne senior had a son Aspelon junior and a daughter Deonisia. It seems likely that Aspelon senior gave to the nuns the rent on one of the messuages in St Mary's, while Aspelon junior may bought one of the shops from the nuns for a perpetual rent.[xiii] Both father and son died, leaving Deonisia to inherit both properties. She had sold on the properties by 1279. A third messuage, also in St Mary's, where Walter the barber resided, had been acquired from the nuns by Walter of Oxford serving at the University of Cambridge The fourth property was a messuage in St Sepulchre that had been bought from the nuns by Leon Dunning or a previous owner.[xiv] A fifth property, another shop in St Mary's, was purchased from the nuns by Robert Odierne, who was presumably a relative of Aspelon senior.[xiv] This shop did not pay rent to the nuns, but to St Mary's Church; presumably it had been bought outright from the nuns (for gersuma) at an earlier stage.
Stratford Priory Near the banks of the River Lea, about 200 metres south of Bow Bridge next to the present church Founded c.1051–75	The priory received a rent of 2s from a piece of vacant land in St Mary's held by Richard Bateman senior. Richard bought it from Richard Burs, who bought it from his uncle who bought it through ancient acquisition.

(continued)

Table 2.23: Institutions outside Cambridge receiving rent from Cambridge in 1279 (continued)

Name, location and foundation date	Source of rent
Swaffham Priory The village of Swaffham Bulbeck, 7 miles north-east of Cambridge Probably founded in the second half of the 12th century	They held a shop in St Mary's given to them by William Herre from his inheritance, together with rental income totalling 30s and a liability for 20s 5d hawgable.[xlvi] The rent was generated from a portfolio of 11 properties: A messuage in St Clement's held by William of Pickering paying half a mark which was originally purchased from the nuns by Hugh Eldcorn.[xlvii] A house in St Benedict's held by Henry of Barton paying 2s that was was given to Henry by his uncle, who bought it from Radulph le Cuver, who acquired it from the nuns.[xlviii] A messuage in St John's held by Margaret daughter of Ranulph at the Gate paying 32d.[xlix] A messuage in St Benedict's held by Osbert the farrier and his wife Berota paying 2s rent.[l] A messuage in St Sepulchre held by Henry Toylet paying 2s to lord Roger of the Exchequer and 3s to the nuns.[li] A messuage in St Edward's held by Gilbert Bernard paying 8s to the nuns through the heirs of William Wulsi, who inherited the property.[lii] A messuage in Holy Trinity held by Henry Page who bought it from Richard Bateman senior who inherited it from his uncle Wade, paying 1d to St Radegunds and 3s to the nuns of Swaffham. It is possible that Wade acquired the property from St Radegund's, and that they had been given it by someone who had previously given the rent on the property to the nuns of Swaffham.[liii] Some vacant land in St Andrew's held by John Godsone paying 6d to Barnwell Priory and 18d to the nuns.[liv] It is possible that that the land was given first to Barnwell, who sold it to Swaffham, who sold it to Robert of Lanselle, from whom it descended to John Godsone. Two houses in St John's held by William Eliot paying 28d (14d each), one of which was originally held by Richard Bonney and the other by Maurice le Rus. It seems that the nuns sold the two properties as one, that they were subsequently divided and then reunited by William's father Henry.[lv] A messuage in Holy Trinity held by John Bradeye paying 4d. It descended from the Aleyn family through Emma daughter of Roger and wife of Henry the cooper. The low rent suggests that the nuns may have sold the property at an early date.

(continued)

Table 2.23: Institutions outside Cambridge receiving rent from Cambridge in 1279 (continued)

Name, location and foundation date	Source of rent
Hospitals	
Hospital of St Mary Longstowe Longstowe is a small village 12 miles west of Cambridge towards Biggleswade Founded pre–1250	The sisters acquired a messuage in Holy Trinity by gift of John of Barton though burdened with a rent of 8s payable to John. John had acquired the messuage through inheritance. The sisters sold the messuage, presumably for an undisclosed gersuma, to Simon, brother, who held it in 1279. It is possible that Simon was connected with the Hospital. The sisters received a token rent of 1d.[lvi]
Hospital of Balsham Balsham is a village 11 miles south east of Cambridge Founded 1200s	Held three shops in St Edward's and two messuages in St Andrew's.

Sources: [i] HR P25; [ii] HR P25; [iii] HR 608/9; HR 693; [iv] HR 848; [v] HR 719; [vi] HR R7; [vii] HR 101; [viii] HR 139; [ix] HR 201; [x] HR 114; [xi] HR 133; [xii] HR 170; [xiii] HR 174; [xiv] HR R5/6; [xv] HR 408; [xvi] HR A13/5; [xvii] HR P3; [xviii] HR P26; [xix] HR F60; [xx] HR 82; see also HR R11; [xxi] HR 144; [xxii] HR 580; [xxiii] HR 850; [xxiv] HR 504; [xxv] HR 744; [xxvi] HR F22; [xxvii] HR R8; [xxix] HR 274; [xxx] HR 218; [xxxi] HR 455; [xxxii] HR 501; [xxxiii] HR 528; [xxxiv] CCCC09/07/5; [xxxv] StJ 338; [xxxvi] HR 500; [xxxvii] VCH2 Lincs; [xxxix] HR 211; HR 436; [xl] HR 237, 265; [xli] Appendix 2; [xlii] HR 46, 524, 577/9,585; [xliii] HR 585; [xliv] HR 46; [xlv] HR 577; [xlvi] HR P30; [xlvii] HR 214; [xlviii] HR 256; [li] HR 422; [lii] HR 353; [liii] HR 673; [liv] HR 1063; [liii] HR 772; [liv] HR 810; [lv] HR 830/1; [lvi] HR 771

2.10 Conclusion

Using the Hundred Rolls it has been possible to distinguish different types of property, different locations (principally parishes) and different types of tenure. It has been possible to analyse in detail the rents paid on each property and the people or institutions to whom these rents were paid. Using this information it has been possible to determine property hotspots in the town, in other words locations where properties were most expensive. Hedonic regression was used to control for property type and tenure when analysing spatial variation of rents. As a result, one major property hotspot and two secondary hotspots have been identified. Regression analysis can also be used to analyse the variation of rents from their predicted values. This exercise reveals a tendency for rents to be more variable in parishes where average rent was high, suggesting that high-rent parishes may have been socially intermixed.

Hawgable is an important component of rent because, although it is usually small, it can inform on early property holding in a town. Analysis of hawgable showed that, contrary to previous opinion, the level of hawgable rent varied considerably across different properties and across different parts of the town. Regression analysis revealed spatial patterns in both the propensity to pay hawgable and the actual amount of hawgable paid.

The rolls provide histories of ownership for each property, going back as far as memory allowed. They also provide information on the modes by which property changed hands. Some involved purchases and sales while others involved inheritance. Gifts were also important but their interpretation is ambiguous. Using this information it is possible to assess the role of market-based transactions in effecting property transfers. They accounted for over 30 per cent of all property transfers, and possibly more depending on whether gifts involved undisclosed payments. Thus, market-based property transactions were a significant feature of Cambridge economic life.

The rolls also indicate the family relationships between those who transferred property. It is therefore possible to link the mode of property transfer to family relations. The results suggest that, while gifts often took place between family members, purchases did not. This result is qualified in Chapter 4, where family trees reveal that a significant number of transactions took place between 'in-laws' within extended families. Purchasers seem to have exploited family connections that are not explicitly recorded in the rolls.

Rent was paid not only to private individuals but also to a range of institutions, including abbeys and priories, churches and hospitals. About half the total rent paid on Cambridge properties accrued to charitable institutions of one sort or another, indicating a substantial flow of income from local citizens to charitable causes. Furthermore, this does not include potentially significant direct donations to local churches and the friars.

Different types of institution attracted endowments from different types of people who donated different types of property located in different parts of the town. Abbeys and priories tended to attract a larger number of donations with, on average, a higher rent per property. This probably reflects the greater wealth of their benefactors. The spatial patterns for the different types of rent do not replicate the spatial papers for total rent, however. This is plausible because the individual components of rent are not governed by the same economic forces that act on total rent.

Notes

[1]   For a general review of the evolution of property holding up to the time of the Hundred Rolls see Frederick Pollock and Frederic Maitland, *The History of English Law Before the Time of Edward I* (Cambridge, 1895). For an authoritative study of medieval conveyancing methods see J. M. Kaye, *Medieval English Conveyances* (Cambridge, 2009) especially pp 278–300. For a comparison of freehold rents and customary rents see N. Neilson, 'Customary Rents', *Oxford Studies in Social and Legal History* ed. Paul Vinogradoff (5 vols) II (Oxford, 1910), pp 97–219, and Pollock and Maitland, *Law*.

[2]   M. A. Boyle and K. A. Kiel, 'A Survey of House Price Hedonic Studies of the Impact of Environmental Externalities', *Journal of Real Estate Literature* 9 (2) (2009): 117–44; Casson and Casson, 'Location'; G. Clark, 'Land Rental Values and the Agrarian Economy: England and Wales 1500–1914', *European Review of Economic History* 6 (3) (2002): 281–308; N. Dunse and C. Jones, 'A Hedonic Price Model of Office Rents', *Journal of Property Valuation and Investment* 16 (3) (1983): 297–312; M. E. Turner, J. V. Beckett and B. Afton, *Agricultural Rent in England, 1690–1914* (Cambridge, 1997).

[3]   N. Baker, J. Brett and R. Jones, *Bristol: A Worshipful Town and Famous City: An Archaeological Assessment* (Oxford, 2017); N. Baker, P. Hughes and R. K. Morriss, *The Houses of Hereford 1200–1700* (Oxford, 2017); C. Dyer, 'The Archaeology of Medieval Small Towns', *Medieval Archaeology* 47 (1) (2003): 85–114; K. D. Lilley, 'Urban Planning after the Black Death: Townscape Transformation in Later Medieval England (1350–1530)', *Urban History* 42 (1) (2015): 22–42; B. Jervis, 'Assessing Urban Fortunes in Six Late Medieval Ports: An Archaeological Application of Assemblage Theory', *Urban History* 44 (1) (2017): 2–26; Butcher, 'Newcastle'; G. Demidowicz, *Medieval Birmingham: The Borough Rentals of 1296 and 1344–5* (Stratford-upon-Avon, 2008); Harding and Wright, *London Bridge*.

[4]   M. de Wolf Hemmeon, *Burgage Tenure in Medieval England* (Cambridge, MA, 1914), 61–87; Hilton, 'Urban', pp 326–37.

[5]   Richard F. Muth and Allen C. Goodman, *The Economics of Housing Markets* (London, 1989), p 60.

[6]   Goddard, *Coventry*.

[7]   The role of hawgable and other ground rents in the evolution of English towns has attracted considerable attention and some controversy. A classic work is

Thomas Madox, *Firma Burgi* (London, 1726), which has never been completely superseded. The standard work on landgable is Hemmeon, *Burgage*. Some controversies over the evolution of towns are discussed by Tait, *Medieval English Borough*. Legal aspects are considered by Martin (1971) and evidence from Domesday Book is presented by Adolphus Ballard, *The Domesday Boroughs* (Oxford, 1904). For an analysis of rents based on class conflict over property see Rodney H. Hilton, 'Towns in English Feudal Society', *Urban History Yearbook* (1982), pp 7–13, reprinted in Hilton, *Class Conflict and the Crisis of Feudalism* (London, 1985), pp 175–86. An interesting long-period view of town development is expounded by David M. Palliser, *Towns and Local Communities in Medieval and Early Modern England* (Aldershot, 2006).

8   See Casson, Casson, Lee and Phillips, *Business and Community*.

9   HR 201.

10 HR 75.

11 HR P11.

12 A house was probably a substantial building, but not necessarily of stone; stone buildings are not separately identified in the rolls. Shops, stalls and selds are difficult to distinguish: a shop was probably a residential building with a showroom or workshop downstairs, opening onto the street through a window or a door; a stall was probably a free-standing portable building, or possibly a lean-to on the side of another building or against a wall. A seld may have been a passage off the street down the side of a building, with stalls along the passage or to the rear; only one seld is mentioned in the rolls. A grange was a group of agricultural buildings for storing and processing grains and vegetables, or stabling livestock, while a granary was probably a warehouse for threshing and storing corn ready for shipment to market. Few granges and granaries are identified in the rolls. A curtilage was a (potentially irregular) piece of land, possibly bordering a road, which could be put to various uses, while a croft could be, for example, an orchard, flower garden or herb garden.

13 Edward Miller (trans) and Frances Willmoth and Susan Oosthuizen (eds), *The Ely Coucher Book, 1249–50: The Bishop of Ely's Manors in the Cambridgeshire Fenland* (Cambridge, 2015); M, pp 119–33.

14 Jeffrey M. Wooldridge, *Introductory Econometrics: A Modern Approach*. 5th ed. (Mason, OH, 2013).

15 When analysing variation it is appropriate to measure variation from the estimated conditional mean, which in practical terms means estimating the variance using squared residuals from the level of rent regression. This is the same method as used in standard tests for heteroskedasticity. Wooldridge, *Econometrics*.

16 The overall results of the regressions were broadly similar irrespective of whether or not logarithms were used. There is one striking difference, however: the proportion of sample variation that is explained is doubled by using logarithms, from 37.6 per cent to 74.6 per cent. Explaining three-quarters of sample variation is an impressive result for a hedonic regression and it gives strong support to the multiplicative view of rent determination. The logarithmic transformation is particularly useful in accommodating the difference between low-value rents, which were often paid on hawgable only, and larger rents that aggregated several components paid to different people.

17 Lawrence Butler, *Church of St Peter off Castle Street Cambridge* (London, 2007).

18 The diagnostic statistics for the first regression confirm that heteroskedasticity is present (as revealed by the second regression); they also show that the residuals are

not normally distributed, which means that the stated significance levels must be treated with caution. Despite these limitations, the logarithmic regressions reported in Table 2.2 suggest that the overall results are robust. There are no substantial changes in the signs and significance of the variables discussed here. The overall 'fit' to the data is much improved, however, especially for low-value properties; this is because the logarithmic regression postulates a more plausible multiplicative mechanism as to how location and property characteristics interact. The pattern of unexplained variance appears to be different from before, however, but this is because Holy Trinity parish (the control) now has higher unexplained variance relative to other parishes. Once this is taken into account, the view that higher-rent parishes have higher variability is also confirmed.

[19] Bonney, *Lordship*, pp 27–9.

[20] Goddard, *Coventry*.

[21] Casson and Casson, 'Bristol'.

[22] Casson and Casson, 'Location'.

[23] Horrox, *Plan*; Platt, *Medieval Southampton*, pp 43–5.

[24] H. Clarke, S. Pearson, M. Mate and K. Parfitt, *Sandwich: The 'Completest Medieval Town in England': A Study of the Town and Port From its Origins to 1600* (Oxford, 2010), pp 226–7.

[25] Hilton, 'Urban', pp 326–37.

[26] Rosser, *Medieval Westminster*, p 45; Rutledge, 'Landlords': 11–13;

[27] Hilton, 'Urban'; for example, properties in Sherborne were zoned, see Joseph Fowler, *Medieval Sherborne* (Sherborne, 1951). For other examples of variable landgable see Mary Rogers and May Wallace (eds), *Norwich Landgable Assessment, 1568–70* (Norfolk Record Society, 58 (Norwich, 1999), pp 2–7; Hemmeon, *Burgage*.

[28] HR 38, 41; HR 35, 37, 39; HR 40; HR 33; HR 34, 36.

[29] HR 31, 33, 38.

[30] HR 45; HR 212.

[31] HR 360, 537, 657; HR 417.

[32] HR 571.

[33] HR 608.

[34] D. and B. Martin, *New Winchelsea, Sussex: A Medieval Port Town* (King's Lynn, 2004); TNA SC11/674 New Winchelsea; Casson and Casson, 'Location'.

[35] S. H. Rigby, *Medieval Grimsby: Growth and Decline*, 119; TNA SC11/674 New Winchelsea; Horrox, 'Plan'; Catherine Casson and Mark Casson, 'Property Rents in Medieval English Towns: Fourteenth-Century Hull', *Urban History*, 46 (3) (2019): 374–97.

[36] Casson and Casson, 'Location'.

[37] Martin, *New Winchelsea*; TNA, SC11/674 New Winchelsea.

[38] LB.

[39] LB, pp 282–90.

[40] Gifts in marriage are excluded since almost all of these are from the wife's parents.

[41] The scholars of Merton are excluded as they are discussed elsewhere. The table employs messuages as a control for type of property and Holy Trinity parish as a control location.

[42] Brittain Bouchard, *Holy Entrepreneurs*; Guerriero, 'Culture of Corporation'; Rosenwein, *Neighbour*.

[43] Brittain Bouchard, *Holy Entrepreneurs*; Rosenwein, *Neighbour*.

[44] Bonney, *Durham*, p 123.

[45] Rees Jones, *York*.

[46] Dorothy M. Ellis and L. F. Salzman, 'Religious Houses', *A History of the County of Cambridge and the Isle of Ely, II: Victoria History of the Counties of England* ed. L. F. Salzman (10 vols) III (Oxford, 1948), pp 197–319, 218–20; StR.

[47] J. C. Hodgson, 'The "Domus Dei of Newcastle Otherwise St Katherine's Hospital on the Sandhill', *Archaeologia Aeliana* 3rd series 14: 191–220.

[48] Clarke et al, *Sandwich*, p 76.

[49] Marie-Hélène Rousseau, *Saving the Souls of Medieval London: Perpetual Chantries at St Paul's Cathedral c. 1200–1548* (Farnham, 2011), pp 11, 53.

[50] C, pp 20–1; Roy Midmer, *English Medieval Monasteries: A Summary (1066–1540)* (London, 1979), pp 3–4; Marmaduke Prickett, *Some Account of Barnwell Priory in the Parish of St Andrew the Less, Cambridge* (Cambridge, 1837).

[51] StR, p 13; Elizabeth Van Houts, 'Nuns and Goldsmiths: The Foundation and Early Benefactors of St Radegund's Priory at Cambridge', *Church and City, 1000–1500: Essays in Honour of Christopher Brooke* ed. David Abulafia, Michael Franklin and Miri Rubin (Cambridge 1992), pp 59–79.

[52] Ellis and Salzman, 'Religious Houses', pp 218–20; StR.

[53] Gray suggested that the dual dedication of the nunnery occurred in c.1160, and that prior to that the dedication was only to St Mary. The addition of St Radegund may, he argued, have been made as a result of a second charter from King Malcolm of Scotland of c.1160. In 1159 King Malcolm seems to have visited Poitiers, the site of Radegund's Abbey of the Holy Cross, while on campaign with Henry II, and it is possible that the new dedication and this event were linked, pp 5–7, 12, 14. For another explanation see Van Houts, 'Nuns and Goldsmiths', pp 75–6.

[54] StJ, pp x–xi; Charles Cardale Babington, *History of the Infirmary and Chapel of the Hospital and College of St John the Evangelist at Cambridge* (Cambridge, 1874); Craig Cessford, 'The St. John's Hospital Cemetery and Environs, Cambridge: Contextualizing the Medieval Urban Dead', *Archaeological Journal* 172 (2015): 52–120.

[55] StJ, pp ix–x.

[56] StJ, pp ix–x.

[57] StJ, pp xv.

[58] Ellis and Salzman, 'Religious Houses', pp 303–7.

[59] Rubin, *Charity*.

[60] Chester H. Jones, 'The Chapel of St Mary Magdalene at Sturbridge, Cambridge', *Proceedings of the Cambridge Antiquarian Society* 28 (1927): 126–50.

[61] Ellis and Salzman, 'Religious Houses', pp 307–8; Taylor, *Hidden History*, pp 72–3.

[62] Alison Dickens, 'A New Building at the Dominican Priory, Emmanuel College, Cambridge, and Associated Fourteenth Century Bawsey Floor Tiles', *Proceedings of the Cambridge Antiquarian Society* 87 (1998): 71–80; Ellis and Salzman, 'Religious Houses', pp 269–76; F. H. Stubbings, 'The Church of the Cambridge Dominicans', *Proceedings of the Cambridge Antiquarian Society* 62 (1969): 95–104.

[63] Michael Robson, 'The Commemoration of the Living and the Dead at the Friars Minor of Cambridge', *Commemoration in Medieval Cambridge* ed. John S. Lee and Christian Steer (Woodbridge, 2018), pp 34–51.

[64] From 1304 onwards the friars received a regular grant from the Crown, probably in connection with their contribution to the town's educational sector – they are one of the orders credited by historians with establishing the Theology School in Cambridge. Ellis and Salzman, 'Religious Houses', pp 276–8; Midmer, *Monasteries*, pp 12–13.

[65] Ellis and Salzman, 'Religious Houses', pp 282–6; Taylor, *Hidden History*, p 67.

66 Taylor, *Hidden History*, p 67.
67 Taylor, *Hidden History*, pp 67–9.
68 Ellis and Salzman, 'Religious Houses', pp 290–1.
69 VCH 3, pp 122–3.
70 Taylor, *Hidden History*, p 71; Ellis and Salzman, 'Religious Houses', pp 290–1.
71 HR P27.
72 Ellis and Salzman, 'Religious Houses', pp 264–7.
73 Holt, 'Society'.
74 VCH 1 Huntingdon, pp 391–2; VCH 3, 29–31; StR 4–6, 74–5; HR A12.
75 HR 690.

3

Economic Topography

Introduction

Chapter 2 demonstrated that variation in rent levels between parishes was one characteristic of the Cambridge property market. This chapter examines the economic topography of late 13th-century Cambridge and considers the features that may have contributed to that variation. It analyses both the occupational structure and the parochial structure of the town, and relates the two. It presents a statistical profile of occupations and parishes, based on the information in the Hundred Rolls. It examines locational specialization in both trades and professions. It distinguishes between parishes that specialized mainly in trade and those that were mainly professional. It compares the Cambridge evidence with that for other towns and identifies similarities and differences.

The second part of the chapter provides profiles of every parish in the town (Figure 3.1). This is the first comprehensive set of parish profiles ever published for the town because it is the only one that is based on a complete set of the Cambridge Hundred Rolls. In particular, it conveys important new information about the parishes to the south and east of the town. The evidence on parishes revealed in the Hundred Rolls is compared with the relative wealth of the town's parishes as revealed in the valuations of the income of the English Church produced during the 13th century.

Overall, the chapter affords insights into occupational diversity and geographical clustering of occupations, and the extent to which particular parishes specialized in particular trades and professions. It considers some of the factors that may explain the specific patterns of specialization found in Cambridge.

3.1 The diversity of occupations

The Commercial Revolution of the 13th century generated a remarkable increase in the variety of occupations within the English economy, which led to successful specialization for some and to increased casualization of work for others.[1] Medieval towns with the greatest range of skills and specialities in this period were those where opportunities coexisted for serving large households, supplying the surrounding region and servicing overseas trade.[2] In the case of Cambridge, Barnwell Priory and the nascent university generated demand; the town was a natural market centre for its surrounding region and the riverside trade with its coastal links provided opportunities for overseas trade.

The Hundred Rolls specifically record the occupations of many owners and previous owners, and these allow us to relate the occupation to the type of property held and to the places in which this property was located. Where no occupation is specifically stated, a nominal occupation can be established in cases where a family had an occupation name such as Smith or Carter, although it was not necessarily the case that members always practised the occupation from which their name derived. As the Hundred Rolls only record property holders, they generally omit members of those poorer trades who were unlikely to hold property, such as the potters, cooks and vendors of commodities such as cheese and butter, who we know from street names were operating in the vicinity of the marketplace by this period or shortly afterwards.[3]

Table 3.1 lists trade occupations, whether stated or nominal, as reported in the rolls. The occupations are listed in descending order by the number of people associated with that occupation. Adjustments are made to compensate for people owning multiple properties. The columns provide the names of individuals, together with the parishes in which their properties were located. These parishes were not necessarily those where they practised their trades; the properties concerned could be places of residence, or acquired through dower, or simply investment properties leased out for income. It is useful to identify Newnham, Barnwell and the marketplace as separate locations, and so in the text they are treated as notional parishes. While the ranking provides a reasonable indication of the relative numbers of people practising particular occupations, it is not absolute as it includes people from different generations (biasing the number upwards) and only those who held property (biasing the number downwards), leaving absolute numbers uncertain. Special skills could be concealed beneath simple occupational descriptions such as 'smith' or 'carpenter'. There were also men and women who practised more than one craft.

The professions are analysed in Table 3.2. This repeats the previous

Table 3.1: Occupations by parishes: trade

Occupation	People	Names	Parishes
Trades			
Baker (pistor)	13	Anketin, Arnold, Geoffrey, Gervase, Gilbert, Nicholas, Richard of Stowe, Roger, Stephen, Thomas (2), Walter, William	All Saints in the Jewry, Holy Trinity, St Benedict, St Edward, Newnham
Tailor (cissor)	9	Bartholomew, Hamon, Geoffrey, Maurice, Philip, Richard, Sewallus, Walter, Warin	All Saints at the Castle, All Saints in the Jewry, Holy Trinity, St Andrew, St Clement, St Giles, St Mary, St Michael, St Peter at the Castle
Barber	8	Adam son of Geoffrey, Geoffrey (same family), John, Richard, Roger, Wakelin, William, Matilda (barberess)	Holy Trinity, St Benedict, St Botolph, St Edward, St Mary, St Peter at the Castle
Carter	8	Albert, Eustace, Herbert, Luke, Michael, Osbert, Simon, Walter	All Saints in the Jewry, St Mary, Barnwell, Newnham
Shoemaker (cordwainer, corde(r), sutor)	8	Fulk, Hugo, John, John Halte, Peter, Radulph, Stephen, Walter	Holy Trinity, St Andrew, St Benedict, St Clement
Butcher (carnifius)	7	Aubrey, Harvey, Hugh, John Yve, Richard Bateman senior, Robert le Ke, William Herre	Holy Trinity, St Edward, St Mary, The Butchery in the market
Goldsmith (aurifaber)	7	Bartholomew, Gilbert, John of Barton, Nicholas, Roger, Samson, Walter	St Mary, Holy Trinity
Smith (fabro, ferun)	7	Ernulph, Geoffrey, Henry, John, Robert, Simon, William	Barnwell (mainly), All Saints at the Castle, St Andrew, St Benedict, St Botolph, St Mary
Apothecary (family name Potecar or Potekin)	6	Hugo, Geoffrey, Gilbert, John, Simon, Thomas	Holy Trinity, St Andrew, St Mary

(continued)

Table 3.1: Occupations by parishes: trade (continued)

Occupation	People	Names	Parishes
Marshall (mariscallo)	6	John, Matthew, Peter, Thomas (son of Peter), Reginald, Robert	St Benedict, St Clement, St John
Merchant, mercer (mercator)	6	Benedict, Ernest, Henry, Ketel, Thomas, Walter	St Mary, St Benedict, Barnwell, All Saints in the Jewry, All Saints at the Castle
Carpenter	5	Alexander le Gresbi, Robert, Thomas (2), William	All Saints in the Jewry, Holy Trinity, St Andrew, St Benedict, St Mary, Newnham
Cooper (cupere, cuver(e))	5	Geoffrey, Henry, Norman, Radulph, Stephen	All Saints at the Castle, Holy Trinity, St Benedict, St Clement, St Giles, St Sepulchre
Miller	4	Acelina, Edmund, William of Biggleswade, William Lucke	St Andrew, St John, Marketplace, Newnham
Mason, mazun	5	Adam, Alexander, John, Thomas, Warin	All Saints in the Jewry, Barnwell
Cutler	3	Henry, John, Thomas	St Clement, St Mary
Farrier	3	Geoffrey, Osbert, Thomas	St Bene't, St Mary
Fisher	3	Aunger, Clement, Simon	St Giles, St Peter at the Castle
Savener, sauver (soap-maker)	3	Algar, Gregory, Richemann	St Edward, St John
Whitesmith	3	William, Robert (son of William), Robert (son of Robert) (one family)	St Mary
Brewer (breuer, braci', braciator)	2	William, Winfrid	All Saints at the Castle, St Benedict, St Botolph, St Mary
Draper	2	Auwre, Ketel	All Saints at the Castle, St Botolph

(continued)

Table 3.1: Occupations by parishes: trade (continued)

Occupation	People	Names	Parishes
Fitter(e)	2	Geoffrey, William	Holy Trinity
Glover, chirothecar	2	Eudo, Jacob	St Andrew
Plumber	2	Gilbert, Walter son of Gilbert (same family)	St Clement, St Mary
Porter	2	Elye, Oliver	St Mary, Barnwell
Skinner, skin	2	Jordan, Richard	All Saints in the Jewry, St Mary, St Peter outside the Trumpington Gate
Tanner	2	Richard, William	Newnham, St Benedict
Weaver	2	Nicholas, William	St Botolph, St Peter outside the Trumpington Gate
Cap-maker	1	Radulph	St Peter at the Castle
Castellan (castelyn)	1	William	St Peter at the Castle, St Mary
Cofferer (keeper of the coffer)	1	Richard	St Andrew
Felterer	1	William	Holy Trinity
Fuller	1	Robert	Barnwell
Horsemonger	1	Leon	St Peter at the Castle
Linen-seller	1	Henry	Not specified
Lorimer[a]	1	William	St Mary
Money-changer (monnier)	1	Baldwin	Holy Trinity

(continued)

125

Table 3.1: Occupations by parishes: trade (continued)

Occupation	People	Names	Parishes
Mustarder	1	Simon	Holy Trinity
Painter	1	Robert	Not specified
Palfreyman[b]	1	John	St Botolph
Parchmenter	1	William	St Mary
Ploughwright	1	William	St Peter at the Castle
Stabler	1	Alan	Barnwell
Taverner	1	Richard	Not specified
Turner	1	Fulk	Holy Trinity
Upholsterer (upholder)[c]	1	Thomas Arinvene	St Michael

Notes

[a] A lorimer was a maker and seller of spurs, mouth-bits, and other metal attachments to harness and tackle.

[b] A palfreyman was a keeper of saddle-horses

[c] Upholders were initially dealers in second-hand clothes, furs and skins. Subsequently they carried out not just the manufacture and sale of upholstered goods but were cabinet makers, undertakers, soft furnishers, auctioneers and valuers. The Worshipful Company of Upholders was founded in London in 1360

Source: TNA SC5/CAMBS/TOWER/2 Barnwell Hundred Roll; TNA SC5/CAMBS/TOWER/1/Parts1–3 Cambridge Borough Hundred Rolls; Catherine Casson, Mark Casson, John S. Lee and Katie Phillips, *Business and Community in Medieval England: The Cambridge Hundred Rolls Source Volume* (Bristol, 2020)

Table 3.2: Professions and titles by parish

Occupation and number of people	Names	Parishes
Chaplain 51	William of Preston, Geoffrey of Barnwell (M), Radulph of St Clement's, Richard of Newnham, John of Thriplow, Radulph of Cotes, Sir Alan of Little Bradley, Richard Payn of Balsham, Anthony of Stocton, Simon son of Henry Barton, John Frost, Richard Aldgod, John of Ditton, William of Sawston, Gilbert of Berden Essex, Stephen of Cottenham, Geoffrey of Aldreth, Elisius grandson of Nicholas the weaver, Reginald nephew of Roger Borers of Kerlinge, Henry Coynard, Lord Roger of Hinton, Walter of Hinton, Abraham, Roger [of Newnham] nephew and heir of Master Nigel (M), Adam Coynterel, Henry son of William Palmer, Simon Cademan, Richard of Shelford, Roger of Redlingfield, nephew of Master Nigel, doctor, John of Barking, John son of Aubrey the butcher, Lord William Grim, Geoffrey of Welles, Robert father of Margaret of Abington, William of Ditton, Adam de la Grene of Walpole, William de la Bruere, William of St Edmunds, Walter son of Robert of St Edmunds, John of Norton, Robert of Thorndon, William of St Radegund's, Edward, Radulph, Robert, Roger, John of Huntingdon, Robert of Ely, William of Wilbraham, Radulph Flori, Godfrey of Impington	St Andrew (8) St Edward (7) St Benedict (6) Holy Trinity (5) St Botolph (5) St Michael (5) Barnwell (5) St Mary (4) St Peter outside the Trumpington Gate (4) All Saints at the Castle (3) All Saints in the Jewry (3) St Giles (3) St John(3) St Clement (2) St Sepulchre (1) Newnham(1)
Rector 10	John le Ry, Former R of chapel of St Edmund, Robert R of the chapel of St Edmund, Guy de Mortimer R of Kingston, John of Huntingdon former R of St Peter at the Castle, Lord Alan R of st Benedict's, Lord Thomas former R of St Bendict's, Lord Richard R of Hinton, Robert former R of Hardwick, Master Stephen of Haslingfield R of St Michael (M), Robert former R of Willington, Henry R of Barrington, Radulph R of Eltisley	St Benedict (3) St Michael (2) All Saints at the Castle (1) St Andrew (1) St Botolph (1) St John (1) St Peter outside the Trumpington Gate (1)

(continued)

Table 3.2: Professions and titles by parish (continued)

Occupation and number of people	Names	Parishes
Vicar or priest 8	Henry V of St Benedict's, Henry former V of St Benedict's, Robert former V of St Edward's, John former V of All Saints in the Jewry, Robert V of Soham, Thomas of Samford V of Walden, Lord Roger V of Hinton, Nicholas the priest	St John (2) All Saints in the Jewry (1) St Benedict (1) St Botolph (1) St Edward (1) St Peter at the Castle (1) Newnham (1)
Clerk or cleric 28 + Clerks of Merton	William of Rudham*, William son of John Mason, Michael of Huntingdon nephew of Master Robert of Huntingdon, Nicholas of Hedon, Roger of Stanton, Harvey Gogging, William of Rudham, Thomas Swin, Thomas of Wimpole, Nicholas of Hitchin, nephew of Master Nicholas of Hitchin (M), Philip de Bergelun, Master John of Histon (M), Geoffrey of Histon, Henry of Norwich, Alan son of Baldwin of Stowe, Robert of Teversham, Walter of Newnham, Andrew son of Andrew, William of Ely, William, Godfrey, John Adelhard, Thomas father of Johanna wife of Lord Simon Constable of Holderness, John Cant', Roger, John father of Lord Master Walter, Clerks of Merton, Henry of Crissale, Walter of Hauxton	Barnwell (6) St Bene't (5) St Andrew (4) St Edward (3) St Peter outside the Trumpington Gate (3) St Botolph (2) St John (2) All Saints at the Castle(1) All Saints in the Jewry (2) St Giles (1) St Mary(1) Howes (1) Marketplace (1)

(continued)

Table 3.2: Professions and titles by parish (continued)

Occupation and number of people	Names	Parishes
Master 58 + Master of the Hospital of St John, Master of the University	Nigel, Lord Roger his nephew (Ch), Lord Walter, Guy of Barnard Castle and John, his brother, Bartholomew of the Larder and Stephen of the Larder his son, William doctor of Balsham, Warener, Laurence of Gresbi, Robert of Huntingdon, Henry of Hinton, Pagan of Docking, William of Beeston, Nicholas of Tuttington, Simon Prat son of Geoffrey Prat, Henry of Notley, William le Blunt, Reginald le Blund of Welles, Bartholomew son of Radulph of Fordham, Nicholas of Hitchin (Cl), Martin of Lynn, Robert of Skidbrooke, Andrew of Middilton [Middleton], William of Norwich, Thomas of Tydd (Ch), Henry of Notley, Richard of Gedney, William de la Lade, Thomas of Hingolphorp, William le Blund, Eustace of Shelford, John of Histon (Cl), Adam of Lincoln, Adam de Bondone, Walter of Tyrington, Martin of St Radegund's, Walter of Histon, Stephen of Haslingfiled (R), Andrew of Gisleham, Radulph de Walpole Archdeacon of Ely, Simon of Huntingdon, Robert Engayne, Nicholas doctor, Radulph of Nottingham, William of Salop, William Golde, John of Histon, Radulph Tullel, Nicholas of St Quentin's, Richard Crocheman, Bartholomew Wombe, Thomas Toylet, Thomas of St Edmund's, Alexander of St Edmunds, Thomas Eliot, Robert Aunger, Geoffrey of Barnwell (Ch)	St Andrew (15) St John (11) St Mary (10) Holy Trinity (9) St Michael (7) St Botolph (6) Barnwell (6) St Clement (5) St Benedict (4) All Saints in the Jewry (3) Marketplace (3) St Sepulchre (2) All Saints at the Castle (1) St Peter outside the Trumpington Gate (1)

(continued)

129

Table 3.2: Professions and titles by parish (continued)

Occupation and number of people	Names	Parishes
Lord 37	Simon de Insula, William of Hemmingford, Gilbert Peche, Reginald de Argentin, Giles de Argentin, Count of Huntingdon, Radulph of Chokesfield, Robert of Greyle, Richard de Frevile of Little Shelford, Philip de Colevile, Henry de Colevile, William Buckworth soldier, Lord John soldier of Hinton, Roger (V of Hinton), Roger of Trumpington son of Robert of Trumpington, son of Everard of Trumpington, Peter de Chavent, Robert of Mortimer, William of Mortimer senior, Radulph Pirot, Alan (R), Richard (R), William Grim, John de Scalar' of Thriplow, Berenger the monk, Roger of the Exchequer, Simon de Furneus, John de Engayne, Radulph de Turbelvile, Lady Emma de la Leye heir of Reginald de Grey, Robert de Brus, Lord of Rushden Northants, Geoffrey chaplain (M, Ch), Lady Albarissa of Madingley,	Barnwell (4) Holy Trinity (3) St Andrew (3) St Peter at the Castle (3) St Bene't (2) St Botolph (2) St Edward (2) St Mary (2) St Michael (2) St Sepulchre (2) All Saints at the Castle (1) All Saints in the Jewry (1) St Giles (1) St John (1) St Peter outside the Trumpington Gate (1)
Medical	Surgeon: Robert Medical doctor: Master William of Barsham, Master Nicholas Midwife: Agnes	Surgeon: All Saints in the Jewry Medical doctor: St Andrew, Barnwell, Holy Trinity Midwife: Holy Trinity

Key: Ch: chaplain; Cl: clerk or cleric; L: lord; M: master; R: rector; V: vicar.

Notes: The parishes listed indicate the locations of properties once held by one or more of the persons listed. The number of entries relating to relevant parishes is given in brackets. Other jobs and titles such as 'knight' and 'brother' (of an institution) add only one or two names to these lists.

Other singular professionals include Peter the triumvir (constable of three counties) and Walter the bedel.

Source: TNA SC5/CAMBS/TOWER/2 Barnwell Hundred Roll; TNA SC5/CAMBS/TOWER/1/Parts1–3 Cambridge Borough Hundred Rolls; Catherine Casson, Mark Casson, John S. Lee and Katie Phillips, *Business and Community in Medieval England: The Cambridge Hundred Rolls Source Volume* (Bristol, 2020)

exercise undertaken for trades using four categories of profession, namely chaplains, clerks, rectors and vicars, and two titles indicative of status, namely master and lord. There is a very large number of chaplains and a substantial number of clerks. There is also a large number of 'masters' and a significant number of lords. In some cases, the title master or lord may be no more than a courtesy title bestowed upon an important individual by the jurors of the Hundred Rolls. 'Master' could also signify a graduate of the university or a learned monk, while 'lord' could signify a major tenant-in-chief, a royal courtier or a knight.

3.2 Geographical specialization of trades and professions

The parishes in which the professions held property seem to differ from parishes where tradesmen held property. This suggests that some parishes may have specialized in trades and others in professions. Tables 3.1 and 3.2 clearly demonstrate that some parishes specialized in *particular* trades and some in *particular* professions, but this does not mean that these parishes specialized in trades or professions as a whole. As noted, evidence from other medieval towns has suggested that people from different trades, or different professions, were motivated to agglomerate in particular parts of the town because they carried out complementary tasks or served similar sorts of customer.

To investigate this further, Table 3.3 presents two rankings of parishes, the first by the number of different trades carried on by property owners and the second by the number of professionals who held property in the parish. The first is a measure of trade intensity and the second a measure of profession intensity. Although other measures are available, these are the easiest to construct given the nature of the source material. The table also lists the particular trades represented in each parish and identifies the dominant professions in each parish.

Table 3.4 uses these rankings to determine whether certain parishes specialized in either trade or professions. It also distinguishes parishes that had strong connections with trades and professions from those that had little connection with either. It classifies each parish into three categories along each of two dimensions; the categories are high ranked (ranks 1–4) middle ranked (5–10) and low ranked (11–18), while the dimensions relate to trade intensity and professional intensity. The rankings are based on absolute number of trades and professionals and are not adjusted for parish size. The tables show that specialization in trades and professions occurred at two levels.

Table 3.3: Ranking of parishes by number of trades and by numbers of professional people in the parish

Rank	Parish	Trades		Parish	Professions
1	St Mary (18)	Tailor, carter, barber, goldsmith, apothecary, butcher, merchant, smith, carpenter, cutler, farrier, whitesmith, brewer, plumber, skinner, lorimer, parchmenter, porter	1	St Andrew (28)	Master (15), chaplain (8) clerk (4) rector (1)
2	Holy Trinity (14)	Baker, tailor, shoemaker, barber, goldsmith, apothecary, butcher, carpenter, cooper, fitter, felterer, money-changer, mustarder, turner	2	St John (19)	Master (11) chaplain (3) clerk (2) vicar (2) rector (1)
3	St Benedict (10)	Baker, shoemaker, barber, merchant, smith, carpenter, cooper, farrier, brewer, tanner	3	Barnwell (17)	Master (6) clerk (6), chaplain (5)
4	St Andrew (8)	Tailor, shoemaker, apothecary, smith, carpenter, glover, miller, cofferer	4	St Benedict (15)	Chaplain (6) clerk (5) others (4)
5	All Saints in the Jewry (7)	Baker, tailor, carter, merchant, carpenter, mason, skinner	4	St Botolph (15)	Master (6) chaplain (5) others (4)
6=	All Saints at the Castle (6)	Tailor, merchant, smith, cooper, brewer, draper	6	Holy Trinity (14)	Master (9) chaplain (5)
6=	St Botolph (6)	Baker, brewer, draper, weaver, smith, palfreyman	6	St Michael (14)	Master (7) chaplain (5) rector (2)
6=	St Peter at the Castle (6)	Tailor, barber, cap-maker, ploughwright, horsemonger, fisher	8	St Edward (11)	Chaplain (7) clerk (3) vicar (1)
6=	Barnwell (6)	Carter, merchant, smith, mason, fuller, stabler	8	St Mary (11)	Master (5) chaplain (2)
10	Newnham (5)	Baker, miller, carter, carpenter, tanner	10	All Saints in the Jewry (9)	Master (3) chaplain (3) others (3)

(continued)

Table 3.3: Ranking of parishes by number of trades and by numbers of professional people in the parish (continued)

Rank	Parish	Trades		Parish	Professions
11=	St Clement (4)	Tailor, shoemaker, cutler, plumber	10	St Peter outside Trumpington Gate (9)	Chaplain (4) master (3) others (2)
11=	St Edward (4)	Baker, barber, butcher, soapmaker	12	St Clement (7)	Master (5) chaplain (2)
13	St Giles (3)	Tailor, cooper, fisher	12	All Saints at the Castle (7)	Chaplain (3) clerk (2) others (2)
14=	St Michael (2)	Tailor, upholsterer	14	St Giles (4)	Chaplain (3) clerk (1)
14=	St Peter outside Trumpington Gate (2)	Skinner, weaver	14	Marketplace (4)	Master (3) clerk (1)
14	Marketplace (2)	Butcher, miller	16	St Sepulchre (3)	Master (2) chaplain (1)
14=	St John (2)	Miller, soapmaker	17	Newnham (2)	Chaplain (1) vicar (1)
18	St Sepulchre (1)	Cooper	18	St Peter at the Castle (1)	Vicar (1)

Notes: Parishes with equal numbers are given equal rank; this is indicated by an equality sign in the left-hand column. Trade occupations with only one representative in a parish do not have a number after their names.

Two occupations are omitted from this analysis because they are more concerned with law and enforcement than they are with trade: marshall and castellan.

The title 'lord' is omitted from this analysis as it does not necessarily signify membership of a learned profession. Its inclusion makes little difference to the rankings, however, as properties owned by lords are fairly evenly distributed across the town: Barnwell, Holy Trinity, St Andrew, St Edward, St Michael (3 each); St Benedict, St Botolph, St Giles, St Mary, St Peter outside Trumpington Gate, St Sepulchre (2 each); all other parishes one each and Newnham none.

Source: Tables 3.1 and 3.2

Table 3.4: Relationship between trades and professions across parishes

Ranking of parishes by trade-intensity	Ranking of parishes by profession-intensity		
	High: 1–4	Medium: 5–10	Low: 11–18
High: 1–4	St Benedict (3,4)	St Mary (1,8) Holy Trinity (2,6)	All Saints in the Jewry (5,10) All Saints at the Castle (6,12) St Peter at the Castle (6,18) Newnham (10, 17)
Medium: 5–10	St Andrew (4,1) St Botolph (4,4) Barnwell (6,3)		
Low: 10–18	St Edward (11,3) St Michael (14,6) St Peter outside the Trumpington Gate (14,10) St John (14,2)		St Clement (11,12) St Giles (13,14) Marketplace (14,14) St Sepulchre (18,16)

Source: Table 3.3

It is useful to begin by comparing the high- and medium-intensity parishes as a group with the low-intensity parishes. Table 3.4 shows (from the first two rows and the first two columns) that six parishes were specialized in both trades and professions, namely St Benedict's (sometimes referred to as St Bene't's), St Mary's, Holy Trinity, St Andrew's, St Botolph's and Barnwell. With the exception of Barnwell, these are all fairly central parishes. Four parishes were specialized in trades but not professions (from the first two rows and the third column), namely All Saints in the Jewry, All Saints at the Castle, St Peter's at the Castle and Newnham. Three of these four parishes are on the edges of the town. Four parishes were specialized in professions but not trades (from the first two columns and the third row), namely St Edward's, St Michael's, St Peter's outside the Trumpington Gate and St John's. With the exception of St Peter's, these parishes are fairly central. Four parishes show little specialization in either trades of professions (from the third row and the third column), namely St Clement's, St Giles', St Sepulchre (also known as Holy Sepulchre) and Marketplace; these are relatively central locations.

At first sight it seems remarkable that marketplace, with lots of business premises, did not specialize in trade, but this is probably because those who traded there did not own properties there; many of them may have occupied stalls or selds associated with other people's properties. Those who owned property in the marketplace probably held 'investment' properties, which they leased out to traders at high fixed-term rents. Furthermore, the marketplace is a specific retail area within the parish of St Mary's, which is highly trade-intensive; traders in St Mary's as a whole do indeed seem to have owned the premises from which they traded. By contrast, the high degree of specialization in trade in the peripheral parishes is probably accounted for by traders who practised their trade from their own premises, where they may also have resided.

Many of the traders in the peripheral parishes practised trades that may have involved some degree of nuisance (noise and smells in particular), but then some of the trades in St Mary's and other central parishes did so too (Table 3.1) However, there is some evidence that 'nuisance trades' were, on balance, carried out more often in peripheral parishes than in central ones.

It is also instructive to compare the high-intensity parishes with the medium-intensity parishes. This involves focusing on the first two rows and columns of Table 3.4. It shows that St Benedict's was unique in being highly specialized in both trades and professions; it ranked third for trades and fourth for professions. Other parishes also specialised in both, but to a lesser degree. This shows that property holders in St Benedict's were, relative to those in other parishes, extremely active in the local economy as either traders or professionals. In St Mary's and Holy Trinity specialization was more intensive in professions than trades, while the opposite was true in St Andrew's, St Botolph's and Barnwell.

Overall, therefore, there was a tendency for trade-specialized parishes to be more peripherally located than professionally specialized parishes, but this pattern is only weak. This may be linked to the suggestion that traders in the centre of the town, and especially around the market, did not own the premises from which they traded, while in peripheral locations they did.

3.3 Explaining the patterns of specialization: a comparative analysis

There was a certain degree of social and occupational clustering in medieval English towns. Homes of single people and widows tended to be clustered in the suburbs or poorer areas of the town. Sellers of food and drink tended to congregate in the centre of towns to provide refreshment to travellers, although they were also scattered through the town. Some industries encouraged clustering, an example being those requiring access to water. Merchants' houses were found in the commercial centre. The most physically distinct sectors of urban society were clergy in communities where their rule (and often a physical wall) segregated them from the outside world.[4]

The statistical analysis has identified 55 different occupational categories in Cambridge, of which 47 are associated with trade, and 8 with professions (Tables 3.1 and 3.2). This compares with other 13th-century towns such as Durham, with 53 different occupational descriptions listed in the deeds, and Winchester, where 67 occupations can be identified. The city of Norwich supported nearly 70 different occupations by 1300.[5] A diversity of non-agricultural employment, albeit on a smaller scale than in urban areas, could also be found in the countryside at this time, as the occupations and craft surnames of the villagers recorded in the Cambridgeshire Hundred Rolls show. These included the occasional shipwright, glover and goldsmith, in addition to the many smiths, carpenters and tailors.[6]

Detailed studies of individual medieval towns have identified specific occupational clusters within particular geographical locations.[7] Trades requiring water for manufacturing, such as the dyers and the tanners, were usually located close to water sources. This was the case in late medieval York, where the occupational topography of the city has been mapped through poll tax and testamentary sources. Fishmongers had stalls at two main bridges. There was a distinct commercial quarter in York, which appears to have shrunk and become more closely defined between 1381 and the later 15th century.[8] Similarly in medieval Durham, concentrations of butchers, tanners and skinners have been identified. The city's bridgeheads were good sites for traders and shopkeepers because traffic built up at crossing points, while many of the victuallers lived alongside the main route to the castle and priory. The small community of Durham goldsmiths also lived as close as possible to their main clients, near the main gateway to the castle and monastic precinct.[9]

The spatial distribution of occupations in the city of London between the 1370s and the 1550s has also been explored. This found that the most extreme clustering, which occurred among the butchers and the fishmongers, was a result of civic regulation. Two smaller guilds of the city, the Bowyers and Fletchers, also clustered, as customers generally wanted to purchase the two items together. Retailers of perishable staples, bread and ale, benefited from dispersal rather than clustering in order to be close to their consumers. Those engaged in the same or similar occupations clustered together where they could gain economic advantage through interdependencies, or where they could best access their customers. The more specialized their trade, the more likely they were to be organized in these ways.[10] Similarly, evidence from Norwich has shown how different trades and professions converged in particular areas of the city, as they were associated with related tasks (such as the smith and the farrier) or related customers (such as the carpenter and the upholsterer).[11] The Hundred Rolls reveal similar patterns of occupational topography in Cambridge.

3.4 Locational clustering of individual trades

This section examines individual trades in detail. Some trades were widely distributed, with little locational clustering, others demonstrated greater locational clustering. The food and drink trades, notably the 13 bakers, were distributed across several parishes, and so too were the 9 tailors, 8 barbers, 8 shoemakers, 5 carpenters and 5 coopers. Specialist craftsmen demonstrated greater clustering, however. Several specialist tradesmen held properties in St Mary's parish. These included William le Lorimer (a maker of bits and metal mountings for horses' bridles) and William le Parchmenter (a maker or seller of parchment) who had held property in the parish, and may have supplied the academic community.[12] There were seven goldsmiths holding property, confined to St Mary's and Holy Trinity parishes, and six apothecaries, confined to these two parishes plus St Andrew's. Contemporary street names confirm this evidence, with a Goldsmith's Row in St Mary's parish recorded in 1285 and a reference to an Apothecaries' Row, although with no location given, in the following year.[13] A number of the shoemakers were property holders in Holy Trinity parish, where 'Cordwaneria', later Cordwainers' Row, was recorded in 1322.[14] Simon le Mustarder (a maker of or dealer in mustard) held a messuage in Holy Trinity.[15]

The butchers held property in Holy Trinity, St Edward's and St Mary's parishes. The Butchery, referred to in the Hundred Rolls as the place where Richard Bateman held two shops, is known from deeds to have been located immediately east of St Edward's Church in the late 13th century, while immediately to the west of this lay Tripers' Lane. The Hundred Rolls also describe two shops in the marketplace, held by John Ive, 'where he sells meat'.[16] Civic authorities often restricted butchery to particular areas, as stated in a later Cambridge market regulation of 1376, because of the potential nuisance, as well as allowing meat to be inspected more easily.[17]

The location of metal-working was varied. More specialized metal-working craftsmen, though, were focused within the more central parishes in Cambridge. Three cutlers and two plumbers held property in St Mary's and St Clement's. The Whitesmith family, which held property in St Mary's parish, may have made items from tin-plated iron or made iron tools with a sharp edge.[18] William le Lorimer has already been mentioned.[19] Street name evidence again correlates with the material in the Hundred Rolls. A deed of 1299 mentions 'le Lorineresrowe', although with no clue to its location, while a deed of 1271 refers to a piece of land stretching from St Mary's churchyard to 'Smitherowe', and one of 1297 to 'Cuteller', later known as Cutlers' Row, north of Great St Mary's Church.[20]

Many other metal trades were on the town's periphery because of the risk of fire, smoke and noise. The prevalence of smiths in Barnwell recorded in the Hundred Rolls is notable because recent archaeological excavations at Brunswick, adjacent to Midsummer Common and the site of Barnwell Priory, have found evidence of medieval iron smelting. The excavated site may have been owned by Barnwell Priory or simply adjacent to the priory's holdings. It has been suggested, given the lack of local deposits of iron ore, that this, together with pig iron, was transported by river from the Rockingham Forest area of Northamptonshire to Cambridge. The River Cam, adjacent to the excavated site, would have facilitated the transport of ores and fuel.[21]

Agricultural occupations were generally found in the more peripheral parishes. The only ploughwright recorded holding property, William le Plowritte of Madingley, held messuages in St Peter's by the Castle.[22] Similarly, the only fishers listed as holding property were in the parishes of St Giles and St Peter by the Castle.[23] The Hundred Rolls also stated that the townspeople of Cambridge had a communal fishery in its waters.[24] Little record survives of this, although Lyne's Map of Cambridge of 1574 shows fishing in the river, both from the banks and by boat (Figure 1.3). Two horse mills are recorded, including one, somewhat surprisingly, in the marketplace.[25] This was possibly for milling specific commodities purchased in the market, as there were designated sites for selling malt, peas, oats and corn within the central market area.[26]

3.5 Locational clustering of merchants and professionals

Merchants held property in several Cambridge parishes, and were sufficiently numerous and well organized to have a guild of merchants with trading privileges described in the Hundred Rolls.[27] A number of merchants were probably associated with the grain trade, and granaries were recorded in the riverside parishes of St Michael and All Saints in the Jewry held by Anglesey Priory and the Prior of Ely, and by townsmen William Seman, Richard de Hockley, Nicholas Morice, Simon Godeman, and Henry and Thomas Toylet. Five of these granaries had been held by the Dunning family, highlighting the importance of this family in the town's grain trade.[28]

The professional occupations recorded in the Hundred Rolls are harder to define, but many seem to have been associated with the Church courts and university. Cambridge was home to two ecclesiastical courts, the Ely consistory court and the Archdeacon of Ely's court. By the 14th century, the bishop's official-principal, or chief judicial officer, habitually lived in Cambridge and presided over the consistory court there; it regularly met in Cambridge parish churches and drew on a substantial body of men with advanced legal training and courtroom experience. It seems likely that many of their 13th-century predecessors were based in Cambridge too, although records of the court are scant until the late 14th century. The consistory court employed advocates, proctors, a registrar and notaries, and apparitors or summoners.

The Archdeacon of Ely's court in Cambridge provided additional employment for canon lawyers, proctors, notaries and other officials.[29] Master Radulph de Walepol (Walpole), Archdeacon of Ely, held messuages in the parishes of St Michael, St Andrew and Holy Trinity. He was a Cambridge Master of Arts and Doctor of Theology.[30] Two of his officials were university masters and property holders in the town: Richard Crocheman held messuages in St Michael's and All Saints by the Hospital; William de Beston held a messuage in St Michael's parish, and may have been the previous owner of two others.[31] Another official of Ely diocese in the 1220s, and probably a university master, Walter de Tyrington, had held a messuage in St Mary's parish.[32] The Archdeacon of Ely also had oversight of grammar schooling in Cambridge, appointing a 'master of glomery' or grammar master, who could judge disputes between scholars of grammar; there was also a 'bedel of glomery'. The members of this community seem to have been regarded as associates, but not full members, of the university.[33] The original and authorized grammar school in the town is likely to have been in Glomery Lane, to the north of the present King's College Chapel, first recorded as a street name in 1295.[34]

3.6 Members of the university

Members of the university had also started to hold property within Cambridge. The Hundred Rolls pre-date the earliest college within the university, Peterhouse, founded in 1284, although Merton College, Oxford, already had its Cambridge estate centred on the stone house now known as the School of Pythagoras.[35] The Hundred Rolls state that Thomas and Matilda Servient of the university had held a messuage in St Andrew's parish and Walter of Oxford, who had served at the university, in St Mary's parish.[36] There were many others, though, mentioned in the Hundred Rolls but not identified as university members, who can be traced through the list of medieval alumni. These property holders included two university chancellors: Master Andrew de Gisleham (Gilselham), chancellor of the university in 1283, who owned a messuage in St Michael's parish, and Master Stephen de Aseligfeld (or Haslingfeld), rector of St Michael's Church in 1279, and the university's chancellor by 1300, who held a messuage in the same parish.[37]

University members bought and sold urban property: Master Nicholas de Totington held two messuages and vacant plot in Straw Lane in St John's parish, and had sold an acre in the Cambridge fields and a messuage in St Michael's.[38] Many of the holdings were probably relatively small. Master Pagan de Dockinge owned a rent of 20s in Holy Sepulchre parish.[39] Chaplain Richard Aldgod (or Alzod) owned a messuage in St Clement's parish.[40] Master Alexander of St Edmund's had a messuage in St Michael's parish.[41] Master Henry Hinton had held 4 acres in Barnwell field and an acre in Cambridge field.[42]

Among the largest property portfolios held by university members were those of Master Robert Aunger de Cambridge, who held over 60 acres in the Cambridge fields as well as receiving rents from other properties in the town.[43] Master Adam de Bouden owned what became the main part of the site of Michaelhouse.[44] Master Thomas de Tyd was sufficiently wealthy to own a stone house in St Sepulchre parish in 1273, as well as holdings in St Andrew's and St Benedict's parishes.[45] Perhaps the most notable of all was Master Guy of Barnard Castle, who practised law in Cambridge and speculated in property, acquiring many of the properties of the Dunning family through mortgage (see Chapter 6).[46]

Some of the university members holding property probably had family connections, including Master John de Histon, who had held a messuage in St Edward's parish, and Master Walter de Histon, who had 20 acres in the Cambridge fields.[47] Master Robert de Huntingdon (Huntedon) had owned 8 acres in the Cambridge fields and Master Simon de Huntingdon two messuages in All Saints' parish.[48] Some of this property had been inherited, an example being the two messuages in St John's and St Mary's parishes that Master Bartholomew Lardario had acquired from his father, Master Stephen.[49] Master Nicholas of Hitchin (Hicche) had held a messuage in St John's, which he gave to his nephew and namesake, a clerk.[50]

The University of Cambridge had also begun to hold some property corporately. The chancellor and masters held three messuages, the gifts of Nicholas de Hedon and John de Thriplow. The rents from these properties appear to have been used to maintain a university chaplain to celebrate mass for the soul of Roger Heedon; John Geyste had been appointed chaplain in 1276. The chancellor also received rent for a messuage in All Saints in the Jewry.[51] The oldest known properties that the university owned around the Old Schools site were not, however, described as being in their ownership in the Hundred Rolls. These were messuages that the

Hundred Rolls stated were held by Roger de Redelingfield, also known as Roger de Thornton, from his uncle Nigel, a physician. Master Nigel may have been a Cambridge graduate, who died between 1270 and 1279. These messuages were subsequently proved to belong to the university; Roger de Redelingfield's connection was only as chaplain of a university chantry that his uncle had founded, but it took repeated litigation until 1294 before the university finally secured its claim.[52] As well as revealing the limited property portfolio held by the university at this time, these properties indicate the central importance of remembering the souls of founders and benefactors within the medieval university, which was an institution of commemoration as well as of education.[53]

3.7 Parish profiles: introduction

Having examined the economy of the town as a whole, it is now appropriate to 'drill down' to the parish level. The information in the Hundred Rolls can be pooled to construct a comprehensive profile of each parish. This exercise is particularly valuable for those parishes covered by the missing roll, as it enables their true size and significance to be fully appreciated. These profiles, together with the earlier results, provide a wide range of insights into the economic topography of the town and suggest some significant revisions to previous views. A map of the parishes is presented in Figure 3.1.

Each parish had its own particular character, which was reflected in the types of property it contained and the kinds of people who held them. Most property owners in Cambridge held only one or two properties, although leading families held more (see Chapter 4). It is therefore probable that many properties were inhabited by their owners, although the rolls only occasionally mention where people resided. This section examines the town parish by parish, beginning at the north and finishing at the south, with some adjustment to put together parishes that share a lengthy boundary. Each parish profile focuses on urban properties rather than lands in the fields. The Hundred Rolls are not ideal for analysing the ownership of fields as it is not always clear which lands are in which particular parishes. Issues specific to fields, such as tithing, are not addressed in this book.

Definitive information on parish boundaries in the 13th century is not available, and so it is assumed, following previous writers, that little has changed since then. Thus boundaries from c.1800 can be used instead.[54] The main differences are that the parish of All Saints at the Castle has been merged into St Giles' and St John's has been merged into St Edward's.

Figure 3.1: Cambridge parishes, c.1500

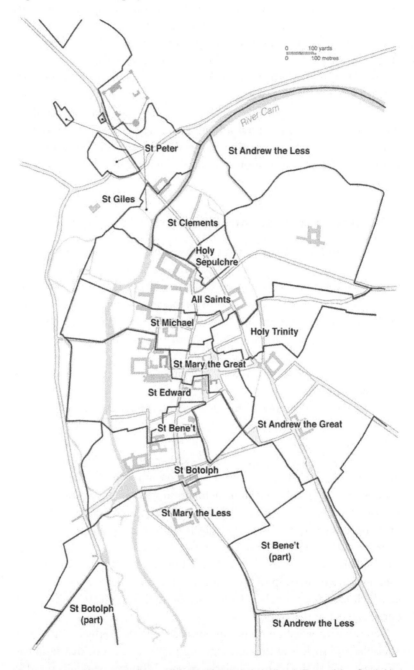

Source: Adapted from a map first published in Mary D. Lobel, *Historic Towns Atlas: Cambridge* (London, 1975) © Historic Towns Trust, 1975 (Reproduced with the permission of the Historic Towns Trust)

The church and parish of St Peter's outside the Trumpington Gate has also been rededicated to St Mary the Less.

3.8 North of the river

All Saints at the Castle

All Saints at the Castle was the most northerly of the Cambridge parishes. It no longer exists, having been merged into St Giles' in 1364 on account of its depopulation. It lay mainly along the west side of the Huntingdon road opposite the castle, which was the king's domain and outside the liberty of the town. It also included a large plot of land north of the castle on the opposite side of the road known as Sale Piece, which abutted Chesterton to the north and east. It is believed that the church pre-dated the building of the castle. Prisoners escaping from the castle gaol often sought sanctuary there. Baldwin Blancgernun granted the advowson to Barnwell Priory in 1219. The church was appropriated to Barnwell Priory by Hugh of Balsham, Bishop of Ely.[55]

The Hundred Rolls begin by itemizing four properties in the fee of the castle. Although the tenant-in-chief was the king rather than the town, only three of them paid rent to the sheriff (as the king's representative); the fourth paid hawgable to the town, presumably by gift of the king: 'Mabilia heir of Henry Hyrp possesses a certain piece of land in fee from the castle for which she pays per annum to the bailiffs of Cambridge 4 pence.'[56]

Two of the properties paying rent to the sheriff were held by Leon Dunning and the other by Robert, heir of Robert Seman. Leon paid 4d for a messuage and 6d for land while Robert paid 2d for land. This identifies the Dunning and Seman families as among the oldest and most venerable in Cambridge (see Chapter 4).

In 1279 the properties in the parish proper comprised 15 messuages, 4 granges, 6 shops, 3 houses and 4 pieces of land (2 vacant). The granges probably consisted of a farm complex comprising a farmhouse and outbuildings, as distinct from the granaries on the south side of the river, which were probably barns and warehouses. The granges were held mainly by leading families; the holders were Henry Toylet, Michael Pylat, Sabina Hubert and Stephen Baker.

Much of this parish was originally held by the Dunning family, although they must have disposed of much of their land fairly early, because other families seem to have acquired it and then given some of their properties to Barnwell Priory from the late 12th century onwards. Barnwell in turn sold off its land for perpetual rents. The Blancgernun family, however, retained some properties; Henry held a house, two messuages and some vacant land.

Barnwell was not the only institution to receive rents from the parish, however, as the parish church, the Hospital of St John and St Radegund's Priory were also recipients. Eva daughter of Christian of Huntingdon, undertook to sustain a candle in St Peter's Church nearby in perpetuity.

Sabina Hubert held five properties, comprising two messuages, two shops and a grange, the last being held on a lease for her life. Apart from Sabina Hubert and Henry Blancgernun, most of the property owners held only small and localized portfolios. Other owners possessed larger portfolios, and their holdings in All Saints' were overshadowed by more strategically located properties south of the river; these owners included Richard Laurence, John Porthors and Henry Toylet (noted earlier).

Female owners were prominent: Margaret Warin held four shops and a messuage; Sabina Hubert held a grange for life; Eva, mentioned previously, who was a relative of John of Huntingdon, former rector of St Peter's Church, held a messuage; while the sisters and daughters of William Braci, namely Margaret, Johanna, Avicia and Elena, jointly held two messuages and individual properties besides. It was a trade-intensive parish, ranking 5th for tradesmen and 12th for professionals. The rolls also identify four properties in the hamlet of Howes, all of them messuages, three with a croft attached and one with an acre of land.

It is widely accepted that All Saints' parish stagnated economically in the 13th century as the centre of gravity of urban commerce shifted to the south, and the evidence given here is consistent with that view. Nevertheless, the parish was neither desolate nor decayed in 1279. The leading families were still represented in the parish, and the granges seem to have been active.

St Peter's at the Castle (or St Peter's beyond the Bridge)

St Peter's at the Castle lies mainly west of the Huntingdon road below the castle. The church is halfway up the hill from the river to the castle. The church, first mentioned in 1217, is small, having been much reduced in size, but still retains some original features. The core area around the church is bordered to the south by St Neots Way (the Madingley road). There is also a detached part along the north bank of the river, including part of the plot on which Magdalene College now stands.

In 1279 the parish contained a mere 19 messuages, one house, a shop and a croft attached to a messuage. Most of the properties were held by a small number of well-established Cambridge families. Michael Wulward held two messuages and a house, John Warin held two messuages and the daughters of Thomas de Froyslake, Matilda and Isabella, held a messuage each. Two members of the Seman family also held messuages. Robert Wymund, another member of the Seman family, also held two messuages. Some of these families were connected (see Chapter 4).

St Peter's was also a trade-intensive parish, ranking 6th for tradesmen and 18th for professionals (see Table 3.3). William the ploughwright of Madingley held two messuages that had been part of the Dunning fee. There was a shop held by Alice, wife of William the Barber, and messuages held by Maurice the tailor and Agnes, daughter of Philip the tailor. Alan of Howes held three messuages and a croft, and may have been a farmer. Walter of Howes also held a messuage there, with an acre of land attached.

The Hundred Rolls tend to group properties by parish and also by owner, but in the case of St Peter's there is a clear pattern of grouping properties by family too. Messuages held by different members of the same family are listed consecutively, suggesting that they may have been adjacent to each other. In the case of the Froyslake sisters this is confirmed by the rents. Both messuages paid rent to both Lord Philip de Colevill and Lady Alicia, widow of Lord William of Bokesworth. Rents on the other messuages were paid to different people, however; for example, rent on one of John Warin's messuages was also paid to Lord Philip de Colevill, but rent on his other was paid to St Radegund's Priory. The rent to St Radegund's was 3s, which seems to have been a fairly standard rent on St Radegund's properties in whatever parish they were located. The most likely explanation of the ownership and location pattern of the messuages is that existing holders of a messuage often took advantage of an opportunity to purchase properties nearby (though not necessarily adjacent) to expand their businesses or for the use of a relative.

The dominance of 'old wealth' in this parish confirms, to some extent, the impression that the casual visitor gets today: that it is a parish where time has stood still. But the opinion is perhaps exaggerated. It might be more accurate to say that the parish looked outwards towards its surrounding fields as well as inward towards the centre of the town.

St Giles'

St Giles' is the third of the three parishes lying north of the river and below the castle. It lies between the two portions of St Peter's parish. It has an irregular shape, with a small amount of river frontage, and was bordered by fields to the west. The traditional date of its foundation is

1092. It hosted a group of canons for about 20 years, who were sponsored by the sheriff's wife; they then moved east across the river and developed Barnwell Priory on a new site.

The church stands at the intersection of the Huntingdon road and St Neots Way; it was remodelled in the early 19th century and in c.1875 it was completely rebuilt. The advowson was held by Barnwell Priory. Barnwell also seems to have held much of the land in the parish from an early date.

The parish has more properties than St Peter's but fewer than St Clement's on the opposite bank of the river. Unlike these parishes, it was almost entirely residential. It comprised 35 messuages, two half-messuages, four houses and three vacant plots of land. There was a single grange, built by John Porthors on land that he purchased from Peter Wulward. The older families were again much in evidence as holders of property.

Geoffrey Andrew was the largest property owner, holding no fewer than nine properties, including a house, two messuages and two plots of vacant land. Most of these properties were inherited from his father. Five properties paid only hawgable: a nominal amount of 1d or less. The others paid modest rents. Leon Dunning and John Dunning also held messuages. Amicia Dunning, daughter of Roger Warin and widow of Richard Dunning, held four messuages, also paying very low rents. Robert Wymund, of the Seman dynasty, held three properties, while Robert son of Robert Seman held one messuage and Laurence Seman and his wife held half a messuage. These properties paid higher rents. The properties paying the lowest rents were probably those whose owners (or their predecessors) had purchased them outright. Some other names that are familiar from St Peter's also appear, examples being Michael Wulward, Isabella Froyslake and Maurice the tailor. Patterns of property ownership do not seem to have been influenced by parish boundaries in this part of the town.

'New money' was represented by Norman the cooper, who held two messuages, and gave a third to his daughter Sarah. These properties also paid higher rents: 4s to the Hospital of St John, 3s to Barnwell Priory and 1s to the Prior of Ely. Tradesmen and professionals were few; the parish ranked 13th for tradesmen and 14th for professionals (see Table 3.3).

The evidence suggests that St Giles' developed as a residential centre from an early date, probably from about the time when the canons were there. By comparison, its 'twin' across the river, St Clement's, appears to have become more of a commercial centre. As the town developed, and the commercial centre of gravity moved south, St Giles', like its neighbouring parishes to the north, ossified to some degree. The existence of three vacant plots in the parish suggests that people were in no hurry to develop property in the area at the time of the Hundred Rolls.

3.9 South of the bridge

St Clement's

St Clement's parish is bordered to the north-west by the river, and by All Saints in the Jewry and St Sepulchre to the south. To the east it abuts on the estates of Barnwell Priory and St Radegund's Priory. The parish church is on Bridge Street, leading from the Hospital of St John to the Great Bridge. The church building dates only from the 13th century, although its dedication suggests Scandinavian links.[57] The controversy over the advowson is discussed in Chapter 4. The site on the east bank of the river now occupied by St John's College was the site of the hospital, founded in the mid-12th century. The site borders St Clement's but is mainly in All Saints'.

In 1279 the Great Bridge was described as being in very poor repair, so that large carts crossing it fell into the river and many others crossing with horses were placed in great danger.[58] The bridge seems to have been broken by flood, and the sheriff, Robert del Estre, had placed the unprecedented pontage levy of 2s from every hide, when the customary charge was 6d. He had seized timber from poor men at Barnwell Fair. Estre had apparently promised a new bridge of stone rather than wood, but had then merely patched up the existing bridge and diverted building materials to his own purposes. One of his officers, the keeper of the castle prison, Richard Prest, even came out at night and removed planks from the bridge. Estre allegedly kept a boat on the Cam and profited from ferrying travellers across the river. The issue, which clearly caused great resentment, was mentioned by seven hundreds across the county as well as in the returns of the borough.[59]

Trades and professions were in a minority; the parish ranked only 11th for trades and 12th for professionals. The parish properties in 1279 comprised 40 messuages, 14 shops, two houses and one plot of vacant land, making this one of the larger parishes in the town. Despite its location on the river, there were no granges or granaries; but it was not purely residential as there were several shops.

A high proportion of the rent paid on properties in this parish accrued to religious institutions. Private individuals received only a small proportion of rents, but this income included a small number of rents that were very large. The principal private recipient of rent was Master Robert Aunger, son of Aunger, but even this rent was assigned, in large part, to the church. Radulph, the chaplain of St Clement's Church, received 5 marks annually from Master Robert, sourced from various messuages and incomes.[60] Rents also accrued to members of some of the old Cambridge families, notably Childman, le Rus, Seman, Wulward and Wombe. Some of these rents were large: Juliana, wife of Humphrey of Clopton, received 20s from Stephen Baker for a messuage, while William Pikerel received 18s from Richard de Parham for a messuage.

The 14 shops paid almost no rent to either individuals or institutions, except a nominal amount of hawgable. Ownership was concentrated in a few hands. The shops were held by Robert Mathefray and Margaret his wife (six), Robert Aunger (four), Nicholas Morice (two), Thomas the Marshall and Richard Prest with Alicia his wife (one each). It seems that they were owned outright and run for profit, with one exception; Robert Aunger's profits went to the church.

St Clement's parish was the focus of large-scale charitable giving in Cambridge. It was not only the place where many major families held properties but in many cases it was also the place where they chose to live: one of the best addresses in town. Their objects of charity were not confined to the hospital in the parish, nor to institutions in the town. Yet there was a parochial dimension; the parish church benefited enormously. It seems that the parishioners lavished their gifts on St Clement's Church rather than on St Mary's near the marketplace. The highest value and most specialized trades in the town, however, were located not in this parish, but in St Mary's.

All Saints in the Jewry (or All Saints by the Hospital)

All Saints in the Jewry lies south of St Clement's, St Sepulchre and a detached part of St Peter's south of the river, and north of St Michael's and Holy Trinity. It is very wide from east to west but narrow from north to south. The church no longer survives (it has been replaced by a small memorial garden), but All Saints' Passage, once known as Pilate's Lane, is now a footpath from the High Street (St John's Street) to Conduit Street (Sidney Street). The parish was also known as All Saints by the Hospital and All Saints above the water. The advowson was given by Sturmi of Cambridge to St Radegund's Priory in 1180.[61] The east of the parish became the parish of St Radegund's in c.1250, and remained separate until the Dissolution, but because St Radegund's was so small it is included with All Saints in this study. It must also be borne in mind that the Jews, many of whom had lived in or around Pilate's Lane, had been expelled from the town in 1275. Jewish property was escheated to the queen and then sold on by her agents, and it is not clear that this property was itemized in the Hundred Rolls.

The parish occupies a key position near the meeting of several roads and its property rents were relatively high. Nevertheless the uses of property were fairly mixed. This is partly because parish boundaries in Cambridge are very irregular compared with many other towns, so that the area of any given parish does not map neatly into an area of economic specialization. Each part of the parish seems to have been similar to its adjacent parishes, so that the different parts of the parish are not that similar to each other. In particular the area of the parish nearest St Michael's seems more similar to St Michael's than it does to the part nearest St Clement's, which is quite similar to St Clement's.

The parish contained the Hospital of St John, which had been founded on 'a very poor and empty place' according to jurors of an inquest in 1274.[62] Archaeological evidence at the Chapel Court site has shown that after a prolonged period of alluviation, a major programme of land reclamation was initiated in the late 11th or early 12th centuries.[63]

Excluding St Radegund's, the parish included 13 messuages, four granaries, a grange, four shops, two houses and two plots of vacant land. St Radegund's accounted for five messuages (one of which was occupied by the nuns) and two plots of land, one of which was vacant. Both trades and professions were well represented; the parish was somewhat trade-intensive, ranking 5th for tradesmen and 10th for professionals.

The grange was located at Dame Nicholas Hythe and was held by Robert Toylet. The granaries were held by Thomas Toylet, Henry Toylet, William Seman and Richard of Hokele (probably Hockley, a village in Essex), all of whom held properties elsewhere in Cambridge. Two of the shops were held by Lord Simon Constable, soldier of Holderness, whose wife Johanna inherited them from Thomas Stanton, clerk, her father, and paid 2s rent to Richard Wombe and 6s to the almoner of Ely; the other shops were held by William Seman and Alicia, daughter of Simon Godeman. The messuages were held by members of some well-known families, such as Michael Pilat, Walter Pilat and Richard Wombe, and paid rent to a variety of institutions, including Ramsey Abbey, Fordham Priory, Thremhall Priory and the Almoner of Croyland, as well as local institutions.

The properties in St Radegund's parish seem to have been held by people of somewhat lower status, such as William Carpenter, Hubert son of Geoffrey the cook, and Emma, his wife, and Alice, widow of Hamon the tailor. There were seven messuages and two plots of land, one of them vacant. All the messuages paid either 3s or 4s rent to St Radegund's

Priory. The wealthiest owner was probably Henry Page, who owned shops in Holy Trinity close to the marketplace, on which he paid 3s rent to the priory.

There is no doubt that many of the people who held land in All Saints' came from wealthy families, and the high rents in the parish might to some extent reflect the size and status of the properties they occupied. However, the people in St Radegund's parish also paid reasonably high rents, even though they were of lower status. It may be that property in these parishes was expensive simply because it was a desirable place in which to live, and those who could afford it lived there whatever their status.

St Sepulchre (or Holy Sepulchre)

St Sepulchre is a small and compact parish lying between St Clement's to the north and All Saints in the Jewry to the south. The church has long been known as the Round Church because of its distinctive configuration. Reinald, Abbot of Ramsey, in c.1114–30 granted a fraternity land adjoining the graveyard of an earlier church dedicated to St George on which to build, but nothing of the original church remains. Architectural features suggest that the present church was built in c.1120–40.[64] The advowson was held by Barnwell Priory from c.1250.[65]

In 1279 the parish contained 13 messuages, one with a croft attached, a half-messuage and two houses. Two of the messuages and the croft had been given to Barnwell Priory by Adam Weriel son of Walter, and were still, apparently, in the priory's hands. The priory may have used them for priory business or leased them on a short-term basis, perhaps to their lay employees. The two houses were held by the Hospital of St John; they were the gift of William Toylet (probably William II, see Chapter 4) and paid 6s rent to Barnwell Priory. This is an example of how properties burdened with rent to one institution, when given to another institution, could generate inter-institutional payments of rent.

Other properties were held largely by members of leading families, including the Bartons, Pilats and Toylets. Bartholomew Gogging held what must have been a very grand messuage that his wife Johanna had received in dowry from her father, Henry of Barton (see Chapter 4), and which, like many messuages in Cambridge, had originally been held by the Malerbe family. A rent of £1 was paid to Master Pagano of Docking, Norfolk, by assignment of Michael Malerbe, and in addition 7d hawgable to the town.[66]

Three of the messuages were held for life; two were held by men (one a widower) and one by a husband and wife. None of them were held by widows, although two of the three messuages were acquired through dower. This suggests that the parish might have been a retirement location for parents whose children had taken over the ownership and management of the family portfolio. Another possibility is that some of the property owners had sons and daughters serving as brothers and sisters in the neighbouring priories.

Properties in the parish paid substantial rents to religious institutions. The principal beneficiary was Barnwell Priory, which received rents from no fewer than five properties, which is not surprising given that it bordered the parish. Other beneficiaries included the nuns of St Radegund's (also local), the nuns of Swaffham and the nuns of St Mary de Pré.

St Sepulchre was a small parish that shared many of the characteristics of St Clement's. It had very few tradesmen or professionals, ranking 18th for the former and 16th for the latter. Its property owners were mostly from established wealthy families and they paid substantial rents to religious institutions. But the parish was smaller and less commercial than St Clement's (it had no shops) and did not border the river. It was closer to the local priories, however.

St Michael's

St Michael's lies mainly to the west of the High Street towards and beyond the present course of the river; it also includes a portion of what is now Green Street. The church is on the High Street, where some of the most prestigious properties were located. The controversy over its advowson is discussed in Chapter 4. Towards the river lay three granaries; the other properties comprised 24 messuages and two plots of vacant land. Half a century later, Michaelhouse and Gonville Hall were to be established in this parish and its church was rebuilt by the founder of Michaelhouse for use by his college. Even in 1279 though, scholars, churchmen and administrators held many of the messuages in this parish. Master Andrew of Giselham, future chancellor of the university, Master Adam de Bouton and Master William of Beeston held messuages in which they probably resided. Master Radulph of Walpole, Archdeacon of Ely, Adam de la Grene of Walpole, chaplain, William de le Bruere, chaplain, and Master Stephen of Haslingfield, rector of the church, also held property. Another high-status owner was Lord Simon of Constable, soldier of Holderness. It is not surprising, therefore, that the parish rates as profession intensive, ranking 6th for professionals and 14th for tradesmen.

Several women held property: Matilda, daughter of Isanti, Cecilia, daughter of Simon Potecar, and Margaret, daughter of Fulk of Barnwell, all held messuages, while Alicia, sister of Ernest the merchant, held a grange. Leading families in the town were represented by Richard Wombe and Richard Crocheman, both of whom had long-standing links with the parish.

The Wombe family not only held property but also received rents from property. The family was in decline and had sold off several of the properties that it once held, receiving rents from the new owners instead.

A number of religious institutions received rents from property in the parish, including Barnwell Priory, Thremhall Priory, Anglesey Abbey, the Templars of Denny, St Radegund's Priory, Hatfield Priory, the Hospital of St John and the scholars of Merton. In addition Anglesey Priory and the Prior of Ely both held messuages in their own right.

3.10 Central area

St John's (St John Zachary)

The church of St John the Baptist, commonly called St John Zachary, stood on the west side of Milne Street, within a parish that occupied a key position between the High Street and the river. It lay south of St Michael's, north of St Botolph's and west of St Mary's, St Edward's and St Benedict's. Its properties comprised 44 messuages, three houses, three plots of vacant land and two curtilages (one with land). There were no shops. Many of the properties had addresses in Mill Lane, Milne Street and Strawylane.

The parish is notable for the number of institutions that held property (as opposed to receiving rents). The Prior of Ely held two messuages, Anglesey Priory some vacant land, while the Abbot of Warden, the Abbot of Titley and the Hospital of St John of Jerusalem held one messuage each. The parish was very intensive in professions, ranking 2nd for professions and 14th for tradesmen.

The dominant private property owners were William Eliot, Richard of Hockley and his son Simon, William Seman and Simon son of John Bradley. Three people held two properties in the parish, namely Roger of Redlingfield, Matilda, daughter of Isanti, and Nicholas Drayton and Margaret his wife. Roger held two prestigious properties. One came with 26 acres of land attached. It was given by Master Nigel, doctor, his uncle, who bought it from Cassandria, daughter of Christina Warin. The other messuage was known as Dagenhale, and is referred to by name in several deeds and in other entries in the rolls. A messuage held by John of Barking, chaplain, is described as lying outside the Trumpington Gate; this may allude to a detached portion of the parish.

Despite its proximity to the river, St John's seems to have been more favoured by clerks and institutions than by tradesmen. Trade seems to have been concentrated on the quays in St Michael's and St Clement's to the north. These trends were to be reinforced by the arrival of the Carmelite Friars from Newnham who, it was claimed, had destroyed houses in the parish in 1291, and, much later, by the college foundations of Trinity Hall (in 1350), Godshouse (in 1439) and the second site of King's College (in 1446). The founder of the last of these colleges, Henry VI, relocated both Godshouse and the church of St John Zachary, and caused the parish to be amalgamated with St Edward's.[67] St John's Church, demolished to construct King's College Chapel, was rebuilt at the north-west corner of the Old Court of King's College, but quickly fell into disuse and had disappeared by the mid-16th century.[68]

St Mary's (now known as St Mary the Great or Great St Mary's)

St Mary's is and was a compact and densely populated parish. It borders St Michael's, Holy Trinity, St Andrew's and St Edward's, and previously St John's. Together with St Edward's, it encompassed the market and its surrounding streets. The church is located on High Street/Trumpington Street at the west end of the market. It is the only church in Cambridge where the king held the advowson in 1279. The church was first mentioned in 1205.[69]

St Mary's contained 54 messuages, 27 shops, a half-shop, four stalls and six plots of land (five were vacant). Some of these properties are specifically mentioned as being in the marketplace, and are discussed in more detail later in this chapter. Barnwell Priory held much of the land in St Mary's, and received a substantial amount of rent.[70]

Property ownership was fairly diffuse. The largest property owners were William le Comber and Matilda his wife. They owned three messuages, a shop and a stall. One of the messuages paid rent to no fewer than four people: 3s to Alicia, wife of John Kirkeby, 2s to Robert son of Robert the whitesmith (lead-worker), 10d to Nicholas Morice and 8d to Walter the Plumber. Another messuage paid 1 gallon of oil to St Radegund's for a lamp in their church and half a mark to Nicholas Morice. Otherwise no-one owned more than three properties. Ten people held three properties each. Nicholas Goldsmith, for example, held a messuage paying 6s to John of Stanton through the heirs of Henry Nado and 1d hawgable; a messuage paying 2d hawgable and 0.5d to Jordan the skinner and Cecilia his wife; and a shop paying 9d to the heirs of William de Novacurt.

Some specific properties are of interest. Wakelin the barber resided in a messuage that he bought from Walter of Oxford 'serving at the University of Cambridge', which Walter acquired from the nuns of Pré (near St Albans). William of Norfolk and Margaret his wife held a shop in the market that paid 4s 6d to the Anchorite of Trumpington, as well as 2s 6d to the heirs of Ernest the merchant by assignment of Richard son of Ivo.

Overall the parish exhibited significant diversity in the type of people holding property and the range of institutions to which these properties owed rent. These institutions included, in addition to those already mentioned, Anglesey Priory, Hatfield Priory, Thorney Abbey and, locally, St Michael's Church, St Edmund's Chapel and the high altar in St Mary's Church. The diversity of people is reflected in the fact that it contained a wide variety of occupations.

St Edward King and Martyr

The parish of St Edward King and Martyr is one of the oldest in Cambridge. The church's dedication suggests Anglo-Saxon origins, and a Saxon coffin stone has been found there. The advowson was granted to Barnwell Priory by Hugh of Northwold, Bishop of Ely 1229–54.[71] The church lies south-west of the market. The original parish (as described here) occupied a relatively small area south of the market. The modern parish incorporates St John's parish (mentioned earlier).

The parish was highly commercialized. It included 35 properties, comprising 25 messuages, 18 shops, one stall, one house and two plots of land (one vacant). Several of the messuages had shops attached. Many different people held property in the parish, and most of them held just a single plot.

The largest parish portfolios were held by Isabella Morin, Thomas son of Edmund Miller and Gilbert Bernard. Isabella held three messuages and a stall (one of the messuages being held for life) on land first acquired by John Aubrey. Two of her properties paid rent to St Radegund's and one to Barnwell. Thomas held six shops, all paying rent to private owners.

The main institutions receiving rent were St Radgund's, the Hospital of St John and the Almoner of Ely. Rents were also paid to Barnwell Priory, the nuns of Swaffham and Anglesey Priory. Eleven properties paid hawgable; it is unclear what distinguished them from other properties: three paid 8d, one paid 6d and the others all paid a maximum of 2d. The highest levels of hawgable, namely 6d and over, were paid on shops. The parish was profession intensive, ranking 8th for professions and 11th for tradesmen (Table 3.3).

St Benedict's (now known as St Bene't's)

St Benedict's is, like St Edward's, a parish of great antiquity. Architectural features suggest that its church is the oldest in Cambridge. It has been suggested that later parishes were carved out of this parish as other churches were built. It was primarily residential; it consisted mainly of messuages and had no shops. St Benedict's was intensive in trade as well; it ranked third for tradesmen and fourth for professionals, making it very much a 'working' parish.

The parish contained 42 messuages, one house and ten plots of land, nine of which were vacant. The vacant plots of land could be the consequence of a fire, of redevelopment or of rents that were too high to be affordable. There are no records of a fire (although the borough records are scant) and it seems unlikely that nine plots would be undergoing redevelopment at the same time. The most plausible explanation is that this part of the town was in decline, and that properties had been vacated by people unable to pay the rents. Under these conditions a property would revert to the previous owner, who might in turn be liable for rents, although not, of course, for any rents that they themselves had imposed. The process of repossession could take considerable time, however. Whatever the cause, it seems to have afflicted some neighbouring parishes too, such as St Mary's and Holy Trinity, which also had significant numbers of vacant plots.

The pattern of ownership is again fairly diffuse. Two people held four properties: Osbert the farrier and John of Braintree; Cecilia, widow of Peter de Welles, held three plots, five people held two and everyone else held just a single plot. Osbert the farrier and Berota his wife held two messuages and two pieces of vacant land. Three of the properties paid rent to Luke of St Edmund's, while the remaining property paid 5s to Henry of Hauxton and 1d hawgable. One of the vacant plots was said to be opposite the Friars Preachers, who were based on the present site of Emmanuel College in St Andrew's. This suggests that either the rolls are mistaken (which seems unlikely) or something must have changed: perhaps the friars were in temporary accommodation or, more likely, the parish boundary has changed. Perhaps there was a detached portion of St Benedict's in what is now St Andrew's parish. There may have been other detached portions; land held by Margaret Abiton from Walter of St Edmund's is described as being in St Benedict's parish outside the Trumpington Gate.

It is difficult to draw firm conclusions about St Benedict's parish because its boundaries are uncertain, and it is difficult to be sure whether it was developing, declining or rebuilding at the time of the Hundred Rolls.

The most plausible assessment is that it was a stagnating area occupied by a mixture of professionals and tradesmen. Many of those who held property in the parish, and perhaps lived in the parish, may have worked elsewhere in the town.

The marketplace

The marketplace has always retained its focal position in the centre of the town. There are 17 records in the Hundred Rolls concerning properties located in the market. Fifteen of these paid rent, while the other two were owned by institutions: the hospital held a shop given by Eustace of Wimpole and Anglesey Priory held a shop given by Harvey son of Selede. Both properties were probably rented out, but only on a short-term basis.

Seven of the 14 records relate to St Mary's parish and two to St Edward's. Six shops, a half-shop and two messuages were described as being in St Mary's. The most notable were a pair of shops in the Butchery held by Richard Bateman senior, which paid 8s to St Edmund's Chapel (on Trumpington Street), the same to St Mary's Church and 2s to Alan Segin by assignment of Robert Aunger.

Four shops were described as being in St Edward's. These comprised three shops held by Thomas son of Edward Miller, for which he paid 10s rent to William Toylet, and a shop held by Nicholas Morice, on which he paid 8d hawgable.

Six properties were not ascribed to any parish. John Ive held two shops that sold meat and paid hawgable of 8d; Bartholomew Gogging held a stall paying 6s to Lord Peter de Chavent; Geoffrey the farrier a shop paying 5s to John above the Market and 2s to the hospital; Henry Page a shop paying 5s to the Sacristan of Ely; and Geoffrey Spartegrave and Agnes his wife a messuage paying 16d to Agnes of Madingley. Finally Leon Dunning held a horse-mill in the market as part of a large portfolio of inherited properties on which the total rent was 2.5 marks to Radulph Pirot and Cassandria his wife, 2.5 marks by assignment of Giles of Argentin and over 25s to the town.

Rents were generally high and hawgable on shops, when levied, was also high at 8d. The market ranks low on both trades and professions, ranking 14th for each, even though most of their properties were used for trading purposes. It is likely that many property owners did not trade there themselves and that many properties were leased out to traders on a short-term basis.

St Andrew's (St Andrew the Great)

St Andrew's parish has never been fully researched because much of the evidence on its medieval properties is in the missing portion of the Hundred Rolls. Stokes, in his book on the parish, had access only to information on four messuages in the parish held by St Radegund's Priory and six others held by private individuals.[72] He noted a major discrepancy between the records of the Hundred Rolls and deeds of St Radegund's, but concluded that the numerous St Radegund's deeds referred to the same few properties at different times. In fact St Andrew's was one of the most populous parishes, in which lived many aristocrats and scholars. Similar problems of missing evidence affect Holy Trinity and, to a smaller extent, most other parishes too.

The development of the parish was stimulated by the arrival of the Dominican order in Cambridge in or shortly before 1238. The site (now occupied by Emmanuel College), was out beyond the Barnwell Gate, away from what was then the town centre. The success of the early preaching mission may be gauged by the friars' piecemeal acquisition over the next few decades of surrounding properties to create a site covering some 10 acres. By 1296, through the generous benefaction of Alice de Sanford, the Countess of Oxford, the friars were able to greatly enlarge their original buildings. By 1260, several friars were acknowledged lectors in the university's Theology Faculty. In c.1314 the Cambridge priory was made into a 'studium generale' for the Order.[73] The Hundred Rolls record that land formerly subject to geld and feudal aid was now held by the friars in perpetual alms 'by purchase and by gifts of many people'.[74] The friars seem to have had a major impact on the parish. In 1279 it ranked first for professionals and fourth for tradesmen (Table 3.3), suggesting that many of the tradesmen may have catered for a local professional clientele.

The parish lay outside the Barnwell Gate along the main road that now leads to the station and on towards Colchester. It was known in medieval times as Hadstock Way or Friars Preachers Street, and today as St Andrews Street and Regent Street. It seems likely that much of the early development was along this road. It may well have followed a similar path of development to that still visible along Trumpington Street in the parish of St Peter's outside the Trumpington Gate (discussed later). In the case of St Andrew's much of the visible legacy has been lost through later retail development. The church is located near the site of the gate opposite the junction with Hobson's Lane; it has been rebuilt several times. The advowson was presented to the Prior of Ely by Absolon son of Algar, the rector and patron, in 1225–8. Bishop Geoffrey of Ely appropriated the church to the sacrist.[75]

The rolls record no fewer than 48 messuages, together with one half-messuage, three houses, four curtilages, a shop and six plots of land (three vacant). Seventeen of the properties paid hawgable. Among the important people holding property were Master Radulph of Walpole, Archdeacon of Ely, Master Andrew of Middilton, Master William of Norwich and Walter le Rus of Waldene.

A total of eight properties paid rent to St Radegund's. The priory also held four messuages and a piece of vacant land that they had been given by Robert Crocheman and Cassandria his wife in return for a chaplain celebrating mass for their souls, and another messuage given by William Sweteye on which they paid 1d hawgable.[76]

Several families held multiple properties, although their portfolios were of modest size. William Eliot, a prominent burgess, held a capital messuage, a house, three curtilages and a small amount of land, all of which paid hawgable. Walter of Hauxton, clerk, held two messuages, paying rent to St Radegund's and the Almoner of Ely, William of Astrocam held two messuages (one for his life) paying rents to the Almoner of Barnwell and Anglesey Priory; and Sarah Alsope held two messuages paying modest rents to individuals. Robert Godsone held a messuage and a shop, and Cecilia, daughter of William Godsone, held a messuage; these properties paid modest rents to private individuals. Most properties, however, were held by people who had only one property in the parish. Sir Alan of Little Bradley held two messuages given by Hugo of Balsham, Bishop of Ely, for the maintenance of the newly founded Hospital of Balsham (the bishop also gave three shops in St Edward's for the same purpose) (see Chapter 6).[77]

St Andrew's appears to have been a popular parish for professionals and tradesmen alike. Several learned and aristocratic individuals held property there, and some of them lived there too.

Holy Trinity

Holy Trinity is another parish that is only partially covered in the Record Commission edition of the Hundred Rolls. It has received less attention from scholars than St Andrew's parish and its neighbour St Mary's. Yet it too ranked high in professionals and tradesmen. Compared with St Andrew's, however, it was more biased to trade; it ranked 2nd for trade and 6th for professions.

The church lies east of the market and the parish stretches further east across Conduit Street (Sidney Street) and Walis Lane (Hobson Street) towards what is now Christ's Pieces. The church burned down in 1174; parts of the present tower date from about the time of the Hundred Rolls.

William of Yarmouth, a Cambridge vintner, gave the advowson to the Premonstratensian canons of West Dereham in c.1199–1254.[78]

Like St Mary's and St Edward's, the parish was densely built and presumably heavily populated. It contained a variety of properties, but messuages predominated. There are 56 records in the Hundred Rolls of which only 11 were noted by the Record Commission. They comprise 46 messuages, a one third share of a messuage, a house, a building, four shops, a seld and three vacant plots. Many of the messuages bore multiple rents, which suggests that they had changed hands several times without ever being purchased outright. Henry Page, for example, held two shops on which he paid 4s to the Almoner of Titley, 3s to St Radegund's and 1d to Isabella, widow of Albric the butcher.

Some of the properties appear to have been relatively grand and others quite modest. The Archdeacon of Ely paid one mark to John Porthors for his house. Margaret Warin paid 10s rent for her messuage to Isabella and Agnes (possibly sisters), the respective wives of Albric the butcher and Roger Cun. By contrast, Nicholas in the Ditch paid only 10d rent to St Radegund's for his messuage. The four shops were quite valuable. Both Nicholas son of Geoffrey Potecar and John son of Hugo Potecar paid John of Barton 6s. rent, while Henry Page paid over 7s for the other two shops, comprising 4s to the Almoner of Titley and 3s to St Radegund's.

Ownership was widely distributed. Only one person held four properties, and only two held three. John son of Hugo Potecar held two messuages, a shop and a seld; Simon Potecar held a building, a messuage and part of another messuage, and Roger, chaplain, held two messuages and a vacant plot. Five individuals held two properties and everyone else held just a single property in the parish.

Overall, Holy Trinity was a diverse parish. Like similar parishes, this was probably in part because of its geographical configuration. Properties to the west were fairly close to the market and the church, while those further east, bordering St Radegund's Priory, were probably more rural in character. The parish seems to have been mainly residential, but with residents strongly represented in the trades and professions. It had a wider social mix than some of the other residential parishes.

3.11 The south of the town

St Botolph's

St Botolph's, like All Saints in the Jewry, slices east to west across the town. To the north it borders St Edward's, St Benedict's and St Andrew's, and to the south St Peter's outside the Trumpington Gate and a detached portion of St Benedict's. The church sits in the middle of the parish at what is now the junction of Trumpington Street and Silver Street (formerly Smallbridge Street), just north of Trumpington Gate and the King's Ditch. Its dedication may have been stimulated by a local cult of St Botolph, which would suggest an early foundation. Bishop Eustace of Ely (1198–1215) gave the advowson to Barnwell Priory. In 1235 Peter of Bottisham, chaplain, paid 4 marks rent to Barnwell for his income from tithes and so on, and this arrangement was perpetuated for later incumbents.[79]

In 1279 the parish of St Botolph comprised 38 messuages, one half-messuage, two houses, two shops and two plots of vacant land. Most properties were held by people who held only a single property in the parish and no other property in the town. The two largest property owners were Gerard de Vivar and Saer de Feruyngges and Mariota his wife. Gerard, whose name suggests the owner of a fishpond, was a juror of the Hundred Rolls. All his property lay in St Botolph's; it comprised four messuages and two shops. Likewise Saer, a local aristocrat, held four messuages in St Botolph's and, apart from land in Newnham, nothing elsewhere in Cambridge. Few of the old families held land in the parish; only Seman (two), Gogging (two) and Barton and Morice (one each). Trades and professionals were well represented; the parish ranked 4th for professionals and 6th for tradesmen.

Religious institutions received relatively little rent. Some modest rents were paid to Barnwell Priory, two substantial rents of 9s and 6s to the hospital and smaller sums (under 5s) to St Radegund's, Berden Priory, Sawtry Abbey and Markyate Priory (two rents). An unusually large proportion of properties paid hawgable (19 or 43 per cent).

The largest recipient of private rent was Leon Dunning; he received a total of 4s 10d from four properties. The largest payments to individuals were 10s rent for a messuage held by Alice, daughter of William Lucke, paid to the heirs of Robert of Hauxton, and half a mark paid by Walter Berchar to Alicia, widow of William de Kirkeby.

The high proportion of properties paying hawgable could reflect the relatively late development of this part of the town. The bailiffs of the newly chartered borough may have noted the potential of this area and decided to develop it. The area may not have attracted much interest from the older families because it was too remote from the older part of the town near the river.

St Peter's outside the Trumpington Gate (now St Mary the Less or Little St Mary's)

St Peters outside the Trumpington Gate is the most southerly of the town parishes, lying either side of Trumpington Street (the London road). The course of the River Cam, flowing north from Grantchester into Cambridge, lies to the west, near the settlement of Newnham, part of which lies in the parish. Properties in Newnham are analysed separately, however, as they seem to be rather different in character (see the next section). The northern boundary of the parish is where the King's Ditch crosses Trumpington Street at the site of the Trumpington Gate, just south of St Botolph's Church. St Peter's Church (rebuilt in the 1350s and renamed Little St Mary's or St Mary the Less) lies just south of the gate. To the east, the parish is bordered by St Botolph's and St Benedict's.

The parish had a distinctive pattern of property ownership. Excluding Newnham it comprised 25 messuages, one croft and two small pieces of land. Most of these were strung out along both sides of Trumpington Street, where the Fitzwilliam Museum and Old Addenbrooke's Hospital now stand. A substantial group of properties was held by Henry de Ho and another by John of Aylsham and Sabina his wife.[80] Many properties paid rents to either St Radegund's Priory or the Hospital of St John, and in some cases both. The major private recipient of rent was Luke of St Edmunds, the main heir of the St Edmunds dynasty. The advowson of the church was held by St John's Hospital, and transferred to Peterhouse on its foundation in 1284, which subsequently rebuilt the church and rededicated it to St Mary.[81]

The area included major properties held by the St Edmunds family and the le Rus family, as described by Stokes in colourful detail.[82] Some of the messuages were of major historical significance. One was the home of the Friars of the Sack, who arrived in England in 1257 and were established in Cambridge by the following year.[83] John le Rus arranged with Barnwell Priory to hand over his property to the friars, and the house became their headquarters.[84]

Robert, the rector of the chapel of St Edmund, held a messuage with 12.75 acres of land attached. It was the site of St Edmund's Chapel, the advowson of which passed to the White Canons of the order of St Gilbert of Sempringham in 1290.[85] The rector also held 2 acres of land given by John le Rus and an acre given by Lord William of Mortimer senior.[86] The advowson of the chapel was later transferred to the White Canons of St Gilbert of Sempringham, whose members wished to study in Cambridge.[87] Other messuages were held by Luke of St Edmunds and Anglesey Abbey.[88]

The remaining 18 messuages were held by a variety of people. Some, such as William of Sawston, chaplain, were probably of a religious or scholarly disposition, like the members of the St Edmunds and le Rus families. But others appear to have been successful entrepreneurs, such as John of Aylsham and his wife Sabina. Neither professionals nor tradesmen were strongly represented; the parish rated 10th for the former and 14th for the latter (Table 3.3). The parish seems to have been mainly residential, as no shops are recorded, although there may have been some industry near the river. The concentration of property holding by de Ho, the Aylshams and the friars in 1279 enabled Peterhouse to acquire a compact landholding in the parish by 1300.[89]

Newnham

Newnham was a small settlement along the river south of the town, part of which was in St Peter's parish. A detached part of St Botolph's lay nearby. The area gives its name to Newnham College on modern Sidgwick Avenue. The Carmelite Friars were based in Newnham, where they had a church.[90] Their 3-acre plot was given by Michael Malerbe and a consortium of many other people. The friars were uncertain whether their ownership had been confirmed by the king, unlike the Friars of the Sack on the Trumpington road nearby.

The rolls identify 20 properties in Newnham, which comprised 13 messuages, four crofts, three shops and six plots of land (one vacant) (several properties had two separate uses). Ten of the properties paid rent to the Hospital of St John, and one to Barnwell Priory. Eleven paid rent to individuals, three of them to Leon Dunning. Two of the eleven paid rent to the Hospital as well. Rents were relatively low, often just a few pence; the largest rent to the Hospital was 4s and the largest to a private individual was 6s to Michael son of John Michael.

The largest property owners were John Martin, who was mayor on several occasions, and Ambrose son of John Godrich, who was apparently a local man. John Martin held four messuages and 7 acres of land, while Ambrose held two messuages and three shops. The other owners were a mixture of Cambridge people, such as William le Stereman and his wife Rosa, daughter of Richard Dunning, and local people, such as William the tanner. Few professionals lived in Newnham; it ranked 10th for tradesmen and 17th for professionals (Table 3.3).

Barnwell

Barnwell is described as a suburb of Cambridge in the Hundred Rolls. It lay to the east and south-east of the town centre, bordering on All Saints in the Jewry, Holy Trinity and St Andrew's parishes. Its church, Barnwell St Andrew (the less), is on the north side of the Newmarket road about a quarter of a mile south of the River Cam. It may have been founded in the early 13th century as a parish church in order to reserve the priory church for the use of the canons.[91]

Barnwell was very different from the other parishes in that local property consisted almost entirely of messuages and plots of land of varying sizes in the Barnwell fields. There were 86 messuages, two half-messuages, one house, one croft and one piece of vacant land. The main differences were between people who held several messuages and those who held only one. Most people owned a separate plot of land, and generally those who owned most messuages owned most land as well (though not invariably so). With a few exceptions, those who held messuages in Barnwell generally did not hold messuages in Cambridge as well. Neither did they hold land in the Cambridge fields. However, several people who held messuages in Cambridge held land in the Barnwell fields.

The largest holder of multiple messuages was Hugo Mainer, who held five.[92] Next came Hugo le Brun with four, John son of John le Crul with three messuages and a house, Hugo son of Geoffrey Fabro with 3.5 messuages and 12 other people with two.[93] Most properties paid rent to Barnwell Priory, as would be expected.

The first impression of Barnwell is that it was a predominantly rural parish, but it nevertheless ranked third in terms of professionals and sixth in terms of tradesmen (Table 3.3). The presence of professionals may be explained by the proximity to Barnwell Priory, while the presence of trade was connected with metal-working and agricultural services. Many of the property holdings were recorded as being bought from the priory, and a number still owed rents to the priory. It was common practice for many monasteries to establish or reorganize associated settlements in order to generate additional income, and it seems that Barnwell was laid out in the early 13th century as a planned development by the priory. There seems to have been similar redevelopment by the priory at Chesterton, a mile to the north-east of Cambridge, granted to Barnwell Priory in c.1200 and which had 80 messuages in 1279 (see Chapter 6). In both cases, it appears that the priory was capitalizing on the town's growing economic importance by converting part of its agricultural holding to residential use.[94]

3.12 Parish assessments

There is less material available to make comparisons of changes in wealth of the parishes. Taxes were usually levied on a ward basis rather than by parish: in Cambridge; there were ten wards referred to in Domesday Book and seven used for taxation in the early 14th century.[95] Several valuations were made, however, of the income of the English Church on a parish basis during the 13th century. Valuations of parishes for taxation purposes were based largely on tithe income, predominantly reflecting patterns of agricultural wealth. Town churches were relatively low in tithe income and income from glebe land, and more dependent on offerings at the altar, which were difficult to assess.[96] Nonetheless, in the absence of other data, they form a useful source for comparisons alongside the evidence from the Hundred Rolls.

The earliest valuations of parish wealth were simply estimates made by clergy as to the value of their livings, but in 1254 these appraisals were verified by rural deans, and in 1291 specially appointed assessors compiled a far more comprehensive valuation of ecclesiastical wealth. This *Taxatio*, as it became known, was used as the basis of assessment for all papal and clerical subsidies to 1523.[97] The chronicler of Barnwell Priory noted that the assessors of 1291 in the diocese of Ely of the spiritualities (the income from each benefice), did their work 'faithfully and carefully', in contrast to the 'evil' assessors of temporalities (ecclesiastical lands).[98] The pope carefully instructed all items of income to be included for taxation, including the smallest oblations for burial. Exemptions were also carefully listed though, and included rents and revenues of leper hospitals, houses of God and hospitals, whose income was reserved for the poor and sick. The other major exemption in 1291 was churches valued at 6 marks or less, although they would be included if they were held in plurality, that is, the benefice holder held other benefices and the overall annual income totalled more than 6 marks.[99]

Several Cambridge churches were excluded from the *Taxatio* in 1291, although some were omitted because their livings had been appropriated and served by vicars whose income was valued at 6 marks or less. The 1276 values, though, were given without any clarification regarding income divided between rectors, vicars, portion holders and pension holders. As the extent of exemptions may have varied between different subsidies, direct comparisons of value from different assessments are problematic, but assessments can be ranked to explore *relative* changes in the wealth of parishes. This is a technique that has been successfully used with records of lay taxation.[100]

Table 3.5 shows that although there are changes in the ranking of

Table 3.5: 13th-century valuations of Cambridge parish income

Parish	1217		1268		1276		1291	
	£	rank	£	rank	£	rank	£	rank
St Mary	6.67	1	12.00	1	6.67	1	10.00	1
St Bene't	5.00	3	10.00	3	5.33	3	6.67	3
St Giles	3.33	7	5.33	12	3.33	9	6.67	3
St Clement	5.33	2	11.33	2	3.33	9	4.67	5
All Saints by the Castle	3.33	7	1.00	15	3.33	9	4.67	5
St Andrew	3.33	7	9.33	6	3.33	9	4.17	6
St Botolph	3.33	8	9.33	6	5.33	3	2.67	7
St John	3.00	10	6.00	11	3.00	10	1.00	9
St Peter without the Gate	3.00	10	6.67	10	4.00	5	1.00	9
St Edward	2.67	12	6.67	10	2.00	13	0.67	10
St Michael	4.00	4	7.33	8	4.00	5		
Holy Trinity	1.50	15	8.00	7	1.50	14		
All Saints by the Hospital (in the Jewry)	2.00	13	9.33	6	2.00	13		
Holy Sepulchre	1.67	14	4.67	13	0.67	15		
St Peter by the Castle	2.67	12	4.00	14	2.67	11		

Sources: W. E. Lunt, *The Valuation of Norwich* (Oxford, 1926), pp 218–19, 538, 557; J. H. Denton, 'The 1291 Valuation of the Churches of the Ely Diocese', *Proceedings of the Cambridge Antiquarian Society* 90 (2001): 69–80

several parishes between assessments, certain trends stand out. St Mary's was consistently the wealthiest parish. The relative poverty of St Peter's by the Castle is clear. Indeed the relatively lower values of the other parishes north of the river (All Saints by the Castle and St Giles') is also evident in some assessments. The area to the north of the river was adversely affected by the construction of the Norman castle. The number of properties declined and the relative importance of the area continued to decline throughout the medieval period. Apart from the castle and the churches the main activities appear to have been agriculture and quarrying for gravel and marl. Archaeology has also uncovered some small-scale domestic occupation in this area.[101]

A similar pattern, with the poorer parishes on the periphery, remained in Cambridge in later centuries. As noted earlier, lay taxation within the town was usually assessed by wards. The ward boundaries are unclear, but Market Ward was always the wealthiest and most densely peopled, surrounding the market and including the parishes of St Mary, St Edward and (probably) St Benedict. Barnwell Ward was the smallest, and paid least subsidy, covering Newmarket road, and the parish of St Andrew the Less.[102] In 1664, the poorest parishes, with the largest percentage of households with single hearths, were St Peter's and St Giles', while the wealthiest was still Great St Mary's.[103]

3.13 Conclusion

The Hundred Rolls reveal that Cambridge had both a diversity and geographical concentration of occupations that were similar to those found in other medieval towns. Specialized and higher value trades tended to be found in the central parishes of the town. Trades that were particularly noisome were restricted to particular areas. Agricultural occupations tended to be found in more peripheral parishes. The Hundred Rolls reveal university members buying and selling property and bequeathing it to relatives. Town and gown were interlinked through the Cambridge property market as they were through so many other facets of the town's economy and society. These links have often been obscured by the exclusive focus of many historical studies of the town on the disputes and conflict between these two bodies.[104]

The parish profiles reveal that many of the trends found in Cambridge in the later Middle Ages, and even into the early modern period, were already evident in the late 13th-century town. Great St Mary's was the wealthiest parish, where the leading townspeople resided, and the base for two religious guilds that had the resources to found in 1352 their own academic college, Corpus Christi, albeit sited outside the parish. The relative poverty of the parish of St Peter's by the Castle is apparent. Certain parishes had a greater concentration of landholding by professions in 1279, and several of these were later to become the sites of colleges. St John's parish subsequently accommodated Trinity Hall, the initial site of Godshouse, and the second site of King's College, the latter necessitating the demolition of the parish church. St Michael's parish was where Michaelhouse and Gonville Hall were to be established. St Benedict's came to accommodate Corpus Christi College and St Botolph's Queens'. The colleges were not, for the most part, founded in the wealthiest parishes where traders were most concentrated. The town was already focused more on the marketplace than the riverside.

Notes

1   R. H. Britnell, 'Specialisation of Work in England, 1100–1300', *Economic History Review* 54 (2001): 1–16.
2   Richard Britnell, 'The Economy of British Towns 600–1300', *Cambridge Urban History* ed. D. M. Palliser (3 vols) I (Cambridge, 2000), pp 105–26.
3   Bryan and Wise, 'Reconstruction': 73–87.
4   H. Swanson, *Medieval British Towns* (Basingstoke, 1999), p 114.
5   Swanson, *British Towns*, p 24.
6   Edward Miller and John Hatcher, *Medieval England. Towns, Commerce and Crafts 1086–1348* (London, 1995), p 132.
7   Swanson, *British Towns*, p 114.
8   P. J. P. Goldberg, *Women, Work and Life Cycle in a Medieval Economy: Women in York and Yorkshire c. 1300–1520* (Oxford, 1992), pp 64–71.
9   Bonney, *Durham*, pp 161–8.
10 Justin Colson, 'Commerce, Clusters, and Community: A Re-Evaluation of the Occupational Geography of London, c. 1400–c. 1550', *Economic History Review* 69 (2016): 104–30.
11 Elizabeth Rutledge, 'Economic Life', *Medieval Norwich* ed. Carole Rawcliffe and Richard Wilson (London, 2004), pp 157–88.
12 HR 619, 755.
13 Bryan and Wise, 'Reconstruction': 84–5.
14 Bryan and Wise, 'Reconstruction': 83.
15 HR 770.
16 HR 561, 566. Bryan and Wise, 'Reconstruction': 82, 85.
17 Cambridgeshire Archives, City/PB Box 1/4 Cross Book, fols 8a–9a.
18 HR 590–1; *OED*: Whitesmith.
19 HR 619.
20 Bryan and Wise, 'Reconstruction': 83–5.
21 Atkins, 'Between River, Priory and Town': 7–22.
22 HR 59–60.
23 HR 26, 102, 111.
24 HR F24.
25 HR 7, 49, P35.
26 Bryan and Wise, 'Reconstruction': 75.

27 HR F28.

28 HR P25, P28, 224, 363, 469, 498, 674, 743.

29 BR, 21-41; VLAE, pp xi–xxvii.

30 *BRUC*, p 612; HR 161, 698, 845.

31 *BRUC*, pp 59, 167; HR 398, 691, 722–4, 755; BR, p 43.

32 *BRUC*, p 603; HR 635.

33 The bedel of glomery had the right to bear a rod or mace, but not at ceremonies involving the chancellor and the regent or teaching masters of the university. The university chancellor and regent masters had to attend the funerals of regent masters, non-regent masters and scholars, and suspend disputations on the day of burial, but this was not to apply to funerals of teachers of grammar, except on a voluntary basis, see VLAE, pp 20–3; Hackett (ed.), *Statutes*, pp 216–17; Nicholas Orme, 'The Medieval Schools of Cambridge, 1200–1550', *Proceedings of the Cambridge Antiquarian Society* 104 (2015): 125–36.

34 Orme, 'Medieval Schools': 127.

35 HR P26–7.

36 HR 579, 864.

37 *BRUC*, pp 259, 292; HR 697, 693.

38 *BRUC*, p 592; HR 458, 497–9, 697.

39 *BRUC*, p 189; HR 308.

40 *BRUC*, p 8; HR 178.

41 *BRUC*, p 501; HR 691.

42 *BRUC*, p 325; HR 238, 373.

43 *BRUC*, p 24; HR R1, 50, 163–8, 174, 199, 209, 297, 520, 566, 581, 592, 598, 719, A50.

44 *BRUC*, p 81; HR 692–3, 697.

45 *BRUC*, p 600; HR 205, 407.

46 *BRUC*, p 39; HR P26, 42, 162, 250, 291, 337–40, 364; SP, pp 6–8, 18, 34, 44–8, 62.

47 *BRUC*, p 307; HR 512, 660.

48 *BRUC*, p 321; HR A40, 716.

49 *BRUC*, p 353; HR P31.

50 *BRUC*, p 304; HR 500.

51 HR A46, 721. H. P. Stokes, *The Chaplains and the Chapel of the University of Cambridge (1256–1568)* (Cambridge, 1906), pp 3, 81.

52 *BRUC*, p 585; HR 491–3; Willis and Clark, *Architectural History*, iii, p 3, n 1; Stokes, *The Chaplains and the Chapel*, pp 5–7, 81, 88–91; Hackett (ed.), *Statutes*, pp 29–30.

53 Lee, 'A University Town'.

54 Lobel, *Atlas*, map 6.

55 VCH 3, p 123.

56 HR 2.

57 Christopher Brooke, *Churches and Churchmen in Medieval Europe* (London, 1999), pp 52, 71.

58 HR F 53.

59 Scales, 'Ragman Rolls', p 114.

60 HR R2.

61 StR 93a.

62 Rubin, *Charity*, p 107.

63 Cessford, 'The St John's Hospital Cemetery', p 57.

[64] Catherine E. Hundley, 'Holy Sepulchre, Cambridge in the Twelfth Century' (unpublished paper presented at the British Archaeological Association conference, Cambridge in 2018) argued that the church was originally a pilgrimage destination staffed by canons of the Order of the Holy Sepulchre, an order based in Jerusalem.

[65] VCH 3, p 124.

[66] HR 308.

[67] LB, pp 209–11.

[68] VCH 3, pp 129, 386.

[69] VCH 3, pp 129–30.

[70] HR P12.

[71] VCH 3, pp 128–9.

[72] OBG, p 13.

[73] Blackfriars, Cambridge, available at http://www.blackfriarscambridge.org.uk/medieval-priory/ (accessed 9 January 2018).

[74] HR A31.

[75] OBG, pp 9–10; VCH 3, pp 125–6.

[76] A 28/9.

[77] HR 1071.

[78] VCH 3, pp 124–5.

[79] VCH 3, p 126.

[80] Catherine P. Hall, 'In Search of Sabina: A Study in Cambridge Topography,' *Proceedings of the Cambridge Antiquarian Society* 65 (1973–4): 60–78.

[81] Brooke, 'Churches', pp 71–2.

[82] OTG.

[83] HR A43.

[84] OTG, p 23; Catherine P. Hall and Roger Lovatt, 'The Site and Foundation of Peterhouse', *Proceedings of the Cambridge Antiquarian Society* 78 (1990): 5–46, 12–15, 23–4.

[85] HR P35a; OTG, pp 58–63.

[86] A48/HR 297.

[87] OTG, pp 60–1.

[88] HR P25; HR P35.

[89] Hall and Lovatt, 'The Site and Foundation of Peterhouse': 12–15, 23–4.

[90] HR A44.

[91] VCH 3, p 126.

[92] HR 895–900.

[93] HR 996–1001; HR 943, 945, 946, 947; HR 960–3.

[94] Richard Newman, 'Planned Redevelopments in Medieval and Early Post-Modern Chesterton', *Proceedings of the Cambridge Antiquarian Society* 104 (2015): 89–106.

[95] VCH 3, pp 111–13.

[96] J. H. Denton, 'The 1291 Valuation of the Churches of the Ely Diocese', *Proceedings of the Cambridge Antiquarian Society* 90 (2001): 69–80.

[97] Maureen Jurkowski, 'The History of Clerical Taxation in England and Wales, 1173–1663: The Findings of the E 179 Project', *Journal of Ecclesiastical History* 67 (2016): 53–81.

[98] LB, pp 200–3.

[99] J. H. Denton, 'The Valuation of the Ecclesiastical Benefices of England and Wales in 1291–2', *Historical Research* 66 (1993): 231–50; W. E. Lunt, *The Valuation of Norwich* (Oxford, 1926).

[100] See, for example, John S. Lee, 'Tracing Regional and Local Changes in Population and Wealth during the Later Middle Ages Using Taxation Records: Cambridgeshire, 1334–1563', *Local Population Studies* 69 (2002): 32–50.

[101] Cessford and Dickens, 'Castle Hill': 95–7.

[102] VCH 3, pp 111–13.

[103] Nesta Evans, *Cambridgeshire Hearth Tax Returns Michaelmas 1664*, British Records Society Hearth Tax Series, 1; Cambridgeshire Records Society, 15 (London, 2000), p xlv.

[104] VCH 3, p 97; Alan H. Nelson (ed.), *Records of Early English Drama: Cambridge* (2 vols) (Toronto and London, 1989), p 707; Lobel, *Atlas*. For an alternative view, see John S. Lee, 'Monuments and Memory: A University Town in Late Medieval England', *Commemoration in Medieval Cambridge* ed. John S. Lee and Christian Steer (Woodbridge, 2018), pp 10–33, and John S. Lee, 'Trinity and the Town', *History of Trinity College, Cambridge* ed. E. Leedham-Green and A. Green, I: 1317–1742 (forthcoming).

4

Family Profiles

Introduction

This chapter uses the Hundred Rolls to reconstruct family dynasties of late 13th-century Cambridge, focusing on the transmission of property between generations. The families that feature in this chapter are not a representative collection of Cambridge families. They are families that achieved significant wealth through property holding. They either held substantial property or derived substantial rental income from properties held from them by others. To feature in this chapter a family had to hold at least four properties in 1279 and to have at least five members who were related to each other.

The Hundred Rolls present detailed information on the descent of properties, which often takes the narrative back to c.1200 or even earlier. This unique feature means that for each family a tree can be constructed showing how different individuals related to each other, both within the same generation, for example, as brothers and sisters, and between generations, as mothers and fathers, sons and daughters, uncles, aunts, and nieces and nephews. Some families rose to prominence during the period 1200–79, while others were in decline. Some peaked in their fortunes during the period, while others maintained stability. By comparing the profiles of different families it is possible to identify different groups of families that were at different stages of maturity.

Information from the Hundred Rolls has been supplemented from a wide range of additional sources, several of them specially translated for this purpose (see Chapter 1 and *Business and Community in Medieval England: The Cambridge Hundred Rolls Source Volume*). As a result, this chapter is exceptionally rich in detail. Some of the families have never been described before, while others have been described only partially and sometimes erroneously. The new evidence not only reveals new secrets but shows that several conjectures made by previous authors are false. But the amount of detail can be overpowering. Cambridge antiquarians will, we hope, be fascinated by the new evidence, but other readers may not. General readers may wish to skip this chapter on a first reading and proceed directly to Chapter 5, where thematic issues, such as family survival and success, are discussed. They can refer back to this chapter as required. Readers who wish to get a flavour of family life before they move on are recommended to study the histories of the Barton, Blancgernun, Dunning, Gogging, le Rus, Toylet and Aylsham families.

4.1 Methodology

There is a substantial literature on family reconstruction and an even larger literature on family history.[1] Most family historians work back from the present day, whereas this book works back from 1279. There are certain generic problems, however, that relate to the use of family names whatever the period. There are four main problems with the sources employed here.

Conflation. Two different people with the same name appear as one. This can occur when sons are named after their father. The problem can be detected from conflicting information, such as one being alive after the other has died.

Split personality. The same person has two different names. Apart from the issue of women and marriage, this can occur when people gain a nickname or become named after their occupation, place of origin or place of residence. Split personalities can be detected from the fact that both people have the same relatives and the same relationships to them.

Missing daughters. It is relatively easy to link parents with sons but not parents with daughters. Members of extended families regularly became related as in-laws through marriages, and while this may be clear in the male line it may be obscure in the female line. Sometimes it is necessary to postulate the existence of an unnamed daughter in order to explain relations between or within extended families.

Remarriage. High mortality rates mean that remarriage was common for both men and women even though divorce was virtually unknown. This creates particular difficulties when a man had children by different wives. Family tensions can be created by remarriage, as children of a previous marriage may be wholly or partially disinherited. Similar tensions arise when parents give properties to religious or charitable institutions instead of bequeathing them to their children. These tensions may lead to court cases that create records, but untangling from the records who was exactly related to whom can be difficult.

The basic principle used here has been to provide the simplest possible account that is consistent with the available evidence, making clear which evidence is taken to be reliable and which has been excluded as potentially unreliable. There are often 'alternative dynasties' that could be constructed by incorporating some of the more questionable evidence, but in the interests of simplicity these alternatives are not discussed in detail.

Records management

Reconstructing a single family over several generations can be a daunting task. Reconstructing all the leading families of a town is even more challenging. Medieval studies of population have examined family structures in specific settlements, but hitherto they have focused on small units such as manors and vills, and on rural rather than urban communities. Clarke, for example, used deeds conveying customary land to analyse family structures in Chesterton, a village adjacent to Cambridge, and constructed some partial family trees for families that appear in the present study.[2] Perhaps the closest analogue to the present study, though, is Kermode's analysis of Beverley merchants and their families; however, her analysis is confined to merchants and relies on sources such as guild records, which are not available for 13th-century Cambridge.[3]

While the Hundred Rolls have long been recognized as a valuable source, their systematic exploitation has been comparatively rare. Their main use has been to investigate the influence of tenurial systems on agricultural productivity.[4] Their use for family reconstruction was pioneered by Cicely Howell in her analysis of land ownership in the Leicestershire village of Kibworth Harcourt.[5] Her subsequent work on Cambridgeshire, however, was never completed.

Whatever the context, collating all the information from different sources on different families requires careful organization. Previous researchers on family structure have relied on card indexes or even coloured slips of paper.[6] This study uses computerized records management in place of card or paper. All the sources, both qualitative and qualitative, were entered into a single master document, which was then searched by keywords (e.g. family name, property location, occupation), and the output recorded in separate files. The only exceptions were the calendared deeds of St Radegund's Priory and the Hospital of St John, and the *Liber Memorandum* of Barnwell Priory, which were consulted in hard copy using their excellent indexes.

Computerization reduces a lifetime's work to six months' systematic study. This is obvious when the results are compared with those achieved by previous scholars such as Miller, Maitland, Stokes and Gray. Despite their best efforts, these fine scholars had no access to computer search algorithms, nor to the recent transcriptions and downloadable documents used in the preparation of this book. They could not reconstruct families with the same degree of accuracy as is possible today.

4.2 The family profiles: leading families

The Cambridge Hundred Rolls provide the most comprehensive coverage of any town in England, as noted earlier. As a result, 36 families can be profiled in detail. Together they were involved, in one way or another, with over half the properties in Cambridge. They are classified into three groups. There are 13 large families with significant pedigrees, and these have received most attention in previous literature. Next come ten successful families that made good through various strategies discussed in the following chapter. Last come 13 of the smaller families that are most typical but to some extent least interesting.

This chapter focuses on 23 of these families that between them illustrate almost all the features found in the full set of families. These families are of greatest intrinsic interest to the reader. They comprise all 13 large families and five each of the medium-size and smaller families. Within each group families are discussed in alphabetical order. Because this study is comprehensive and systematic, the 13 remaining families are described in the same amount of detail in Casson, Casson, Lee and Phillips, *Business and Community* at Appendix 14.

Barton dynasty

The Barton dynasty was extremely wealthy. Its most entrepreneurial member was John of Barton, who died in c.1274. He accumulated considerable property, which he left to his family. Barton is a village about 3 miles west of Cambridge, beyond the Cambridge fields. All the people that appear in the Hundred Rolls take their name directly or indirectly from John of Barton, but the rolls provide little information on John's ancestry. He may have been the son of William Barton.

John purchased most of his property himself, though a small amount was inherited. John owned several selds in the marketplace, including a property abutting on Smith Row and the chancel of St Mary's Church.[7]

Barton dynasty

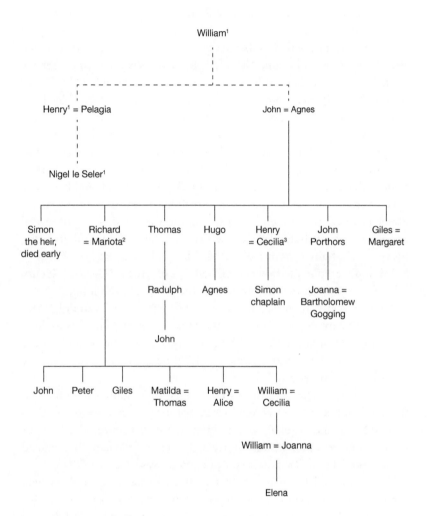

Notes:
[1] This part of the family tree is conjectural.
[2] Daughter of William Bagge.
[3] Daughter of Richard Laurence.

In 1236 he was in debt to the Cambridge Jews Isaac son of Samuel and Jacob son of Deulesaut for 12 marks.[8] John married Agnes, who survived him and was alive in 1279. She held land in Cambridge and in Madingley from Barnwell Priory.[9]

Henry of Barton was John's contemporary and possibly his older brother. Henry sold land in St Giles' parish to John and they witnessed deeds together.[10] Henry held a messuage and some land in All Saints at the Castle from Baldwin Blancgernun.[11] He lived in a house on the king's highway opposite the Hospital of St John; it was adjacent to a house that Alice, John Ruald's widow, gave to the hospital.[12] He sold a messuage to the Crutched Friars of Cambridge for a rent of 12d.[13] Henry married Pelagia and they had a son, Nigel le Seler, who was given land near the castle by the Hospital of St John that had previously been held by Henry from Baldwin Blancgernun.[14] Together with Eustace Eldcorn, Nigel was in debt to Isaac son of Samuel and Jacob son of Deulesaut for 20s in 1237.

John and Agnes had at least seven sons: Simon, Richard, Thomas, Hugo, Henry, John Porthors and Giles. Some of the sons and their descendants continued the family's involvement in the property market. Simon, the heir, was vicar of St John the Baptist's Church and became a very wealthy man, acquiring a large portfolio of property in the Milne Street area near the church.[15] In 1268 Simon was listed as one of several people who contributed land to the Friars of the Sack, the others being his brother Thomas, Maurice le Rus, Master Thomas son of Walter of St Edmund, Stephen le Bercher, Gilbert son of Michael Bernard, Henry Pikerel, and the master and brothers of the Hospital of St John.[16]

Thomas seems to have died young. He left a son, Radulph, who witnessed many deeds relating to the Hospital of St John.[17] Radulph's son John inherited a close and buildings called Lemanespichtel on the great street in Grantchester, which in 1279 he granted to Lucy, widow of William of Appelford.[18]

Master Hugo held land from the Hospital of St John. He continued the family support for local religious institutions by giving a messuage in Newnham to the hospital on condition that they paid him 12d for his lifetime and exempted him from paying 8d rent on the land that he held from them.[19] He had a daughter, Agnes, who was alive in 1279.[20]

Henry married Cecilia, daughter of Richard Laurence and his wife Sabina, who were themselves an important dynasty of property owners (to be discussed later). The couple lived opposite the Hospital of St John and had a son named Simon, who became a chaplain and was alive in 1279.[21]

Giles owned a great deal of property in 1279, accumulated through inheritance and purchase.[22] He purchased a messuage in St Clement's parish and was given by his father 18 acres of land in several plots in the fields around Cambridge. He died between 1307 and 1314, leaving a widow, Margaret.[23]

John, son of John, was known as John Porthors. He was bailiff at various times in the period 1273–7, and in 1282–3, 1286 and 1291, but apparently was never mayor.[24] John may have made a career out of property speculation as there is evidence that he bought and sold many properties in Cambridge and received rent from quite a few as well. He lived at one time in a stone house opposite the church of St Sepulchre, on which he paid a rent of 2.5 marks.[25] This house, it has been suggested, was one of several houses in this area that had belonged to the Cambridge Jews before their expulsion, and which were acquired in about 1276 by Robert of Fulbourn, chancellor of the university, who gave some of them to Barnwell Priory in return for the services of a chantry priest.[26] John's brother Henry lived in a neighbouring house.[27] John left 13d per annum from a messuage in All Saints in the Jewry to the nuns of St Radegund's to commemorate the souls of his parents.[28] John himself probably died in c.1312.[29] John's daughter Johanna married Bartholomew Gogging, creating a connection with another important local dynasty of property owners (discussed later).[30]

Richard of Barton became John's heir after the death of his brother Simon.[31] Richard acquired a great deal of property during his lifetime, inheriting relatively little from his father. Some of this property came from the Dunning family through Master Guy of Barnard Castle.[32] Richard married Mariota, daughter of Walter Bagge and his wife Johanna (daughter of Michael Malerbe).[33] Richard and Mariota had at least five sons and a daughter. Three of their children owned property in 1279: Peter, Giles and Matilda (also known as Maud).[34] It seems that their brother John was a goldsmith; he gave his property to his mother, who was by then a widow.[35] In c.1292 Peter gave an acre of land in Cambridge fields, along the Huntingdon road, to his brother Giles.[36] About the same time he gave 3 acres in the same fields to his sister Maud.[37] Also at this time Maud was left a messuage in Milne Street, opposite St John's Church, by her mother.[38]

The other two siblings were Henry and his brother William.[39] Henry of Barton is described as a goldsmith in a deed of 1295 and as bailiff in 1298.[40] He seems to have held a number of shops. It may be this Henry, with his wife Alice, who sold a shop in St Mary's parish. William married Cecilia, daughter of Walter Glaseneix, and they had a son, William junior; this William married Joanna and had a daughter, Elena.[41]

The Barton family was extensive, a situation that could have resulted in fragmentation and disputes over property. However, family members seem to have networked effectively with each other, particularly in the case of the brothers. The family had social standing in Cambridge, with brothers John Porthors and Simon holding positions of responsibility in the town and the local church. The family adapted well to the commercialization of Cambridge by retaining and enhancing their existing holdings. There are some indications that property may have operated as a business asset, perhaps as a security for John of Barton's debt in 1236.[42] There are also indications that the family's portfolio may have contained properties that had been used by others as security for loans; for example, some of Richard's property appears to been acquired as a result of the Dunning family selling their property because they had become encumbered with debt.

John and his sons Richard and John Porthors accumulated significant property on their own initiative. They appear to have succeeded by spotting opportunities in a commercializing economy. Some opportunities may have been more legitimate than others, as in 1274 Agnes (John's wife and mother of the seven sons) was accused, together with others, of concealing goods and chattels of Saulot the Jew, deceased, which were forfeit to the king.[43] After an inquest in Cambridge she was eventually acquitted.[44] Opportunities could also come from strategic marriages, as when Henry married Cecilia, daughter of the wealthy Richard Laurence.

The success of John and his seven sons also benefited the third generation. Three of the six children of Richard and Mariota, for example, owned property in 1279.[45] As well as supporting other family members, two members of the family were important patrons of religious orders; Henry of Barton (the Crutched Friars residing in Cambridge) and John Porthors (nuns of St Radegund's).[46]

Baldwin Blancgernun and his family

Edward Miller characterized the Blancgernun family as blending the roles of burgess and squire and suggested that they were more property owners than tradesmen.[47] They are one of the oldest Cambridge families to figure prominently in the Hundred Rolls. In the early part of the 13th century they held property along the Huntingdon road in the parish of All Saints at the Castle, along St Neots Way (the Bedford road), near the Barton road (towards Biggleswade) and down near the bridge in St Clement's parish.[48] They also had property in St Edward's parish near the Guildhall, in the market, and in Newnham. By the time of the Hundred Rolls, however, many of their properties were in the hands of other families, largely because Baldwin junior had sold property to cover debts.

The two key members of the family were Baldwin senior and his son Baldwin junior. Baldwin senior was the founder of the dynasty; he was possibly the 'man with the white moustache' referenced by the Norman family name. He supervised the repair of Huntingdon Castle for Henry II in 1174.[49] He held valuable land around a croft near the castle known as The Sale, and in the parish of All Saints at the Castle. In 1199 he acquired a messuage and 9 acres of land from Harvey son of Eustace (Dunning),

Blancgernun dynasty

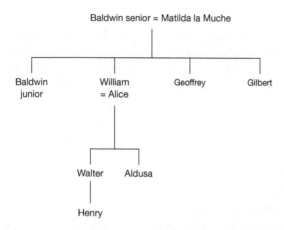

for an annual rent of 14d.[50] In the same year he petitioned against Aunger of Cambridge in a plea of land, and was also called to warrant for Martin Wulward in a case of morte d'ancestor against Absolon son of Absolon, suggesting a possible connection with those families.[51] In 1204 he was involved in a dispute over novel disseisin (recent dispossession) with Anketil son of Herbert and Juliana his wife.[52] Baldwin was tallaged for 10 marks in 1211, which was a very considerable sum, placing him in the top five of those tallaged in Cambridge.[53] He must have been genuinely wealthy, as he paid off nearly all of his tallage by 1224 (92 per cent, which is a higher proportion that most of his contemporaries). It should be noted that he was not tallaged in 1176–7, which suggests either that he was a newcomer at that time or, unlike many of his neighbours, was not involved in river trade.

A Baldwin Blancgernun held land in the village of Conington, in Papworth hundred. Some or all of his land there was granted to the Earl of Salisbury in 1216.[54] Baldwin still held some land there later, namely a quarter of a knight's fee, held from Picot the sheriff, on which he paid pontage.[55] Meanwhile in Cambridge Baldwin sold a messuage and some land in All Saints at the Castle to Henry of Barton, and a rent of 3s 2d to Geoffrey of Ely for 2 silver marks (an implicit interest rate of 12 per cent).[56] He gave 9 acres of land in the fields of Cambridge to the Hospital of St John in perpetual alms,[57] and in 1219 he gave the advowson of All Saints at the Castle to the Prior of Barnwell.[58]

Baldwin married Matilda, who was also active in property transfers. In c.1240 Matilda la Muche, described as the widow of Baldwin Blancgernun, sold property, probably in St Clement's parish near the bridge, to Henry of Barton.[59] In 1250 Matilda petitioned a number of tenants who occupied land that she was claiming in dower.[60] The couple had at least four sons: Baldwin junior, William, Geoffrey and Gilbert. They may also have had a fifth son, Absolon, but this is conjecture.

Baldwin junior is judged by the historian Miller to have been a failure; he suggests that he frittered away a substantial inheritance, borrowing from the Jews and selling off land to support an unduly extravagant lifestyle.[61] In 1230 he borrowed £11 from Maurice le Rus and gave 12.5 acres in the West fields as security for repayment within five years, but he was unable to repay. In 1223–31 he leased to Harvey Dunning a property adjoining the School of Pythagoras for 12 years for 22 marks and sold it to him outright in 1240–50 for an additional 34 marks.[62] In 1234 he owed two separate sums – £16 and 10 marks – to Jacob Crespin of London.[63] In c.1240 he borrowed £15 from Richard, the Master of St John's Hospital, to repay the Jews. The security was 30s 8d rent from Cambridge properties in the marketplace, Bridge Street and along the riverbank.[64] The ratio of the rent to the capital sum borrowed indicates an implicit rate of interest of 10 per cent. Baldwin also gave away a large amount of land, in particular to the Hospital of St John and to his relative Geoffrey.[65]

Baldwin (presumably junior) had a brother William.[66] William, it seems, was a merchant, who married Alice, and together they held land in All Saints at the Castle.[67] William and Baldwin held neighbouring plots of land near to the St Neots road, which they may both have inherited from Baldwin senior.[68] In 1228 William was sued for 3.5 marks of rent arrears by John of Stowe, and when he failed to appear the sheriff was ordered to attach him, but it seems that the bailiffs would not cooperate, and the outcome is unclear.[69] William was a generous benefactor of the hospital; he gave them a messuage and 20 acres of land that was held in fee from Ely Priory, and a messuage and 72 acres of land near a large wharf on the river.[70] William had a son, Walter, and a daughter, Aldusa, who became a nun at St Radegund's.[71]

Geoffrey Blancgernun, described as Baldwin's son, seems likely to be another of Baldwin junior's brothers.[72] This is consistent with Geoffrey and Baldwin junior sharing intertwined plots of land north of the river.[73] Geoffrey bought land and buildings near All Saints at the Castle from his father for the substantial sum of £1 per annum rent and 40s gersuma.[74] Geoffrey gave to the hospital a messuage in St Giles' that he had inherited from his father.[75] According to Miller, Geoffrey succeeded William to a family property in Doddington in 1251.[76] This would suggest that William was the elder of the two and died first. Miller suggests that Geoffrey was William's son, but this is inconsistent with a deed where Geoffrey is described as Baldwin's son.[77]

There is less information on the fourth son, Gilbert, but he held property near the market and sold a messuage in Cambridge in c.1262–70 to William of St Edmunds, whitesmith.[78]

Stepping down a generation, Walter Blancgernun was the son of Alice Blancgernun (and presumably her husband William) and held land near Coton.[79] Walter died before 1279 and his son Henry inherited his properties. These included a messuage at All Saints at the Castle, the gift of Baldwin, and properties he purchased himself, mostly from his neighbour Juliana, daughter of Thomas Longis, namely a house, another messuage, some vacant land and four plots of land in the Cambridge fields.[80]

It is difficult to know when the Blancgernuns first acquired their large properties around the castle and the river, but it seems quite clear that Baldwin senior played an important role in either creating or consolidating their position in the town. It is equally clear that Baldwin junior lost most, if not all, of what Baldwin senior had gained. He incurred debts and was forced to sell property to pay them off. It is possible that Baldwin junior's behaviour was perceived by his brothers to be damaging the family name and that they did not want to associate with him. Whatever the reason, each of Baldwin's sons seems to have followed their own inclinations. William was the only one of Baldwin senior's four sons who seems to have shown much initiative. Overall, Miller's judgements on the family are borne out by more detailed scrutiny.

Leon Dunning and his family

The Dunning family were one of the oldest in Cambridge. Dunning is a patronymic name that is almost certainly pre-Conquest in origin. Dunning, great-grandfather of Leon, who figures prominently in the Hundred Rolls, lived in Cambridge in c.1140 and held land there and in Chesterton. The Dunnings may have held land in Cambridge from the time of the Conquest.[81] Dunning's original residence may have been at Sale Piece, north of the Castle. He may have moved down to the river when the castle was built, or later, when Pain Peverel was Sheriff of Cambridgeshire. Gray considers Dunning to have been 'a man of wealth and consequence'.[82] His property included 15 acres of land and 10s 2d rent held from the Earl of Leicester, with liability for scutage; also a messuage with 45 acres of land and 50 shillings of annual income in the town and fields of Cambridge.[83] Dunning was a benefactor of Barnwell Priory, giving them 50 acres of land north of the river.[84] Other properties he acquired remained in the family and were passed down to

Dunning dynasty

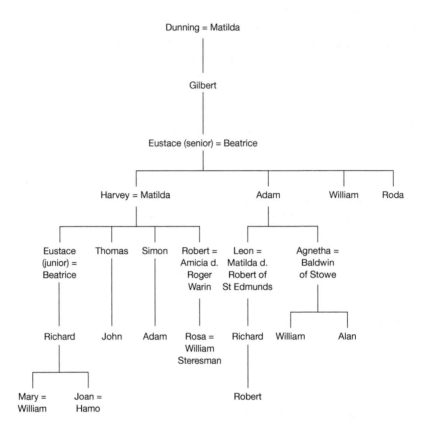

his grandchildren. However, poor management by Dunning's children and grandchildren meant that the family holdings were eventually acquired by the scholars of Merton residing in Cambridge and used to endow Merton College, Oxford.

Dunning married Matilda, and the couple had a son, Gilbert. Gilbert was well connected and possessed land in Little Gransden, Gamlingay and elsewhere.[85] He witnessed two important deeds: together with Nigel, Bishop of Ely, he witnessed a grant of land to St Radegund's Priory and, with Saher de Quincey, uncle of the Earl of Winchester, a grant of half a mark of rent to the same nunnery.[86] Gilbert and Saher fell out, however; in 1165; Gilbert was fined 10 marks in connection with a dispute between them.[87] Gilbert seems to have had little to do with the borough of Cambridge thereafter.

It seems that Gilbert had a son Eustace. Some accounts imply that Eustace was Gilbert's brother, but a genealogy in a contemporary writ implies that Eustace was Gilbert's son.[88] Eustace's son inherited a virgate of land from Gilbert in 1199.[89] In any event Eustace became Dunning's heir, either as his grandson, his elder son or his surviving son.[90]

Eustace married Beatrice and had three sons and a daughter, Roda, who entered St Radegund's nunnery. The three sons were Harvey, Adam and William. William appeared in court in 1199 as attorney for his brother Harvey.[91] Harvey and Adam seem to have been joint heirs, inheriting roughly equal amounts of property on the death of their father, although Harvey was the sole heir of Gilbert. Harvey (also known as Harvey Dunning, Harvey Fitz-Eustace and Dominus Harvey the Alderman) was alderman of the Gild Merchant shortly after it was chartered by King John in 1201. Harvey was mayor, it seems, in 1231.[92] He claimed the rank of a knight, and his seal was a mounted knight with a drawn sword. He lived in the stone house that is now within the precincts of St John's College and was later known as Merton Hall and then as the School of Pythagoras. He seems to have been a litigious person. In 1199, in the course of a legal dispute over his uncle Gilbert's lands in Gamlingay, Harvey challenged Geoffrey Picot to wager of battle; the battle never took place but Harvey successfully defended his claim.[93]

Harvey's inheritance included property in Babraham, Girton, Cheveley, Chesterton and Madingley, but much of it was later sold off.[94] In 1196 he sold a large amount of land in Newnham to William Ruffus.[95] In 1199 he sold land in Cambridge to Baldwin Blancgernun, and at the same time bought three messuages there from Michael Malerbe and another three from Harvey son of Edward.[96] In 1199 he gave land to Barnwell Priory. He also gave 7 acres of land to the Hospital of St John, and in return he and his heirs had rights to two beds in the infirmary and a chaplain to celebrate mass. He also gave houses and 15 acres of land in the Cambridge fields to St Radegund's, where his sister was a nun (mentioned earlier).[97] Harvey was tallaged for 5 marks in 1211.[98] In 1236 Harvey was in debt to the Jew Isaac son of Samuel, for 6.5 marks. Adam was in debt at the same time to the same person for 50s and a quarter of corn, and three years later he was in debt again for £15.[99]

Harvey and his wife Matilda may have had four sons.[100] Two are well documented: Eustace (the younger) and Thomas.[101] Harvey died in or before 1241 and his estate was inherited by Eustace, who was presumably his eldest son.[102] Eustace, like his father, incurred debts to money-lenders, but unlike his father the debts were large. He mortgaged a lot of his properties to Master Guy of Barnard Castle.[103] Eustace and Master Guy both died in c.1264–5, which was a troubled time in Cambridge, and Master Guy's property eventually came into the hand of his nephew, William of Manefield (see Chapter 6).[104]

Eustace's son Richard (d. 1278), meanwhile, sold a lot of the property he inherited, including the stone house, which was eventually acquired by Walter Merton for his college.[105] Richard had two daughters: Mary, who married William Drinkwater of Gamlingay, and Joan, who married Hamo of Croydon, Cambridgeshire; neither appears in the Hundred Rolls.[106] Eustace's brother Thomas was bailiff in 1263, and his son, John, was mayor in 1296–8, 1305, 1307 and 1309, and alderman of St Mary's Gild in 1309.[107]

The Hundred Rolls also identifies a Simon, son of Harvey Dunning, who in turn had a son, Adam. A fourth son may have been Robert Dunning, who held property from Leon Dunning as tenant-in-chief; he married Amicia, daughter of Roger Warin, and his daughter, Rosa, married William Stereman, son of Geoffrey Cissore.

Adam, Harvey's brother, is twice recorded as being in debt to the Jews. The first occasion has already been noted; the second was in 1239 when he owed £15 – a very substantial sum – to Jacob Crispin of London.[108] Adam married Olive and had a son, Leon, who figures prominently in the Hundred Rolls, and a daughter, Agnes, who married Baldwin of Stowe and had two sons, William and Alan, cleric.[109]

Leon (d. 1305) married Matilda, daughter of Robert of St Edmunds.[110] He seems to have had a reputation as a volatile character and never held civic office. He maintained his own court in Newnham, and refused to pay hawgable due on his properties to the bailiffs of Cambridge.[111] He allied himself with the dispossessed barons of the Isle of Ely and was pardoned for this in 1268. Leon's son Richard was a bailiff in 1300; Richard in turn had a son, Robert, who was bailiff in 1311, mayor in 1317, 1318 and 1323 and a Member of Parliament for Cambridge in 1320.

In 1336 a Robert Dunning licensed the sale of 5 acres of land to the nuns of St Radegund's.[112] After this date the family held little or no property in Cambridge and disappear from local records.

The Dunnings appear to have been an aristocratic family that had difficulty coming to terms with the Commercial Revolution in 13th-century Cambridge. The older generation seem to have acquired their property, at least in part, through military service. The younger generation typically inherited their property from the older generation, displaying little commercial acumen. Like Baldwin Blancgernun junior, they lived beyond their means, incurring debts and selling properties to pay them off.[113] Eventually they disposed of the ancestral properties in which they lived, and possibly left Cambridge altogether.

Luke of St Edmunds and his family

The Hundred Rolls trace the St Edmunds dynasty back to Robert of St Edmunds (d. by 1279), who witnessed many deeds in the first half of the 13th century. He was described as a clerk in a deed of 1246 and was mayor in 1258.[114] He is recorded as being in debt to the Jews for three consecutive years. In 1234 he was indebted to Jacob Crespin and Josce le Prestre for 100s, in 1235 to Isaac son of Samuel, Jacob son of Deulesant, and Aaron son of Isaac, for 2 marks, and in 1236 to Isaac son of Samuel, for 12 marks.[115]

Robert had at least three sons and one daughter. Matilda, his daughter, married twice; her first husband was Richard son of Gregory, and her second Leon Dunning, heir of the Dunning properties.[116] The first marriage produced a son, John.[117] It seems that Matilda retained some of her own property and may have been alive in 1279.[118]

St Edmunds dynasty

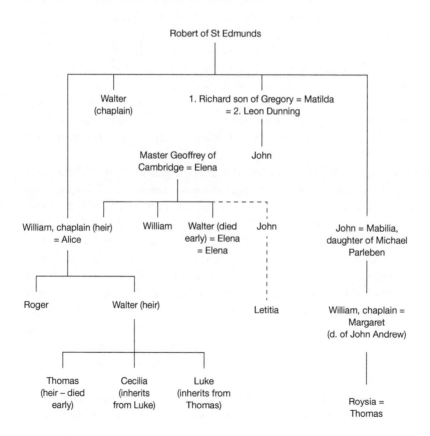

Robert's three sons were Walter, John and William, his heir. Walter, chaplain, seems to have been the poorest (perhaps the youngest) of the three. He purchased an acre of land in the fields of Cambridge, which he later gave to his nephew William son of John (discussed later).[119] He seems to have had no children.

John was a juror for the Hundred Rolls, and must have been quite old at the time.[120] He is probably the person described as a Canon of Barnwell, who appears twice in the *Liber Memorandum*, on the second occasion in connection with a legal case in 1298.[121] He inherited a small amount of land (1 rood) from his father.[122] In 1279 he held a messuage in St Sepulchre for the term of his life.[123] John probably became a canon in later life as he married Mabilia, daughter of Michael Parleben, a prominent townsman (discussed later), and they had a son, William.[124] William married Margaret, daughter of John Andrew, and had a daughter, Roysia, who married Thomas of Impington (a village close to Cambridge).[125] All of this suggests that although John was a juror, he was, like his brother Walter, not particularly wealthy.

The third son, William, was Robert's heir and married Alice, daughter of Master Geoffrey of Cambridge and his wife Elena.[126] Alice had a brother who died young, namely Walter, the heir, whose wife was also called Elena.[127] Walter held land in St Benedict's parish and a messuage and croft in Barnwell.[128] He confirmed the grant of the advowson of St Clement's to the nuns of St Radegund's made by his ancestor Hugh Absalon and previously confirmed by his uncle Walter (who was presumably Alice's deceased brother).[129] Alice also had a brother, William, who held 7 acres of land in the fields of Cambridge and whom she survived.[130]

William and Alice (son and daughter-in-law of Robert) held some valuable property, that was subsequently inherited by Leon Dunning. This included a messuage in St Peter outside Trumpington Gate and a horse mill in the marketplace with 70 acres of land in the fields of Cambridge, all inherited by Alice; for this they paid 2.5 marks rent to Radulph Pirot and Cassandria his wife by assignment of Lord Giles of Argentin, who held the advowson of St Benedict's Church by hereditary descent.[131] The couple had two sons, Walter junior (the heir) and Roger.[132]

Walter junior had at least three children: Master Thomas, Luke (d. 1282–4) and Cecilia.[133] Thomas (d. by 1279) was the heir, and when he died Luke succeeded him. Luke was a major property owner at the time of the Hundred Rolls. He possessed a large stone house, a court and a chapel – the chapel of St Edmund styled *ecclesia* and with a *custos* (warden).[134] These properties were located on the east side of Trumpington Street, roughly opposite where Peterhouse now stands. He also owned fields to the west. He was renowned for pious gifts. Later, Cecilia, his sister and heir, gave this estate to the Canons of Sempringham.[135]

The St Edmunds family are mainly noted for their religiosity and their charitable endowments. This activity was to a large extent funded out of the legacy of Robert, founder of the dynasty. Robert purchased three properties that he gave away to people with family connections: a messuage in St John's that he bought from Peter son of Radulph, and gave as dowry to his daughter Matilda on her first marriage to Richard Gregory; another messuage in the same parish that he gave as dowry on Matilda's second marriage to Leon Dunning; and a messuage in All Saints in the Jewry that he gave to William his heir.[136]

Robert was, without doubt, the most entrepreneurial member of the family. He acquired considerable property, but also seems to have been a risk-taker as he incurred significant debts along the way. As he sold very little property, however, it may be assumed that he was successful in paying off his loans. Robert's sons acquired additional properties, partly by purchase and partly through marriage. Following the death of Master Thomas, most of these properties came to Luke. In later years many of these properties were sold, often for quite high perpetual rents. This is reflected in the many properties paying rent to Luke of St Edmunds in 1279. Luke enjoyed a substantial income but no longer stood to profit from capital gains when property values rose.

Bartholomew Gogging and his family

The Gogging dynasty begins with Harvey, cleric, who became a canon of Barnwell Priory, probably late in his career.[137] He held a substantial amount of land from the priory, which eventually descended to his grandson Bartholomew.[138] He was almost certainly involved in commerce too; he was amerced, with his associates, for 6 marks in 1209 and tallaged for £2 in 1211.[139] He had two sons, Michael, who seems to have been the heir, and John (senior).[140] He also had a daughter, Isabella, who married William Morice and had a son Nicholas Morice.[141]

John (senior) had two children, a son and a daughter. His son Harvey (junior) married Matilda, daughter of Bartholomew Cissor and his wife Matilda, daughter of Geoffrey Potekine.[142] His daughter Sarah married Robert Wulward, son of Martin Wulward.[143]

Harvey (junior) and Matilda had a son, John son of Harvey, who was alive in 1279.[144] It was probably Harvey (junior) who was indebted to Isaac son of Samuel, and Jacob son of Deulesaut, for 30s in 1235; his son John had a similar debt the following year (possibly because his father

Gogging dynasty

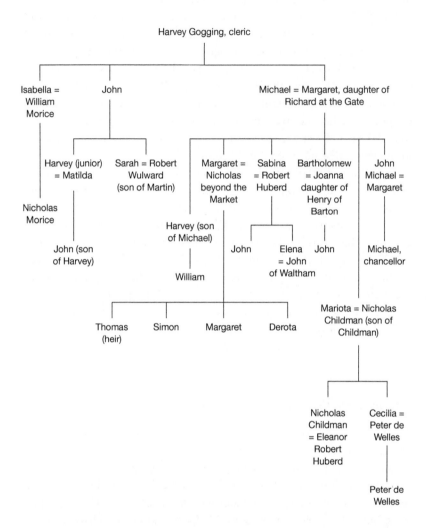

was unable to repay). John was again indebted (this time to Aaron son of Abraham of London) for 60s in 1239.[145]

Michael, the heir, married Margaret, daughter of Richard at the Gate, who was one of the wealthiest people in Cambridge (mentioned later). This marriage provided Michael with access to additional property through his wife, as she, along with her sister Sabina, inherited much of Richard's property as a result of the deaths of their other siblings. Margaret's sister, Sabina, married Richard Laurence, a wealthy landowner who was mayor on several occasions (discussed later). The couple had a son, Richard, and a daughter, Cecilia, who made a good match by marrying Henry of Barton, son of John of Barton (mentioned earlier). Henry and Cecilia had a daughter, Johanna, who married Michael's son Bartholomew, who was a blood relative through Margaret, Michael's wife.

Michael and Margaret had at least three sons and three daughters: Harvey, Margaret, Sabina, Bartholomew, Mariota and John Michael.[146] Bartholomew married Johanna, as mentioned earlier.[147] As the daughter of Henry of Barton, Johanna was related to John Porthors and probably to Eleanor of Gurney, who may have been her aunt; both these relatives provided dowries.[148] Bartholomew may have been in the cloth trade. He is described as a draper in the Cambridge eyre of 1260, owning a mill in St Bene't's parish and a messuage in the cloth market.[149] At some stage he became a clerk as well. Bartholomew was mayor of Cambridge on at least three occasions.[150]

In 1290 Bartholomew was accused of murder, along with three other men, one of whom was his relative Richard Laurence (or his son Richard Laurence junior). Bartholomew and Richard, both clerks, were acquitted by purging their innocence before the Bishop of Ely, but one of the other accused was hanged.[151] Bartholomew's goods and chattels, seized on his indictment, were valued at £42 14s 10d. There was considerable delay in getting them restored, even after the king had authorized it, because it was alleged that after being detained he had escaped from gaol.

Bartholomew and Joanna had a son, John, who became a bailiff in 1296.[152] It may be John who was accused of forgery in 1277.[153] The king ordered the sheriff to produce 'William, son of Bartholomew, mayor of Cambridge', to answer why he had delivered false plates, made of metal other than pure silver, to Benjamin son of Isaac, and Aaron son of Benjamin, who were now imprisoned in London. The bailiffs of Cambridge answered that there was no-one of that name, but the king replied that he would have Bartholomew and his son before the court anyway.

John (junior), also known as John Michael, was another of Michael and Margaret's sons.[154] John Michael married Margaret, and they had a son, Michael.[155] The father or son is described as 'chancellor', suggesting a connection with the law or the university.[156] Since John is elsewhere described as a goldsmith, and was probably bailiff in 1297, it seems likely that Michael was the chancellor.[157]

Margaret, daughter of Michael and Margaret, married Nicholas beyond the Market and they had four children: Thomas, the heir, together with Simon, Margaret and Derota, all three of whom were alive in 1279.[158] Simon, it seems, had a daughter, Sabina, who married John of Westwick.[159] Margaret purchased property from her grandmother, Margaret, widow of Michael Gogging.[160] The second daughter, Mariota, married Nicholas

Childman (son of Childman) and they had two children: a son, Nicholas, who married Eleanor, who survived him and died in 1279, and a daughter, Cecilia, who married Peter de Welles, and had a son, Peter, who was also alive in 1279.[161]

Michael and Margaret's third daughter was Sabina, who married Robert Huberd (d. pre-1285), a very wealthy man (mentioned later).[162] She had a son, John, and a daughter, Elena, who married John of Waltham.[163] In 1285 Sabina, Robert's wealthy widow, left a valuable property, Sedge Hall, on the River Cam near the Bridge, which possessed its own quay, to Bartholomew's son, John. Bartholomew was her brother-in-law and John her nephew. Sabina's right to dispose of the property in this way seems to have been challenged by Bartholomew's wife, Johanna, whose son was the beneficiary, although the matter was finally resolved in John's favour in 1292.[164]

Bartholomew was successful in accumulating wealth. The valuation of his goods when seized by the Crown was high when compared with other leading townsmen. In 1279 he held 5 houses and 22 acres of land. The houses were in St Botolph's, St Sepulchre and St Benedict's. He also held a stall in the marketplace, and had leased out a messuage in St Clements and a grange in All Saints at the Castle to his sister Sabina, widow of Richard Huberd.[165] Most of these properties were acquired from his relatives or his spouses, and most are recorded as gifts during the donor's lifetime. The most likely explanation is that he used his income, probably generated from various sources, to purchase property from relatives who had inherited properties but needed money instead.

Ivo and his family

Ivo is a mysterious figure. He had five sons who figure prominently in the Hundred Rolls. He is not Ivo son of Absolon, nor Ivo Pipestraw (mentioned later), nor Ivo Quarrel, a prominent member of the town community, but he could be Ivo carnifax, who was tallaged 2 marks in 1211, or Ivo son of Matilda, tallaged £1 at the same time.[166] What is fairly certain is that Ivo held 'a piece of land with a house situated above in the parish of All Saints (in the Jewry) above the water at Dame Nicholas Hythe', which remained in the family until 1279.[167]

Richard was Ivo's heir. He purchased a house in St Michael's jointly with Thomas Toylet, taking the western half, and Thomas then gave the eastern half to the Hospital of St John.[168] Richard had two daughters, one of whom, Alexandria, married William Eliot, a member of another influential family in c.1272–8.[169] Richard presented her with a handsome

Ivo and his family

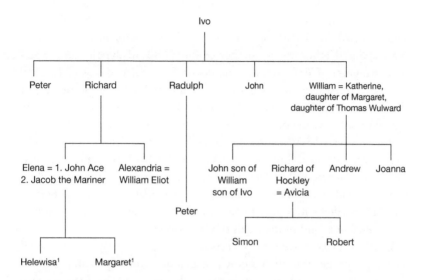

Note: [1] These daughters are from the first marriage.

dowry, comprising a stone house with solar and cellar and 3 acres and 1 rood of land in Cambridge and Barnwell fields.[170] The other daughter married twice. Her first marriage, to John Ace, produced two daughters, Helewisa and Margaret.[171] Her second marriage, to Jacob the Mariner, may have been childless.[172]

John son of Ivo gave a messuage to William Eliot on his marriage to Alexandria, his niece.[173] John's brother Radulph bought a messuage in the parish of St John Zachary from St Radegund's Priory, which his son, Peter son of Radulph, sold to Robert of St Edmunds.[174] Radulph's brother Peter son of Ivo, held land in St John's near the land of Absolon son of Roger the priest, and half an acre in Newnham that he purchased from St John's Hospital for a rent of 6s and 16s gersuma.[175] The land was between Trumpington Street and the river, and carried summer and autumn services of hoeing and harvesting. He granted this, in c.1258, to his daughter Katherine. The two relevant deeds were witnessed by three of his brothers: Richard, William and John. In 1279 Anglesey Priory held 5s rent from a messuage formerly of Peter son of Ivo, suggesting that Peter may have been dead by this date.[176]

William was the most successful of the five sons, acquiring an impressive portfolio of properties, including several purchased from members of the Dunning family.[177] These included two granaries, one in St Michael's and the other in All Saints in the Jewry, and about 14 acres of land distributed widely in the fields around the town.[178] He bought land from Radulph de Trubevill, who was connected with the le Rus family.[179] In 1249–50 he was defendant in a court case instigated by Margaret, widow of Michael Parleben (mentioned later). William made a good marriage to Katherine, a member of the Wulward dynasty and great-granddaughter of Wulward, the founder of the dynasty (discussed later).[180] They had three sons and a daughter. All inherited some property. Two of the three sons sold off some of their inheritance; John inherited a granary, which he sold to Nicholas Morice,[181] while Andrew sold off both a house and a messuage.[182] William's daughter Johanna sold some of the land she inherited to the third son, her brother Richard. Richard, who was known as Richard of Hockley, married Avicia, daughter of John Bradley, and they had two children, Simon, the principal heir, and Robert.[183] Simon inherited a messuage in St John's while Simon and Robert jointly inherited some land in the fields of Cambridge.

The sons of Ivo owe their success to a first generation that occupied a strategic property in the commercial area of Cambridge and produced five sons, and a second generation that included a dynamic entrepreneur. Of the five sons, Richard, the heir, added little to his father's inheritance and concentrated on marrying off his daughters. In contrast, William acted as the entrepreneur, focusing on the grain trade.[184] However, Ivo's other children and grandchildren chose to dispose of their inheritance.

Richard Laurence and his family

The Laurence family's holdings appear to have been accumulated by Laurence of Littlebury, who held substantial lands in Chesterton from the Prior of Ely.[185] Littlebury is a small parish near Saffron Walden in north-west Essex, about 15 miles south of Cambridge and lying on the medieval London road. Laurence's inheritance included 2.5 acres of land that he gave to St Radegund's Priory in exchange for an equal amount of land elsewhere.[186] In 1199 he petitioned a plea of land against Aunger (le Rus) of Cambridge.[187]

Laurence married Isabella, daughter of Robert Seman, and the couple had a son, Richard, who became a major property owner in both Cambridge and Chesterton. Isabella's dowry included a messuage in the parish of St Peter at the Castle, which Richard inherited and sold to Robert Wymund.[188] Richard also inherited a messuage at Holme from his father, together with two messuages in Holy Trinity and half a messuage in St Edward's parish.[189]

Richard Laurence and his family

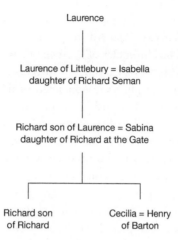

Laurence

Laurence of Littlebury = Isabella
daughter of Richard Seman

Richard son of Laurence = Sabina
daughter of Richard at the Gate

Richard son   Cecilia = Henry
of Richard   of Barton

He also inherited his father's land in Chesterton (see Chapter 6),[190] and he made purchases, such as a house in the parish of All Saints at the Castle.[191] Richard held rights of pasture over the meadow near St Radegund's, and built a bridge over the King's Ditch, to move his cattle to and from the pasture.[192] The bridge was regarded as a public benefit in some accounts and as an encroachment on common land in others. Richard seems to have had high standing in the town, serving as mayor in 1263, 1270 and 1278 and bailiff in 1283.[193] He witnessed many deeds over the period 1245–85, especially with respect to lands acquired by the scholars of Merton.[194]

Richard married Sabina, daughter of Richard at the Gate and sister of Margaret, who married Michael Gogging (previously mentioned). Richard and Sabina had a son, Richard, and a daughter, Cecilia, who married Henry of Barton.[195] His son seems to have been known first as Richard son of Richard Laurence, then as Richard Laurence junior and finally as Richard Laurence, possibly after his father's death. Cecilia had an 'uncle Wade' who may have been Richard's younger brother.[196]

In 1280 Richard (senior or junior) was a tenant of John le Rus when John died in debt to the Jews. In 1295 he held a messuage at Holme from Barnwell Priory. A deed of c.1305 shows that Richard (junior presumably) held a tenement adjoining that of Aunger; the same deed refers to a meadow of the nuns of St Radegund's in Grenecroft and the adjoining *curia* of Richard Laurence.[197] This may have been the same land concerned in the plea of 1199 already mentioned.

In 1290 a jury reported that Richard held in chief 54 acres of arable land in the fields of Barnwell, yielding the priory an income of 18d and sale value of 20s, and also held 3 acres of meadow fit to mow yielding 2s income with sale value 24s (an implicit rate of interest of about 8 per cent in both cases).[198] That year Richard (or possibly his son) was convicted of a serious crime. The chronicler of Barnwell Priory reports that two of their tenants, Richard son of Laurence, and Robert of Withersfield (in north Suffolk near Haverhill) were convicted of felony and their lands escheated to the priory.[199] Richard, described as a clerk, is said to have been convicted of the murder of Geoffrey de Griseleye, and Robert was hanged in connection with the same. In fact Richard had been charged but was acquitted after purging his innocence before William of Louth, Bishop of Ely, in accordance with the benefit of the clergy. Bartholomew Gogging (a relative by marriage) was also charged and acquitted for this crime (as noted earlier). Richard's goods and chattels, valued at £26 9s 1d, were restored to him four years later.[200] In 1295 Richard remained in possession of the tenement in Cambridge that he held from the priory.[201]

Richard's career is difficult to assess because it is not easy to distinguish him from his son. Richard senior was of minor aristocratic parentage and added properties to his inherited portfolio. He built a bridge for the benefit of himself or the town, or possibly both. He seems to have enjoyed the respect of his peers, as he was mayor on several occasions.

Michael Pilat/Pilet/Pylat/Pylet/Pilate and his family

Michael Pilat, who was active at the time of the Hundred Rolls, took his name from his mother's side of the family, from whom he derived much of his property holdings. However, he also benefited from property holdings accumulated from his father's side of the family, including property purchased in Fordham in 1208/9.[202] Michael was the son of Reginald of Fordham and his wife Margaret.[203] Michael's father inherited property from his father, Reginald of Fordham senior.[204] The family were relatively wealthy, as Reginald of Fordham was tallaged for £1 in 1211 and amerced half a mark *pro fuga* (for flight) in 1219.[205]

However, the most significant property holding came from Margaret, Michael's mother. Margaret was the daughter of William Pilat and his wife Mabilia.[206] On her marriage her father gave Reginald of Fordham, his son-in-law, a messuage in St Edward's parish, 5 acres in Trumpington meadow and half an acre in the Cambridge fields. William's wife Mabilia may be the person later described as Michael's 'friend' who left property to him.[207] William Pilat acted as attorney for the burgesses of Cambridge

Michael Pilat/Pilet/Pylat/Pylet/Pilate and his family

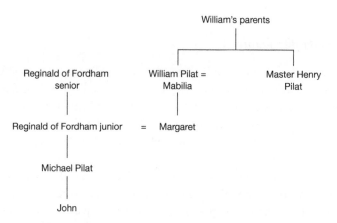

in 1232 in a dispute concerning Sturbridge Fair, which was resolved by the Prior of Barnwell paying the burgesses half a mark annually in respect of their rights.[208] He held an estate in the Jewry that he acquired in parts, probably from 1210 onwards.[209] This estate was centred on Pilat's Lane, possibly named after the family, connecting High Street (St John Street) to Conduit Street (Sidney Street), and now known as All Saints Passage.[210]

Michael held a messuage from Barnwell Priory opposite the hospital gardens and a grange near the church of All Saints at the Castle.[211] He gave a messuage in St Peter's at the Castle and 4 acres in the fields of Cambridge to Thomas Godeman, and also purchased a messuage in St Clement's from him.[212] He also derived rents from a messuage in St Sepulchre, which was divided into two portions.[213] Michael gave land to Barnwell Priory in 1272.[214]

Michael was a bailiff in 1273, 1282 and 1286, a 'guardian' of the town (together with John Butt) in 1290 and mayor in 1293, and joined the Guild of St Mary before 1300.[215] He served as one of the borough's representatives in Parliament in 1302, 1305 and 1311. Records from 1303/4, 1304/5 and 1314/15 suggested that he lived in St Clement's parish.[216] Michael's son John became a leading citizen.[217] He was mayor in 1330 and 1332 and witnessed many deeds between 1300 and 1340.[218]

William Pilat and his grandson Michael were the driving forces in accumulating the family wealth. The main beneficiary was John, whose inheritance allowed him to occupy prestigious roles in the town community from 1300 onwards. Michael may have taken his mother's name, perhaps at William's insistence, in order to obtain William's inheritance.[219] The Pilats were a small and cohesive family. They performed consistently well in terms of maintaining wealth and reputation from one generation to the next.

le Rus/Ruffus family

The name le Rus is linked to Ruffus and traditionally has meant 'red hair'. It seems to have been a name particularly favoured by leading families that aspired to knightly status. Its cachet in England may have originated from William Rufus, younger son of William the Conqueror and his short-lived successor on the throne. However, William Rufus had no direct descendants.

Relations between the le Rus family are difficult to disentangle as there seem to have been several families with the same name – or different branches of the same family – living in different parts of the country. Early Pipe Rolls, for example, refer to Geoffrey, Hubert, Milo, Radulph, Reginald, Robert, Godard and Ernaldus.[220] One branch of the family, led by Eustace of Madingley, originated in Madingley and was well established in Cambridge by 1200. Another branch, led by Aunger, originated in the town but may have been connected to the Madingley branch, while a third, led by William and Simon, originated in a group of villages about 12 miles west of Cambridge, namely Clopton, Bassingbourn, Eversden and Mordon (present-day Steeple Morden and Guilden Morden).

The family members who appear in the Hundred Rolls are descended mainly from Eustace of Madingley. Madingley is a village about 2 miles to the west of Cambridge, south of the Huntingdon road and to the north of St Neots Way. Eustace of Madingley had at least two sons, Albric (or Aubrey) and Eustace.[221] Albric married Mabilia and they had a son Maurice, who in turn had a son John.[222] Albric was apparently one of the first members of the family to be named Ruffus, possibly because he had red hair. He was amerced at Cambridge in 1177 for 1 mark as part of a general levy on Cambridge merchants for unlicensed import or export of corn.[223] Albric held land in St Clement's that was later the *curia* of Richard Laurence (previously mentioned), and by 1220 this property was in the hands of his son Maurice.[224] It seems that Albric was in debt to the Jews when he died. Maurice was accused of taking land from Albric's estate that should have reverted to the king, but the inquest found that the land had been held by Maurice from before his father had incurred the debt, so that it was not a gage of the king.[225] Notwithstanding this decision, Maurice paid the king 1 mark 'for the Jews' in 1223.[226]

Maurice seems to have been an only son. He was probably born before 1175 and may have been dead by 1232, in which year his son John was active.[227]

le Rus/Ruffus dynasty

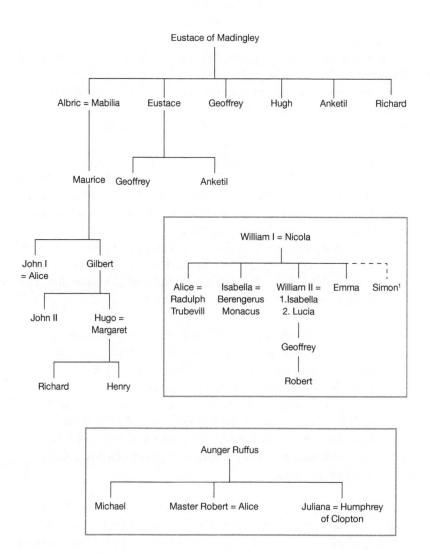

Note: [1] denotes possible link.

He held property in All Saints in the Jewry and 5 acres in the fields of Cambridge. He gave 15 acres of land to the Hospital of St John.[228] He gave land in the Jewry 'towards Barnwell gate', which suggests that Jews lived not only near All Saints' but also near St Andrew's.[229] He also gave 12d. per annum to the nuns of St Radegund's in c.1208 to compensate them for the loss of income to their parish of All Saints in the Jewry when chantry and burial rights were given to the hospital.[230] Maurice lived in a large stone house on the west side of the Trumpington road near the present site of the Fitzwilliam Museum. Adjacent to this, in c.1245, he built a private chapel dedicated to St Lucy.[231] It was inherited by his son John, who gave it to the Friars of the Sack in 1259 (discussed later).[232]

It seems that Maurice had two sons, John, the heir, and Gilbert, who held property in Oakington from the Prior of Barnwell.[233] John le Rus I, the heir, was probably mayor in 1249–50, and possibly in other years too.[234] He sold 28 acres of land and a croft to Thomas Toylet, which Thomas gave to Barnwell Priory.[235] He is recorded in the fines for Cambridgeshire in 1232, 1240 and 1248.[236] He was in debt to the Jewish moneylender Jacob Crispin of London for 50s in 1234.[237] In 1253 he offered himself against Isaac, son of Moses of Cambridge, touching a plea of account; Isaac did not appear and the case was deferred.[238]

John married Alice, but it seems that they had no children.[239] In 1259 John gave his principal messuage near to his chapel on Trumpington Street to the Friars of the Sack, who had recently arrived in Cambridge. This led to a controversy with Prior Jolan of Barnwell:

> The Friars of the Sack purchased the principal messuage of John le Rus opposite the chapel of St Edmund, but this messuage belonged to the fee of the canons of Barnwell. Prior Jolan impeded their right of possession. Then came John le Rus with his brothers to the Prior and petitioned with tears for his license and permission etc. And he referred to a charter of 1258 in which his tenure was recognised for 28s.11d annual rent and obligations regarding his horse mill in Milne Street etc.[240]

Gilbert, John's brother, had two sons, John II and Hugo.[241] John II, like his father, had dealings with the Jews.[242] He seems to have had no children. He was dead by 1279, and Hugo became the heir.[243] Hugo married Margaret, daughter of Louis, and they had two sons, Richard son of Hugo, and Henry Eliot (mentioned later).[244]

John's last recorded activity seems to be a final concord concluded with Josce son of Robert, in 1262.[245] His horse mill in Milne Street was inherited by Hugo. Hugo also received Heycroft, a 10-acre property in Trumpington that he sold to the But family. He was known as Hugo le Rus of Oakington in 1279 and in 1306.[246]

Hugo was involved in a curious incident involving a mill.[247] The mill paid a heavy rent to the Prior of Barnwell and had fallen into ruin. Hugh therefore disassembled it and moved it to a new site near to the student hostel of Guy Mortimer. The prior took Hugo to court, and won his case:

> John son of Maurice le Rus held many tenements in Cambridge from the Prior of Barnwell and much land in the fields, and he used to render 28s.11d. rent. However John sold off much of his land in small portions. Eventually John obliged the Prior to reduce the rents or to distrain the mill. On his death he was succeeded by his nephew Hugo le Rus. The mill was ruinous and owed much rent. Hugo uprooted it and carried it off, with grinding stones and wheels, to the residence of Guy, rector of Kingstone, and deprived the prior of his rent.[248]

Richard son of Hugo had a more serious brush with the law. Roger of Ely claimed that Richard entered his house in Cambridge on the evening of 18 January 1257, at about the hour of vespers, and attacked him with a knife. The Bishop of Ely's official, who was present in the court, claimed him as a clerk. Before delivering him to the bishop, however, the jury pronounced him guilty.[249]

The second branch of the family was headed by Aunger le Rus.[250] In 1179 land of Aunger along the quayside in Cambridge was escheated to the Crown, and Wulward of Cambridge was accused of detaining some of the rent.[251] The land was subsequently rented to Simon de Insula on behalf of the king. In 1199 there were a burst of litigation involving the lands of Aunger, which suggests that he may have died and been succeeded by a son of the same name.[252]

Aunger lived just south of the river in St Clement's parish. He purchased a large amount of property and left much of it to his son Master Robert Aunger, who married Alice.[253] This included 41 acres of land that Aunger had purchased from Baldwin Blancgernun.[254] Out of his inheritance Master Robert gave a property portfolio generating 5 marks rent annually to maintain a chaplain to say masses in St Clement's Church.[255] He also gave 15 acres of land in fields south and west of Cambridge to Hugo le Rus.[256] He was also involved in a curious transaction in which he offered rent to the nuns of St Radegund's from his own property in substitution for an equal rent from someone else.[257] He was linked to the scholars of Merton; in 1272 he concluded a final concord with their master, Peter of Abington, regarding properties in Cambridge and Chesterton.[258] In the same year he also recovered a messuage from Barnwell Priory.[259] He may also have been linked to Lord Aldo Pirot.[260] Aunger had another son, Michael, who witnessed a will in c.1235.[261] Aunger's daughter Juliana married Humphrey of Clopton (a village near Croydon, Cambridgeshire, now deserted).[262]

The third branch of the family originated with William le Rus, who was active in Cambridge in 1178 and 1180, at about the time that Albric and others were amerced. It is possible that they were brothers. He was acquitted of 16s 4d of the farm of Cambridge borough in 1178 and Robert de Hou, his man, of Norfolk, was pardoned 11s 8d at the same time for a fine that had been taken from him at the Cambridge Assizes. William's acquittal continued until his death, when it was extended, it seems, to William his heir.[263] It is possible that this land was acquitted of fee farm rent because it was used for some civic purpose (possibly as the quay); on the other hand, it could simply have been a reward for services to the king.

William was an itinerant royal justice. He came to the bench by way of the domestic side of the royal household, becoming a chamber officer.[264] In about 1175–6 he was made *custos* of Berkhamstead Castle. At this time he was involved as king's justice in eyres in Wiltshire, Somerset, Devon and Cornwall.[265] The following year he was busy raising aids from boroughs and towns in the south-west.[266] He continued as a justice in the south-west until 1180.

Like several other justices of Henry II, he served also as sheriff.[267] In 1179 he became Sheriff of Bedfordshire and Buckinghamshire, a role he sustained for many years. By 1182 he had gained the higher rank of *dapifer Regis*, a title he bore for the rest of Henry's reign.[268] William married Nicola, and had three daughters, Alicia (possibly the eldest), Isabella and Emma, and at least one son, William II.[269] Alice married Radulph de Trubevill, Isabel married Berengerus Monacus and Emma married Bartholomew de Lega, who died before 1195.[270] Nicola, it seems, brought property in Cambridge as part of her dowry, along with property in Hemingford and Gilling. In 1220 there was a disagreement between Emma and Alice over the distribution of inheritance from the respective holdings of William and Nicola his wife, and this reignited in 1243.[271]

William may have been a relative of Richard Ruffus, who became royal chamberlain in 1168. Richard appears in the Pipe Rolls only five years earlier than William, which suggests that, if related, he was an elder brother.[272] Richard had property in Hinton (Himmedon), Wiltshire, and William seems to have had strong connections with that county as well. Richard may have had a son, known as William son of Richard, who also became a justice and served with William himself on a Lincolnshire eyre.[273] William and Richard may have been related to Herbert Ruffus, who was also a royal administrator. Herbert Ruffus was described as *serviens meus* in a royal grant of 1159.[274] He was responsible for £8 of royal expenditure in Staffordshire in 1160–1.[275] He seems to have been much older than either William or Richard, as he disappeared from the records at this time.[276]

In 1194 William accompanied the king's army on an ill-fated campaign to recover Normandy.[277] At the same time he sold 1 acre of land and 3s rent to Harvey son of Eustace (Dunning), possibly to finance his trip.[278] He appears to have returned the following year in bad health because he died in 1195 near Southampton, probably on his way home from Normandy. The hundred of Redbridge, near Southampton, was fined 40s for concealing the details of his death.[279] Shortly before he died in 1195 William bought 50 acres of land and a 3s rent in Cambridge from Harvey son of Eustace (Dunning), for 60 marks of silver.[280] William died owing a considerable sum in respect of the sheriff's farm for Buckinghamshire and Bedfordshire.[281] It seems that William son of Richard was responsible for settling some of these debts.[282]

William was succeeded by his son William II (d. c.1250), who was possibly a minor. By 1204 his father's debts were still outstanding and it was reported that Ralph de Trubevill, Alice's husband, had custody of him.[283] William II succeeded to the Cambridge property. In c.1207–12 he witnessed a deed in Cambridge, on which he was described as a clerk of the Treasury.[284] In 1209 he married Isabella, daughter of Gilbert Archer, but by 1228 he was married to Lucia.[285] William II seems to have had great social ambition. He held a half-fee in Bassingburn in the honour of Boulogne, 1212–17, which he may have acquired through profits made in royal service.[286] He seems to have been doing well because he excused himself from other obligations: in 1230 he owed 40s scutage for avoiding military service and half a mark for withdrawal from the assizes.[287] In 1235 he was pardoned by the king for trespass, with the qualification that he could stand trial if others proceeded against him.[288] On his death, c.1250, William held 1 hide in chief for a half-fee. He also held 1.25 hides in Clopton of the Abbot of Lesnes for a fifth fee and 50s per annum. and 1.25 hides of William de Cheyni for a fifth fee and 60s rent.[289] He was succeeded by his daughter Alice.[290] There is also a reference to William Ruffus, possibly his son, holding property in Wilbraham in 1254.[291] It should be noted that Aunger le Rus's daughter married Humphrey of Clopton, suggesting a connection between Aunger and William, and therefore between the two branches of the family.

Geoffrey le Rus, William's heir, was about 36 years old when he succeeded him.[292] He may have been an attorney as he represented William in court in 1228. In 1262, he made a final concord involving property in Clopton.[293] Geoffrey le Rus died in c.1267; he held at his death a half-fee in Clopton of the honour of Boulogne, rendering yearly to William de Cheney of Mordon 60s and to the Abbot of Lesnes 50s. He also held a half-fee of the honour of Boulogne in Bassingbourn, for which he paid suit twice yearly at St Martin le Grand.[294] Geoffrey's heir was his four-year-old son, Robert.[295] The wardship and marriage of heirs for the manor of Bassingbourn was granted to Hugh de Bruey, king's yeoman, and was valued at 100s per annum in 1276.[296] In 1276 Robert, presumably then of age, sold his tenement in Clopton to Hugh of Clopton.[297]

The le Rus family continued living in Cambridge. A William le Rus was mayor in c.1279.[298] In c.1293 Michael le Rus, son of John Michael, sold an acre of land in Barnwell Fields and about three years later he sold a further rood of land.[299] In 1364 Alice le Rus and her three children, John, Margaret and Isabella, leased out a dovehouse and curtilage in St Clement's with free access to fetch water in Nun's Lane.[300]

Unlike some of the other great families already described, the different branches of the le Rus family kept their distance from each other, to the point where it is unclear whether they were actually related or not. One branch, headed by Eustace of Madingley, produced the religious patron John Rus, whose piety and virtue were not transmitted to his nephew Hugo and his heirs. The second branch, founded by Aunger, gained reputation through the administrative abilities of Master Robert who, like John le Rus, was a major patron of religious institutions. The fortunes of the third branch were built in royal service. William le Rus was a pioneering justice in eyre, who developed close connections with the court of Henry II. He may have been born in Cambridge or he may have established a connection through his marriage; there must be some reason why he gained possession of a valuable property in the town that was quit of fee farm. Although the connections between the three branches were weak, their members had quite a lot in common, namely an orientation to administrative activity and institutional patronage. Their early wealth was acquired through royal service. The later generations were stewards of wealth; in so far as they disposed of their inheritance, they did so deliberately, to good causes. By the time of the Hundred Rolls, however, the management of debt in one branch of the family had become a serious problem.

Robert Seman and his family (also Wymund)

The Seman family is complex because there were two different branches of the family with different names: Seman and Wymund. Robert Seman and Walter Wymund were brothers. Six generations are recorded, during

Robert Seman and his family (also Wymund)

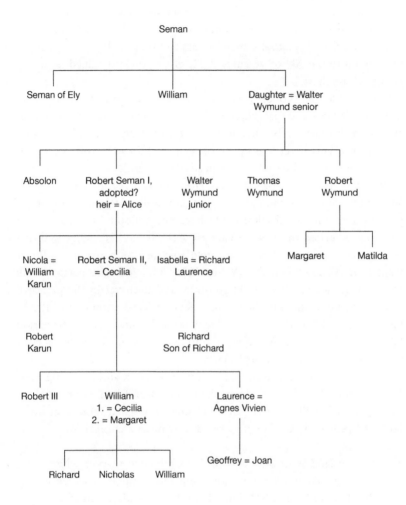

Notes:
[1] Walter Wymund senior may be the husband of an unspecified daughter of Seman or a widow of Seman of Ely or William.
[2] Vivien is transcribed as Fixion in the printed edition of the Hundred Rolls (see F, p 601).

which grandfather, father and son were named Robert; they are identified below as Robert I, II and III respectively.[301]

The Seman dynasty can be traced back to Seman. Seman can be identified with either Seman of the Bridge, who was the king's viewer of the castle during rebuilding work in 1172–3, or with Seman of Trumpington who, somewhat earlier, in 1165, owed 4s 1d to the treasury.[302] Seman had at least two sons, Seman of Ely and William, and may also have had a daughter, who may have married a man named Walter Wymund.[303] Seman of Ely, possibly a cleric, held a property in the parish of St Peter at the Castle, the rent on which was paid in 1279 to Robert Seman III's heirs.[304] His other son, William, inherited a messuage in St John's from his father which he sold to Philip de Burgelun, who in turn sold it to the Abbot of Titley.[305] He also witnessed a deed regarding land in Grantchester.[306]

It is possible that Robert I was the sole surviving son of either Seman of Ely or William and that when his father died he was adopted by Walter Wymund, his father's brother-in-law. He may have retained the name Seman in order to secure his position as heir. Subject to this constraint, Walter junior would have become head of the family.

Walter Wymund senior seems to have had four natural sons: Robert Wymund, Thomas Wymund, Absolon and Walter Wymund junior (or possibly just three – Absolon could have been adopted too). Robert I certainly inherited most of Seman's property. It has been suggested that he was educated as a clerk.[307] He held land on the bank of the River Cam near Blancwyneshythe (White Wine Quay) in the parish of All Saints in the Jewry, between High Street and the river in the parish of St John, and elsewhere in the town.[308] Robert I was essoined in 1199.[309] He was tallaged 1 mark in 1211.[310] He witnessed many deeds in the period 1220–40. It was probably Robert I who owed 11s and a quarter of corn to Jacob son of Deulesaut, in 1235.[311]

Robert I married Alice and had a son, Robert II, and two daughters. His daughter Nicola married William Karun and had a son, Robert Karun, while Isabella married Richard Laurence and had a son, Richard.[312] Robert I provided Nicola with a handsome dowry, comprising:

> all my land with buildings on it in the corn market where there stand stone houses with a mill and all the land which I hold of William of St Edmund's in the same place and all the land which I hold of John de Warom there and with an annual rent of 12d which William of Shelford holds of me and all the land which I hold of William son of William of Trumpington.[313]

Robert II married Cecilia, daughter of Nicholas, son of Everard of Wimpole.[314] It is probably this Robert who was bailiff in 1270, c.1273, c.1277 and 1284.[315] Robert II and Cecilia had three sons: Robert III, William and Laurence. Laurence married Agnes Vivien, daughter of Robert Vivien and granddaughter of Henry Vivien.[316] Laurence and Agnes had a son Geoffrey who married Joan.[317] William was a juror of the

Hundred Rolls and bailiff in 1278 and 1283.[318] He may be the William Seman of Newnham who sold land in Ashmancroft, Newnham, in c.1250.[319] He seems to have married twice. He probably married Cecilia first; they had two sons, Richard and Nicholas.[320] Margaret, daughter of Walter Em, son of Robert Em, was probably his second wife, and William inherited an enormous amount of property from this marriage (mentioned later).[321] His son Richard lived in a messuage in St Clement's in 1279.[322] There was also a third son, William son of William, whose mother is uncertain.[323]

Walter Wymund senior's four natural sons, Robert Wymund, Thomas Wymund, Absolon and Walter junior, can now be considered in turn. In 1279 Robert Wymund held three messuages, all north of the river in the parishes of St Peter at the Castle and St Giles', together with some small amounts of agricultural land.[324] In 1284 he became bailiff. Robert had two daughters, Margaret and Matilda, both of whom were alive at the time of the Hundred Rolls, when they each held a messuage in St Giles'.[325] Neither seems to have married. By this time Robert's brother Thomas may have died. He seems to have held little property, although he gave some vacant land to his niece Matilda. Absolon son of Wymund, held land in the parish of St Peter outside the Trumpington Gate near the Chapel of St Edmund.[326] When witnessing a deed in c.1235 Walter junior is described as a clerk of Paris, suggesting that he may have been educated at the university there.[327]

The view that Robert Seman was adopted by Walter Wymund senior makes sense from two points of view. First, why would Walter otherwise have two sons called Robert? Secondly the Seman branch descended from Robert I was much more successful than the Wymund branch. This was partly because Robert Seman I inherited more wealth, but it is also the case that this wealth was subsequently augmented in various ways, especially through advantageous marriages. The initial wealth diffused through members of a growing dynasty. Family members were typically well educated and developed useful social networks, enabling William, in particular, to hold civic office and act as a juror of the Hundred Rolls. Their social contacts meant that the growth in family size was largely self-financing. The Semans continued living in Cambridge; in 1354 a Geoffrey Seman held a tenement in St Giles'.[328]

Thomas Toylet and his family

The Toylet family were benefactors of both Barnwell Priory and the Hospital of St John. The surname is unusual, and as a consequence has

Thomas Toylet and his family

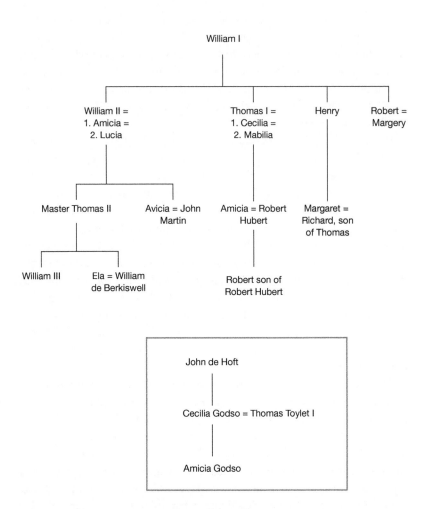

a variety of spellings in the records. It could be a corruption of a French name or possibly a reference to tillet, a form of coarse cloth made in nearby Suffolk. Two members were named Thomas and three William. The line begins with William I, who had at least four sons: William II, Thomas I, Henry and Robert.[329] Henry and Robert may have been the youngest as they were both still alive in 1279. William I acquired an enormous amount of property, which he passed on to his children. In 1279 this property was held by his surviving sons Henry and Robert, and by charitable and religious institutions, as described later.

Little is known of William I's origins. It is possible that he made his fortune out of royal service. One of his properties was purchased from Lord Roger of the Exchequer, who in turn had bought it from Moses, the Jew of Clare; it is possible that it came into the king's hands through the Exchequer of the Jews. William also invested in the grain trade; he bought a granary in the parish of All Saints in the Jewry, which he left to his son Henry.[330] The only property that he did not purchase was given to him by William Brat, who had inherited it from Keal the Draper, his father.[331] William seems to have been an assertive individual: the Prior of Barnwell accused William of blocking up the door to a house that his son Henry held from the priory to stop the prior distraining chattels for arrears of rent.[332]

William's son Thomas I purchased a granary in the parish of All Saints in the Jewry from Leon Dunning, which he gave to his nephew, Thomas II.[333] Thomas advanced the family's fortunes. He married twice. Cecilia Godso, daughter of John de Hoft, was his first wife and they had a daughter, Amicia, who married Robert Hubert.[334] His second wife was Mabilia, otherwise known as Maddi de Balsham. Thomas arranged to become a pensioner at Barnwell Priory and left substantial property, totalling 67 acres of land, to Barnwell;[335] he supported the Hospital of St John too.[336] In 1279 two houses in St Michael's parish were described as having been acquired from Thomas, and one of them had definitely been purchased by him.[337]

Thomas's son-in-law, Robert Hubert, together with his own son, were determined to maximize the value of their share of Thomas's inheritance. Robert claimed that 66 acres of land had been given to the priory for Thomas's life and not in perpetuity, and his son added that Thomas had not intended to injure his heirs by his gift; but the jury found largely in favour of the prior, who retained possession of 58 acres. Thomas's widow, Maddi de Balsham, also entered a plea of dower, but the outcome is not recorded.[338]

Thomas's brother William II married Amicia and then Lucia.[339] He had at least two children: a daughter, Avicia, who married John Martin, an important member of the town community (discussed later), and Master Thomas II, clerk.[340] William may have been involved in commerce; either he or his father sold three shops in the marketplace to Thomas, son of Edmund Miller.[341] He supported the Hospital of St John, leaving them 14 acres and two houses in the parish of St Sepulchre.[342]

In 1279 Master Thomas II held three messuages inherited from his father, in the parishes of All Saints at the Castle, St Clement and St Sepulchre. He also had a financial interest in the grain trade: he held a granary in the parish of All Saints near the hospital given to him by his Uncle Thomas.[343] He was bailiff in 1292.[344] He had two children, for whom he made joint provision: a son, William III, and a daughter, Ela, who married William de Berkiswell.[345] The deed of gift is unusual in the way that it provides for both of them, and in the fact that the properties concerned carry five different rents:

> Thomas Toylet, clerk, to his *pueri*, William and Ela, and the longest liver of them, two messuages in Bridge Street in St Clement's parish between a messuage of his father William to the south, and a messuage late of Koc, the Jew, to the north, abutting on the street and on the lane towards St John's Hospital: rent 1d. to the said Thomas, to Bartholomew Gogging, 2s., to the Nuns 4s., to John Alured 4s. and to St John's Hospital 4s.[346]

Henry was bailiff in 1270 and 1278.[347] He had a daughter, Margaret, who married Richard son of Thomas, nephew of the Prior of Wells; Henry gave her a messuage between St Michael's Church and the river as a dowry.[348] Henry was still alive in 1279 when his brother William's grandchildren had come of age. He inherited much of his father William I's property, namely two messuages, in St Michael's and St Sepulchre, a granary in All Saints in the Jewry and about 34 acres of land in six lots, while from his brother, William II, he received 7.5 acres in the fields of Cambridge.[349] He also acquired a small amount of land himself.

Robert married Margery; he was bailiff in 1273 and 1284, and mayor in 1278 and 1293–4, when he was involved in an action against the Prior of Barnwell over the seizure of goods left behind at the Midsummer Fair by an absconding merchant.[350] In 1279 he held a grange in the parish of All Saints in the Jewry at Dame Nicholas Hythe, a messuage in St Clement's and 1 acre of land that he acquired from Henry, his brother, together with a messuage in Holy Trinity given by his father.[351] In 1295 he held a grange in All Saints at the Castle, near the Barbican, from Barnwell Priory, while his brother Henry held another grange opposite the same church, also from the priory.[352]

The combination of fields, granaries and market shops held by various members of the Toylet family suggests involvement in the grain trade, and possibly even vertical integration from field, through granary, to market stall. At the same time, clerical professions, aristocratic connections, religious patronage and civic service suggest that family enterprise was not confined to the commercial sector.

Richard Wombe and his family

The Wombe family can be traced back to Henry, who had two sons, Radulph and Harvey. Harvey married Alicia who, it seems, later married Henry of Waddon.[353] Harvey and Alicia had a son, Bartholomew, who married Custancia, daughter of Richard the Tailor, and they had a daughter, Isabella.[354] Radulph (also known as Radulph son of Henry) was the key member of the family. He married Nicola, and they had at

Richard Wombe and his family

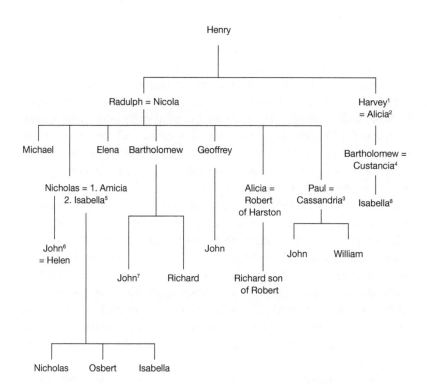

Notes:

[1] Nothing is known of Harvey's ancestors; he could have been Henry's brother or Radulph's son; he is shown here as Henry's son and Radulph's brother.

[2] On Harvey's death Alicia married Henry of Waddon.

[3] Daughter of Gregory Edward.

[4] Daughter of Richard the tailor and Margaret his wife.

[5] Daughter of Michael Bernard.

[6] Heir who sold much of his inheritance.

[7] Heir who died early [presumably with no surviving wife or children], leaving a large inheritance to his brother.

[8] Isabella might have been the daughter of Bartholomew son of Radulph.

least five sons and two daughters.[355] Radulph was tallaged for 4 marks in 1211 and amerced £1 for flight in 1219. He was also fined half a mark for flight in 1221.[356] Radulph held property in St Michael's parish and other parts of Cambridge, in Barnwell fields, near Hinton Way and further afield, for example Gamlingay.[357] Up to c.1247 Radulph witnessed no less than 31 deeds relating to lands acquired by the Hospital of St John.

Radulph's sons were Michael, Nicholas, Paul, Bartholomew and Geoffrey; his daughters were Alicia and Elena. Some of his children prospered more than others. Alicia married Robert of Harston and they had a son, Richard son of Robert, who was alive in 1279.[358] He was not the wealthy 'Richard' though (mentioned later). The other daughter was Elena.[359] She was given a shop in All Saints at the Castle by her mother Nicola, which she then sold to Sabina Huberd.[360] Michael seems to have died young; his brother Bartholomew inherited from him a messuage in St Botolph's that he had been given by his father.[361] Geoffrey Wombe does not appear in the Hundred Rolls, but as 'Geoffrey son of Ralph' he witnessed 14 deeds relating to the Hospital of St John, mostly over the period 1230–40, sometimes with his father and sometimes with his son John. He held land in St Mary's parish.[362] Paul Wombe married Cassandria, daughter of Gregory Edward, and they had two sons. John, who was alive in 1279, inherited a messuage in St Michael's parish from his father.[363] William held a messuage in Milne Street; he witnessed an undated deed giving rent from Oakington to the Hospital of St John.[364]

In the riot of 1235 it appears that Paul Wombe struck and wounded Andrew of Balsham. Harvey Wombe and Nicholas Wombe were also named among the rioters; Nicholas was specifically accused of wounding Richard son of Simon, with a stick. Subsequently Geoffrey Wombe was taken, with three other suspects, to Northampton for trial, where he was bailed.[365] It may be the same Paul Wombe who was convicted of robbery at the county assizes in 1260; the jury found him guilty even though he did not appear.

Nicholas inherited from his father some vacant land in St Michael's parish and was given by him two messuages in All Saints in the Jewry, which were probably quite valuable; to these he added, by purchase, small amounts of agricultural land.[366] These properties were inherited by his son John, who sold most of them. Nicholas married Amicia and then Isabella, daughter of Michael Bernard, who survived him.[367] Nicholas and Amicia had a son, John, while Nicholas and Isabella had two sons, Nicholas and Osbert, and a daughter, Isabella.[368]

John (son of Nicholas and Amicia) sold many of the properties that he inherited from his father, as already described, as well as other properties that he probably acquired by purchase.[369] In particular he sold messuages, barns and a courtyard at various times between 1266 and 1274 to William le Comber and his wife Matilda; these included 'Wombe's messuage with a house on it' that lay along Henney Lane, which ran west from the High Street to the river near the present Garret Hostel bridge.[370] It is almost certainly this John who was involved in the sale of Sedge Hall to John Gogging in 1292, which was the result of a lawsuit.[371] Helen, widow of John Wombe, finally disposed of all claims she might have had to these properties in 1306.[372]

Bartholomew Wombe was Radulph's principal heir. He was also known as Master Bartholomew and as Bartholomew son of Ralph.[373] He had two sons: John, his heir, and Richard, who inherited on John's death.[374] Richard Wombe was a major recipient of property rents at the time of the Hundred Rolls and a bailiff in 1305. In 1279 Richard Wombe held two messuages, one each in St Michael's and St Botolph's, a shop in St Mary's, a plot of vacant land in All Saints in the Jewry and over 33 acres of land in the fields of Cambridge, almost entirely inherited from Radulph through his father.[375] In 1280 Richard Wombe was named as a tenant of John le Rus, deceased, holding 20 acres of arable land in Newnham paying rent of 12s. In 1278 Richard Wombe and John Wombe mainperned Walter le Bercher, who was a member of a jury of six Christians and six Jews inquiring into the validity of a starr.[376] This John must have been the son of Paul rather than Bartholomew, since by this time John son of Bartholomew, had died.

Many members of the Wombe family appear in the Hundred Rolls. But most of the drive and ambition seems to have come from Radulph, who amassed an extensive property portfolio and had seven children. Two of his grandsons inherited most of his property; Richard son of Bartholomew, maintained most of his inheritance, but John son of Nicholas, seems to have squandered his; at any rate, he sold off most of what he inherited in a series of transactions over a 20-year period. By the time of the Hundred Rolls the family still held considerable property, and they also received a large amount of rent from properties that they had sold.

Wulward family

According to the Hundred Rolls, the Wulward dynasty began with a man called Wulward. Wulward (or Wulfward) at the Bridge was amerced for half a mark in 1177, and Ailwin Wulward for 3 marks in the same year.[377] In 1179–80 Wulward of Cambridge was fined £1 for detaining rent due from a house of Aunger in the parish of St Clement. Somewhat earlier, in

Wulward family

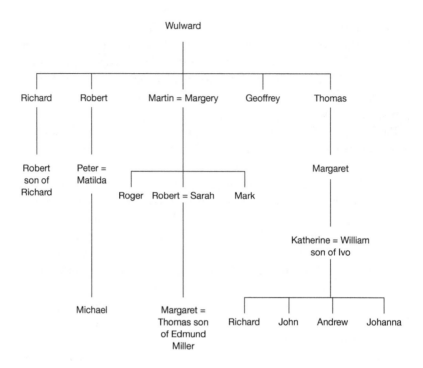

1175–6, a William Wulward owed the king 2s 6d.[378] Ailwin and William may have been Wulward's brothers.[379]

Wulward had five sons: Richard, Robert, Martin, Geoffrey and Thomas. Richard was tallaged for 6 marks in 1211; he had paid off half a mark by 1223, which was probably his last payment.[380] In 1221 he was fined 20s *pro fuga*. At the same time Decana Wulward, probably a customary tenant in Chesterton, was fined half a mark for his flight, possibly because he provided surety. Also that year Radulph son of Fulk son of Theobald, who, it seems, acted for the sheriff, owed the king half a mark for the chattels of Wulward fugitive and 17s for the chattels of Richard fugitive.[381] Richard bought a messuage in St Clement's, which he held from Maurice Ruffus and his heirs.[382] It has been said that Richard had died by 1227, leaving a widow, Cecily, who in 1239–40 held property in Cambridge from Ramsey Abbey.[383] Richard had a son, Robert son of Richard, who held a tenement between the river and the market, paying 18s rent to Baldwin Blancgernun, which Baldwin gave to the Hospital of St John.[384]

Robert, son of Wulward and brother of Richard, held land north of the river from the fee of the castle of Cambridge in 1260.[385] Robert had a son, Peter, who married Matilda, daughter of Margaret, and had a son, Michael, who was alive in 1279.[386] Michael became bailiff in 1294. It seems that Peter was Robert's only son and sole heir and that Michael was Peter's sole heir too. As a result, quite a lot of wealth was consolidated through inheritance in this branch of the family. Peter inherited three messuages, a shop and two plots of land: a messuage in St Peter's at the Castle paying 7s rent to the Prior of Chicksands; a messuage in St Clement's paying 10s rent to St John's Hospital; an unspecified messuage received as dowry; a shop with curtilage in St Clement's and two pieces of land in St Giles's.[387] To this inheritance Michael added a house, which was a gift from Sabina Huberd (possibly a dowry).

Martin Wulward owed tallage of £4 in 1211.[388] He was fined 5s 8d for selling wine in 1221.[389] In 1200 he bought some property from Absolon son of Absolon for 1 mark.[390] He also bought land in a 'little lane' leading to St John's Church from Absolon son of Roger the priest.[391] Martin married Margery. She had a sister, Ella, who was married to William Cholle, who may have been connected with Cholle's Hythe on the river.[392]

Martin and Margery had three sons: Robert, his heir, Roger and Mark.[393] Roger held land inherited by his father from his uncle Thomas, probably in Milne Street, possessing access from the main road to the water, which he granted to his brother Robert.[394] In c.1278 Robert sold this land on to Robert of Hockley and his wife Avicia for 6 marks.[395] Mark bought land from Warin son of Absolon, which was probably near the King's Ditch.[396]

Robert Wulward owed 5s for a *licencia concorandi* in 1230.[397] He held a seld in the market, near the Great Street by St Mary's Church, where meat was sold.[398] He also held a courtyard with free entry and exit near the King's Ditch and Cholle's Hythe.[399] Robert married Sarah, daughter of John Gogging, and they had a daughter, Margaret, who married Thomas son of Edmund Miller.[400] Robert, Margaret and Thomas were all alive in 1279, although it seems that by then Robert was a widower. By that time Thomas had inherited a shop in St Edward's on which Robert received a rent for life of 9s, while Margaret held a rent of 1s, and a messuage in St John's parish that came as dowry with a rent of 20d, which Robert had assigned to St Radegund's. Thomas had also purchased three shops in the market from Thomas Toylet, two shops from John Aure and a messuage in St Peter's outside the Trumpington Gate from Richard Timpon.[401]

Geoffrey Wulward, another of Wulward's sons, paid a tallage of 1 mark in 1211.[402] He was fined 16s *pro fuga* in 1221.[403] He held land from Peter Ruffus in St Clement's that he sold in 1226; it has been suggested that he left Cambridge thereafter, and possibly settled at Tilney, near King's Lynn. He may have had a son John.[404]

Thomas Wulward, Geoffrey's brother, held a seld in the market that he sold to John Barton in c.1270.[405] This suggests that he may have been in the same line of business as his brother Robert, who held a seld nearby, although it is possible that the seld was inherited on his brother's death. Thomas also held land in the parish of St Andrew outside the Barnwell Gate, together with property in St John's, on which he paid 7s rent to Warin Grim, son of Absolon.[406] He also held property in Grantchester fields.[407] He witnessed many deeds over the period 1260–80, often with his nephew Roger. He had a daughter, Margaret.[408] Margaret had a daughter, Katherine, who married William son of Ivo.[409] They had three sons and a daughter (previously mentioned): Richard, John, Andrew and Johanna.[410]

The Wulward family were an economic force to be reckoned with in the mid-13th century, if only because there were so many of them alive at the same time. Wulward, the founder of the dynasty, had five sons, but thereafter family size was relatively small and so individual wealth was not dissipated. The later generations were quite cohesive and often witnessed deeds together. They bought and sold properties among themselves and with other people. Many of these properties were concentrated in the commercial heart of the town, near the King's Ditch and around Milne Street, between the river and the market. The early generations played only a limited role in the civic life of the town. Michael Wulward, however, became a leading figure in the 1280s and 1290s, as a bailiff and as a tenant of Barnwell Priory.[411]

4.3 Middle-ranking families

Crocheman family

The Crocheman family begins with Fulk who was tallaged for £5 in 1211.[412] He and his sister Sybil gave land in the Jewry, which was held from them by Brito the Jew, to the nuns of St Radegund's.[413] The deed was witnessed by Baldwin Blancgernun, which suggests an early date, c.1200.

John Crocheman was tallaged for 5 marks in 1211; a substantial sum, but only two thirds of Fulk's assessment. He was the son of Roger Crocheman.[414] In 1220 he was one of four recorders appointed by the king's justices to hear a case in Cambridge between Mabilia de Novacurt and Adam of Cokefield regarding a plea of dowry.[415] In 1239 he was indebted to the Jews for 11.5 marks and a quarter of corn.[416] John held a messuage in St Benedict's parish, which he sold to William son of Roger.[417]

Crocheman family

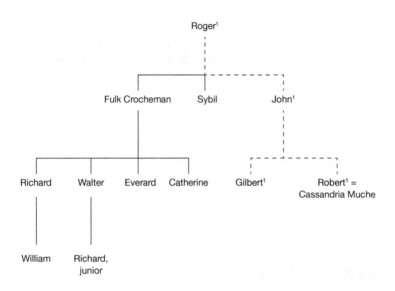

Note: [1] This part of the family tree is conjectural.

There seems to have been a close relationship between Fulk and John; John, together with Fulk and his son Richard, witnessed an early deed giving property in Ely to the Hospital of St John.[418] It is possible that they were brothers. If so, then Roger would have been their father.

Fulk Crocheman had three sons and a daughter: Richard, Walter, Everard and Catherine. Richard, known as Master Richard, witnessed a deed in c.1230 regarding land that Warin Anketil gave to his sister.[419] He became an official of the Archdeacon of Ely from c.1250 to 1275. He also held the office of provost,[420] and was rector of Brington, Huntingdonshire.[421] Walter was implicated in the 1235 riot, but was not punished for it.[422] In 1260 he served on the jury for the Cambridgeshire assizes.[423] He exchanged property with his brother Walter.[424] Richard had a son, William. In 1279 William held a messuage in St Mary's parish and another in St Michael's parish that, together with adjoining land, he had inherited from his father.[425]

Everard was in debt to the Jews for 3.5 marks and a quarter of corn in 1237.[426] Catherine, also known as Cate, died early; she held land in All Saints' that was inherited by her brother Walter.[427] Walter had a son, Richard (junior). In 1279 Richard junior held a messuage in All Saints in the Jewry inherited from his father, who inherited it from his sister Catherine; also a messuage in St Michael's parish and some land bought from Henry Nadon.[428] Richard junior was a bailiff in 1292.[429]

The Crocheman family were apparently very wealthy in 1211 as they were tallaged heavily at that time. King John's exactions were often excessive and they may have been tallaged so heavily that they never fully recovered. Both John and Fulk paid less than 50 per cent of the amount they owed.[430] It is possible that, unlike some other Cambridge families, they lacked a source of profit from trade out of which their fiscal obligations could be met. Apart from John and Fulk, the two most successful members of the family were Master Richard and Robert; the former built a career in church administration, while the latter made an advantageous marriage. Although later generations of Crochemans seem to have lacked a regular income from trade, they found other ways to survive.

Richard at the Gate and his family

In 1211 Richard at the Gate was one of the wealthiest men in Cambridge, being tallaged for £10, the largest amount assessed, and equal to that paid by Richard of Barnwell. It was equivalent to the total sum paid by Baldwin Blancgernun and Harvey son of Eustace, together.[431] Richard had four children: his son John and daughter Seva both died early, leaving his daughters Sabina and Margaret to inherit. Sabina married Richard Laurence and Margaret married Michael Gogging; as a result, Richard's inheritance passed to those two families.[432]

During his lifetime Richard held two messuages in St Botolph's, a messuage and a plot of land in St Benedict's (vacant in 1279), and a messuage with some land in St Edward's The last messuage seems to have divided into two, probably to be shared by his two surviving daughters; each portion of this messuage paid a rent of 27d to the Almoner of Ely. This does not seem to be a very large property portfolio for such a wealthy man.

There is another family named 'at the gate' that does not appear at first sight to be connected with Richard. This line begins with Reginald, whose son Simon had a son, Reginald, and a daughter, Margaret; Reginald bought the properties and his descendants sold them off.[433] The location of these properties is similar to, but slightly south of, those already mentioned: three messuages in St Botolph's and one in Newnham. The implication is that both names refer to the same gate and that the gate in question is the Trumpington Gate on the London road by St Botolph's Church.

Richard at the Gate and his family

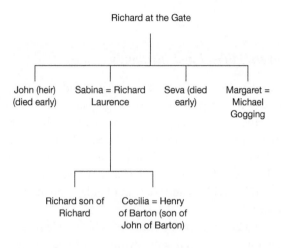

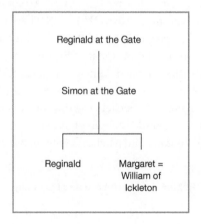

This raises the possibility that Reginald was related to Richard. The notion of a connection is strengthened by the fact that both families traded properties with the Gogging family, to which one of them was definitely related.

It is a curious fact that Richard appears in very few surviving deeds as either a buyer, seller or witness, and that nothing is known about his ancestry. In terms of surviving evidence, he came from nowhere to be the one of the two richest men of Cambridge in c.1200, and then disappeared from view almost as quickly. His son and one of his daughters died and their two surviving sisters married into established Cambridge dynasties. It is possible that he and Reginald were brothers and that there was a family rift between them; this would imply that they shared an inheritance and then went their separate ways.

Robert Hubert/Huberd and his family

Robert Hubert is important because he married into two important families. His wealth seems to have been largely inherited. He is described as the son of Hubert.[434] He appears to have had two brothers, Geoffrey, also described as son of Hubert, and Henry. Henry married Edusa, daughter of Sellarius and sister of Adam, and had two daughters, Eva, who married Thomas Pertehaye, and Margaret, who married William of Norfolk.[435] In 1279 William and Margaret held a shop in the marketplace given by Henry.[436]

Little is known about Hubert, father of Robert. He may be identified with Hubert son of Norman who owned land near the river and the bridge. His purchase of land from Henry Alegod, sometime between 1216 and 1240, was witnessed by Robert.[437] At about the same time Hubert also bought land from Adam Weriel.[438] There is also reference to a brewhouse near the river held by Hubert.[439] These acquisitions were confirmed in 1230–40 by the Hospital of St John.[440]

Robert (d. c.1274) first married Amicia, daughter of Thomas Toylet.[441] They had a son, Robert II, who was a canon of Anglesey Priory.[442] He then married Sabina, daughter of Michael Gogging and sister of Bartholomew Gogging; she was also granddaughter of Richard at the Gate through Margaret, Richard's daughter and Michael's wife (previously mentioned).[443]

Robert Hubert/Huberd and his family

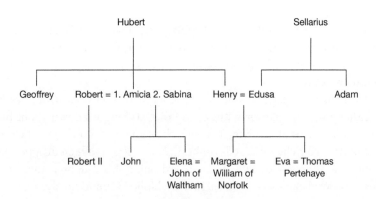

It is probably through Margaret that Sabina inherited one quarter of a knight's fee, comprising 16 acres of land in the fields of Cambridge, from Lady Emma de la Leye, descendant of Lord Reginald le Grey, on which she owed scutage.[444] Robert acquired additional land in St Clement's on his own initiative, some of it jointly with Sabina (presumably using some of her money for the purpose). The new land was close to Hubert's properties; much of it was in the fee of Baldwin Blancgernun and his heirs.[445] Robert and Sabina also held a messuage in Mill Lane, St John's parish, which had belonged to Cecilia Godso, sister of Amicia, Robert's first wife.[446] Robert and Sabina had a son, John, and a daughter Elena, who married John of Waltham.[447] Just before Robert died in c.1274, he was accused, together with Agnes of Barton and Sabina, of concealing Jewish goods and chattels from the king (mentioned earlier).

His son and heir, Robert II, gave two messuages to Anglesey Priory, one in St Michael's parish and one in St Peter's outside the Trumpington Gate; he also gave a granary, 6s rent from Bernard the butcher and some land.[448] Most of this property was inherited. He had an heir, Matilda, daughter of Isanti, although the connection between them is unclear (see the Pipestraw family). She inherited from him a messuage with 2 acres of land in St John's parish.[449] Robert II also granted back to his parents some of his inheritance in a deed that itemized 11 properties.[450]

The Huberts were an old and fairly wealthy family. They were stewards of wealth rather than creators of it. In each generation their property portfolio was controlled by a single male member of the family. Robert I and his son Robert II chose rather different paths in life. While Robert I seems to have followed his father into the grain trade, and perhaps into brewing, his son Robert II chose a career in the Church. Robert I enhanced his wealth through his marriage to Sabina, daughter of Richard at the Gate, while his son gave much of his inheritance to Anglesey Priory, and seems to have given the rest back to his father and his stepmother.

Parleben/Parlebyen family

Two branches of the Parleben family were active in Cambridge in the mid-13th century. One comprised Roger and his son Harvey, the coroner, while the other comprised Robert and his son Michael. Their influence in the town peaked in the 1220s and early 1230s, when Roger, along with other notables, witnessed numerous deeds, including many gifts to the Hospital of St John.

In the first branch of the family, Roger married Mabilia and they had a son, Harvey, who married Margaret.[451] Roger held a lot of land around

Parleben/Parlebyen family

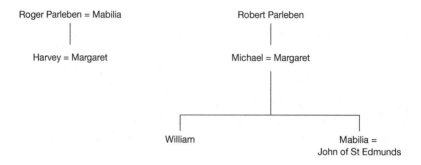

Bridge Street (in St Clement's), but at some stage sold it all to Peter of Lynn for 4d rent and 4 marks gersuma. Peter then sold it to the hospital for a small profit, at 60s gersuma, and Roger then relieved the hospital of the 4d rent charge on the property.[452] This gift may have been made shortly before his death in c.1233, when his widow instigated a claim of dowry. Her claim encompassed portions of several Cambridge properties, including three messuages, 2 acres of land and 30d rent. Part of the claim was directed against Anthony, Master of the Hospital of St John, possibly to retrieve some of the land around Bridge Street that had been given earlier by her late husband.[453]

Harvey held land in St Michael's parish in c.1246–56 and 3 acres of land in Cambridge fields that he sold to John of Barton.[454] He was coroner in 1260, when the assize jury took a very dim view of his competence.[455] He had a record of incompetence: he failed to secure pledges for Henry Russell, accused of stealing from John the Vintner; when the hue and cry was raised for murder in Bridge Street he failed to attach all the watchmen to give evidence; and when a stranger was killed in Littlemore fields he failed to summon the neighbours as witnesses. In each case judgement was made against him. Earlier offences of a similar nature may have led to him being fined 5s by royal justices for 'many transgressions' in 1242.[456]

The second branch of the family was headed by Robert Parleben, who gave 3.5 acres of land to Thomas Toylet, who then gave them to Barnwell Priory. Robert's son Michael sold 2 acres of land to Thomas for the same purpose. Michael, like Harvey, held land in St Michael's.[457] Michael married Margaret and they had a son, William, the heir, and a daughter Mabilia, who married John son of Robert of St Edmunds. Michael seems to have died in c.1249, when his wife instigated a claim of dowry against William son of Ivo.[458] The case hinged on the legal status of her son William, whom John of Barton warranted was a minor in his mother's custody. William died young, however, and his sister Mabilia inherited. Her inheritance included a messuage in St Sepulchre.[459]

The Parleben family seem to have been a very mixed bunch of people. Roger became a highly reputable citizen, but his legacy was undermined; his widow became involved in litigation, and their son, the local coroner, failed, for whatever reason, to invest in local property. Robert and Michael's line never achieved the same degree of success but their decline was less dramatic; it disappeared when his son and heir died young and his daughter married into the St Edmunds family. The family's rise and decline is neatly encompassed by the period 1200–79. They held a significant amount of property but did little with it. Had they been more cohesive, and capitalized on Roger's reputation, they might have achieved greater success.

Pipestraw/Pipestau family

The Pipestraw family was marked by sibling rivalry involving three sisters. The rivalry related to which of their male relatives should inherit the advowson of St Michael's Church and the messuage that was attached to it. This led to extensive litigation in the royal courts.[460] The seeds of the dispute were planted in the reign of John, in c.1200, but matters first came to a head in c.1220. The legal dispute commenced in about 1231 and continued until c.1243. When the court records are compared with the account in the Hundred Rolls, discrepancies arise. The principal surviving property owner in 1279, Matilda, seems to have provided a heavily edited account of the descent of her properties that made her entitlement appear stronger than it really was.

The line of descent begins with Reginald Pipestraw, who had at least five children: Ivo and his four sisters who, in order of birth, were Alicia, Dera, Matilda and Albreda. Reginald held the advowson of St Michael's Church, which his son Ivo inherited. Ivo was tallaged for 1 mark in 1211, but he made only one payment of 3s.[461] Ivo may also have played a part in the management of the Hospital of St John. He claimed, with others, the advowson of St Peter's Church outside the Trumpington Gate. In 1207 a jury was summoned to determine whether he, together with Herbert the chaplain, Reginald, son of Alfred, and William Caldecot, held the advowson, or whether it belonged to the king.[462] Maitland suggests that these four men were representatives of the Hospital of St John.[463] The jury decided that the advowson did indeed belong to the hospital, but through a different line of descent, namely from Langlinus to his kinsman Sigar and then to Henry son of Sigar, who gave it to the hospital.[464]

Pipestraw/Pipestau family

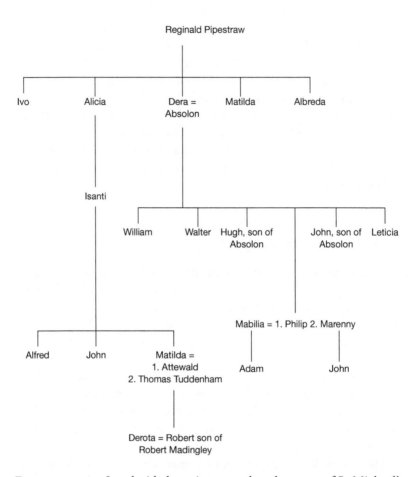

For some reason Ivo decided to give away the advowson of St Michael's Church, which he had inherited. It is possible that he was celibate and wanted to appoint an heir who could take over right away. He gave it to the husband of one his sisters: not the first born sister, Matilda, but the second-born, Dera.[465] Dera was married to Absolon.[466] Dera and Absolon had a number of children, including William and Walter. William was the eldest and Walter was the second-born son. It is possible that Ivo considered William, his nephew, to be best qualified to take the job. There may also have been some expectation that William would become the parson. It appears that Dera's sisters, Alicia and Matilda, initially agreed to this; when Ivo died they confirmed William as heir to the advowson. By this time the youngest sister Albreda had died without heirs.

Matters seem to have come to a head when William died. Walter seems to have taken the view that, as William's younger brother and heir, the advowson would pass to him, but the heirs of Alicia (the first-born sister) took a different stance; namely that the advowson should come to them. It seems that Walter died while the dispute remained unresolved, and William's brother, John son of Absolon, took up the case.

Alicia had a son, Isanti, and this son had three children, John, Alfred and Matilda junior. At this stage of the litigation Matilda, the third-born sister, had also died without heirs. Alice's heirs sponsored John son of Isanti as their candidate. John was still a minor, but it was maintained that this was no obstacle, as the Bishop of Ely could act for him until he attained his majority.

The heirs of Isanti won the case. John son of Isanti must have died young, however, because the family inheritance seems to have passed to Alfred, son of Isanti, and, on his death, to Matilda, daughter of Isanti. Matilda may have married twice; first to a member of the Attewald family and then to Thomas Tuddenham, with whom she had a daughter, Derota, who married Robert, son of Robert of Madingley.[467] It is probably Matilda who ensured the following emphatic statement in the Hundred Rolls:

> Item. It is said that the advowson and donation of the church of St Michael's, Cambridge, belongs de Matilda de Walda, who is the true patron of the aforesaid church and by law patron pertaining to it through hereditary right through the death of her ancestors as is stated in the great roll.[468]

What is not in dispute is that Matilda, as heir to most of the Pipestraw properties, held five messuages and a house in 1279, together with three plots of land and two rents. Some properties were inherited from Ivo, some were purchased by her father Isanti and some were acquired jointly with her husbands.[469] The principal messuage was the old family home in St Michael's parish with the advowson of the church; the other messuages were in St Mary's (2), St Edward's and St John's; the house, bought by her father, was in Strawylane.

Dera and Absolon had at least four other children, but they did not figure in the court case. They were Hugh son of Absolon, John son of Absolon, Mabilia and Letitia. Hugh made various grants to religious institutions. Acting on the advice of Eustace, Bishop of Ely 1197–1215, he gave the advowson of St Clement's Church to St Radegund's.[470] He also acquired the advowson of St John's Church through the death of his brother William, and he gave this to Barnwell Priory.[471] Mabilia, who

223

was also known as Mabilia Marenny, probably married twice. She had two sons, John Marenny and Adam son of Philip.[472] Letitia was Prioress of St Radegund's for the period 1213–28 or longer.[473] Hugh gave 29d from a tenement in Pilate's Lane (*Vico Judaeorum*) in All Saints in the Jewry to the nuns to celebrate her anniversary.[474] He also gave them 6 acres of land in the fields of Cambridge, which he had inherited from his father.[475]

The Pipestraw family represents a combination of devout but possibly incompetent men and litigious women. The men attempted to dispose of an advowson in pursuit of their own agenda and the women disputed their decisions in the interests of their children. Litigation, especially in the royal courts, was expensive, and it is difficult to estimate how much family wealth was dissipated in this way. In 1279, however, one of the litigants, Matilda, held a substantial property portfolio in Cambridge, suggesting that protecting her inheritance, as she perceived it, may have been a rational strategy.

4.4 Smaller families

John of Aylsham and his family

John of Aylsham was a prominent citizen, serving as bailiff on several occasions, but little is known about his origins. The name Aylsham is uncommon in Cambridge, suggesting that he or his parents may have migrated from Aylsham in Norfolk. He married Sabina, daughter of Martin Brithnor', and niece of Martin's brother Harvey.[476] Sabina was the widow of Peter de Wilburham, and after John's death in c.1299 she married Simon Asselof.[477] John held properties both in his own name, and jointly with his wife Sabina.[478] The jointly owned properties had been acquired by Sabina herself, possibly before she married him. Almost all of the properties were either in the parish of St Peter outside the Trumpington Gate or in the Cambridge fields. This is true of both the properties bought by John and those bought by Sabina, suggesting that if John had relatives in Cambridge they may have resided close to Sabina's family. The fact that the properties were outside the gate but reasonably close to the river (they were described as 'towards Newnham' in 1295) is consistent with the family being tanners.[479]

John held five messuages in St Peter's parish, each of them purchased from a different person. He also owned 6 acres of land in the field of Cambridge, four of them being acquired from Eustace Dunning through William Manefield, a middleman who dealt in properties held by people who were burdened with debt (see Chapter 6). Sabina and John mainly

John of Aylsham and his family

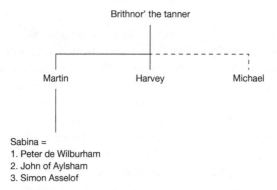

bought from different people, although both bought messuages that had been held by Eustace Selede. Circumstantial evidence suggests that Eustace was a Jew and that he may have been selling up when he was expelled to Huntingdon. In 1279 John served on a jury (one of six Cambridge men) for an inquest into the authenticity of a starr.[480] John served as bailiff in 1270, twice in the period 1273–8 and again in 1286.[481] While he contributed to civic society, he seems to have had no connection (other than tenancy) with religious or charitable institutions.

After John's death Sabina remarried, but was soon widowed again; before her own death she conveyed properties both to Peterhouse and to a local charity. Some of these transactions appear to have been philanthropic, but others not so (see Chapter 7).[482]

John and Sabina appear to have been a pair of successful entrepreneurs from a commercial background who were doing well for themselves. John may have been a relative newcomer who married into an existing family business. Although Sabina had surviving male relatives, she seems to have had considerable latitude to deal in property on her own account. Both their families may have been involved in tanning. It is also possible that the family was engaged in property development on the southern edge of the town.

William Braci and his family

The Braci family were remarkably cohesive. The sisters and daughters of the late William Braci jointly held two messuages in All Saints at the Castle. Four of them shared ownership.

William was the son of Ketel Attewal, a merchant or mercer.[483] Ketel was tallaged for 2 marks in 1211; he had paid about three quarters by 1223.[484] William apparently had a brother, Aldred gener Ketel; he was tallaged 2.5 marks at the same time. The name 'Braci' may be short for *braciator*, which is Latin for brewer. Since Ketel and Aldred were both involved in trade, and probably traded in grain, an occupation as a brewer would fit well with the family's interests. William seems to have had two sisters, Margaret and Emma. After William's death his sister Margaret co-owned with his daughters, possibly because she was a spinster or had become a widow; Emma, on the other hand, did not.[485]

William married Margaret, daughter of Margaret Siyion, who was daughter of Harvey the clerk, and the couple had three daughters, Avicia, Elena and Johanna. Elena married John Gerund, about whom nothing is known.[486] Avicia and Johanna both inherited property in their own right.[487] Johanna married, but it seems likely that Avicia did not.

William held five messuages in Cambridge at the time of his death. Three had been inherited from his father, one had probably been obtained as dowry and one he had bought himself. His sisters and daughters jointly inherited two messuages in All Saints at the Castle.[488] Avicia inherited a further two messuages, one in St Benedict's and the other in St Botolph's, while Johanna inherited a single messuage near the castle.[489] Alicia possibly got more because she was (probably) unmarried.

William seems to have consolidated the family's wealth rather than created it. It was probably his father who was the most enterprising member of the family. The family name did not continue because he had no surviving sons, and his brother carried a different name.

William Braci and his family

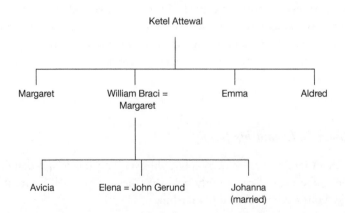

Matilda le Comber and her family

The first recorded member of the le Comber family is Osbert, who was tallaged for 1 mark in 1211. Osbert had two sons, Elias and William. Elias son of Osbert was tallaged at the same time for the same amount. Both had paid their tallage almost in full by 1221, which is more than most of their fellow citizens achieved. William married Matilda, daughter of Robert Whitesmith. Robert was the son of William Whitesmith, and lived in Smith Street adjacent to St Mary's Church. Matilda was an enterprising woman whose property deals are recorded in many deeds.[490]

William and Matilda had a son, John, sometimes known as John son of William the smith. The family traded regularly in properties in the area around Smith Street. They subdivided properties, sometimes keeping half themselves and selling off the other half, perhaps as a means of financing their purchase. They put up buildings on vacant land adjoining St Mary's Church.[491] This activity accelerated after William's death, probably in the 1280s, as mother and son acted as a team of property developers and speculators. The couple acquired property outside the Smith Street area. They bought a couple of properties from the Wombe family (previously mentioned), whose son John was liquidating much of his inheritance at the time. One of these properties was towards the river; another, between the market and the river, was used by Matilda as a brewhouse.[492]

The Hundred Rolls provide a snapshot of this process of business expansion. William held a messuage in St Benedict's that he had inherited from Radulph of Eversden, a messuage in St Mary's that his father had bought from Andrew of Wimpole, and a shop and messuage in the

Matilda le Comber and her family

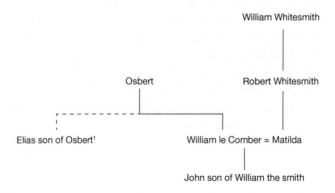

Note: [1] Elias may be the son of another Osbert.

same parish given by Matilda's father.[493] He had bought a stall in the market from John Porthors and a messuage in St John's from John Wombe (mentioned previously).[494] He also held a small amount of land. A later snapshot is provided by the Barnwell rental of 1295, which is more limited in its coverage of properties; it shows that Matilda owned a vacant plot in Glomery Lane, on which she paid rent of 1s plus two capons, and that with John she held 2 acres of land in Newnham croft on which they paid 3s rent. At this time they were buying and selling other properties too.

The evidence suggests that Matilda was the driving force in the family, even though it carried the le Comber name. She continued her own family's involvement in smithing, but also diversified into brewing. Once her husband died her property dealing increased, and she developed a business partnership with her son that lasted into the early 14th century.

Michael Malerbe and his family

The Malerbe family was one of the oldest in Cambridge; they held a lot of property from c.1200 and in 1279 received significant rents from the properties that they had sold. The founder of the dynasty was Michael Malerbe senior, who was a major benefactor of the Carmelite Friars, to whom he gave land in Newnham for their friary. Michael provided half the land required and many townspeople contributed to the other half.[495] Michael sold three messuages in Cambridge to Harvey son of Eustace, in 1198–9 for 60s 8d.[496]

Michael had a son and heir, Michael Malerbe junior.[497] It was probably Michael junior who was indebted to Jacob son of Deulesaut, for 1 mark in 1238.[498] The following year he claimed customary services from a tenant in Newnham, who denied that he was Michael's villein.[499]

Michael junior had a son, Nicholas Malerbe, and two daughters: Johanna, who married Walter Bagge, and Eleanor, who married Richard le Marshal and had a son, John.[500] Michael junior provided dowries for his daughters: two messuages in St John's for Joanna and a messuage in the parish of St Sepulchre for Eleanor.[501] Nicholas was the heir but he seems to have had little involvement in Cambridge. In 1249 he and his wife Alice were involved in a dispute over land in Haslingfield near Cambridge, and later Hawisa, his daughter and heir, contested land in Hampshire with Waverley Abbey, near Farnham, Surrey.[502] The Cambridge properties were sold off; they comprised a messuage in St Mary's, a messuage in St Sepulchre and four plots of land in the Cambridge and Barnwell fields.[503] Two properties were disposed of earlier by Nicholas's father: a

Michael Malerbe and his family

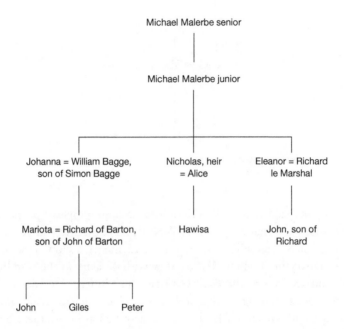

messuage in St Botolph's, sold to Richard Wombe, and another messuage in St Sepulchre, sold to Walter Pago.[504]

The Malerbe family appear to have been aristocratic and to have inherited much of their wealth from 12th-century ancestors. In Cambridge the dynasty was established (at least within living memory) by the two Michaels, father and son. The father was generous in his support of the friars. His son sustained the family fortune, but became indebted to the Jews. The third generation simply sold up and left. They may have used the proceeds of the sale to purchase lands in Hampshire, and perhaps elsewhere.

Morice family

Nicholas Morice is the key figure in the Morice dynasty. His grandfather was Morice.[505] His father was William Morice, who married Isabella, daughter of Harvey Gogging, clerk, and Alicia, his wife.[506] They had two children: Nicholas was the heir and held almost all the family property in 1279, while his sister Mariota married twice: first to Elisio Textor and then to Saer de Feruyggnes.[507]

Morice family

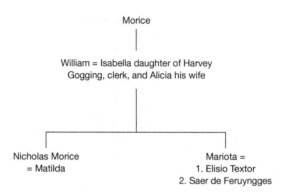

Nicholas married Matilda.[508] He built up a large property portfolio by purchasing from many different sellers. By 1279 he had purchased two messuages in St Botolph's, two shops in St Clement's, a shop in the market and a granary in St Michael's, together with 43 acres in the Cambridge fields and 15 acres in the Barnwell fields. His inheritance was small by comparison: a messuage in St Botolph's from his grandfather, and another messuage with an acre of land that was acquired as his mother's dowry. Some of his land was purchased indirectly from the Dunning estate through William of Manefield, and some was even sold by Manefield to John Porthors and then sold on to Nicholas as the final buyer (see Chapter 6).

The Morice family continued to flourish in Cambridge well into the 14th century. Bartholomew Morice became mayor in 1317, and many members of the family held property in the town. But after 1279 it is difficult to keep track of the relations between them.

The Morice family was a small family spanning three generations in which every member of the family pulled their weight. Unlike some of the larger families, where low-performers or even 'free riders' were conspicuous, the Morice family was compact and cohesive. The driving force was Nicholas, but his parents, grandparents and sister all seem to have played a useful role.

4.5 Conclusion

This chapter has presented 23 case studies of Cambridge families, with their family trees. These studies illustrate how different sources of information can be combined to discover new links between family members and to cross-check information on particular individuals. Together with 13 other case studies in Casson, Casson, Lee and Phillips, *Business and Community*, Appendix 14, they provide the evidence base for Chapter 5, which addresses the bigger issues concerning these family dynasties and the growth of the town.

Notes

[1] See, for example, the journal *Medieval Prosopography: History and Collective Biography*. For prosopographical research of other groups see, for example, Stephen Alsford, 'The Men Behind the Masque: Office-Holding in East-Anglian Boroughs, 1272–1460' (MPhil thesis, University of Leicester, 1982), available at http: //www.trytel. com/~tristan/towns/mcontent.html (accessed 7 February 2018).

[2] Clarke, 'Peasant Society'.

[3] Kermode, *Merchants*.

[4] Kosminsky, 'Hundred Rolls'; Kanzaka, 'Villein Rents'.

[5] Howell, *Land, Family*.

[6] Howell, 'Contrasting Communities'.

[7] Corpus Christi College Archive, University of Cambridge CCCC09/08.

[8] Casson, Casson, Lee and Phillips, *Business and Community*, Appendix 8; J, p 253.

[9] HR 249–53; LB, p 178.

[10] HR 247; StJ 16, 75. Henry's father was William, who appeared in court as an attorney in 1198: Casson, Casson, Lee and Phillips, *Business and Community*, Appendix 6.

[11] StJ 9, 10.

[12] StJ 75.

[13] HR A45.

[14] StJ 20, CCCC09/15; StJ 26.

[15] Much of it was from the estate of Richard Hockley, who was survived by his wife, Eva of Madingley, and their two sons, John (the heir) and Richard (CCCC09/16C/26, 28, 29, 31–4).

[16] HR 884; OTG, p 23, HR A41.

[17] HR 157, 800; StJ 157,162.

[18] Merton 1622.

[19] StJ 130.

[20] HR 130, 803.

[21] StJ 75; HR 31, 253/4. It is probably Henry son of John, who witnessed many deeds in the period 1270–1310. In 1281 Henry petitioned a plea of debt against Josce son of Saulet (Casson, Casson, Lee and Phillips, *Business and Community*, Appendix 8; EJ VI, p 281).

[22] HR 237–48.

[23] CCCC09/1119, CCCC09/14/30.

[24] Casson, Casson, Lee and Phillips, *Business and Community*, Appendix 12; F, p 265; M, pp 134–5.

[25] F, p 265; LB, p 285.

[26] J, p 119, 166: LB, p 223.

[27] StJ 75.

[28] StR 97.

[29] F, p 265.

[30] HR 314.

[31] HR 334, 959, 1080. In 1260 Richard was amerced for selling wine in Cambridge contrary to the assize (Casson, Casson, Lee and Phillips, *Business and Community*, Appendix 11).

[32] HR 337/8/40.

[33] HR 334.

[34] HR 338; HR 339; HR 340.

[35] HR 641; HR 336/7.

[36] StR 306.

[37] StR 307.

[38] StR 189.

[39] HR 44; StJ 240/2; StR 105, 130.

[40] Casson, Casson, Lee and Phillips, *Business and Community*, Appendix 12.

[41] HR 29; CCCC09/14/31. Savary of Barton was the father of William the Goldsmith (StJ 165). There are other persons whom it is difficult to place in the family tree: 1) Geoffrey of Barton, clerk, may have been another of John's sons. In c.1250 he bought some land in Newnham from the Hospital of St John, which was previously owned by Gilbert the baker, for a payment of 38s and an annual rent of 4s. 2) Richard of Barton witnessed a deed transferring property in Madingley from Albric son of Eustace, to Roger de Burdeleys in c.1184–1204 (CCCC09/17/2/2). In view of the early date it is possible that he might be John of Barton's grandfather, the father of William. If so then Henry son of Richard of Barton, witness to an early deed (StJ 240), would be William's brother, and in fact 'William his brother' witnessed the deed. 3) Alan of Barton witnessed a deed for 100 acres of land in Madingley, c.1200–1233 (CCCC09/17/2/4). He held considerable land in Barton, on which he paid rent of 3s 2d and 12d in frankpledge (LB, pp 252, 277). He married Roheys (Rose) (PDR, p 9), and they had a son, Radulph (J, p 253; StJ 161). Roheys had a sister, Matilda. It seems that Matilda and Roheys had a father Elye and a mother Alice (PDC, p 309). In 1219 Alan, Rose and Matilda were involved in a dispute with the Prior of Merton over the presentation of a priest to Barton church (F. W. Maitland (ed.), *Bracton's Note Book*, II (3 vols, Cambridge, 1897), p 28, plea 34). Alan was in debt to the Jews for 8 marks and two quarters of corn in 1238 and 22s 6d in 1239 (Casson, Casson, Lee and Phillips, *Business and Community*, Appendix 9; J, pp 253, 258). John son of Adam of Barton was in debt to the Aaron son of Isaac for 10s and one bushel of corn in 1238 (Casson, Casson, Lee and Phillips, *Business and Community*, Appendix 9; J, p 258). Peter of Barton (not the same Peter as above) was in debt to the Jews (Isaac son of Samuel and Jacob son of Deulesant) for 12s 6d and half of one quarter of corn in 1238 (Casson, Casson, Lee and Phillips, *Business and Community*, Appendix 9; J, p 257). Hugh, son of Bartholomew of Barton, gave land to the Hospital of St John (StJ 214).

[42] Casson, Casson, Lee and Phillips, *Business and Community*, Appendix 8; J, p 253.

[43] Casson, Casson, Lee and Phillips, *Business and Community*, Appendix 8.

[44] EJ III, p 179. In 1274, when Agnes, together with the Prior of Royston, Geoffrey Spartegrave, Robert Hubert, Abraham Biscop and Muriel, widow of Saulot Motun, were accused of concealing goods and chattels of Saulot the Jew, deceased, which were forfeit to the king (Appendix 8). Robert died shortly after the indictment. The others failed to appear in court when summoned, and the sheriff was ordered to distrain them. John Porthors, Agnes's son, paid in the Kings Receipt 32s, as did Geoffrey 5s and Agnes herself 2s 6d. Suspicion also fell on

Sabina, Robert's widow. It was alleged that Sabina, Agnes and John had between them received goods and chattels worth a total of £24, and a jury was called to decide the matter. Sabina and John gave the king 20s for the inquest to be held at Cambridge. The verdict favoured the accused and amercement was remitted.

45 HR 338; HR 339; HR 340.
46 HR A46; J, p 202.
47 MR, pp 74–6.
48 StJ 41.
49 Casson, Casson, Lee and Phillips, *Business and Community*, Appendix 5, 20 Hen II, p 287; MR, p 74.
50 Casson, Casson, Lee and Phillips, *Business and Community*, Appendix 10; PDC, p 284.
51 Stenton, *Pleas I*, 2170 and Casson, Casson, Lee and Phillips, *Business and Community*, Appendix 6, I, p 431.
52 Casson, Casson, Lee and Phillips, *Business and Community*, Appendix 5.
53 Casson, Casson, Lee and Phillips, *Business and Community*, Appendix 2; M, pp 168–9.
54 Thomas Hardy (ed.), *Rotuli Litterarum Clausarum in Turri Londoniensi Asservati* (2 vols), I (London, 1833), p 252, cited in FC, p 103.
55 LB, pp 239, 277, T. 354, cited in FC, p 103, who gives a date of 1234.
56 StJ 9/10; StJ 11. The implicit rate of interest is calculated by dividing the rent by the payment and expressing the result as a percentage.
57 HR A33/4.
58 M, p 176.
59 CCCC09/15/4a.
60 Casson, Casson, Lee and Phillips, *Business and Community*, Appendix 6; Curia Regis Rolls XIX, p 362.
61 MR, p 78.
62 Merton 1543; 1544.
63 Casson, Casson, Lee and Phillips, *Business and Community*, Appendix 9; EJ I, p 267, which does not agree with MR, p 77.
64 StJ 59; MR, p 77.
65 StJ 71; MR, p 77.
66 StJ 41.
67 StR 271. He witnessed a number of deeds; for example, CCCC09/17/3 and 4.
68 StJ 64.
69 Casson, Casson, Lee and Phillips, *Business and Community*, Appendix 6; Curia Regis Rolls XIII, p 187.
70 HR P3/4.
71 StR 211c.
72 StJ 64–8; StR 266.
73 StJ 64, 66–70.
74 StJ 67.
75 HR 10.
76 MR, p 75.
77 MR, p 75; StR 266.
78 StR217. CCCC09/08/48. There is an earlier reference to a Gilbert Blancgernun, which almost certainly refers to a different person, possibly a brother of Baldwin senior. In 1199 Edith, wife (or widow) of Gilbert agrees to let Eva, wife of Segar, hold her messuage in Cambridge for life (Casson, Casson, Lee and Phillips, *Business and Community*, Appendix 7.1; Curia Regis Rolls, I; FC, p 289).

[79] StJ 41. He held land near Coton. He witnessed a deed in c.1269 concerning land in the Sale, near the Castle, and another involving St Radegund's Priory (Casson, Casson, Lee and Phillips, *Business and Community*, Appendix 10; StR 270).

[80] HR 49–56.

[81] SP, p 1.

[82] SP, p 2.

[83] HR P26–8.

[84] HR P1.

[85] SP, p 2; PDC, p 290.

[86] SP, p 2; StR 19.

[87] Casson, Casson, Lee and Phillips, *Business and Community*, Appendix 5, 11 Hen II, p 60.

[88] The Hundred Rolls offer three contradictory accounts, but evidence from other sources suggest he was his son, despite assertions to the contrary (HR P1, A18, 1034; SP, p 2).

[89] Casson, Casson, Lee and Phillips, *Business and Community*, Appendix 6; Stenton, *Pleas I*, 3536.

[90] Gilbert may have had other sons: Walter son of Gilbert was tallaged half a mark in 1176 while William son of Gilbert was put in pace of Harvey, son of Eustace, in a court case in 1199 (Casson, Casson, Lee and Phillips, *Business and Community*, Appendix 2; Stenton, *Pleas I*, 2504).

[91] SP, p 3; Stenton, *Pleas I*, 2240.

[92] StJ 72.

[93] PDC, p 278; SP, p 4.

[94] PDC, pp 285, 290, 298; SP, p 3.

[95] PDC, pp 285, 290, 298; SP, p 3.

[96] PDC, p 284; PDC, p 264; PDC, p 276.

[97] HR A18; SP, p 5.

[98] Casson, Casson, Lee and Phillips, *Business and Community*, Appendix 3; M, pp 168–9.

[99] J. p 260; J, p 268.

[100] HR 740; HR 784/5. F, p 348 claims to identify two further sons, Michael son of Harvey and John son of Harvey, who witnessed 13th-century deeds, but his sources do not seem to corroborate this.

[101] HR 71.

[102] SP, p 5.

[103] HR 162; SP, p 6.

[104] SP, p 8; HR P26, 42, 250, 290, 364–5.

[105] HR R11.

[106] SP, p 9.

[107] Casson, Casson, Lee and Phillips, *Business and Community*, Appendix 12; BNM, p 7; M, pp 135–6.

[108] Casson, Casson, Lee and Phillips, *Business and Community*, Appendix 9, p 268.

[109] StJ 23.

[110] HR 108.

[111] SP, p 10; M, p 184.

[112] StR 235.

[113] M, p 164; SP, p 7.

[114] Casson, Casson, Lee and Phillips, *Business and Community*, Appendix 12; BNM; OTG, p 59.

[115] Casson, Casson, Lee and Phillips, *Business and Community*, Appendix 9, pp 267, 257, 261.

[116] HR 454; HR 110.

[117] HR 454.

[118] HR 458.

[119] HR 729.

[120] In 1260 John made a pledge for Simon son of John of Barton, accused of mayhem and robbery, at the county assizes, and Simon failed to appear. He also mainperned John Saleman and Simon son of Geoffrey of Ely, both accused of murder, and again they did not appear, leaving John and his seven colleagues in mercy (Casson, Casson, Lee and Phillips, *Business and Community*, Appendix 11).

[121] OTG, p 59; LB, pp 166, 218.

[122] OTG, p 59; LB, pp 166, 218; HR 69.

[123] HR 729.

[124] HR 729.

[125] HR 58.

[126] StR 169c. A William of St Edmunds, described as a king's justice, was involved in ratifying an agreement in 1232 by which the Prior of Barnwell agreed to pay half a mark per annum to the town of Cambridge in respect of their rights in a four-day fair at Barnwell granted by Henry III in 1229 (LB, p 88). He could be the same William as above, as the dates are reasonable, were it not that William is elsewhere described as a chaplain rather than a royal justice (although one does not exclude the other). Master Geoffrey, Alice's father, seems to have been a person of some importance. Stokes thought that he may have been an official under the Bishop of Ely; a gift of land by Reginald de Argentin to St Radegund's was witnessed by 'Mr. Geoffrey, official', who might have been the said Geoffrey (StR, p 50; OTG, p 57). But he could also be Master Geoffrey, the chaplain of Barnwell, who endowed a chantry in the Almonry with a great messuage facing both the town and the fields, 5 acres of land and 100 silver marks in return for 1 mark per annum rent sometime before 1251; this would imply that he had retired to a life of celibacy after bringing up his three children (LB, pp 96–7).

[127] OTG, p 57, fn 3.

[128] StR 283.

[129] StR 239b.

[130] HR 71; PDR, p 22. She may also have had a brother (or brother-in-law) John, whose daughter Letitia was described as the granddaughter of Master Geoffrey, which would make John Geoffrey's son (or son-in-law). In 1225 Letitia entered a plea against Richard de Argentin, regarding a messuage in which William and Alice may have lived (Casson, Casson, Lee and Phillips, *Business and Community*, Appendix 6; Curia Regis Rolls XII, p 165).

[131] HR P35b.

[132] HR 632, 646; PDR, p 16; StR 329; OTG, p 57.

[133] OTG, p 58. Other members of the family, about which little is known, include 1) Master Alexander bought a messuage in St Michael's from the Templars of Denney, which he gave to Ermina of Hardwick (HR 691). 2) Humphrey (HR 799/80) served on an inquest jury comprising Christians and Jews into the property of Belecote, widow of Samuel Gabay (Casson, Casson, Lee and Phillips, *Business and Community*, Appendix 7). Humphrey had a son, Richard, who owned property near Holy Trinity (HR 799). In 1279 Richard held two messuages in Holy Trinity parish, one leased for the occupier's life, both of which were inherited from his

father, who had purchased them. 3) William of St Edmunds, whitesmith, bought and sold property in and around Smith Row, near St Mary's Church; his name may allude to Bury St Edmunds (e.g. CCCC09/08/14). 4) Dru was the first husband of Alice, whose second husband was Walter le Rus of Walden (HR872). Dru and Alice bought a messuage in St Andrew's from St Radegund's that the nuns had been given by Robert of Trumpington because he could not bear the burden imposed on the messuage of maintaining the watch. Dru may be 'Dru the chaplain' who was involved in the riot of 1235 (Casson, Casson, Lee and Phillips, *Business and Community*, Appendix 7; Curia Regis Rolls, XV, pp 358–9).

[134] HR P35a, b; OTG, p 56.

[135] HR 530; StR 31; CPR 1290, p 363; 1293, p 25; 1299, p 421; OTG, p 58, fn 5.

[136] HR 454; HR 110; HR 721.

[137] LB, p 134.

[138] HR 309.

[139] Casson, Casson, Lee and Phillips, *Business and Community*, Appendices 2 and 5; M, p 168.

[140] StJ 98, 114.

[141] HR 358.

[142] HR 408, 589.

[143] HR 412–14; F, p 379.

[144] HR 405, 406.

[145] Casson, Casson, Lee and Phillips, *Business and Community*, Appendix 9, pp 254, 271.

[146] Little is known about Harvey, other than that he had a son called William (CCCC09/18/1–3).

[147] HR 308.

[148] HR 314; HR 307; F, p 379.

[149] CCCC09/18/5; Casson, Casson, Lee and Phillips, *Business and Community*, Appendix 11.

[150] Casson, Casson, Lee and Phillips, *Business and Community*, Appendix 12; PDR, p 56; VCH 3, p 39; BNM, p 7.

[151] BNM, pp 6, 7; CCR, 8 July 1290, p 91; 17 May 1294, p 348; 12 November 1296, p 499.

[152] BNM, p 7.

[153] Casson, Casson, Lee and Phillips, *Business and Community*, Appendix 8, Exchequer of the Jews, III, p 277.

[154] HR 386, 680; F, p 379.

[155] HR 386, 680; F, p 379; HR 304.

[156] HR 309.

[157] CCCC09/15/10.

[158] HR 517; HR 518; HR 516; HR 519; HR 522.

[159] HR 519.

[160] HR 519.

[161] HR 398–403.

[162] HR 261, HR 305. Sabina, it has been suggested, had previously been married to Stephen Baker, although there is no evidence for this in the Hundred Rolls (F, p 379). Robert may also have been married before – possibly to Amicia, daughter of Cecilia Godso (HR 636). Robert may have had a son from this first marriage, namely Robert son of Robert, who was a canon of Anglesey Abbey.

[163] StR 364; HR 262.

[164] CCCC09/15/5–10.

[165] HR 190/1, 302–14; VCH 3, p 39.

[166] Another possibility is Ivo of Lynn, son of Master Martin of Lynn (HR 384); however, Peter, one of Ivo's sons, styled himself Peter son of Ivo of Cambridge, which suggests that Ivo as well as Peter may have come from Cambridge (CCCC09/13/1b).

[167] HR 705.

[168] StJ 57.

[169] HR 836/7; Casson, Casson, Lee and Phillips, *Business and Community*, Appendix 14.

[170] CCCC09/12/4a; see also StR 333.

[171] HR 497.

[172] HR 251.

[173] HR 363; HR 833.

[174] HR 451. A Radulph brother of Ivo was tallaged 1 mark in 1211; it is possible that Radulph was named after Ivo's brother.

[175] StR 177, 185a.

[176] HR P25.

[177] William witnessed many deeds c.1250 (St J35/6).

[178] HR 238, 287, 363, 370, 471, 474/5, 715; StR 364; StJ 41.

[179] HR 370.

[180] HR 233/7, 287, 471, 475.

[181] HR 363.

[182] HR 237, 712.

[183] HR 470.

[184] There are four other 'sons of Ivo', but none of them appear in the Hundred Rolls. It is likely that they belonged to different families. Philip son of Ivo acted as attorney for William Frisselak, a leading member of the town community, in 1199 (Casson, Casson, Lee and Phillips, *Business and Community*, Appendix 6). Geoffrey son of Ivo was amerced half a mark *pro fuga* in 1219 and half a mark concerning a pledge in 1220 (Casson, Casson, Lee and Phillips, *Business and Community*, Appendix 3). Robert son of Ivo was amerced half a mark in 1221 (Casson, Casson, Lee and Phillips, *Business and Community*, Appendix 4). It is possible (especially in Geoffrey's case) that they may have left the town. Gregory son of Ivo witnessed a deed in c.1250 (CCCC09/13/1).

[185] HR 144. Laurence of Littlebury was the son of Laurence (HR A16).

[186] StR 63.

[187] Stenton, *Pleas I*, 2179.

[188] HR 65.

[189] HR 145–8.

[190] In 1259 a royal writ directed the Cambridge bailiffs to remove to Westminster a dispute between Richard and Walter de Berkeay over a messuage in the town (C, p 48, citing Rot. Claus. 44 Hen III).

[191] HR 263.

[192] HR F46, 47.

[193] Casson, Casson, Lee and Phillips, *Business and Community*, Appendix 12; VCH 3, p 39.

[194] See Chapter 6.

[195] HR 253.

[196] HR 255.

[197] StR 247.

198 LB, p 228.

199 LB, pp 228–9.

200 CCR, 19 October 1290, p 105; 12 June 1294, p 351.

201 LB, pp 282–90.

202 F, p 529, citing PDR, p 7.

203 HR 1070.

204 HR 735; StR 363.

205 Casson, Casson, Lee and Phillips, *Business and Community*, Appendices 2 and 3;
     M, p 168. William may have had a brother called Henry. There is evidence of a
     Master Henry Pilat who was a contemporary of William, and the pair witnessed
     deeds together c.1210–18, StR 249, 285. Henry may have had a son named Henry
     who appears in the Hundred Rolls. Henry (father or son) may also be the Henry
     who was married to Sarah (HR 737).

206 HR 736; R14.

207 HR 725.

208 LB, p 88.

209 See, for example, StR 91; F, p 529.

210 It has been conjectured that William acquired much of the land from a well-
     connected lady in Sawston who was his employer; the evidence for this is
     debatable, however (F, pp 529–30).

211 LB, pp 130, 283; HR 733.

212 HR 201–3; HR 734.

213 HR 750/1.

214 F, p 530.

215 Casson, Casson, Lee and Phillips, *Business and Community*, Appendix 12; F, p 530.

216 F, p 530.

217 StJ 189.

218 CCCC09/08/9; CCCC09/09/8. There are several other members of the Pylet
     family who are almost certainly related to those noted here, but are difficult to
     place in the family tree. They all held property in the area around the Jewry. The
     most obvious conjecture is that they are sons or younger brothers of William
     and Henry. Walter Pylet bought a messuage in All Saints in the Jewry from the
     nearby Hospital (HR 718). Walter's garden bordered on land in Grenecroft, near
     St Radegund's, where Hugh Pylet held land (StR 50). Walter and Hugh may
     have been brothers. Walter's messuage may be the same as a messuage 'formerly
     of Walter Pylet' near the Hospital and Kings Lane (StR 97). Harvey Pylet owned a
     messuage in nearby St Sepulchre parish (HR 737; LB, p 285). Harvey was married
     to Sarah; they also held a half-messuage in Newnham (CCCC09/13/3A).

219 F, p 530.

220 PR, pp 1159–66.

221 StJ 194; StJ 191, 196.

222 StJ 40, 195.

223 Casson, Casson, Lee and Phillips, *Business and Community*, Appendix 1; M, p 171;
     OTG, p 35.

224 F, p 591.

225 J, p 142; OTG, p 36; EJ I, p 31; Casson, Casson, Lee and Phillips, *Business and
     Community*, Appendix 8.

226 PR 1223, p 147.

227 OTG, p 39; F, p 591.

228 HR A36; StJ 40/2, M, pp 171–3.

229 StJ 41/2.

230 StR 181; OTG, p 37.

231 StJ 80; OTG, p 39.

232 There were several men in Cambridge in c.1220 identified as 'son of Eustace' and it is not entirely clear whether they were sons of Eustace of Madingley or Eustace his son or, indeed, of some other Eustace altogether. Four other men, however, appear to have a distinct connection to Eustace of Madingley, namely Richard, Geoffrey, Hugh and Anketil (StJ 192, 195, 206, 301). Geoffrey and Hugh were certainly brothers and it is possible that Richard was their brother too (StJ 206). It is possible that Anketil removed to Henlow, Bedfordshire (StJ 197). The most probable explanation is that they were all sons of Eustace of Madingley; indeed it seems that Geoffrey son of Eustace also became known as Geoffrey of Madingley (probably on the death of his father). This suggests that Eustace of Madingley had six sons altogether. (Harvey son of Eustace, discussed previously, seems to have no direct family connection to Eustace of Madingley, although the two families held properties that were close to each other.)

233 HR 660; StJ 118.

234 F, p 592.

235 HR P9.

236 PDR, pp 16, 23, 29.

237 Casson, Casson, Lee and Phillips, *Business and Community*, Appendix 9; J, p 268.

238 Casson, Casson, Lee and Phillips, *Business and Community*, Appendix 8; EJ I, p 119.

239 OTG, p 42; F, p 529.

240 LB, p 218.

241 HR 170.

242 Casson, Casson, Lee and Phillips, *Business and Community*, Appendix 9; EJ VI, pp 131, 137.

243 OTG, p 42.

244 HR 269, 827.

245 PDR, p 40.

246 F, p 529.

247 OTG, p 43.

248 LB, pp 160–1, summary translation.

249 Casson, Casson, Lee and Phillips, *Business and Community*, Appendix 11.

250 In 1226 Peter Ruffus bought nearby land in St Clement's parish from Geoffrey Wulward and Aunger himself (or his son) witnessed the deed (StJ 77). Peter Ruffus witnessed several deeds relating to lands in Trumpington and Grantchester, but his relation to Aunger is unclear (StJ 166, 169, 172, 211–12).

251 Casson, Casson, Lee and Phillips, *Business and Community*, Appendix 5, 26 Hen II; F, p 593.

252 Stenton, *Pleas I*.

253 OTG, p 42.

254 HR 163.

255 HR R2.

256 OTG, p 42.

257 StR 198.

258 PDR, p 47.

259 LB, p 131.

260 HR 734.

261 StJ 21.

[262] HR 180.

[263] Casson, Casson, Lee and Phillips, *Business and Community*, Appendix 5; PR various; FC, p 288.

[264] T, p 49. In 1167–8 he executed a royal writ in Hampshire when he and another royal servant were accounting for £10 for the queen's maintenance (PR 1167–8, p 191). In 1170 he was charged with spending £20 in Staffordshire for the maintenance of the young king, Henry II (PR 1169–70, p 128), and in the following year he spent money in Gloucestershire for carting goods to Scotland on the king's behalf (PR 1170–1, p 88). In 1171–2 he was among those handling funds for the young king's coronation. In 1172–3 he commenced his role as an itinerant justice, working as part of a team, normally with two other justices. He began by visiting Devon and Somerset. In 1173–4 he was involved in an assize at Windsor, and in supervising expenditure in Hampshire, Leicestershire and Warwickshire, much of it apparently connected with improving and garrisoning castles (PR 1173–4, pp 116, 136, 140). In 1174–5 he was fined in Gloucester for a false claim (PR 1174–5, p 161), for which he was pardoned by the king the following year (PR 1175–6, p 72). He witnessed about ten of Henry II's charters, the earliest dated 1171, and occasionally witnessed final concords at Westminster too (T, p 50).

[265] PR 1175–6, pp 153, 156, 174.

[266] PR 1176–7, pp 16–179.

[267] T, p 49; PRO, pp 1, 34, 141.

[268] T, p 49. In 1182–3 he extended the scope of his judicial activity: he became involved in eyres in Surrey, Sussex, London and Middlesex, Berkshire, Hampshire, Northamptonshire and the eastern counties (Norfolk, Suffolk, Cambridgeshire, Essex and Hertfordshire) (PR 1182–3). He also participated in the eyre for Bedfordshire and Buckinghamshire, where he was also sheriff. It is possible, though by no means certain, that this extension of his work coincided with a relocation of his principal residence from Wiltshire to Cambridge. In 1184–5 he also conducted eyres in Worcestershire and Kent (PR 1184–5, pp 123, 228). At this point he seems to have been at the height of his powers. In 1187–8 he renewed his role as Sheriff of Bedfordshire and Buckinghamshire on new terms (PR 1187–88, p 185), and took on the role of Sheriff of Sussex for a short time (PR 1187–8, p 185). He seems to have owed the king 38 hawks as a result of his previous seven and a half years as sheriff, and he seems to have owed even more when his second term came to an end. In 1189–90 he was pardoned 40s for scutage in Essex and Hertfordshire, but held liable for over £9 scutage of the honour of Arundel, with respect to military service in Wales (PR 1189–90, pp 109, 130). In 1191–2 he was involved in the Norfolk eyre (PR 1191–2, p 44) and the following year in the Lincolnshire, Northamptonshire and Bedfordshire eyres (PR 1193, pp 48, 97, 146).

[269] PR 1189–90, p 115.

[270] PDH, p 5, entries 3 and 4.

[271] Casson, Casson, Lee and Phillips, *Business and Community*, Appendix 6; Curia Regis Rolls XVII, p 485; PDH, p 8, entries 31, 34.

[272] PR 1165–6, 1170–1.

[273] PR 1187–8, p 20; PR 1193, p 48.

[274] T, p 26.

[275] PR 1160–1, p 41.

[276] It has been suggested that Herbert was Richard's father, and by implication William's father too, but another possibility is that William was Eustace's son and Albric's brother (T, p 26). It has also been suggested that William's family

background was 'administrative and knightly' and that William was the son of Radulph de Rufus, one of the Conqueror's knights, but the timing seems to be wrong (T, p 27, especially fn 5, p 26; VCH Staffs 17, p 169; Edward Foss, *Biographia Juridica: A Biographical Dictionary of the Judges of England from the Conquest* (9 vols) I (London, 1870), p 303). A Herbert Ruffus reappears in the Pipe Rolls in 1192 (Itinerary of Richard I, p 71), but this person is likely to be a member of a later generation.

277 PR 1194, p 210.
278 PR 1194, p 79.
279 PR 1195, p 241.
280 Casson, Casson, Lee and Phillips, *Business and Community*, Appendix 10; PDC, pp 259–60; FC, p 289; see also PR 1194, p 79, which gives a somewhat different account of the transaction.
281 Casson, Casson, Lee and Phillips, *Business and Community*, Appendix 6; PR 1195, p 199.
282 PR 1196, p 152.
283 Casson, Casson, Lee and Phillips, *Business and Community*, Appendix 5.
284 StJ 218.
285 PR 1209, p 11; PR 1228, p 11.
286 FC, p 23; see also LB, p 248.
287 Casson, Casson, Lee and Phillips, *Business and Community*, Appendix 5.
288 CPR 28 Feb 1235.
289 FC, pp 12, 24.
290 Fine Rolls, C60/47, 7/299, 20 April 1250, available at https://finerollshenry3.org.uk/home (accessed 17 October 2018).
291 PDR 1254, p 35.
292 FC, p 12.
293 PDR, p 40.
294 FC, p 24.
295 FC, p 12.
296 FC, p 24.
297 FC, p 12. Another Clopton connection concerns Simon Ruffus, who held a half-fee in Clopton of the Honour of Boulogne, 1198–1201 (PDC, pp 276–7; PR 1198, p 138; FC, pp 11–12). This could be the same fee that was later held by Geoffrey le Rus (FC, p 12). He also had an interest in a mill in Clopton. At about the same time Simon sold to William Pevel 2 virgates of land in Morden for 20s in 1199 (PDC, p 270, PDR, p 2). Simon's connection to William and Geoffrey is unclear. As he became active in the property market shortly after William's death, he may have been William II's younger brother. Several other members of the family were alive at about the time of the Hundred Rolls and are difficult to place. Alan Ruffus jointly held land in Hinton near Cambridge of the honour of Earl Conan in 1183 (FC, p 81). Robert Ruffus petitioned against Stephen Ragedale in grand assize concerning half a hide of land in Wratting, a village east of Cambridge in 1199; the case was respited for default of visors (Casson, Casson, Lee and Phillips, *Business and Community*, Appendix 7; FC, p 108). He may be unrelated to the others as none of them held much land in this area. Hugo Ruffus jointly purchased with Philip son of Robert, a virgate of land in Eversden in 1204 (PDC, p 307), but little else is known about him. Walter le Rus of Waleden married Alice, widow of Dru of St Edmunds; they held a messuage in St Andrew's that Dru and Alice had bought from the Prioress and Convent of St Radegund's

(HR 872). Maurice Ruffus of Horningsea, a village about 4 miles downstream from Cambridge, owed 40s to Salomon son of Josce in 1272 (J, p 278). Henry le Rus was one of a number of tenants of Robert de Hastings in debt to the king in 1276 in respect of Robert's debts to Moses of Clare, the Jew (EJ III, p 117). Thomas le Rus was the father of Helewisa, wife of John of Orwell (HR 726–7), and had a son, Thomas (HR 875).

[298] Casson, Casson, Lee and Phillips, *Business and Community*, Appendix 12.

[299] StR 334–5.

[300] StR 218.

[301] HR 133, 134.

[302] Casson, Casson, Lee and Phillips, *Business and Community*, Appendices 2 and 5; F, p 287.

[303] Information about the daughter is inferred from the fact that Robert I is described both as the son of Walter Wymund and as Seman's grandson (HR 133; HR 134). This suggests that Seman had another son, Walter, or a daughter who married Walter. The latter is most likely, since Walter is never actually described as Seman's son. Robert is also described as Walter's brother, and Walter, conversely, as Robert's brother (HR73; StJ 15). This suggests that Walter had a son, Walter junior.

[304] HR 116.

[305] HR 501.

[306] StJ 175. Either William or his son could be the 'Seman of Newnham' who, with Gunhilda his wife, were involved in a plea regarding land in Newnham in 1219 (Pipe Roll, Casson, Casson, Lee and Phillips, *Business and Community*, Appendix 5).

[307] For example, F, p 596.

[308] StR 90; StR 233; StR 252, 254a, 364.

[309] Casson, Casson, Lee and Phillips, *Business and Community*, Appendix 6, Curia Regis Rolls, I, p 278.

[310] Casson, Casson, Lee and Phillips, *Business and Community*, Appendix 2; M, p 168.

[311] Casson, Casson, Lee and Phillips, *Business and Community*, Appendix 9; J, p 263.

[312] CCCC09/08/11; HR 543; HR 65.

[313] CCCC09/08/10.

[314] HR 216, 218.

[315] Casson, Casson, Lee and Phillips, *Business and Community*, Appendix 12.

[316] HR R10, 136.

[317] CCCC09/17/15, 16, 25.

[318] HR F2; Casson, Casson, Lee and Phillips, *Business and Community*, Appendix 12.

[319] CCCC09/13/1.

[320] HR 187; HR 188.

[321] HR 216, 218–36.

[322] HR 187.

[323] CCCC09/15/19.

[324] HR 65–71.

[325] HR 72–4, 261.

[326] HR 132; StR 161.

[327] StJ 15.

[328] StR 262.

[329] HR 182–6, 739, 743.

[330] HR 935; HR 669.

[331] HR 938.

[332] LB, pp liii, 158.

[333] HR 939. Thomas may be the person recorded as paying 4s to the fifteenth levied in the parish of Chesterton, adjacent to Cambridge, in 1225 (CC, p 1). Thomas witnessed a number of deeds up to his death in c.1259. In 1260 a county jury reported that the late Thomas had encroached on a common thoroughfare by obstructing Alwines Lane; this conflicts with the published date of 1264–5 for his corrody.

[334] HR 636. When Robert remarried on her death to Sabina Gogging this established a three-way link between the Toylet, Hubert and Gogging families.

[335] StJ 355; LB, p 85. 'Item the said canons have by gift of Thomas Toylet 24 acres of land in fee from Baldwin Blangernun, which he held from the prior of Barnwell by charter and by service of 26 pence per annum, and 28 acres and one croft which the same Thomas bought from John le Rus, and seven and a half acres and half a rood which he bought from Geoffrey Melt, and half an acre which he bought from Walter Baker, and three and a half acres which he acquired by gift of Robert Parleben, and two acres which he bought from Michael son of Robert Parleben, and one acre which he bought from John son of Roger the Infirmarer, and two roods which he acquired by gift of Radulph, son of Henry, in exchange for another two roods. And one rood which he bought from the aforesaid Geoffrey Melt. And 15 pence of income paid annually which Winfr' son of Hamo of Barnwell owed to him for half an acre of land which he held from him in the fields of Barnwell; for this land he made to the said canons, tenant-in-chief of the lord's fee by service owed and by custom of which they are unaware and gave to the their almoner of Barnwell a chapel for perpetual celebration of divine mass for his soul and for the souls of all their deceased faithful' (HR P9).

[336] HR 692.

[337] HR 692, 698. One of these houses came to be known as the Archdeacon's House (MH, pp 2–7).

[338] LB, pp liii, 115–18.

[339] HR 721.

[340] HR 382, 739; BNM, p 8. states that Avicia was William's sister rather than his daughter, but this implies that she received her dowry from her brother rather than her father.

[341] HR 536. William witnessed many deeds in the period 1250–80.

[342] HR A39, 13.

[343] HR 734.

[344] Casson, Casson, Lee and Phillips, *Business and Community*, Appendix 12.

[345] StJ 31, 55, 58.

[346] StR 245a.

[347] Casson, Casson, Lee and Phillips, *Business and Community*, Appendix 12.

[348] CCCC09/12/3.

[349] HR 671–5, 678–81; HR 683.

[350] Casson, Casson, Lee and Phillips, *Business and Community*, Appendix 12; BNM, p 8; LB, pp 89–90.

[351] HR 183–6.

[352] LB, p 284. Robert may have had a son, Robert, although there is no record of this. A Robert Toylet was bailiff in 1309 and represented the town in Parliament in 1315 (BNM, p 8). In 1330 Margery, widow of Robert Toylet, sold land in All Saints by the Castle (StR 272). A Robert Toylet, who was probably of an earlier generation, was fined half a mark in 1220 and 1 mark in 1223 for selling wine

contrary to the assize (Casson, Casson, Lee and Phillips, *Business and Community* Appendix 5). He is listed as one of the rioters in 1235 whose actions led to the king taking control of the town, although he does not seem to have been punished (Casson, Casson, Lee and Phillips, *Business and Community*, Appendix 6). He may have been a younger brother of William I.

353 HR 482; HR 713.

354 HR 622.

355 HR 193, 361.

356 Casson, Casson, Lee and Phillips, *Business and Community*, Appendices 2, 3 and 5.

357 StJ 35/6/8, 43, 105/6, 306/13.

358 HR 173.

359 HR 193.

360 HR 193.

361 HR 658.

362 StJ 90.

363 HR 879; HR 687.

364 CCCC09/16C/3; StJ 264.

365 Casson, Casson, Lee and Phillips, *Business and Community*, Appendix 6; Curia Regis Rolls XV.

366 HR 610; HR 716; HR 286; HR 368.

367 HR 117/18, 1054, R9.

368 HR 874; HR 1078; HR 440.

369 HR 286, 403, 605, 610, 716.

370 CCCC09/16C/13–15, 21–2.

371 CCCC09/15/10.

372 CCCC09/16C/40.

373 StJ 36, 142; HR 561. Matters are complicated, however, by the fact that there were apparently two men called Bartholomew Wombe, who belonged to different branches of the family. The other Bartholomew was the son of Harvey Wombe. Harvey and Radulph may have been related. Harvey could have been Henry's brother or his son; in the latter case Harvey and Radulph would have been brothers. Dating evidence supports the latter case.

374 John confirmed a grant to St Radegund's Priory (StR 244b).

375 HR 656–70; possibly HR 372 too.

376 A starr is a Jewish deed or bond, especially one of release or acquittance of debt; a receipt given on payment of a debt (OED).

377 Casson, Casson, Lee and Phillips, *Business and Community*, Appendix 1; M, p 171.

378 Casson, Casson, Lee and Phillips, *Business and Community*, Appendix 5.

379 Casson, Casson, Lee and Phillips, *Business and Community*, Appendix 5; F, p 692.

380 Casson, Casson, Lee and Phillips, *Business and Community*, Appendix 2; M, pp 168–9.

381 Casson, Casson, Lee and Phillips, *Business and Community*, Appendix 5.

382 StJ 76.

383 F, p 692.

384 StJ 59.

385 Casson, Casson, Lee and Phillips, *Business and Community*, Appendix 2.

386 HR 103–5.

387 HR 103–6, 156, 159.

388 StR 179; Casson, Casson, Lee and Phillips, *Business and Community*, Appendix 2.

389 Casson, Casson, Lee and Phillips, *Business and Community*, Appendix 5.

390 PDC, p 280; Casson, Casson, Lee and Phillips, *Business and Community*, Appendix 6; Curia Regis Rolls I, p 431.
391 StR 179.
392 Casson, Casson, Lee and Phillips, *Business and Community*, Appendix 10, 1206.
393 HR 417; HR 477; CCCC09/16C/8.
394 CCCC09/16C/9, 12.
395 CCCC09/16C/19.
396 CCCC09/16C/8a, 11.
397 Casson, Casson, Lee and Phillips, *Business and Community*, Appendix 5.
398 StJ 28, 95.
399 CCCC09/16C/20/3.
400 HR 415; HR 541.
401 HR 536–42.
402 HR 122; StJ 5; Casson, Casson, Lee and Phillips, *Business and Community*, Appendix 2.
403 Appendix 5.
404 StJ 79; F, p 694.
405 CCC09/08/1.
406 StR 121a, 187, 370; F, p 694.
407 StJ 168.
408 StJ 224.
409 HR 237.
410 There is also Stephen Wulward, who witnessed a deed (StJ 175), and Andrew Wulward who held a tenement in Tripereslane in 1306 (StR 200).
411 HR A5.
412 Casson, Casson, Lee and Phillips, *Business and Community*, Appendix 2; M, pp 168–9. Fulk should be distinguished from Fulk son of Theobald, who was Sheriff of Cambridgeshire 1207–12, and had a son, Radulph, who was fined for unpaid debts to the king incurred in the final years of John's reign, and again in 1221 for detaining chattels (Casson, Casson, Lee and Phillips, *Business and Community*, Appendix 5). Confusion is possible because Fulk the sheriff also held property in All Saints in the Jewry and witnessed local deeds (StJ 13).
413 StR 83.
414 StJ 50.
415 Casson, Casson, Lee and Phillips, *Business and Community*, Appendix 6; Curia Regis Rolls IX; BN, case 1393; M, pp 184–5.
416 Casson, Casson, Lee and Phillips, *Business and Community*, Appendix 9; J, p 256.
417 StR 50.
418 StJ 271.
419 StJ 3.
420 BNM, p 4; StR 172a.
421 LB, p 148; BRUC, p 167; VLAE, pp xxxvii, 287; BR, p 43.
422 Casson, Casson, Lee and Phillips, *Business and Community*, Appendix 6; Curia Regis Rolls XV, p 358.
423 Casson, Casson, Lee and Phillips, *Business and Community*, Appendix 11.
424 HR 684.
425 HR 684–6.
426 Casson, Casson, Lee and Phillips, *Business and Community*, Appendix 9; J, p 267.
427 HR 722; StR 95.
428 StR 96/8; HR 722–4; HR 715–17.

[429] Casson, Casson, Lee and Phillips, *Business and Community*, Appendix 12. Two people who do not fit into this line of descent are Robert and Gilbert Crocheman, who could be sons or brothers of John Crocheman, mentioned in the Crocheman family tree. Robert Crocheman married Cassandria, who may have been the daughter of Simon Cademan (HR 441). Robert and Cassandria gave four messuages and some vacant land in St Andrew's parish to St Radegund's (HR A30). Robert witnessed a deed concerning a gift to St John's Hospital of rent from a stall in the butchery in 1246 (StJ 96). Cassandria may have had a brother, Richard of Lanselle, or Lawshall, who had sons Simon and William (HR 441, 810). In 1242 Gilbert Crocheman owed the king £20 1s 6d for debts to the Jews (Casson, Casson, Lee and Phillips, *Business and Community*, Appendix 3; Pipe Rolls).

[430] Casson, Casson, Lee and Phillips, *Business and Community*, Appendix 2.

[431] Casson, Casson, Lee and Phillips, *Business and Community*, Appendix 2.

[432] HR 148, 257–8, 262, 305, 460, 519.

[433] HR 294, 303, 352, 460.

[434] StR 21.

[435] StR 54, 193, 194b; HR 576–7.

[436] HR 576.

[437] HR 576. Robert also witnessed many deeds in the period 1250–70.

[438] CCCC09/4.

[439] CCCC09/15/8.

[440] StJ 21.

[441] HR 367, 636.

[442] CCCC09/16C/18, item 10.

[443] HR 261, 262.

[444] HR 261, 262.

[445] CCCC09/15/5–8.

[446] HR 468.

[447] HR 262; John son of Robert should not be confused with a John Hubert who was in debt to the Jews for 10s in 1235 (J, p 253), who is more likely to have been Robert's brother.

[448] HR P25.

[449] HR 636.

[450] 1. a messuage formerly of Reginald Godshoe, probably in St John's parish; 2. a messuage called Ragenhall adjacent to land of the convent of Chatteris, extending lengthwise from the main road to Henney ditch in the same parish; 3. a nearby tenement called Revereles in St Michael's parish; 4. land in All Saints' parish (probably the Jewry); 5. 8 acres of land in Cambridge and Newnham fields; 6. a rent of 6s and two capons from Thomas Plote and his heirs for a capital messuage on the corner of Segrimslane; 7. a rent of 2s from Alicia Herves for 4 acres of land in Cambridge fields; 8. a rent of 3s from land in St Andrew's parish; 9. a rent of 6d for a messuage in St Andrew's parish; 10. a rent of 12d for a shop in Smith Street (*via fabrorum*); and 11. a messuage at the Bridge (CCCC09/16C/18).

[451] HR 240, 241, 252.

[452] StJ 101/3.

[453] Casson, Casson, Lee and Phillips, *Business and Community*, Appendix 6; Curia Regis Rolls XV, p 97.

[454] StJ 37; HR 240/1.

[455] Casson, Casson, Lee and Phillips, *Business and Community*, Appendix 11.

[456] Casson, Casson, Lee and Phillips, *Business and Community*, Appendix 5.

[457] HR P9; StJ 47.

[458] HR 728; Casson, Casson, Lee and Phillips, *Business and Community*, Appendix 6; Curia Regis Rolls XIX, p 68; XX, p 100.

[459] HR 728. There are also references to two John Parlebens, one of whom is described as the son of John le Marscal (HR 371) and the other as the son of John Fabro (1038/9). A John Parleben is described as holding land abutting on Smith Row and St Mary's churchyard; this is presumably John son of John Fabro (CCCC09/08/104); John Fabro held two messuages in the parish of St Andrew. Roger Parleben held land in Bridge Street adjacent to the land of John the Smith (StR 101), who may have been John Parleben's father. This suggests that John Parleben may have been Roger's adopted son. Hugh Parleben witnessed a deed in c.1250 relating to land in Newnham granted to Peter son of Ivo (CCCC09/13/1). He may be connected to Michael and Margaret Parleben, previously discussed.

[460] Casson, Casson, Lee and Phillips, *Business and Community*, Appendix 6; Curia Regis Rolls, V, XIV, XVII; M, pp 175–6.

[461] Casson, Casson, Lee and Phillips, *Business and Community*, Appendix 2.

[462] Casson, Casson, Lee and Phillips, *Business and Community*, Appendix 6; Curia Regis Rolls V, p 39.

[463] M, p 175.

[464] M, p 175.

[465] BN Plea 307.

[466] BN Plea 523. It is difficult to identify Absolon with certainty. It is possible that he was a fifth son of Baldwin Blancgernun senior, who may have dropped the family name to dissociate himself from his brother Baldwin junior, the heir (see above). But there are other possibilities. There are three plausible candidates. They all have links to the Church, which is a characteristic of the family as a whole. Maitland notes that Absolon is a popular name in Cambridge in c.1200 and suggests it may represent Breton influence (M, p 175, fn 4). The first candidate is Absolon son of Walter. He and his father were jointly amerced for 16s 8d in 1177, and then pardoned by writ of the Bishop of Ely (Casson, Casson, Lee and Phillips, *Business and Community*, Appendix 1; M, p 171). The second is Absolon son of Segar, who was tallaged for 1 mark in 1211. Segar was a kinsman of Langlinus, who held the advowson of St Peter's Church at the Trumpington Gate, and served as its parson for many years. He had a son, Henry, who also held the church for many years before giving the advowson to the Hospital of St John (Casson, Casson, Lee and Phillips, *Business and Community*, Appendix 6; Curia Regis Rolls V p 39; M, p 175). The third candidate is Absolon son of Roger the priest (or presbyter). He is the least likely candidate. He held property in Milne Street in St John's parish, near land of Peter son of Ivo. He sold some of his land in the parish to Martin Wulward, who was also his tenant (StJ 179, 380). Absolon had a wife, Maud, a brother Hugh, a son Reginald, and daughters Isabel and Margaret (StR177/8, 380). All of them lived near to each other in St John's parish. Absolon also held rents elsewhere, including a messuage in St Botolph's and lands in Cambridge fields. It seems that Absolon outlived his brother Hugh (StR 380). There is no direct reference to a son named Hugh, however (StJ 178).

[467] HR 624, 631.

[468] HR F55.

[469] HR 633–41; R14–15.

[470] StR 239a.

[471] BN Plea 307.

472 Casson, Casson, Lee and Phillips, *Business and Community*, Appendix 6, VIII, p 288; M, p 176; BN Pleas 103, 104.

473 StR, p 30.

474 StR 88.

475 HR A19.

476 HR 289–90. Brithnod the tanner was tallaged at 10 marks in 1211, of which he paid half immediately. In 1239 Michael Brithnod, possibly another of Martin's brothers, or his father, owed 10.5 marks to Aaron son of Abraham of London (Casson, Casson, Lee and Phillips, *Business and Community*, Appendix 9).

477 OBG, pp 18–19; Hall, 'Sabina': 60–78.

478 It has been suggested that Sabina was the widow of Peter of Wilburham, one of the Cambridge bailiffs, but the Hundred Rolls clearly state that Sabina bought the properties herself; perhaps her previous husband was edited out of the rolls on her initiative (OTG, p 18, citing Peterhouse Treasury, Citus Collegii, A26).

479 LB, pp 282–90.

480 Casson, Casson, Lee and Phillips, *Business and Community*, Appendix 8, V, p 130.

481 Casson, Casson, Lee and Phillips, *Business and Community*, Appendix 12.

482 Hall and Lovatt, 'Peterhouse': 25–6, 38–43.

483 HR 350/1.

484 Casson, Casson, Lee and Phillips, *Business and Community*, Appendix 2.

485 HR 40.

486 HR 651.

487 HR 348, 453.

488 HR 348–9.

489 HR 349–51.

490 CCCC09/66/7.

491 CCCC09/08/19 and following.

492 CCCC09/2/5; CCCC09/16C/13–15, 21–2; CCCC09/08/56.

493 HR 439.

494 HR 439.

495 HR A44.

496 Casson, Casson, Lee and Phillips, *Business and Community*, Appendix 10, p 263; PDC, p 264.

497 HR 335.

498 Casson, Casson, Lee and Phillips, *Business and Community*, Appendix 10.

499 Casson, Casson, Lee and Phillips, *Business and Community*, Appendix 6, Rotuli Curia Regis XVI, p 188; PDC, p 264.

500 HR 308, 488; HR 335; HR 341.

501 HR 335.

502 Curia Regis Rolls, XIX, p 68; Casson, Casson, Lee and Phillips, *Business and Community*, Appendix 6.

503 HR 247, 308, 393, 488, 627, 1070.

504 HR 658; HR 847.

505 HR 356.

506 There was also William Morice who witnessed a deed in c.1235 (StJ 82).

507 HR 358, 371; HR 390.

508 StJ 31.

5

Family Dynasties:
Success and Failure

Introduction

This chapter analyses the successes and failures of Cambridge family dynasties. The evidence is derived from the family profiles presented in the preceding chapter and in Casson, Casson, Lee and Phillips, *Business and Community*, Appendix 14. The chapter begins by considering the concepts of success and failure. Two main dimensions of success are distinguished, namely wealth and reputation. The wealth of a family is assessed from its property portfolio, while its reputation is assessed by using the indicators of civic office holding, a responsible job in a prestigious institution and the title of Master.

Different family characteristics are then identified: these include the age of the family (the number of generations that it can be traced back), its size (the average number of people in each generation), gender balance (the ratio of brothers to sisters in a given generation), sources of income (trade, royal service, etc), philanthropic activity (gifts to charitable institutions) and vulnerability to debt, crime and litigation. Each of these family characteristics can be derived from the family profiles.

The chapter then explores whether certain types of family were more successful than others. Some characteristics emerge as particularly important; source of income, for example, was very important, while gender balance was not. Overall, the evidence from Cambridge suggests that there were a number of key resources to which families needed to gain access in order to be successful. These resources were both economic and social; they included the skills to work in various industries and occupations, membership of social networks where useful contacts could be made and the ability to manage property portfolios efficiently. Families did not need to have access to all of these resources, but they did require access to some of them, and the more of them they accessed the more successful they seem to have been.

Families faced various risk factors. In many respects medieval life was subject to greater risks than modern life, and so risk management was very important for medieval families. Some risks were external to the family, such as wars, taxes and diseases, but others were internal, such as sibling rivalry and disputes over inheritance, which could lead to a general lack of family cohesion.

The analysis in this chapter suggests a trade-off involving size of family. Large families were more likely to have substantial resources available, particularly when different members of the family had different occupations that gave them access to different resources. On the other hand, large families provided greater scope for rivalry and discord, and a consequent lack of cohesion. This could prevent the various resources from being combined efficiently.

This chapter confirms the importance of the distinction between old wealth and new wealth.[1] Economic changes in the 13th century, linked to the Commercial Revolution described in earlier chapters, created particular problems for old wealth and additional opportunities for new wealth. To remain successful, old-wealth families needed to make the transition to new wealth. They needed to spot new opportunities to increase the resources at their disposal. On the other hand, families creating new wealth could often benefit from alliances with old wealth, thereby gaining access to these families' inherited property and elite social connections. Old wealth and new wealth did not just compete for resources, therefore; they could build alliances and collaborate. These collaborations could be mediated by social networks centred on the local churches and the civic community, but most especially through intermarriage.

An important qualification must be noted, however. The family is a largely private sphere of social life. The functioning of any family is necessarily a matter of conjecture so far as outside observers are concerned. This chapter does not offer definitive statements about what happened inside specific families; instead it presents an overview of how Cambridge families functioned, and the factors that contributed to their success.

5.1 Family characteristics

Success and failure

Some Cambridge families were undoubtedly more successful than others, but when deciding who was successful it is important to specify the criteria involved. Two main criteria of success can be applied using the evidence available, namely wealth and reputation.

Wealth. The wealth of families can be assessed from the properties they held and the rents they received from them in 1279. The rents they paid on the properties they occupied may also be an indication of wealth. To be a meaningful indicator, however, wealth needs to be evaluated on a per capita basis. A large family is likely to possess greater wealth than a small family because there are more potential earners. It is therefore appropriate to divide family wealth by the number of adult family members in order to measure economic success. However, while rental income can be measured, income from trades and professions cannot; furthermore, the number of adults alive in 1279 is uncertain too. Wealth is therefore measured using three categories: very high, high and modest. This terminology reflects the fact that all the families identified as property owners were wealthy to some degree.

In 1279 the very wealthy dynasties were the Barton, Gogging, Toylet, Wombe, Aylsham, Eliot and Martin families, and those of Richard Laurence and Richard at the Gate. Also wealthy were the surviving Blancgernun, Dunning, St Edmunds, sons of Ivo, Pilat, le Rus, Seman, Wulward, Hubert, Pipestraw, Braci, le Comber and Malerbe families, and the family of Robert of Madingley. The modestly wealthy were the Crocheman, Parleben, Morice, Bateman, Bernard, Childman, Andrew, Aure, Braintree, Godeman, Morin and Potecar families, and the family of Walter Em.

It turns out however, that the very high-wealth families behaved in a quite similar way to the ordinary high-wealth families, and so the two categories are merged into a composite high-wealth category in the analysis that follows.

Reputation. It is important to distinguish between good reputation, bad reputation and reputation in general. Large families with substantial property portfolios tended to have a reputation of some kind simply because they exerted a significant influence on urban life and were therefore perceived as powerful. The criterion for success used here, however, is based on good reputation. This means being widely recognized as honourable and trustworthy. Holding civic office or a responsible job in a prestigious institution can be used as an index of good reputation. For men, the title Master may be taken as an indicator of professional success. Reputation can, however, be tarnished in various ways; for example, a leading family member may be accused, or convicted, of a crime or be known to be heavily in debt. A powerful family with some 'black sheep' could easily acquire a bad reputation. Families with bad reputations may be shunned, and their economic prospects may be impaired as a result.

The Barton, Dunning, St Edmunds, Pilat, le Rus, Toylet, Wulward, Crocheman, Aylsham, Eliot, Martin families and those of Walter Em and Robert of Madingley all had a good reputation. Those with bad or tarnished reputations were the Blancgernun, Gogging, Wulward, Hubert, Parleben and Pipestraw families and Richard Laurence and his family. The remaining families appear to have had little or no reputation (whether good or bad).

Old and new families

An old family may be identified from the number of generations for which it can be traced back. It is old if it can be traced back at least three generations, or to 1200 and before. The family profiles identify 16 that can be defined as old: the Barton, Blancgernun, Dunning, St Edmunds, sons of Ivo, Pilat, le Rus, Seman, Toylet, Wombe, Wulward, Pipestraw, Malerbe and Bernard families, and those of Richard Laurence and Robert of Madingley.

For old families, survival may be regarded as an achievement. This does not apply to new families, however. The survival of new families can, in principle, be assessed using deeds and civic records from after 1279, but these sources are nowhere near as comprehensive as the Hundred Rolls. The success of new families is assessed chiefly from the speed with which they accumulated property.

Size of family

It is useful to have a measure of size of family that is independent of the number of generations shown in the family tree. A suitable measure is the number of siblings in each generation. This factor is significant for two reasons. First, a large number of siblings creates a larger base from which new branches of the family can develop in the next generation, and secondly, it can act as a spur to enterprise. Sons with no prospect of becoming an heir may be driven to explore new opportunities for making a living, while an heir with many sisters may be stimulated to seek out profit in order to make provision for their dowries.

The number of siblings varies between generations, however. What is required is a simple measure of size that makes a binary distinction between large and small families. Fortunately, the family profiles presented in Chapter 4 demonstrated that most large families were created in a single generation by a man who had many children. A suitable measure of family size is therefore the largest number of siblings in any recorded generation. A threshold size is needed to distinguish between large and small, and the family profiles suggest that four is an appropriate number. The following families had four or more children in some generation and therefore meet this condition: Barton, Blancgernun, Gogging, sons of Ivo, Seman, Wombe, Wulward, Pipestraw, Bateman, Bernard and Eliot.

Gender balance

The ratio of women to men (the gender balance) is important for two obvious reasons. Men, not women, carry the family name, so a family name can disappear quickly if there are no surviving sons. Secondly, certain occupations could only be taken up by men, whether for pragmatic, social or doctrinal reasons. For most women, making a good marriage was the main route to accessing resources for the family; even so, much of their wealth would be controlled by their husband who belonged to a different family. Men could access wealth through marriage too, but this was lucrative mainly when they married into a family with no surviving male heir. Gender balance is difficult to measure exactly because daughters are not normally recorded in the Hundred Rolls unless they owned (or part-owned) property. In its place a *gender indicator* is used, which shows whether, in any generation, the family had female heirs because it lacked surviving male heirs. The indicator is positive for the following families: Wulward, Pipestraw and Aylsham, and the families of Walter Em and Richard at the Gate.

Sources of income

Five main sources of family income can be distinguished. Four of these concern incomes obtained from following a trade or professions, while the fifth is unearned income achieved through a strategic marriage.

Commercial profit from trade represents income accruing from business ventures involving wholesale or retail trade or large-scale artisan production. Participation in profit-making activities can be inferred from deeds and from the probable uses of the types of properties owned by the family. Trades were discussed in Chapter 3. The following families accessed commercial profit: Barton, Gogging, sons of Ivo, Toylet, Wombe, Hubert, Aylsham, Braci, le Comber, Morice, Bateman, Eliot, Andrew, Aure, Braintree, Godeman and Martin, and the families of Robert of Madingley, Walter Em and Richard at the Gate.

Property management and speculation generated income from rents and also capital gains from buying and reselling of properties that appreciated in value. Active management and speculation can be inferred from systematic buying and selling of property as recorded in deeds and in the Hundred Rolls. The following families seem to have been heavily engaged in managing their property portfolios: Barton, St Edmunds, Gogging, Pilat, Aylsham, le Comber, Morice, Bateman, Eliot and Martin, and the families of Richard Laurence, Robert of Madingley and Walter Em.

Professional activities, including administrative activities concerned with religious institutions and royal service, and teaching or administration in the nascent university. The classification of professions was discussed in Chapter 3. The following families were particularly active in the professions: St Edmunds, Gogging, Pilat, le Rus, Seman, Toylet, Crocheman, Hubert, Parleben and Pipestraw.

Craft production, specifically small-scale artisan work of a specialized nature (e.g. goldsmith). The Barton, Gogging, Aylsham, Braci, Bateman, Aure, Braintree and Potecar families were involved in this.

Strategic marriage involved the marriage of a family member to a person from a wealthy or highly reputable family. It includes the marriage of a son, daughter, widow or widower to a spouse with substantial personal wealth of their own. The Barton, Gogging, sons of Ivo, Seman, Toylet, Wulward, Crocheman, Hubert, Bernard, Childman, Andrew and Martin families were the main ones involved.

Philanthropy

Philanthropy was widespread in medieval Cambridge, as noted in previous chapters, but some families were more philanthropic than others. Philanthropic families can be identified from gifts of property to the priories, friaries and hospitals. Some of these were recorded in the Hundred Rolls, while others were recorded in charters and deeds. The most philanthropic were the Blancgernun, Dunning, St Edmunds, Pilat, Le Rus, Seman, Toylet, Wombe, Andrew, Aylsham and Eliot families.

Family behaviour: debt, crime and litigation

Debt was remarkably common in medieval Cambridge. Most of the recorded debts were long-term loans secured on personal property and, with one exception, all the recorded debts were owed to Jewish moneylenders. There may have been short-term credit extended from one businessman to another, but the surviving records do not inform on such situations. The Barton, Blancgernun, Dunning, St Edmunds, Gogging, le Rus and Crocheman families and the family of Richard Laurence were those involved in the recorded debts.

Leading families were also involved in criminal proceedings to a surprising degree. There seem to be two main reasons why their family members were prosecuted for crimes. First, members of leading families had opportunities that were denied to others, notably opportunities for fraud in handling large payments and valuable goods. Secondly, the nature of their crimes meant that they were held before royal justices. Relevant records are often incomplete, however, and so the final judgment passed on these crimes is often unclear. Six families had members who were accused of serious crimes: Barton, Gogging, Wombe, Wulward, Parleben and the family of Richard Laurence.

Three families initiated litigation, namely the Dunnings, Parlebens and the Pipestraws. These were mainly concerned with the protection or restitution of property, although it is not always clear whether those who initiated the litigation won their case.

5.2. Patterns in the evidence

The 36 families in this study have been now been placed into a range of different categories. For example, some are much wealthier than others. Some are engaged in commercial trades and some in professions. The question naturally arises as to whether there are links between these characteristics. For example, is the occupation in which the family mainly engaged connected with their level of wealth?

The most systematic way to search for patterns is to correlate all the factors identified and then search for significant positive or negative pair-wise correlations. This results in a table of pair-wise correlation coefficients, one for each pair of factors. The result is shown in Table 5.1. There are 15 different factors, so this results in a table with 15 rows and 15 columns. The table is shown in two parts because it is too large to display all the columns in a single table. Each cell in the table represents a correlation coefficient. As in Chapter 2, the numbers in

Table 5.1: Correlations between family characteristics

	Old	Children	Gender	Debt	Crime	Litigation	Profit	Property
Old	1.00							
Children	0.38 (0.02)**	1.00						
Gender	-0.04 (0.84)	0.08 (0.63)	1.00					
Debt	0.33 (0.05)**	0.08 (0.64)	-0.21 (0.21)	1.00				
Crime	0.20 (0.24)	0.35 (0.04)**	0.04 (0.84)	0.30 (0.08)*	1.00			
Litigation	0.13 (0.43)	0.24 (0.17)	0.17 (0.32)	0.08 (0.64)	0.13 (0.43)	1.00		
Commercial profit	-0.44 (0.01)***	-0.01 (0.94)	-0.04 (0.84)	-0.33 (0.05)**	-0.05 (0.77)	-0.34 (0.04)**	1.00	
Property management	-0.25 (0.13)	-0.03 (0.84)	-0.01 (0.96)	-0.02 (0.93)	-0.05 (0.77)	-0.24 (0.16)	0.48 (0.00)***	1.00
Professional activity	0.19 (0.26)	-0.01 (0.97)	-0.07 (0.69)	0.27 (0.12)	0.06 (0.75)	0.26 (0.12)	0.32 (0.06)*	-0.11 (0.51)
Craft/artisan work	-0.34 (0.04)**	0.08 (0.64)	0.02 (0.90)	0.04 (0.84)	0.12 (0.49)	-0.16 (0.35)	-0.16 (0.35)	0.12 (0.48)
Strategic marriage	0.08 (0.65)	0.30* (0.08)	-0.11 (0.51)	0.05 (0.78)	0.16 (0.36)	-0.21 (0.21)	0.04 (0.82)	-0.20 (0.24)
Reputation	0.22 (0.20)	0.06 (0.75)	0.08 (0.63)	0.53 (0.01)***	0.30 (0.08)*	0.30 (0.08)*	-0.11 (0.51)	0.11 (0.51)

(continued)

Table 5.1: Correlations between family characteristics (continued)

	Old	Children	Gender	Debt	Crime	Litigation	Profit	Property
Good reputation	0.13 (0.43)	-0.05 (0.77)	-0.09 (0.58)	0.37 (0.02)**	-0.13 (0.43)	0.02 (0.93)	0.11 (0.51)	0.34 (0.04)**
Wealth	0.43 (0.01)***	0.14 (0.41)	0.07 (0.69)	0.18 (0.29)	0.11 (0.52)	-0.04 (0.83)	-0.06 (0.75)	0.11 (0.51)
Philanthropy	0.38 (0.02)**	0.08 (0.63)	-0.27 (0.12)	0.23 (0.17)	-0.13 (0.43)	0.02 (0.92)	-0.13 (0.43)	-0.03 (0.84)

	Profession	Craft	Marriage	Reputation in general	Good reputation	Wealth	Philanthropy
Profession	1.00						
Craft	-0.18 (0.29)	1.00					
Marriage	0.22 (0.20)	-0.09 (0.58)	1.00				
Reputation in general	0.37 (0.02)**	-0.14 (0.41)	0.12 (0.49)	1.00			
Good reputation	0.13 (0.43)	-0.06 (0.75)	0.04 (0.84)	0.66*** (0.01)	1.00		
Wealth	0.11 (0.53)	-0.27 (0.12)	0.04 (0.79)	0.25 (0.13)	0.14 (0.41)	1.00	
Philanthropy	0.26 (0.12)	-0.21 (0.21)	-0.09 (0.58)	0.18 (0.29)	0.35** (0.04)	0.28 (0.10)*	1.00

Sources: Chapter 4 and Catherine Casson, Mark Casson, John S. Lee and Katie Phillips, *Business and Community in Medieval England: The Cambridge Hundred Rolls Source Volume*, Appendix 14 (Bristol, 2020)

brackets under the coefficients represent a p-value and the stars indicate levels of significance. Interpretation focuses on the starred cells, where the coefficient is significantly different from zero. The table is 'lower-diagonal'; that is, all the top right-hand cells are empty. This is because the correlation coefficients are symmetric, so that each missing coefficients is equal to the coefficient that appears as its 'mirror image' in the main diagonal.

Note that correlation does not imply causation. For example, the link between occupation and wealth can run in both directions. A wealthy person may have a preference for certain occupations or certain occupations may tend to make a person wealthy; either could generate a pattern linking occupation and wealth.

There are 21 significant coefficients. Readers who are not interested in the specific results can proceed to the following section where their wider implications are considered.

Age of family

1. Older families tended to have more children. This may reflect a trend over time towards a deeper rather than broader investment in children's education and training. High rates of infant mortality may have encouraged the early generations of older families to produce many children, while, by contrast, lower infant mortality, rising incomes and greater concern for education may have encouraged later generations, who are more prominent in newer families, to have fewer children. Improved medical skill and the growth of an early form of 'knowledge economy' may have underpinned this. Caution is warranted, though; the sample of families may be biased towards families that had many children because families that had small numbers of children may have died off and therefore do not appear in this study.

2. Older families were more prone to debt. This is consistent with the view that older families were mostly in decline and were maintaining their living standards by recourse to debt. Ultimately their inability to fund their lifestyle would require them to sell off parts of their property portfolios.

3. Older families did not rely on commercial profit as a source of income. This underlies the distinction between old wealth and new wealth, which is examined in more detail later. Whether older families considered trade and commerce to be low status, or whether they simply lacked the skills to carry it on, is unclear, but a cultural explanation based on status is certainly consistent with the results in what follows.

4. Older families tended to avoid artisan crafts. This conforms to the stereotype of old wealth attitudes to manual work.

5. Older families were on average wealthier than newer families. This result suggests that by 1279 new wealth had not equalled, let alone surpassed, old wealth. The older families may have been in decline, and the new families in the ascendant, but they had yet to change places in the top ranks of wealth. This is not true of all families, though; for example, the Bernards were old but not wealthy, while the Goggings were wealthy but not old.

6. Older families engaged heavily in philanthropy. This is the main positive characteristic of the older families. It invites a cultural explanation, based on *noblesse oblige*, but the explanation could be more mundane: many of them were simply wealthier than other newer families (as mentioned earlier). It is also possible that they made larger gifts, and specifically gifts of property, that were more likely to be recorded. It is difficult to say how altruistic their underlying motives were, but the community undoubtedly benefited from their contributions, in particular the Hospital of St John.

Family size

7. Families with many children had a propensity to engage in crime. This result seems somewhat bizarre, but it may have a simple explanation. The larger the number of children in a family, the fewer children stood to inherit any substantial property. In a family with a strong work ethic this may have encouraged the younger siblings to embark on profit-seeking or a professional career, but in a family without that ethic they may have resorted to crime. The type of crime considered here is not normally violent crime, but crime that took advantage of other people, for example by supplying defective goods or concealing taxable assets from the king (see Chapter 4).

8. Families with many children tended to engage in strategic marriage. This result accords with the intuition that if children cannot inherit from their parents then it may pay them to marry an heir from another family. They may also have received parental support: parents of unmarried children who were unlikely to inherit may have assumed responsibility for finding their children a 'good match'. This effect seems to be gender neutral: the propensity to engage in strategic marriage is statistically unrelated to the gender balance between siblings.

Gender balance

9. Gender balance had no significant interaction with any other factors. This is a surprising result, given that a high ratio of daughters to sons implies a substantial commitment to paying dowry. The implication seems to be that marriages into the right sort of family could pay handsome dividends for male members (i.e. fathers and brothers), possibly through access to the social networks of the husband's family.

Sources of income

10. Profit-seeking trade and property management were complementary activities. Families that were involved in one of them were likely to be involved in the other. The combination of profit-seeking trade and property management seems to have been most characteristic of highly entrepreneurial families where profits were reinvested, not only in commerce, but also in property. Profit from trade could finance the acquisition of property; conversely rents from this property, and the occasional sale of property, could finance trade.

11. Profit-seeking trade was also linked to professional activity, though to a much smaller extent. It is easy to see the potential advantage to a family from combining the skills of a merchant with the skills of a lawyer and administrator; one would contribute flair and the other administrative capability. Family profiles suggest that large families in commerce often had a member who was engaged in a profession; thus, while individuals did not normally combine the two activities, families did so.

12. Profit-seekers avoided debt. The debts recorded in the sources were generally long-standing debts and debts that were overdue. Profit-seeking traders may have borrowed money, but if they repaid it promptly their debts were unlikely to appear in the sources. It seems to be those who lacked a source of profit income, and who could not therefore repay their debts, that were mostly recorded as debtors. Conversely, it seems that the growth of merchant business was funded mainly by reinvested profit; in other words, those who engaged in commerce were relatively frugal and saved in order to invest in their businesses.

13. Professions were strongly associated with family reputation. Many of the most reputable families in Cambridge had at least one family member engaged in a religious or lay profession. How far the profession conferred status on the family, and how far the status of the family encouraged entry into the profession, is difficult to say. Profiles suggest that both effects were significant.

14. Property owners had a good reputation. This result relates not to reputation in general but specifically to good reputation, which is reputation untarnished by crime or debt. This result reflects the fact that older families with a good reputation had retained their property portfolios intact by avoiding crime or debt. By contrast, families without a good reputation had been obliged to sell off their properties to pay fines or repay debt.

15. Older families did not specialize in property management. This is technically a 'non-result'; that is, it is inferred from an insignificant coefficient. It is important, however, because it demonstrates that a pattern that might be expected to show up in the evidence does not in fact appear. While older families tended to avoid trade and crafts they were not more heavily involved in property management than those who did. This seems counter-intuitive, as property management was a major requirement for older families that had inherited large tracts of mainly agricultural land. But the evidence from Cambridge is they did not actively manage their urban property portfolios. Indeed, in many cases the family strategy was simply to mortgage or sell off their urban properties to repay debts or make philanthropic donations. Some families eventually liquidated all their Cambridge holdings and settled down on rural estates elsewhere.

Philanthropy

16. Philanthropy was linked mainly to the age of the family and to wealth. Causality seems to have run from wealth to philanthropy. It appears that families engaged in commerce and property management waited until they had become wealthy before they engaged in large-scale philanthropy. There is evidence of much small-scale philanthropy in Cambridge, but it is reported in the Hundred Rolls as a general phenomenon and not attributed to specific families. Only large-scale philanthropy is attributed to specific families and these are generally the older and wealthier ones. It seems that families accumulating new wealth from commerce first acquired a property portfolio, and only when they had achieved considerable wealth did they engage in large-scale philanthropy of the kind recorded in the Hundred Rolls.

17. The next result is a rather trivial one: families that undertook philanthropy had a good reputation. As noted earlier, this result is driven by the behaviour of leading families, who the main families were that undertook philanthropy and possessed reputation. By avoiding crime and debt these families retained enough property and resources to fund large-scale philanthropy.

Debt, crime and litigation

18. Debt was associated with criminality. There are two main ways of interpreting this result. The first is that certain families had the misfortune to have a 'black sheep', who perpetrated crimes and got into debt. Thus crimes and debts were both generated by the same person. An alternative interpretation is that underlying family characteristics were responsible. Two such characteristics are suggested by previous results. Older families were prone to debt, and families with many children (which included several older families) were prone to crime. Resort to both debt and crime could therefore be traced to underlying tensions in older families with many children. The family profiles indicate elements of both. Tensions within families could lead to the emergence of black sheep, while black sheep created tensions in families.

19. Reputable families were prone to debt. This seems paradoxical. Ostentatious consumption and living beyond your means were condemned by medieval religious teachings.[2] Furthermore, debtors to the Jews paid interest on their loans, and were therefore implicated in usurious transactions. It seems, however, that attitudes in Cambridge were pragmatic. For merchants involved in the corn trade, for example, short-term loans could be useful in bridging the gap between payments made to purchase supplies and payments received from customers. Debt, from this perspective, was only a problem if it could not be repaid. Other families (often older ones) took out long-term debt, backed by mortgages on their properties. Even so, those who could not repay often seem to have elicited sympathy rather than censure from the community, especially when they were recognized as benefactors of the town (see Chapter 4). The toleration of debt, therefore, may have encouraged its use. Eventually, it seems, the lenders rather than the borrowers were blamed for the debt, and the Jewish moneylenders were expelled from the town.

20. Reputable families were more likely to engage in crime. It has already been noted that debt and crime are related. Indeed, the status of crime is superficially similar to that of debt discussed earlier: it seems to have been tolerated. It is nevertheless puzzling how reputation could withstand allegations of criminality. The explanation may lie partly in relations between the king and the town. It seems that when the king was displeased with the town he tended to blame the bailiffs and accuse them of some crime. The converse of this is that bailiffs accused of crime could plausibly suggest that they were the victims too. Some criminality may, indeed, have been motivated by the perceived interests of the town rather than the personal interests of the individual concerned. Another possibility is that the extent of criminality among reputable families has

been exaggerated by the sources used. These sources are mostly the royal records, and crimes may appear in the royal records only when reputable people were involved; petty crimes by ordinary people were recorded elsewhere.

21. Litigation was mainly undertaken by reputable families who were not involved in earning commercial profit. Cases of litigation initiated by families were relatively few, and they focused on property and its inheritance.[3] Sibling rivalry was an important issue in at least one case. But why were commercially oriented families not involved? The answer may be that, although commercially oriented families held property, they did not hold sufficient property to make expensive litigation worthwhile. Furthermore, since these families were engaged in commerce, they had plenty of other risks to deal with without creating additional risks by initiating litigation.

5.3 Family strategies for success

The remainder of this chapter places the statistical results in a broader context. It draws out some general themes that underpin the results. Correlations describe patterns very well, but they cannot identify the underlying forces that generate these patterns. A full understanding of the role of families in medieval Cambridge requires some discussion of what these underlying forces may have been. Unfortunately, though, these underlying forces cannot be directly observed. It is, however, possible to construct a plausible account of what they may have been. We cannot observe them, but we can infer them from a careful analysis of the evidence.

These forces are examined here in terms of how a representative Cambridge family may have perceived the options available to them, and why they may have chosen particular options under particular circumstances. This section considers six main strategies available to an ambitious Cambridge family. The advantages of each strategy are spelled out. A large family could deploy multiple strategies simultaneously using different members of the same generation to pursue different careers. A long-lived family could deploy different strategies sequentially, by having one generation focus on one strategy and the next generation on another. A large long-lived family could do both.

Pursuit of commercial profit. Many family dynasties had at least one member who was involved in trade. In several cases the reinvestment of income from trade created a virtuous circle in which the flow of income from past investments continuously augmented the funds available for new investment.

Three main fields of commerce and industry may be identified. *Retail trade* was often short distance and took place in urban markets regulated by local lords or civic authorities. Food and drink were important retail commodities, with food preparation (e.g. baking, butchery and large-scale brewing) requiring considerable skill. Retail trade of this kind was concentrated in and around the market in St Mary's, St Benedict's and Holy Trinity parishes.

Wholesale trade was also often long distance, such as the corn export trade, and was concentrated on the riverside in St Clement's and St John's. Artisans manufactured clothing, household goods, jewellery and so on, sometimes supplying middlemen and sometimes selling direct to the public. *Artisan manufacture* seems to have been more widely dispersed, with different types of production dominating different parts of the town. Choice of commercial activity was often reflected in the location and use of family property.

Property finance and speculation. Wealth could also be increased through capital gains. Many of the properties in which families invested appear to have appreciated in value as the urban economy developed (as revealed by the pattern of multiple rents described in Chapter 2). Freehold property could be readily sold, and so capital gains were easy to realize. They could be realized in a single lump sum, through reselling a property with existing rents attached for a large gersuma (or consideration) or through instalments, by attaching an additional perpetual rent to the property, payable to the vendor. Speculation, like commerce, required good judgement; like an ill-judged trading venture, a reckless speculation could result in heavy loss. Property speculation revealed itself in the recurrent buying and selling of properties. The Hundred Rolls show that many properties were indeed bought and sold several times within living memory, while evidence from deeds shows that some properties – particularly commercial properties such as shops and granaries – were resold at frequent intervals.

Careers in education, lay administration and the law. Universities were at the cutting edge of the 13th-century 'knowledge economy', offering a more secular syllabus than priories, friaries and private schoolmasters. They required administrators, officials (e.g. bedels) and teachers. Although Cambridge was on the front line of university development in England, the university itself was still consolidating its position in the late 13th century; while hostels were already established, the collegiate system was not yet developed.

The reforms of Henry II extended the scope of the law and provided great opportunities for the peaceful resolution of disputes. The legal process created a demand for literate and articulate individuals to act as clerks, scribes, attorneys and judges. Royal service could be highly profitable, as those who were deemed to excel could gain wardships and other perks. It was also possible to bid for franchises such as tax collection: sheriffs, for example, held tax farms of their counties, as the career of William le Rus indicates. The 'contractor state' of the 13th century also posed political risks, however, for those who defaulted on their obligations or otherwise offended the king.

Membership of religious institutions. While a career in the law was open only to men, a career in the Church was also open to women. Daughters from aristocratic families could enter nunneries, such as St Radegund's, and rise to the rank of prioress, in which they would control large property portfolios (although not directly for personal gain). Abbeys and priories offered many other positions of responsibility, such as sacrist or almoner, which involved the management of property. Similarly, the Church provided jobs for bishops, archdeacons, rectors, vicars, chaplains and chantry priests, and, of course, had its own system of canon law and ecclesiastical courts. Jobs in the Church were more secure than jobs in the law because lawyers typically received fees while church ministers received a steady income and often had a job for life, while those who served in abbeys could also obtain a pension.

Civic engagement. Civic government gained importance in 13th-century Cambridge. New charters were obtained conferring important privileges on the town. The mayor, bailiffs and burgesses aggressively defended their rights against the Bishop of Ely, the university authorities and local lords who had established rival markets or exacted tolls. As civic authority became stronger it was to every merchant's advantage to participate in civic life. Personal expenses would be incurred in attending meetings, and new responsibilities would impose additional demands on time, but on the other hand election to civic office was a signal of peer esteem, even though it did not always imply peaceful and lawful behaviour.

Strategic marriage (including remarriage). Marriage played a crucial role in the transmission of property between generations. All of the profiled family dynasties faced issues concerning who their members should marry. Sons that married heiresses could augment the family fortunes at a single stroke. In principle daughters who married wealthy heirs could do the same, but in the process the family name usually disappeared. However, where the wife was the dominant partner in a marriage (which often seems to have been the case) the culture and traditions of her family may have continued into future generations even if their name did not. Unmarried daughters could also be found occupations, for example by entering a nunnery.

The relatively high risk of death in medieval England made remarriage an important issue. Marrying a wealthy widow or widower was a smart move for the individual concerned but could damage the prospects of children of the first marriage. Marriage and remarriage were also complicated by the crucial role of dower. Possessive fathers could be very suspicious of their sons-in-law and so the negotiation of the dowry, and the terms attached to it, had to be carefully managed. Dower was an important subject of litigation in the 13th century.

These six strategies fall into three groups. The first two strategies exploited opportunities created by the growth of the market economy. The first, based on trade, exploited the growth of wholesale and retail commodity markets, and markets for artisan products. Growing demand for artisan products in turn reflected both rising population, which generated demand for basic clothing and household equipment, and increasing affluence, which generated demand for luxury products. The second strategy, property speculation, exploited opportunities created by the subdivision of urban property into burgage plots of modest size, and the development of a legal framework in which such plots could be readily bought and sold. Both of these strategies therefore exploited the widening scope and growing scale of the market economy as a whole.

The next two strategies involved building careers in the emerging knowledge-based economy. The knowledge-based economy had both lay and secular sectors. The universities, the law and the Church were all expanding in the 13th century. They offered remunerative careers for people with relevant qualifications. While entry into these careers might require some initial patronage, subsequent advancement could usually be achieved through hard work, peer-to-peer networking and natural ability (see Chapter 6).

The last two strategies were social as well as economic; the pursuit of civic status and advancement through marriage. As the autonomy of town government increased and the town grew in size, so the power conferred by civic status increased too. Bailiffs had access to information on the town finances and opportunities to share confidential information with each other. Information about the property market could be gained from witnessing charters and deeds. Indirectly, therefore, civic status promoted personal wealth. Marriage, by contrast, was a much more traditional method of social advancement. The growth of the urban economy, however, meant that advantageous marriages could be made within the town rather than between potentially distant villages, as had previously been the case.

Overall, therefore, the growth of the urban economy strongly encouraged the pursuit of a versatile strategic approach to the advancement of wealth and reputation by the family unit.

5.4 Risks of failure

Having discussed alternative routes to success, it is necessary to examine the risks of failure. Three main types of risk can be identified. The first was over-ambition. This includes excessively risky business investment, excessive philanthropy and excessive consumption associated with living beyond your means. Provision of excessive dowries could also create problems. The second risk was loss of family cohesion, which could take two main forms. If different members of the same family followed different career trajectories, driven by different ambitions and different aptitudes, they could drift apart. This could fragment the family; dissident members could change their surnames, especially if they thought that the family was losing reputation, and take an occupational name, place name or nickname instead. Alternatively, members might remain attached to the family but quarrel with their relatives; for example, when different siblings had plans to invest in different areas, disputes over the division of inheritance could break out. The third type of risk has already been discussed, namely involvement in debt, crime or litigation.

Over-ambition: excessive consumption. Living beyond their means was a major issue for aristocratic families trying to come to terms with the commercial spirit of the 13th century. Maintaining social status out of rents from land fixed at 12th-century values in the face of competition from upwardly mobile traders earning steady profits was a difficult task. The problem was particularly acute when the heir was a 'waster', as in the Blancgernun family. Families could insure against a potential problem with an heir by dividing inheritance between siblings. Eustace Dunning senior, for example, seems to have divided his inheritance between his sons Harvey and Adam, thereby mitigating the risks associated with Harvey's impulsive behaviour; but Harvey then left much of his property to his son Eustace, a waster, with dire consequences.

Over-ambition: excessive philanthropy. As noted, small-scale acts of philanthropy appear to have been common in medieval Cambridge, but large-scale benefactions were mainly the prerogative of the larger and older families. Some philanthropy seems to have been carefully calculated and to have secured tangible benefits in return. Philanthropy could be an alternative to strategic marriage, as when an unmarried daughter was placed in a nunnery. It could also be used to purchase a pension in the form of a corrody. Reputation could be enhanced by endowing a chantry or, more modestly, sustaining a candle at an altar in the local parish church. Some gifts, however, seem to have been made at times of heightened emotion; these were extravagant gestures made when people were grieving for the loss of a relative or contemplating their own mortality. Such expensive gestures could not only weaken families financially, but also sow dissention by disinheriting heirs, who then squabbled over the few remaining family assets.

Over-ambition: excessive commercial investment. Cambridge had a substantial group of merchants who were involved in shipping corn, and in the river trade in general. Given the risks to shipping, and the speculative nature of wholesale agricultural markets (see Chapter 6), there was a significant risk of losses, even if merchants operated a cartel. There is, however, little evidence in the Hundred Rolls suggestive of specific commercial losses. While losses from excessive consumption and excessive philanthropy are well documented, commercial losses are not. The only plausible indicator of such losses is that many of the names that appear in early tallages and fines for unlicensed export of corn do not appear in later records, suggesting that the several businesses of the early 13th century may have failed. It seems, however, that conditions improved during the reign of Henry III, and that in the second half of the 13th century trade in Cambridge prospered. So long as prosperity continued, business losses may have been low enough to be manageable. There were sufficient profits in good years to offset losses in bad years, and sufficient support from family members, business partners or creditors to ride out a run of bad luck.

Over-ambition: excessive dowry. Over-ambitious strategic marriage could create a problem with financing a dowry. Marrying a daughter into a wealthy family might well ensure the daughter's future prosperity but the cost of funding a substantial dowry could impoverish the parents and, by implication, her siblings and the heir. Marrying a son into a wealthy family, by contrast, was an unambiguous gain, as the son retained the family name and the wife's family paid the dowry.

Loss of cohesion. Loss of family cohesion manifested itself in two main ways. One was the splitting of the family, with children deserting their parents or, more often, siblings choosing to go their own way and losing contact with each other. The other was family disputes, which often seem to have been fuelled by sibling rivalry. These could come to a head when there was no obvious heir and different family members had rival claims. Adoption seems to have been fairly common in Cambridge, an example being the adoption of an orphaned nephew, but this does not seem to have created problems, possibly because the child was indisputably the parents' heir.

Most of the smaller Cambridge families seem to have been reasonably cohesive, an example being the Braci family, where siblings co-owned properties. Cohesion starkly differentiates some of the larger Cambridge families, however. The Bartons, Goggings and Toylets, for example, seem to have been quite cohesive, while the Crochemans, the sons of Absolon and the sons of Ivo were not. Not surprisingly, the cohesive families appear to have been the most successful.

Debt, crime and litigation are factors that have already been discussed. They may be viewed as intermediating factors, translating the effects of failed strategies into tarnished family reputation and loss of cohesion.

Debt was often a consequence of failed ambition, and in particular of excessive consumption. In the 13th century capital sums were often paid in instalments because cash (reputable coinage) was often in short supply. But borrowing short term to finance a long-term imbalance between income and expenditure was a dangerous strategy. Property pledged as collateral could be forfeited on default, and so miscalculation could have fatal consequences. Professional moneylenders were often involved in property speculation; the object of the lender was not that the borrower should repay but that they should not; their property would be seized, and perhaps improved or redeveloped by the lender, before being resold for a higher rent.

Crime. Crime could be the last resort for a family whose strategies had failed. As noted earlier, the consequences of criminality were not so severe as might be expected. Clerks could escape punishment through the benefit of clergy and burgesses were treated leniently by their fellow burgesses. The costs of crime may have been localized: default on payment may have damaged reputation with trading partners, and illegal encroachments with neighbours, but whether others knew or cared is debatable. However, resort to crime does not appear to have solved the problems of failing families. Taking short-term advantage of other people was no solution to long-term problems of failing family strategies.

Litigation. Taking people to court (or being sued in court) was just as expensive in the 13th century as it is today; even more so probably, given the costs of hiring scribes, purchasing writs, travelling to court and providing sureties, not to mention the inconvenience of delays created by frequent adjournments. Nevertheless, it could be worthwhile if valuable property was at stake and the litigation was successful. Evidence from cases of dower (which were very common) and advowson (which were rare) suggest that litigation might succeed as a calculated gamble, but the pursuit of a petty grievance was likely to lead to a loss.

5.5 Characteristics of successful families

The key to success in many families, it may be suggested, was the presence of an individual entrepreneur. An entrepreneur has been defined as someone who is good at taking strategic decisions in risky situations – a capability that is described as good judgement.[4] The previous section has explained how families faced a range of strategic options regarding members' careers. Without pursuing viable careers, family members' contribution to family income would be diminished. Maintaining a high standard of living without the requisite income would get the family into debt, and in the long run force them into selling their assets.

It is unrealistic to suppose that every family member could be an entrepreneur, because entrepreneurship is a relatively scarce quality. The main requirement for family success, the evidence suggests, was that at least one family member in each generation was an entrepreneur. The Barton dynasty is a good example of a family in which entrepreneurship was sustained from one generation to another.

At the very least, one entrepreneur in alternate generations was necessary to keep a leading family in stasis; in this case each entrepreneur was forced to focus on repairing damage done by the previous generation. The evidence suggests that very few Cambridge families maintained themselves in stasis. Almost all the profiled families were in a state of either rise or decline, as new wealth challenged old wealth in pursuit of profit, property and power. The main exception was some of the smaller commercial families, which operated under the umbrella of larger families to which they were connected by marriage. In return for the security of this arrangement, they comprised their own ability to grow into large and wealthy families themselves.

The role of the entrepreneur was to participate actively in either trade or administration, but it did not really matter which, as each could be a rewarding activity in its own way. An entrepreneur generated a flow of income from profits, salaries or fees that could be used by their family to finance property acquisition. Administration could be lay or clerical or both; royal administration was the most lucrative, but local administration in the county, the diocese or the town could be rewarding too. The le Rus family, for example, was extremely successful in profiting from civil law, county administration and contacts with the Church.

Some families specialized in trade or administration, but a few engaged in both. The Gogging family, for example had both a trading branch and a clerical branch. Combining the two through different members of the family proved very powerful in promoting success. It was normally families rather than individuals that engaged in both.

A specific threat to entrepreneurial families was the ageing of the entrepreneur. This was especially serious if the entrepreneur was also the head of the family. Sickness could impose a burden, and loss of entrepreneurial vigour was problematic too. An ageing entrepreneur might be reluctant to allow the new generation to take over, or might choose the most compliant successor rather than the most enterprising one. In some successful families the entrepreneur surrendered the management of business affairs to their heir(s) by giving away their property in return for a lifetime lease on the principal family residence.

5.6 Old wealth and new wealth

A useful way of summarizing many of the previous observations is to employ the well-known distinction between old wealth and new wealth. This concept can be applied to any era: old wealth is simply legacy wealth generated before the period in question, while new wealth is wealth generated during that period. In periods of innovation new wealth replaces old wealth because old wealth is unable to adjust to new conditions.[5] This is a plausible proposition, but only the evidence can decide whether it is correct.

In a medieval context the distinction can be applied to the Commercial Revolution. Old wealth was the wealth of aristocratic families such as the Dunnings and Blancgernuns. It involved tracts of agricultural land, often measured in large units, such as hides, rather than in the roods and furlongs of the peasant's smallholding or the messuages of the town burgess. Much of this land was granted to the family's ancestors before or just after the Norman Conquest. It may have been granted directly by the king, or more likely by an earl or an influential knight. New wealth, by contrast, was represented by wealth acquired through trade, artisan manufacture or, perhaps, employment in royal or ecclesiastical service.

The problem for old wealth was that in the first half of the 13th century, well before the Hundred Rolls, much of the land it possessed had been subdivided and sold off in return for fixed money rents. As the economy developed during the later 13th century, this land appreciated in value. Rising population increased the demand for food, particularly in fast-growing urban centres, and this increased the value of the land that produced the food, and in particular land that was close to towns. The expansion of mints, and the consequent increase in the money supply, also raised prices through general inflation. Thus the value of the land increased in both real and nominal terms but rents did not.

The rents were fixed in nominal terms (e.g. shillings and pence) rather than real terms (e.g. bushels of corn) so that all the benefit of higher prices for the product accrued to the purchasers of the family's lands and not the family itself. The family might have many rents from different properties in different places, but the total of these small sums was not particularly great. The family was stuck in the middle between the king or the earl from whom they held the land and the local people to whom they had sold it. The king and earl suffered too, because their rents were also fixed, but they had sufficient power to recover some of their income from other sources, such as taxation.

The growth of towns was driven mainly by the growth of markets and by improvements in transport, which encouraged the concentration of market activity in the larger towns, as explained earlier. Aristocratic families perceived a need to secure a base in their local market town, if they did not have one already. To maintain their status in the county and the town they perceived a need for conspicuous consumption, which was increasingly difficult to finance as the real value of their rents declined. They also faced the problem of maintaining their rights over their dispersed rural estates. Illegal occupation of empty fields or farmsteads was a particular problem, as court records of the time reveal (see Chapter 4). But litigation was expensive, both in time and money, particularly if a case was referred from a local court to a higher one.

Matters were made worse by the increasing prosperity of the merchant class, who were gaining control of the towns. Their rising incomes set new standards for conspicuous consumption that aristocrats, it seems, felt obliged to match. It was also necessary for the aristocrats to engage in conspicuous philanthropy by supporting local priories and hospitals. Consumption was increasingly financed by sales of their property. But these sales further eroded their already inadequate rental income. Financial requirements became increasingly urgent, and recourse was had to professional moneylenders. When loans could not be repaid, these lenders foreclosed, often waiting, it seems, for the most appropriate moment when the property could be readily sold on for profit.

New wealth represented the other side of the coin. New wealth had often exploited the benefits of being an earlier settler in an expanding town. New wealth may have moved into the town from another town (perhaps a smaller town) or may have escaped from a rural manor, with or without the consent of the feudal lord. They could also arrive together with their lord as a result of employment as a steward or a clerk. In any case, new wealth would possess an intuitive understanding of the market system. Market regulation may have prohibited forestalling, regrating and other dubious practices, but good business judgement was still rewarded; furthermore, it was not illegal to speculate in property. The problems encountered by old wealth provided just another business opportunity for new wealth to exploit.

In principle old wealth could have adapted their strategy and played new wealth at their own game. There was nothing to stop an aristocrat from engaging in trade, apart, perhaps, from a belief that trade was demeaning. Old wealth preferred to ride about on horseback, making wagers, joining in local tournaments (despite prohibitions by the king) and even going on crusade (often a short-cut to death or bankruptcy).

Family structure may have inhibited adjustment too. Old wealth was often embedded in an extended family, with different branches in different parts of the country. Their in-laws would be another aristocratic family. By contrast, new wealth was often represented by a solitary individual or a small family. New wealth might be an immigrant trader who had married a local girl (preferably one with a dowry of local property). New wealth seems to have embraced something more like a nuclear family structure, involving close relations between parents and children but little contact with siblings or in-laws. In this respect it may have anticipated the later new wealth of the Reformation and the Industrial Revolution. The focus on a small family headed by an entrepreneurial parent is reflected in the structure of some of the smaller and very successful families discussed in Chapter 4. Likewise, the more amorphous structure of aristocratic families is reflected in some of the unsuccessful large families in the same chapter. If this interpretation is correct, it suggests that small families were, on balance, more successful then large ones because they were internally more coherent and were controlled by the driving force of a single entrepreneur.

5.7 Conclusion

Medieval families performed a range of functions. They were not only units of reproduction; but in the absence of public schooling they also educated their children, with boys being apprenticed to their fathers to learn the family trade and girls learning domestic skills from their mothers. Families were also businesses. In the absence of the modern business corporation or joint stock company, families organized trade and artisan production. It was not only children who mastered the family business. Wives too displayed mastery of business, often taking over the business as widows, especially where no son was willing or able to do so. Care of the elderly and infirm was another important role. Although hospital care was available, it was in limited supply, and only the rich could afford to retire to a religious house.

Evidence from Cambridge shows that some families were better than others at managing these issues. Some families produced entrepreneurs who identified business opportunities that provided employment for other members of the family. Some provided basic education that allowed their children to enter knowledge-based careers in royal administration, civic offices, the law or the Church. Some families specialized in particular fields, with several family members following the same career path, but most chose to diversify, with different children choosing different careers. Provided the family was cohesive, different members could help each other in dealing with issues that they could not easily handle themselves. With one sibling in trade and another in a profession the young professional could help out the young trader with legal issues while the trader could provide profits out of which the young professional could finance their education.

In developing their strategies families were constrained by a variety of factors. Small families with few children faced extinction of the family name through the early death of a sole male heir, while larger families faced fragmentation when different branches spun off, having little to do with each other. There is only limited evidence that gender balance was a significant factor, except when the absence of a male heir led to the extinction of the family name.

The dynamics of the family interacted with location. Smaller families tended to remain rooted a single parish, while larger families spread their property portfolio across the town. Families that specialized in trade were likely to focus their property portfolio on areas where their trade was carried out, while families that combined trade and professions held more diversified portfolios.

Notes

1. Rees Jones, *York*, pp 195–7, 315.
2. Diana Wood, *Medieval Economic Thought* (Cambridge, 2002), pp 139, 143.
3. It is also likely that traders used the borough court records to pursue litigation, and few records from those courts have survived (Palmer (ed.), *Cambridge Borough Documents*, pp 1–10).
4. Casson and Casson, *Entrepreneur*, 2–7; Mark Casson and Catherine Casson, 'The History of Entrepreneurship: Medieval Origins to a Modern Phenomenon?', *Business History* 56 (8) (2014): 1223–42.
5. Zvi Razi, 'Family, Land and the Village Community in Later Medieval England', *Past and Present* 93 (1) (1981): 1–36.

Cambridge in a Regional and National Context

Introduction

Cambridge had an important agricultural property market and an active property market, as previous chapters have demonstrated. This chapter considers Cambridge's performance as a town relative to its local and regional competitors. It examines the factors that contributed to making the town an attractive place for investment by existing residents, residents of the Cambridge region and even those from outside the region.

The first part of the chapter, sections 6.1 to 6.4, focuses on the regional context of the town. It examines competition between rival urban settlements in the Cambridge region, with special reference to river and road transport networks. It begins by looking at five important towns within about 20 miles of Cambridge, including some outside the county. It then looks at market centres within the county, and finally considers three satellite villages close to the town. The five large towns were all inland ports involved in wholesale trade. Like Cambridge, they were all on the River Great Ouse or its tributaries; so this river system is considered first. The market centres within the county were mainly concerned with retail trade and were all connected to Cambridge by road (though some had river connections as well); so the road system is considered next. Finally, the discussion focuses on three satellite villages within walking distance of Cambridge. While these villages could, in principle, have been competitors, they were also well positioned to support the town's activities.

The second part of the chapter focuses on the national context.[1] The previous chapters have shown that Cambridge not only had important agricultural markets, but an active property market too. Section 6.5

considers the extent to which these markets operated in isolation from other urban markets or were integrated into national markets. We examine if agricultural prices in Cambridge closely follow national trends or were governed by purely local circumstances. Section 6.6 demonstrate that Cambridge's property market had a national context. A combination of its economic dominance, administrative role as a county town and function as an administrative centre for the Bishop of Ely, and the misfortunes of some of its leading families, attracted external investors to the town.

6.1 Cambridge in a wider context

Cambridge was not the only important town in the area. Cambridgeshire is a relatively small county, and so the borders of neighbouring counties lie quite close to the county town. Norfolk lies north-east, Suffolk south-east and Essex to the south; Bedfordshire is to the south-west and Huntingdonshire to the west. It was therefore possible, in principle, for neighbouring county towns to take trade away from Cambridge.

Cambridge, however, was a relatively large town in its own right, and much larger than some neighbouring county towns, such as Huntingdon and Bedford. Table 6.1 identifies the top 12 towns within easy reach of

Table 6.1: Ranking of Cambridge by taxable wealth in relation to other regional towns in the subsidy of 1334

Rank	Town	Value	Rank in England
1	Norwich	£1,100 (?) [£946]	6
2	Great Yarmouth	£1,000	7
3	King's Lynn, Norfolk	£770	11
4	Ipswich, Suffolk	£550 [£650]	19
5	**Cambridge**	**£500 [£466]**	**21**
6	Bury St Edmunds, Suffolk	£360	26
7	Ely	£315	32
8	Swaffham	£300	37
9	Sudbury, Suffolk	£281	41
10	Huntingdon with Godmanchester	£270 (?) [originally £263]	43
11	Mildenhall	£173	93
12	Thetford, Norfolk	£160	95

Sources: Alan Dyer, 'Ranking Lists of English Medieval Towns', *Cambridge Urban History* ed. D. M. Palliser (3 vols) I (Cambridge, 2000), p 755; R. E. Glasscock (ed.), *The Lay Subsidy of 1334* (London, 1975)

Cambridge (under 40 miles by road) at that time. They can be compared using a metric based on their valuations in the 1334 subsidy returns. Cambridge ranks 5th out of the 12 towns, and ranks 21st nationwide (Figure 6.1). The four towns in the region that were larger than Cambridge were all located on or near the coast, some distance from Cambridge. Cambridge, therefore, was a significant economic force in the region. Far from losing ground to other towns, it could have gained ground at their expense. Whether it realized this potential is one of the subjects addressed in this chapter.

Cambridge's national ranking was high when compared with its ranking today. In medieval England most large towns were in the south-east, with the remainder lying up the east coast or towards Somerset and the

Figure 6.1: Cambridge and the leading 20 English towns in the 1334 subsidy

Source: Alan Dyer, 'Ranking Lists of English Medieval Towns', *Cambridge Urban History* ed. D. M. Palliser (3 vols) I (Cambridge, 2000), pp 755–77, p 755 (Commissioned by authors)

Welsh border to the west. Its ranking today is depressed by the emergence of large industrial towns in the North and Midlands, for example in Lancashire, where no large towns existed in medieval times.

6.2 Competition with other large towns: the influence of river transport

The River Cam is one of several tributaries of the Great Ouse (see Chapter 1). This wide, navigable river flows north into the Wash about 3 miles north of King's Lynn (see Figure 1.1). It gives access to the east coast of England (including London), the North Sea (for the Low Countries) and the Baltic Sea (for Scandinavia and Northern Europe). King's Lynn was one of the most important ports in England in the 13th century. In the 1334 subsidy it ranked 11th among all towns in the country, and 3rd in East Anglia behind Norwich and Great Yarmouth. King's Lynn also lies on the River Nar, which joins the Ouse there from Castle Acre to the east. South of King's Lynn the Ouse flows past the ancient market town of Downham on the east bank. Near Fordham the River Wissey enters from Stoke Ferry to the east. Just north of Littleport, the River Little Ouse enters from Brandon and Thetford, also from the east. A couple of miles further south, a more important river enters from the south-east. This is the River Lark, whose head of navigation is at Bury St Edmunds. Bury was a prominent wool town as well as a pilgrimage centre, and was a major source of the wool exported through King's Lynn.

Once past Ely, on the west bank, the River Cam enters from the south. On its route from Cambridge, the Cam is joined by various lodes, including one from Reach (mentioned later). Past its junction with the River Cam, the Ouse swings due east and proceeds to Huntingdon by way of Swavesey and St Ives. At Huntingdon it swings to the south, and south of St Neots throws off a tributary, the River Hiz, south towards Biggleswade. The Ouse then continues east to Bedford, the county town of Bedfordshire. The source of the river is near Syresham in Northamptonshire. Since the Middle Ages various cuts, drains and relief channels have been built, but the basic configuration of the river and its tributaries has remained unchanged. The limit of navigation today is at Kempston, just west of Bedford.

Three important points emerge from this. The first is that Cambridge formed a key part of a river network that converged on King's Lynn. River boats sailing down the Cam could transship their cargoes to seagoing vessels at Lynn. At the time of Domesday Lynn, then known as Lenn, was held by the Bishop of Elmham and the Archbishop of Canterbury. Lynn acquired a market as early as 1105, granted by Bishop Herbert de Losinga of Thetford, who was actively developing the town at that time. Trade really took off in the early 13th century, however; the town received a charter from King John in 1204, and in c.1220 the course of the River Ouse was diverted from an outlet near Wisbech to the estuary at Lynn. The timing fits in with what is known about the growth of the river trade in Cambridge from the late 12th century onwards. Lynn continued to prosper into the 14th century. It soon attracted Hanseatic merchants, whose warehouse near the quay still survives.

The second point is that Cambridge's monopoly of the corn export trade was not a complete monopoly. The prohibition of exports by other towns (see Chapter 1) only applied to Cambridgeshire. It did not encompass other counties and therefore did not apply to all the towns with access to the River Ouse, examples being Huntingdon, St Ives and Bury. While there is little doubt that Cambridge dominated the corn export trade, this was almost certainly because of its strategic position rather than its statutory monopoly. Its strategic position was enhanced by local investments in mills and warehouses; there is little evidence that the monopoly encouraged complacency among the Cambridge merchant elite.

The third point is that the Ouse and its tributaries connected Cambridge not only to the north, but also to the east and west. There were direct connections as far east as Bury and Thetford, and as far west as Bedford, and possibly beyond. There is no evidence, however, concerning how far these links were commercially exploited.

There are five towns along the Ouse and its tributaries that could have challenged Cambridge. In order to proximity to Cambridge they are Ely, St Ives, Huntingdon, Bury and Thetford (Newmarket is excluded because it was a recent foundation and was not on the river system).

Ely

Ely is a small town located on an island in the Fens about 10 miles downriver north of Cambridge.[2] It was dominated by the abbey and the see of the Bishop of Ely, who were both major landowners, not only in Cambridge but throughout East Anglia.[3] Its isolation by land made it a place of refuge, both after the Norman Conquest and during the Baronial Wars of the 13th century (see Chapter 1). The townspeople derived most of their custom from the abbey. There is little evidence that they themselves participated in the campaigns of those who took refuge in their town. The town was a borough but tight control by the abbey provided little opportunity for local initiative. Ely possessed a quay on the river about half a mile from the abbey, but its trade never challenged that of Cambridge.

St Ives

St Ives hosted a major Easter market, which lasted eight days and was sometimes prolonged even further in order to make more money.[4] Perhaps not surprisingly, the profits of the market were a subject of contention. The Abbot of Ramsey, who had held the town as a gift from a nobleman, Athelstan Mannesone, since the 10th century, naturally had a claim, but had to defend this against both the king and the burgesses of Huntingdon, both of whom made rival claims. St Ives (then known as Slepe), was the first bridging point on the River Ouse and therefore, like Cambridge, was a natural place to develop a market. The wooden bridge, recorded as early as 1107, was not rebuilt in stone until the 15th century.[5] The marketplace, which ran parallel to the riverbank from the bridge to the church, was the site of the fair. The fair attracted foreign merchants selling luxury items of clothing and jewellery, and was patronized by visitors from far afield, including London. The town was not a borough, and so local cases were tried in the abbot's court, although the king had some jurisdiction over the fair.

St Ives could have become a major threat to Cambridge had it not confined itself largely to promoting the fair. It was a major supplier of leather goods but was not a major player in the corn trade. Its merchants were probably too preoccupied with competing against neighbouring Huntingdon to concern themselves with competing against Cambridge as well.

Huntingdon

Huntingdon occupies a strategic position where Ermine Street, the main road from London to Lincoln and York since Roman times, crosses the River Ouse.[6] Roads from Cambridge, Kettering and Chatteris also converge on the town. Huntingdon has a twin town, Godmanchester, across the bridge on the south bank.[7]

Before St Ives bridge was built, Huntingdon was the first bridging point on the river. It had a market by 974 and a mint by 955–9, probably with a single moneyer, and later acquired a Norman castle.[8] Domesday identified 256 messuages. But Huntingdon did not prosper. In the 13th century it faced competition not only from St Ives, but also from Peterborough, a major hub further north on Ermine Street with great ecclesiastical wealth. In 1259 the bridge needed repair and the cost was made a charge on the county, with all county-dwellers being free of toll. Freedom from toll would have boosted the local market but deprived the town of income that could have been invested in attracting custom from a wider area. Despite its good connections, Huntingdon became increasingly parochial, while Godmanchester remained stubbornly rural. At the time of the Hundred Rolls Huntingdon possessed 16 parish churches, and 6 religious houses but, it seems, little long-distance trade.

Bury St Edmunds

Bury is famous for the Shrine of St Edmund, Anglo-Saxon king and martyr, captured and killed by invading Danes in 869. The shrine is now lost, the abbey destroyed, but the precinct remains and the medieval town, with its famous grid of streets, is still intact.[9] A Benedictine monastery was established in 1020. The main north–south road through the town, from Thetford to Sudbury, was diverted to accommodate the abbey precinct on the west bank of the River Lark. Bury played a prominent role in the Suffolk wool trade and served as an inland port for the export of wool, linen and cloth. It was well positioned to consolidate consignments for transport north to King's Lynn. To the south, Sudbury played a similar role, using the River Stour to transport goods to the coastal port of Harwich.

The abbey established a new market, the Great Market, to the north-west of the original town centre, with the original market becoming the Horsemarket.[10] The abbey also developed a substantial pilgrimage trade. The merchants of Bury became very prosperous, but deeply resented the control exercised over the town by the abbot through his obedientiaries, particularly the sacrist.[11] Discontent came to a head in 1327 when the king was forced to intervene after a serious riot. The town survived the Black Death, but its tourist economy was undermined by the dissolution of the abbey.

Bury seems to have developed commercially much earlier than Cambridge.[12] Some Bury citizens invested in Cambridge property from as early as the 12th century, but there is little evidence that Bury and Cambridge competed. Bury had a shrine and Cambridge did not. Cambridge promoted free thinking and encouraged the friars, whereas Bury decidedly did not. The diversity of the English landscape encouraged economic specialization in agriculture, with Cambridgeshire specializing in arable farming and Suffolk in pasture. Thus Cambridge specialized in corn and education, while Bury specialized in wool and tourism.

Thetford

Thetford is an ancient settlement, believed to be the capital of the Iceni, a local Celtic tribe. It is located on the main road from Cambridge to Norwich almost due north of Bury St Edmunds. Like Bury it was an important religious centre. It was the see of the Bishop of East Anglia from 1072 to 1094. A Cluniac monastery was established there in 1104 by Roger Bigod, an associate of William the Conqueror. The number of institutions expanded rapidly; many parish churches and hospitals developed in the town, only some of which survive today. A market is recorded in c.1140 and again in the Hundred Rolls.[13] Charters for fairs were granted in 1140 and 1232.[14]

Domesday Book records 943 burgesses in 1066 and 720 in 1086, making Thetford one of the largest towns not just in East Anglia, but the entire country. Decline seems to have set in fairly early, however, although the market has survived. Archaeological evidence suggests that the town specialized in extraction and processing activities, including chalk-mining, quarrying, sand-extraction, metal-working and pottery-making. There was also some local milling and malting.

Thetford is the most remote of the five towns considered here. Much of the area around the town was sand and gravel, unsuitable for either arable or pasture farming. However, those areas suitable for arable generated a surplus for export because of the low density of population.[15] It was a tribal administrative centre that was transformed into a religious centre through substantial endowments from Norman aristocrats. It had a modest pilgrim trade. Its economic advantage lay in the processing of sand, chalk and clay.[16] Its geology and location afforded no competition to Cambridge. As Cambridge prospered, so Thetford declined.

The conclusion is that none of the neighbouring towns offered serious competition to Cambridge. Two – Ely and Thetford – had inconvenient and somewhat isolated locations, while Bury specialized in completely different trades. Huntingdon and St Ives were locked in competition with each other. It was only St Ives fair, with is influx of exotic luxury products from the Continent, that posed a significant threat to Cambridge trade, and fortunately that lasted (at least officially) for only eight days each year. Cambridge too had a fair, namely Sturbridge Fair (see Chapters 1 and 7), but there was no clash of dates, as Sturbridge was in the autumn and

St Ives in the spring. A policy of mutual toleration was therefore optimal for both parties.

6.3 Competition from smaller towns and villages: the impact of road and river connections

The focus now switches to competition from smaller towns and villages within the county. Many of these towns hosted weekly markets and annual fairs, which potentially posed a threat to Cambridge market. This section examines the strength of this threat.

Table 6.2 lists all the markets in the county that are recorded as receiving charters. It also includes fairs, which may be regarded as annual (and therefore episodic) markets. Their importance resides from the fact that some of them appear to have specialized in certain products, such as horses and cheeses. The table reports the situation leading up to 1279, the period from 1279 until the Black Death and from the Black Death to the present day. It includes only markets and fairs chartered up to 1349. The location of the markets is illustrated in Figure 6.2.

Table 6.3 summarizes key results from Table 6.2. Forty-eight per cent of markets that were chartered up to 1279 had no recorded activity. Only ten markets other than Cambridge are known to have been operating, namely Caxton, Ely, Fowlmere, Gamlingay, Ickleton, Linton, Orwell, Swavesey, Whittlesford and Wisbech. Topographical evidence suggests that Cambridge, Ely and Wisbech were very large, being equipped with dedicated marketplaces off their main roads and surrounded with messuages suitable for artisans. Caxton, Gamlingay, Linton and Swavesey were probably fairly large (and possibly Orwell too), but the others were probably small. In the following period 13 markets were chartered but only 2 – Foxton and Sutton – were recorded as active. Markets chartered in the earlier period were therefore much more likely to survive and prosper.[17] It is well known that many new towns and markets were chartered in this period nationwide, and that in other parts of the country many failed as well.[18]

Table 6.4 summarizes the results for fairs. Cambridge had three fairs: one for the Leper Hospital, one for Barnwell and one for St Radegund's. There were nine other fairs that definitely operated at some time before 1279: Caxton, Ely, Fordham, Ickleton, Linton, Rampton, Reach, Swavesey and Whittlesford. There may have been unchartered fairs at other places, such as Wisbech. Two of these fairs were at places that did not have markets – Fordham and Reach. There were nine fairs or markets

Table 6.2: Chronology of markets and fairs in medieval Cambridgeshire

Location	1279 and earlier	1280–1348	1349 and after
Cambridge £466.09	*Market* from 11th century or earlier. Borough 1086. *Fair* on the Assumption of St Mary granted 1135–54 to the Priory of St Radegund. *Fair* granted to the Leper Hospital 1199–1216. *Fair* of St Giles' Church, Barnwell proclaimed 1229.	*Market* continues; held on a Saturday in 1347 *Leper hospital fair* at Sturbridge recorded in HR and elsewhere.	*Market* continues to 2017. By 1376 the burgesses of Cambridge had established their rights to the profits of *Sturbridge fair*.
Abington Pigotts £48		*Market* chartered 1335 to Warin of Bassingbourne [nearby parish] Friday. It 'came to nothing'.	
Babraham £114		*Market* chartered 1335 to John, Duke of Brittany and Earl of Richmond, tenant-in-chief. Held at the manor. Monday. No evidence of activity.	
Balsham £70	*Market* chartered 1245 to Hugh, Bishop of Ely. Monday. No evidence of activity. *Fair* also chartered 1245. Feast of Holy Trinity.	*Market* chartered 1318 to John Bishop of Ely. Held at the manor. Wednesday. No evidence of activity.	*Fair* survived until early 19th century.

(continued)

Table 6.2: Chronology of markets and fairs in medieval Cambridgeshire (continued)

Location	1279 and earlier	1280–1348	1349 and after
Barham, near Linton, not separately assessed		*Market* chartered 1282 to Simon de Forneus held at manor. Friday. No evidence of activity. *Fair* chartered at the same time. Feast of St Mary.	*Fair* not recorded in 15th or 16th century, but may have been revived in 1664.
Barrington £180		*Market* chartered 1335 to Thomas de Heselarton. Held at manor. Monday. No evidence of activity. *Fair* similarly. Feast of St Margaret.	No evidence for market. *Fair* continued until 19th century.
Bassingbourn £142.50	*Market* chartered 1253 to Peter of Savoy, Earl of Richmond, tenant-in-chief. Held at manor. Monday. No evidence of activity. *Fair* similarly. Feast of St Peter & St Paul.	*Market* and *fair* regranted 1335 and 1344. No evidence of activity.	
Bottisham £172.50		*Market* recorded 1299. Ralph de Monte Hermeri, Earl of Gloucester and Hertfordshire and Joanna his wife. Monday. No evidence of activity.	
Brinkley £99	*Market* chartered to William de Mohun. Held at the manor. Wednesday. No evidence of activity. [Tuesday from 1261] *Fair* similarly. Feast of St Michael.	*Market* and *fair* not recorded.	*Market* disused by 1807.

(continued)

Table 6.2: Chronology of markets and fairs in medieval Cambridgeshire (continued)

Location	1279 and earlier	1280–1348	1349 and after
Burwell £112.50	*Market* granted 1277 to Robert Tybotot. Held at manor. Wednesday. No evidence of activity. *Fair* similarly. Whit Monday. No evidence of activity.		
Caxton £90	*Market* chartered 1248 to Baldwin de Frivill; held at the manor. Monday. Probably active.	*Market* probably active.	Market town in 1600.
Chippenham £120	*Market* granted 1226 to the Prior of the Hospital of Jerusalem in England. Confirmed 1234. Monday. No evidence of activity.		
Clopton £78.75		*Market* granted 1292 to Robert de Ho. Held at manor. Recorded 1298. No evidence thereafter.	Deserted village, enclosed c.1500.
Cottenham £232.50	*Market* granted 1265 to John Walerand, king's clerk, parson of the church. Held at manor. Market similarly. No evidence of activity. *Fair* similarly.	No evidence of activity.	
Eltisley £102		*Market* chartered 1324 to Philip de Stowe. Held at manor. Wednesday. No further evidence.	

(continued)

Table 6.2: Chronology of markets and fairs in medieval Cambridgeshire (continued)

Location	1279 and earlier	1280–1348	1349 and after
Ely £357.61	*Market* 1224 to Bishop of Ely. Wednesday. Planned marketplace. *Fair* granted 1121–9. Feast of St Etheldreda. Regranted 1198 and confirmed 1233.	*Market* continued under the control of the abbey. *Fair* at the manor chartered 1312. Fair on Ascension Day chartered 1318.	All three fairs continued until 17th century at least. Market town 1600 and 2017.
Fordham £105	*Fair* recorded 1233.		
Fowlmere £87	*Market* granted 1207 to the constable of Chester, guardian of Richard Munfchet. Thursday. Market recorded in 1279. *Fair* also chartered 1207. Feast of St John the Baptist.	*Market* held 'from time out of mind' in 1298. Continued until 14th century. *Fair:* No evidence.	In the early 17th century Edward Aldred acquired a new grant of a market but 'the proximity of established markets at Cambridge, Royston, and Saffron Walden soon forced it to cease'.
Foxton £105		*Market* chartered in 1326 to John de la Haye of Shepreth. Friday. *Fair* chartered 1310 to Constantine de Mortuo Mari. Held at manor. Feast of St Lawrence. *Fairs* chartered to John de la Haye in 1326 at the manor. Feasts of St Peter & St Paul and St Andrew.	*Market* survived into early 16th century. *Fairs.* One held at each manor in c.1630.
Gamlingay £145.50	*Market* recorded 1239. Held by John de Plesseto. Held to be detrimental to market at Potton (Beds). In 1279 John de Avenal held a market on Tuesday.	*Market* of John de Avenal continues.	*Market* of John de Avenal continues until 1600, when it was transferred to Potton after a fire damaged the settlement.

(continued)

Table 6.2: Chronology of markets and fairs in medieval Cambridgeshire (continued)

Location	1279 and earlier	1280–1348	1349 and after
Great Abington	*Market* chartered 1257 to Hugh de Vere, Earl of Oxford. Held at manor. Friday. No evidence of activity. *Fair* similarly. Feast of St Lawrence. No evidence of activity.		
Great Wilbraham £23.33		*Market* chartered 1281 to John de Luvetot. Held at manor. Thursday. *Fair* similarly. No evidence of activity.	
Hildersham £27	*Market* chartered 1254 to William de Bolevill and Ela his wife. Held at manor. Friday. No evidence of activity. *Fair* similarly. Feast of St Margaret. No evidence of activity.		
Ickleton £85	*Market* granted 1135–54. Thursday. Other grants 1222, 1227. *Fair* also granted 1135–54.	*Market* recorded 1279 and 1298. *Fair* recorded in 1287 and 1298.	*Fair* recorded in 1536 and 1557. Feast of St Mary Magdalen for five days. Continued until 19th century.
Impington £52.50		*Market* chartered in 1301 to Peter de Chauvent. Held at manor. Thursday. *Fair* similarly. No further evidence for either.	

(continued)

Table 6.2: Chronology of markets and fairs in medieval Cambridgeshire (continued)

Location	1279 and earlier	1280–1348	1349 and after
Kingston £297.50		*Market* chartered in 1306 to Constantine de Mortuo Mari. Held at manor. Thursday. *Fair* similarly. Feast of St Margaret. No further evidence for either.	
Linton £127.50 including two small local parishes	*Market* chartered in 1246 to William de Say. Held at manor. Tuesday. Borough 1279. *Fair* similarly. Feast of St Lawrence.	*Market* survived until c.1850. *Fair* survived until c.1870.	*Market* survived until c.1850. *Fair* survived until c.1870.
Milton £112.50	*Fair* chartered 1229 to Godfrey de Craucumbe. Held at manor. Feast of the Nativity of Mary. No evidence of activity.		
Orwell £139.50	*Market* chartered in 1254 to Ralph de Camoys the Younger. Held at manor. Thursday *Fair* similarly. Holy Trinity.	*Market* survived until 1522 at least.	*Market* survived until 1522 at least.
Rampton £52.50	*Market* chartered in 1270 to Robert de Lisle. Thursday. *Fair* similarly. In 1279 there was a three-day fair.	*Market:* No evidence of activity. *Fair:* Nothing recorded.	*Market* and *fair* confirmed to John, Lord Scrope, in 1534. No evidence of activity.
Reach No assessment	*Fair* recorded in 1201. Monday of Rogationtide. Controlled by Cambridge burgesses, possibly owing to their control of river trade.	*Fair.* Burgesses of King's Lynn complain in 1286 of unjust distraint by Cambridge burgesses. The fair involved a considerable amount of trading, especially in horses.	*Fair.* In 1388 Cambridge held two-third share and the Bishop of Ely one-third share. Also recorded in 1587. *Market* town in 1600.

(continued)

Table 6.2: Chronology of markets and fairs in medieval Cambridgeshire (continued)

Location	1279 and earlier	1280–1348	1349 and after
Sutton £78.75		*Market* chartered in 1311 to Prior of Ely. Thursday.	*Market* continued to mid-16th century or later.
Swaffham Prior £115.50		*Market* chartered in 1309 to Prior of Ely. Thursday. Held at the manor. No evidence of activity. *Fair* similarly. Feast of decollation of St John. No evidence of activity.	
Swavesey £210	*Market* chartered in 1244 to Alan la Zuche. Tuesday. Recorded 1279. *Fair* similarly. Holy Trinity. Another fair granted in lieu in 1261. Feast of St Michael. Both held at the manor. Borough 1279.	*Market* and three-day *fair* recorded 1289.	*Market* recorded 1350. Tuesday market chartered in 1505 to Thomas, Earl of Ormond. Probably disused by 1738 and definitely abandoned by 1840. *Fair* confirmed 1375 and again in 1505.
Trumpington £141		*Fair* chartered 1314 to Giles of Trumpington. Feast of St Peter ad Vincula. Held at the manor.	*Fair* continued to early 19th century.
Whittlesford £142.50	*Market* chartered 1206 to Baldwin de Toney. Tuesday. Market recorded 1242. Re-chartered 1267 to Baldwin de Akeny. Held at the manor. Fair chartered 1267 similarly.	Market and fair continued.	By 1460 neither the Tuesday market nor the fair had any value.

(continued)

Table 6.2: Chronology of markets and fairs in medieval Cambridgeshire (continued)

Location	1279 and earlier	1280–1348	1349 and after
Wicken £67.50		*Market* chartered 1331 to Humphrey of Bassingbourn. Monday. Held at the manor. No evidence of activity. *Fair* similarly. No evidence of activity.	
Wisbech £409.50	From the 12th century there were two *markets* to the east (New market) and west (Old market) of the river. Both held by Bishop of Ely. Recorded 1221.	*Markets* probably continued to operate. *Fair* chartered in 1327 to Bishop of Ely. Holy Trinity. Held at the manor.	A Saturday *market* held by the Bishop of Ely is recorded in 1492. Borough 1549. Market town 1600 and 2017. *Fair* recorded 1492–3 held by Bishop of Ely. Feast of St Peter and St Paul. It may be the earlier fair on a different date. *Fair* 1587. Monday before Lady Day.

Note: The figures in the left-hand columns are the 1334 subsidy valuations for the parish, which correspond to a fixed fraction of the value of the chattels (moveable goods) of the inhabitants of a parish, namely one fifteenth in rural areas and one tenth in urban areas and the royal demesne. The poorest inhabitants were exempt. The Calendar of Patent Rolls is the main source for charters and the VCH for records of market activity.

Source: Samantha Letters, *Online Gazetteer of Markets and Fairs in England and Wales to 1516*, available at http://www.history.ac.uk/cmh/gaz/gazweb2.html (accessed 12 August 2016)

Figure 6.2: Active markets and fairs in Cambridgeshire, c.1279

Source: Samantha Letters, *Online Gazetteer of Markets and Fairs in England and Wales to 1516*, available at http://www.history.ac.uk/cmh/gaz/gazweb2.html (accessed 12 August 2016) (Commissioned by authors)

that probably did not operate, so that half of chartered fairs operated and half did not. This is similar to the ratio for markets.

There is a sharp difference in the following period, 1279–1348, however. Forty-five per cent of newly chartered fairs operated, whereas only 15 per cent of newly chartered markets did so. Part of the explanation may be that fewer fairs than markets were chartered, so that 'over-supply' was lower. Furthermore, competition between the fairs was to some extent lower as the yearly calendar was less crowded because they were only annual events. Fairs could be larger than markets

Table 6.3: Markets: analysis of recorded activity

Period of establishment	Activity		Percentage active
	Yes	No	
1279 and before	11 Cambridge, Caxton, Ely, Fowlmere, Gamlingay, Ickleton, Linton, Orwell, Swavesey, Whittlesford, Wisbech	10 Balsham, Bassingbourn, Brinkley, Burwell, Chippenham, Cottenham, Great Abington, Hildersham, Milton, Rampton,	52
1280 and afterwards	2 Foxton, Sutton	11 Abington Pigotts, Babraham, Barham, Barrington, Bottisham, Eltisley, Great Wilbraham, Impington, Kingston, Swaffham Prior, Wicken	15
TOTAL	13	21	38

Source: Table 6.2

Table 6.4: Fairs: analysis of activity

Period of establishment	Activity		
	Yes	No	Percentage active
1279 and before	9	9	50
1280 and afterwards	5	6	45
TOTAL	14	16	47

Note: The table excludes the three fairs held in Cambridge.
Source: Table 6.2

(e.g. Reach and Swavesey), and therefore more worthwhile for people from across the county to attend. A number of regional fairs grew in the period after the Black Death to serve growing consumer demand and new trading networks.[19] Some fairs may have survived because the entertainments they provided were more important than the products they sold.

Table 6.5 reports the chronology of charters. The period 1240–59 represents the peak for chartering of both markets and fairs. There is a smaller peak over the longer period 1300–39. The first chartering of markets and fairs stops in 1340, although rechartering and charter confirmation continued for some time.

Table 6.5: Dates of first charter or equivalent: analysis

Date interval	No. of markets	No. of fairs
Before 1200	4	3
1200–19	2	1
1220–39	5	2
1240–59	9	7
1260–79	3	4
1280–99	3	2
1300–20	5	6
1320–39	6	4
1340–59	0	0
1360 and after	0	0
TOTAL	37	29

Note: One established market and one fair cannot be accurately dated.
Source: Table 6.2

Location of markets

It is often hypothesized that successful inland urban settlements in non-industrialized areas were located on a major river or at a key point on the river system; on a major road or near a major road intersection; or near an abbey, administrative centre, educational centre or other high-status consumption centre.[20] In the specific context of Cambridgeshire the following position may be added: at an edge between relatively high chalkland suitable for arable or sheep farming and lower-lying clay in river valleys more suited to cattle pasture and meadow.

The locations of the successful markets identified lend some support to this these hypotheses.

Caxton is located on the main road from Cambridge to St Neots, about 9 miles west from Cambridge and 8 miles east from St Neots. Scattered references from the medieval period indicate that it was a popular stopping place for medieval travellers. In the 14th century an oratory was licensed for the use of passing strangers.[21]

Ely, discussed previously, possessed a spacious marketplace and several resident local merchants. There was some local industry, although high-status consumer items were often imported from abroad.[22]

Fowlmere market was active only intermittently. It was near the intersection of the main London–King's Lynn road and the Royston–Newmarket road. A prehistoric trackway from Melbourn to Thriplow passed nearby. By 1686 it had several inns, which provided 13 beds and stabling for 20 horses.[23]

Gamlingay is a local road hub where the Cambridge–Bedford road crosses the Waresley–Potton road close to the St Neots road. For centuries it was a local agricultural services centre housing artisans and craftsmen. In 1279 these included a baker, thatcher, weaver and miller, while in the 15th century there were smiths, glovers and dyers. Until a fire in 1600 it was one of the most populous settlements on the Cambridgeshire/Bedfordshire border.[24]

Ickleton lies on the west bank of the River Cam 11 miles south of Cambridge. The Icknield Way crosses the river close to the village. The principal crops in 1279 were barley and wheat. Later the village fattened sheep for the London market and exported wool. There is limited evidence for the market but much more for the fair, which in the 18th and 19th centuries dealt chiefly in horses and cheese.[25]

Linton lies 9 miles south-east of Cambridge, comprising three adjacent Domesday settlements. It stands at a point where two low chalk ridges come close together at a crossing of the River Cam. Linton Priory, a cell of a Benedictine abbey in Brittany, was suppressed after 1400, while a convent of the Crutched Friars survived until the Reformation. Locally grown timber was used by its artisans. Its market, which moved several times within the town, survived until the 1860s.[26]

Orwell lies just off the main Cambridge–Bedford road about 10 miles from Cambridge. It is an agricultural parish, although several inhabitants in 1279 bore names such as *faber*, *mercator* and *textor*.[27]

Swavesey extends from the River Ouse in the north to the Cambridge–Huntingdon road in the south. It borders local fens and has ready access to the river. It may have hosted a pre-Conquest minster. It was the administrative centre of a large 11th-century estate and was fortified with a castle. It was an inland port by 1177, with a dock whose profits accrued to the local prior. In 1177 two Swavesey men were among many amerced in Cambridge for the export of corn. Later a Swavesey boat was attacked by pirates in the North Sea. By 1279 Swavesey was a recognized alternative to Cambridge as a mart for Long Stanton corn. It remained a populous settlement throughout the early medieval period.[28]

Whittlesford stands by the River Cam 7 miles south of Cambridge, north of the Royston–Newmarket road, formerly a branch of the Icknield Way. Road and river met at Whittlesford Bridge, where tolls were charged. This was a matter of dispute with the burgesses of Cambridge, resulting in a compromise that the local lord would collect the tolls on market day. Market revenues had almost expired by 1460.[29]

Wisbech is situated on the River Nene south of the Wash, between King's Lynn and Boston, 15 miles from Ely and 26 miles north of Cambridge. In this sparsely populated area it is many miles from the nearest rival market. The town stands at the crossing of two major roads: from Peterborough to King's Lynn and from Ely to Long Sutton. It had two marketplaces, the New Market near the castle having long been the more important.[30]

Orbital markets

The markets nearest to Cambridge prescribe an orbit around Cambridge to the west and south, with all of them 8–11 miles from Cambridge. Each was near one of the main roads radiating from Cambridge. The orbit was Swavesey–Caxton–Orwell–Fowlmere–Whittlesford–Ickleton–Linton. The radiating roads led respectively to Huntingdon, Bedford via St Neots, Bedford via Sandy (and also to Biggleswade), Royston, Buntingford, Saffron Walden and Haverhill. The density of markets was greater to the south than to the west. It was least to the north and east. This may be because roads south led towards London and roads west to the Midlands, while roads to the north and east led towards the Fens.

The road system seems to have had three main functions. First, it made it easier for local people to get to market, as a road was more convenient than a track, especially if goods had to be carried by pony or cart. Secondly, being on near a main road encouraged passing trade from people on long journeys; and thirdly, it made it easy for itinerant merchants and pedlars to attend markets on a weekly cycle by travelling directly from one market to the next. The existence of a market was important to a village's economy as visitors brought trade to local inns, artisans and resident shopkeepers.

The distances between pairs of neighbouring markets along the orbit are respectively 7.5 miles, 6.5 miles, 4.5 miles, 4 miles, 3 miles and 6 miles (see Table 6.6). These distances are smallest for markets to the south and west and greatest for those to the north and east. It is particularly notable that these distances are all shorter than the distances from the markets to Cambridge. This suggests that Cambridge market was much bigger than the others because it dominated a larger radius of territory. The size and attraction of Cambridge market made any market closer than 8 miles to Cambridge uncompetitive. The same applied to fairs with one notable exception: Trumpington, 3 miles from Cambridge, had a successful fair that was established in the 14th century, as noted, and may have continued into the 19th century.[31]

Table 6.6: Spatial analysis of markets in operation

Market	Distance from Cambridge	Distance from nearest rival	Distance from second-nearest rival
Established 1279 or before			
Cambridge	–	7m. Whittlesford	7m. Foxton
Caxton	10m.	6m. Gamlingay	6.5m. Orwell
Ely	16m.	13m. Swavesey	16m. [Downham Market]
Fowlmere	8.5m.	2m. Foxton	4m. Whittlesford
Gamlingay	14m.	2m. [Potton]	6m. Caxton
Ickleton	10m.	3m. Whittlesford	5m. [Saffron Walden]
Linton	11m.	5m. [Saffron Walden]	6m. Ickleton
Orwell	8m.	3m. Foxton	4.5m. Fowlmere
Swavesey	9m.	7.5m. Caxton	9m. Cambridge
Whittlesford	7m.	3m. Ickleton	4m. Fowlmere
Wisbech	33m.	8m. [Downham Market]	9m. [Long Sutton]
Established 1280 or later			
Foxton	7m.	2m. Fowlmere	3m. Orwell
Sutton	13m.	6m. Ely	8m. Swavesey

Note: Places shown in square brackets are in neighbouring counties (Bedfordshire, Essex or Norfolk). Suffolk is also a neighbour.

Source: Digimap, Ordnance Survey Mastermap (accessed 10 February 2019) and Table 6.2

6.4 Cambridge satellites: their integration into the urban economy

Having examined the relation of Cambridge to major towns and local market centres, it is useful to consider its relation to settlements close by. In 1279 there were several settlements clustered round Cambridge within a 3-mile radius, including Barton, Madingley, Histon, Fen Ditton and Teversham. Evidence from the Hundred Rolls and other sources makes it clear that these were purely rural settlements. There are three settlements, however, that were particularly close to the centre, all of which lay on or near the River Cam: namely Trumpington and Grantchester to the south of the town and Chesterton to the north. These merit special attention; they may be termed satellite settlements because they were so close to the centre.

Trumpington

Trumpington is located 2 miles south of Cambridge along the London road and was accessed from Cambridge, then as now, down Trumpington Street.[32]

It lies at a crossroads with a minor road from Great Shelford to Grantchester and Madingley. At the crossroads lay a triangular green (now infilled), with the church at the western apex, on the road down to the river. In 1279 there were several important landowners in the parish, the principal one being Simon de Kaleys who had 18 free tenants. Other prominent landowners included Richard of Trumpington, John son of Walter, John Arnold and Avicia de Hauxton. Institutional landowners included St Radegund's Priory and the Rector of Trumpington.[33]

Simon de Kaleys, William de Kaleys, John de Kayleys and Richard his son all held land in Cambridge in or before 1279; so too did Everard of Trumpington, Robert of Trumpington, Roger of Trumpington and Saer of Trumpington; some of their land was given to Barnwell Priory. Walter Crocheman and William le Rus (see Chapter 4) from Cambridge held land in Trumpington, as did Peter de Welles (deceased in 1279). William of Wilburham and William of Shelford, who may have resided outside Cambridge, held land in both Trumpington and Cambridge. Despite its proximity to the river, there is no evidence of any major commercial activity in the village other than the fair.

Grantchester

Grantchester, like Trumpington, lay south of Cambridge but on the opposite bank of the river. It was accessed from Cambridge off the Barton road in Newnham by a road that ran south, parallel to the riverbank. The village and its church were situated where this road met the east–west road from Trumpington to Coton and Madingley.

There were two major landowners in the parish in 1279. Eustace de Sengham and Lucy de Appleford held a knight's fee of the honour of Boulogne with the advowson of the church and a watermill. Their joint ownership was created by the descent of properties once held by two daughters who inherited an estate after the death of their brother. Eustace and Lucy had 15 free tenants and 8 villeins. The other major landowner was the Earl of Lincoln, Henry de Lacy, who had 23 free tenants, 15 villeins and 2 cottars. Two minor landowners were Radulph le Heyr, who had 11 free tenants, and Richard de Harleston, with 8 free tenants.

Several Cambridge property holders held land in Grantchester in 1279, including Richard Wombe (a major landowner), Richard Bateman, John Martin, Hugh le Rus and John son of Richard le Rus; the Hospital of St John held property too. Lord John Engayne held property in both Cambridge and Grantchester, but he probably had little direct involvement with either, other than collecting his rent.

There is no record of any market or fair. Nevertheless, Grantchester seems to have been more closely integrated into the Cambridge economy than Trumpington. While Trumpington appears to have been an elite residential area on a main road into Cambridge, Grantchester lay on a byroad and was more oriented towards the mill and the river. While some Cambridge families, such as Wombe and le Rus, may have originated in Grantchester and moved into Cambridge, it seems likely that other families, such as Bateman and Martin, acquired property in Grantchester because of their involvement in trade. It is possible that they acquired land in Grantchester as part of a strategy of 'backward integration' from the export of corn to the growing of corn; there is no direct evidence for this conjecture, however.

Chesterton

The village of Chesterton is very close to Cambridge; it lies to the north of Cambridge, east of the Huntingdon road beyond the castle; indeed it included part of the castle precinct.[34] It bordered the northern boundary of All Saints' parish, the eastern boundary of St Giles' parish and also included a portion of river bank downstream from the Great Bridge, meaning that Chesterton was well positioned to take advantage of trade on the River Cam.[35] While Barnwell is recognized in the rolls as a Cambridge suburb, Chesterton is treated as just another village. It had close links with Cambridge, however. The Hundred Rolls note 18 people from Cambridge holding land as foreigners in Chesterton (see Table 6.7). They include four who figure prominently in the town property market: John Porthors, Sabina Huberd, Robert Toylet and Henry Blancgernun.

The entire village and manor was in the hands of the king.[36] Much of it was held from the king by Barnwell Priory for a rent of £30 per annum, while the remainder was held by the Rector of Chesterton. These two fees sublet to other large property owners, including the Dunning family and the family of Richard Laurence (see Chapter 4). Some land was held freehold, but much of it by custom. The prior's tenants are documented in the Barnwell Register, or Court Book.[37] Recent archaeological work along the High Street has suggested that Barnwell Priory may have replanned settlement at Chesterton in the early 13th century, laying out new property plots on former open fields, and by the late 13th or early 14th century settlement activity within the vill had intensified.[38]

Overall, it seems that Chesterton was far more strongly integrated into the Cambridge economy than either Grantchester or Trumpington. Trumpington was largely an elite residential area. It may be for this reason

Table 6.7: Foreign tenants from Cambridge in Chesterton in 1279

Name	Status and tenancy
John Porthors	Customary tenant; holds 24 acres in the fields of Chesterton for rent of 5s 6d to Barnwell. Also 6.5 acres from the Rector for 2s 2d; 6.5 acres from the heirs of John le Rus for rent 0.5d; 7 acres from the Dunning fee for 1d and 1 lb cumin; and 3 acres and 1 rood from the heirs of Seinz for rent of 4d. Also 13 acres from various other fees for 21d and one rose.
Sabina Hubert	Customary tenant. Holds 2.5 acres from Barnwell for rent of 11d; 4.5 acres from the Rector for 21d; and one acre and one rood from other fees for 4d.
Robert Toylet	Customary tenant. Holds 10 acres and 1 rood of land for rent of 21d to Barnwell. 5.5 acres and one rood by charter from Barnwell for 11.5d; 0.5 acres of the Nikat fee for 1d; 0.5 acres from the heirs of Muschet for 1d; and 2 acres from the Giles fee for 8d.
Adam Scot	Customary tenant. Also holds one acre from Amicia de Bokesworth and one rood from the Dunning fee.
Margaret daughter of Adam Scot	Holds 0.5 acres from Amicia de Bokesworth
Agnes daughter of Adam Scot	Holds 0.5 acres from the Rector
Norman le Coner	Customary tenant. Also holds land from the rector [record incomplete]
Henry Blancgernun	Customary tenant. Holds 7 acres and one rood from Barnwell for rent of 14d.
Janna Attewo...	Customary tenant [record incomplete]
Benedict de Hawkeston	Customary tenant [record incomplete]
William Ragat	Customary tenant [record incomplete]
Walter de Berdefelt	Customary tenant [record incomplete]
Matilda at the castle [ad castellu]	Customary tenant [record incomplete]
Robert of London	Customary tenant [record incomplete]
John Warin	Customary tenant. Holds 2 acres and 3 roods from Barnwell for rent of 5.5d. Also holds one acre from the rector and other lands [record incomplete]
Amicia and Simon Geth	Customary tenant [record incomplete]
Thomas Godeman	Customary tenant [record incomplete]

Notes: 'Barnwell' refers to the Prior of Barnwell. Customary tenants are tenants of the Prior of Barnwell. Some records are incomplete, as indicated, owing to the poor condition of the rolls.

Foreign tenants who have no connection with Cambridge are excluded. 'The custom of Chesterton used to be to hold half a virgate of land but now it protects the right to sell surplus produce of the tenant's hands' [HR, p 403, column 1].

Comment: For further information on leading residents of Chesterton at an earlier date see CC. Subsidy assessments for Chesterton only are on pp 1–3. Only a few of the family names cross-refer to the Hundred Rolls. There are, however, several names suggestive of trade, e.g. merchant, mercer and miller.

Source: TNA/CAMBS/TOWER/3 as transcribed by the Record Commission, *Rotuli Hundredorum, Vol. II*, pp 402–6

the Trumpington road developed as a residential area in the 13th century and that it attracted religious and scholarly institutions. Grantchester was not quite so well connected to Cambridge as either Trumpington or Chesterton, which is perhaps why it remained a farming settlement until the housing developments of the late 19th century. While Chesterton was dynamic in the 13th century, this dynamism did not last. As the river trade declined, the university grew and the centre of activity shifted south of the bridge towards the marketplace, Chesterton itself became a largely residential area.

6.5 The integration of Cambridge commodity markets into the national market system

It is clear that Cambridge had a major influence on its hinterland for at least 10 miles around, given the dominance of its retail market. Its control of the wholesale market for corn was even wider. But how far did this influence extend? To address this question, the remainder of this chapter explores the links between Cambridge and the wider economy.

If there are strong trading links between different local towns then commodity prices in these towns will tend to keep in step with each other. If any major price discrepancies emerge, merchants will arbitrage between the markets, exporting from low-price towns and importing into high-price towns. To test whether Cambridge was integrated into the national economy, therefore, it is appropriate to consider whether prices in Cambridge moved in step with prices in the rest of the country. By incredible good fortune, sources exist that make this exercise possible for Cambridge, and they begin in the year 1279.

The Hundred Rolls record that the scholars of Merton acquired the estate of the Dunning family, including some farms, and the records of this purchase survive, as well as the bailiffs' accounts of the farms.[39] This section analyses the bailiffs' accounts; the deeds are analysed in the following section.

When Walter Merton acquired a substantial proportion of the Dunning estate, the bailiffs he appointed to manage them sent written reports to Merton College in Oxford.[40] These records were analysed in detail by James Thorold Rogers, Professor of Political Economy at Oxford.[41] Like Frederic Maitland, referred to in Chapter 3, Rogers was a pioneer of historical statistical analysis, but worked on commodity prices rather than property rents.

The Merton estate, like many others in Cambridgeshire, comprised mainly arable land which was used for growing the classic crops of wheat, barley, oats, rye and drage (dredge corn). They provided bread, cakes and beer for human consumption and fodder for animals, especially horses. These are the five key commodities on which this analysis is based, Information on both prices and quantities is available for the period 1279–1301, but after 1301 there is a significant gap in the records.[42]

Table 6.8 compares Cambridge prices and national prices for each of the five commodities. The prices shown are quantity-weighted annual averages of recorded prices for transactions in each commodity in a given year; all prices are per quarter by weight. In some years in Cambridge there were no transactions in certain commodities. The national prices were compiled by Thorold Rogers from information for the full set of Merton estates; in 1301 the college held a total of 143 estates (excluding churches), the largest group being in East Anglia, where agriculture tended to be very prosperous; it also held seven properties in Ireland and two in North Wales.[43]

Table 6.9 examines whether the prices of different crops moved in line with each other over time. The exercise involves correlation coefficients, which were explained earlier (Chapter 5). The top row of the table reports the correlations between national and local prices. They are all high with the exception of wheat. The reason for the discrepancy is indicated in the second row, which reports correlations with time. The wheat price has a downward trend (a negative correlation with time) while the other commodities all have an upward trend (a positive correlation with time). This declining trend may be due to the focus of Cambridge on the export market; it is possible that Cambridge wheat prices were more closely tied to prices in export markets than to prices in the national market as a whole. If the downward trend is removed from the wheat series then the correlations are increased.

Additional insight is provided in the lower part of the table. The first five rows examine correlations between the prices of the main crops. The correlations are fairly high, with one exception: oats do not correlate with either wheat or rye. The lower five rows report national correlations for purposes of comparison. It can be seen that they are similar to local correlations with one exception: the wheat price is now highly correlated with the price of oats whereas the price of rye is not.

The main qualification to this analysis is that local and national prices of commodities may also move in step if common factors, such as weather patterns, influence demand and supply across all towns. A more refined analysis would take account of this, using grain yields to proxy for the weather.

The conclusion is that local and national prices were highly correlated except for wheat, where the correlation was low because trends differed.

Table 6.8: Average annual prices on the Merton estate, Cambridge, with national comparisons

Year	Local					National				
	Wheat	Barley	Drage	Oats	Rye	Wheat	Barley	Drage	Oats	Rye
1279	62	42.25	29.3	24.8	42	61.25	47.37	32.62	24.62	51.75
1280	58	41	32	24	43	59.87	42.75	32	28.37	44.12
1281	85	47.6	41.4			72.75	41.62	39.25	29	55.75
1282	71	48	42	24	68.5	59.5	49.25	34	25.5	59.25
1283	74.6		40	33	65.3	83.25	53.12	43.25	28.25	64.37
1284		42.5	27	24	48	59.75	37.62	27.37	21.87	40.87
1285	54					64.25	42.12	30.62	25.75	49.62
1286						57	39.12	29.62	24.87	44.87
1287						34.25	30.5	24.62	17.75	27.25
1288						36.87	27.62	22	18.5	22.12
1289						51.37	38.5	27	23.75	34.37
1290						77.5	53.62	36	30.75	67.37
1291						67.25	52.5	32.37	26.87	51.25
1292						64.62	47.62	34.5	28.12	47
1293						99.12	61	46.37	33.5	82.87
1294	76.7		44	42	86	109.12	73.37	48.25	34.25	95.62
1295						81	52.62	38.62	28.75	62
1296						57.25	45.12	36.87	27.25	45.67
1297						62.5	50.87	39.62	28.75	36.75
1298	57.1	62	41.3	36.7		62.12	51.62	41.37	29.5	48.5
1299	64	63	47.8	36.8	46.25	72.75	52.5	46.25	33.12	49.62
1300	48	32	24.5	24	34	57	44.5	27.25	23.37	42.62
1301	48	38		26		60.12	43.62	29	24.62	43.75

Note: All figures shown in the able are in pence. Bailiff's accounts for 1286–93 and 1295–7 are missing. For published examples of contemporary Merton bailiff accounts from another manor see P. D. A. Harvey (ed.), *Manorial Records of Cuxham, Oxfordshire, c.1200–1359* (Oxford and London, 1976).

Source: James E. Thorold Rogers, *A History of Agriculture and Prices in England and Wales, II, 1259–1400 (7 vols)* (Oxford, 1866)

Table 6.9: Correlations between prices for grains 1279–1301: local and national comparisons

	Wheat	Barley	Drage	Oats	Rye
Local–local					
Wheat	1.00				
Barley	0.68	1.00			
Drage	0.77	0.95	1.00		
Oats	0.23	0.87	0.73	1.00	
Rye	0.88	0.42	0.64	−0.03	1.00
National–national					
Wheat	1.00				
Barley	0.78	1.00			
Drage	0.98	0.84	1.00		
Oats	0.90	0.77	0.91	1.00	
Rye	0.13	0.62	0.30	−0.33	1.00
Local–national	0.37	0.87	0.89	0.87	0.90
Local–time	−0.47	0.17	0.12	0.56	−0.40
National–time	0.15	0.32	0.25	0.28	0.04

Note: Because of the small number of degrees of freedom very few of the 'local' correlations are statistically significant, and if significant are only marginally so at 5 per cent.

Source: Table 6.8

With few exceptions, prices of the five commodities were positively correlated with each other at both local and national level. This suggests that the market in Cambridge was integrated into the national market and followed similar trends, apart from wheat, where the influence of the export trade was strong.

6.6 The land market and the acquisition of the Merton estate

The discussion so far has focused on networks of trade, but in medieval England, as today, networks of communications were important too. This applies particularly to Cambridge. It was a county town, with a sheriff's court, and also an administrative centre for the Bishop of Ely. The acquisition of the Dunning estates by Walter de Merton, founder of Merton College, Oxford, shows that social networks operating in the royal court and among administrators of the Bishop of Ely communicated information about opportunities in the Cambridge property market to external investors. Walter Merton acquired the Dunning estate from

William of Manefield. Walter Merton was connected to William from their period as colleagues working for the Bishop of Durham. Walter subsequently entered royal service and William became an official of the Bishop of Ely. William had inherited the properties from his uncle Master Guy, who was friends with William of Kilkenny, Bishop of Ely 1255–6. Walter de Merton himself probably knew William of Kilkenny as they moved in the same circle in Durham. To appreciate these connections it is useful to consider in further detail the careers of those involved and the process by which the estates were acquired.

Biography

Walter Merton (1205–77) was born in Basingstoke but named himself from the Augustinian Abbey where he was educated. He founded Merton College, Oxford, with a pioneering constitution that in its final form provided a model for later colleges at both Oxford and Cambridge. A key feature was that the fellows of the college were collectively self-governing; they were a corporate body subject only to the supervision of a visitor.[44] College administration was based in Oxford and the visitor was the Archbishop of Canterbury.[45]

Walter Merton might today be described as an academic entrepreneur. He was a loyal official working for King Henry III for much of his career. He supported the king through the Barons' Revolt of 1265–6. He became very unpopular with Simon de Montfort and his followers during the war, but remained a royal favourite thereafter. There was plenty of opportunity for profit in royal service (as the career of William le Rus demonstrated in Chapter 4). Officials could bid to take over the management of estates during wardship (for example, during the minority of the heir) or when their owners had been dispossessed. After the Barons' Revolt, the main culprits were dispossessed, but many of the king's supporters were impoverished too; they had mortgaged their estates to fund their role in the war. This provided opportunities for speculative acquisition of land that royal officials such as Walter were in a good position to exploit.

Walter began his career seeking to provide for his seven sisters after the death of their parents. He founded a hospital in Basingstoke for the local poor. But his great ambition was to found a college for scholars who would be learned in law and theology but not narrowly committed to careers in either the Church or the law.[46]

Walter entered the service of Henry III in c.1236, which provided him with expertise 'in conveyancing and the routines of the common law'.[47] He served on a commission enquiring into the royal demesne in the

Home Counties. One of his colleagues was William Watervill, an Essex knight, whose manors of Malden, Chessington and Farleigh were probably included in the review because the tenant-in-chief, Richard de Clare, heir to two earldoms, was a minor and a ward of the king. William was in debt and was seeking to dispose of his interest in these three Surrey manors. Walter paid off William's £100 debt to the Jewish moneylender Abraham son of Aaron of London, and made settlements with those, such as Peter son of John of Codinton, who held other interests in the properties, eventually achieving full possession of the manors in 1257. Negotiations were rather tense at times; in 1248–9 Walter and William agreed to defer the settlement of disagreements between them until after the feast of St Mark the Evangelist. In 1249 the king gave to his 'well-beloved clerk' the right of free warren in all three manors.[48]

Meanwhile Walter had moved in c.1245 from royal service into the chancery of Nicholas Farnham, Bishop of Durham 1241–9, former royal physician. Walter and Nicholas had probably met when in royal service together.[49] Walter served as datary and chancellor.[50] He was titled 'dominus' rather than 'magister', suggesting that he was not regarded as an academic. He was rewarded with the benefices of Staindrop and Haltwhistle.[51] It has been suggested that Bishop Nicholas had considerable influence on him.[52] Perhaps as a consequence, Walter maintained contact with a number of officials who served Farnham during this period. While in Durham, in 1247 Walter purchased the manor of Stillington near Sedgefield, County Durham, from the Amundeville family. This involved paying off debts to a Jewish moneylender in York.[53]

In Durham Walter must have met William of Kilkenny, future Bishop of Ely, who was associated with Bishop Farnham over the period 1238–47.[54] Kilkenny was probably older than Merton; he had served under Farnham's predecessor, Richard Poore, and he died in 1256.[55] Kilkenny too was active in the property market. During Nicholas Farnham's time Kilkenny purchased property from Nicholas de Monasteriis 'in his great need' for seven marks, and land in Stanley, County Durham, from Richard son of Thomas son of Bernard, also 'in his great need', for 5 marks. He acquired other properties in the same area at about the same time.[56]

Master Guy of Barnard Castle took his name from the town of Barnard Castle on the River Tees in County Durham, which was founded in c.1133 by Bernard de Balliol.[57] Little is known of Master Guy's origins but it is known that he had a nephew, William of Manefield, son of his brother John. William of Manefield was a colleague of Walter's, working for the Bishop of Durham as an official of the Archdeacon.[58] Master Guy was also connected to William of Kilkenny, future Bishop of Ely.

William of Kilkenny re-entered royal service in 1247 and became keeper of the seal in 1250. He was appointed Bishop of Ely in 1255 but died the following year. Master Guy was one of the executors of his will, together with Master Henry Kilkenny, rector of Balsham.[59] Henry of Kilkenny and Master Guy (in that order) witnessed a grant of a messuage, curtilage, land and advowson in Lydiard Millicent in Somerset to Richard of Kilkenny 1254–5.[60] As William's executor, Master Guy would have been involved in implementing a grant of £20 to Barnwell Priory and the payment of 200 marks to maintain two chaplains studying at the university, who were to celebrate mass for Kilkenny's soul.[61]

Walter returned to royal service at about the same time, and William of Manefield probably left a couple of years later. William subsequently became an official of the Bishop of Ely, possibly through William of Kilkenny's patronage. Walter advanced quickly, eventually becoming chancellor and holder of the Great Seal. His plans were somewhat thwarted by Simon de Montfort and the barons, but after their defeat in the civil war Walter was in a strong position to obtain rewards for his loyal service. The king rewarded his followers, including Walter, with confiscated properties, while entrepreneurs such as Walter could also purchase properties from impoverished knights who had mortgaged them to the Jews.[62] In a short time between 1266 and 1268 Walter acquired four adjacent parishes around the church of St John the Baptist, Oxford, as a site for his college, with provision for two young men to remain as sitting tenants so that they could complete their studies.[63]

The Cambridge connection

In 1269–70 Walter purchased the Dunning estate in Cambridge from his old friend William of Manefield. Eustace Dunning had sold his estate, encumbered with debts, to Master Guy. Master Guy died, leaving his brother John as heir. But he died almost immediately, leaving his property to William of Manefield, then working for the Archdeacon of Ely. Walter then bought the estate from William. In a separate transactions Walter acquired other Dunning properties in Chesterton, Newnham and Over.

The process is well documented and provides insights into the working of the local property market.[64] It involves two main stages: the acquisition of Eustace's property by Master Guy and the sale of these properties by his heir, William of Manefield, to Walter Merton. The process took over 20 years to complete. There are numerous subplots, involving other Cambridge people.

The story begins in 1257, when Eustace son of Harvey leased to Master Guy the messuage in which he lived and all his land around Cambridge, with the exception of his capital messuage, for six years for 14 marks annual rent. Master Henry of Kilkenny and Master Ralph, Master of the Hospital of St John, were the first-named witnesses.[65] It seems that Eustace could not meet the interest payments, probably because the rents from his remaining properties outside Cambridge were inadequate. In September 1258 Eustace mortgaged 7 acres in the Cambridge fields to Master Guy for 14 marks to be repaid at Michaelmas 1264.[66] The payment mentioned here may represent one year's rent that was overdue. If so, then no money would actually have changed hands as a result of the agreement; Master Guy would simply have cancelled Eustace's debt. But there would still have been more rent due the following year.

In January 1259 Eustace mortgaged all his Cambridge lands, now including his capital messuage (see Chapter 4), to Master Guy for £100 to be repaid at Michaelmas 1260.[67] With more rent due imminently, Eustace seems to have been refinancing himself. The earlier lease was cancelled and Eustace took out a mortgage instead. The cost of this move was high, however, as he had to include the capital messuage, and had to raise £100 in a little over one year. From his point of view the situation was now even less sustainable. It seems that Master Guy was 'moving in for the kill'. Needless to say, Eustace defaulted. Master Guy brought in his high-level contacts at Ely to witness the next charter in the following year. Eustace agreed that he must pay Master Guy £100 on 1 May 1261, which he should have already repaid at Michaelmas 1260, or forfeit all his lands. The witnesses were Master Henry of Kilkenny, Master Nicholas of Turri, Jordan of Danyntre (Daventry), Master Richard of Stanes, William of Horsethe (Horningsea) and Robert, Rector of Stanton.[68]

In c.1261 Eustace promised to repay Master Guy 12 marks and 3s at the feast of St Gregory 1262 or forfeit the security he supplied earlier. This charter was witnessed by local townsmen.[69] It is unclear whether Master Guy had granted a stay of execution, or whether Eustace, having just lost his Cambridge lands, was continuing to borrow, albeit on a smaller scale, from Master Guy.

The story resumes eight years later, when Walter Merton appears on the scene. In 1269–70 William of Manefield granted to the House of Merton all his lands and tenements in Cambridge, Barnwell, Chesterton, Howes, Cotes, Newnham and Trumpington. This was witnessed by a very cosmopolitan group of people: Richard Laurence, Mayor of Cambridge; John Porthors, Nicholas Morice, Bartholomew Gogging, Adam Scot (all of Cambridge – see Chapter 4); Richard of Brademere, Surrey; Roger Tayllard; Richard of the More, Buckinghamshire; Eustace the

Flemming; and Robert Edret, Hampshire.[70] This was a large transaction, and it seems that Walter paid in instalments. In 1271 William of Manefield acknowledged receipt from Dominus Walter Merton of 6 marks in part payment for the purchase of his lands around Cambridge.[71] This could have been a credit arrangement; if so, William was presumably content that Walter's credit was good and that they were still friends. It is more likely, however, that William found difficulty getting control of the lands, particularly where sitting tenants were concerned, and so Walter paid instalments only when specific plots of land were delivered up.

At some stage someone instigated an inquiry into the legitimacy of John of Barnard Castle, to whom William was heir. There are reports of a letter from Robert, Bishop of Durham on the subject to King Henry.[72] The letter has been lost, but the fact that it is mentioned in the Merton *Liber Ruber* suggests that someone from the college initiated the inquiry. They evidently wished to check that John's inheritance from his brother Guy, and hence William's title to his lands, was secure. The dating is uncertain: it is from the time of Bishop Robert Stitchill, 1260–74, or Bishop Robert of Holy Island, 1274–83. A date of c.1268 seems most likely. Given Walter's strong connections with Durham it is likely that he initiated the inquiry himself.

Eustace seems to have raised additional finance from Robert Aunger. Eustace granted to Robert son of Aunger le Rus 6 marks of rent. For payment Robert could distrain on lands in the Cambridge fields and scattered strips in Chesterton (both specified in detail).[73] In 1272 the House of Merton bought the rents with a lump sum of 46 marks, equivalent to an interest rate $6 \times 100/46 = 13$ per cent. There is a record of a final concord between Master Peter of Abingdon, Warden of the House of Merton, plaintiff, and Master Robert Aunger for the release to the house of 6 marks annual rent in Cambridge and Chesterton. The warden gave 46 marks in consideration.[74]

It seems that William continued to have difficulty gaining control of the lands that he had sold to Merton. Sometime in 1272–5 William of Manefield granted to the House of Merton 2 acres of arable land in Chesterton that he had recovered before the Justices in Eyre at Cambridge in 1272 by writ of *Mort d'Ancestor* against John of Histon and Agnes his wife. The witnesses were mainly from Chesterton.[75] In 1275 William bound himself to provide sufficient security for the House of Merton, either by fine or otherwise as they could decide, for the lands and tenements he was to convey to them. The witnesses included many who had witnessed the initial charter of 1269–70.[76]

Some progress was made the following year when more land was handed over in return for a further instalment. A final concord was made in 1276 between Master Peter (of Abingdon), Warden of the House of Merton, and William of Manefield whereby William released to the warden 100 acres of land and 14s annual rent in Cambridge and Chesterton. The warden paid £100 in consideration.[77]

By 1 June 1279 the remaining problems had been ironed out in 'a release from William of Manefield to the House of Scholars … of all the lands and tenements that they … have in Cambridge, Barnwell, Chesterton, Howes, Cotes, Over and elsewhere'.[78] The witnesses were again local townsmen: John But, Mayor of Cambridge, Richard Laurence, John Martin, Bartholomew Gogging, William Toylet, Robert Wymund, John Porthors, Nicholas Morice and John of Byri (Bury St Edmunds).[79] The following day the warden agreed to reimburse William for some of the expenses he had incurred in delivering up the properties.[80] William of Manefield died shortly afterwards, it would seem, perhaps exhausted by his legal exertions. There was a claim of dower to settle, however; William's widow Margery had a claim that her son Andrew administered. Andrew reclaimed a property in Over, and after keeping a third of the rent for his mother he returned the balance to the warden.[81] The will was witnessed by people from Cambridge and Over. Somewhat ironically, the first witness was Eustace's relative, John Dunning of Cambridge, mayor.[82]

This tortuous sequence of events is only half the story. At the time that Master Guy was lending to Eustace Dunning he was also lending to John le Rus, and complications arose when John died. Some time after 1270 Eustace died and the residue of his estate passed to Richard Dunning. Richard Dunning was himself indebted to the townsman John Porthors. Master Guy and his brother died.[83] William of Manefield had to sort all that out while he was making other deals at the same time. Some of the other properties that he bought and sold on his own initiative about this time are summarized in Table 6.10 using information derived from the Hundred Rolls. Until William resolved outstanding problems, Walter could not gain full possession of the properties he had agreed to purchase.

Assessment

In 1274 Walter was elected Bishop of Rochester; in 1277 he paid his last visits to Oxford and Durham, and died after an accident later that year. In his will he left property and money to a wide range of people. These included relatives who had lost properties, people from whom he had purchased land and a large number of carters and ploughmen who worked on his manors.[84] The college's estate in Cambridge was formed from a collection of lands that Walter acquired by purchase in 1269–70. Its role

Table 6.10: List of properties in Cambridge intermediated by William of Manefield as documented in the Hundred Rolls

Property	To	Comment
One messuage with 45 acres of land and 50s of income in the town and in the fields of Cambridge	Scholars of Merton	Paying William 1d and hawgable 4s 10d [HR P26]
15 acres of land and 10s 2d income held from the Count of Leicester and thence from Lord Edmund [Crouchback],	Scholars of Merton	Paying Lord Edmund 3s 10d and scutage when required [HR P27]
One piece of vacant land	John Andrew father of Geoffrey Andrew the current holder	Pays 1d to the Scholars of Merton [HR42]
13d rent from the house of John Waubert in All Saints in the Jewry	John Porthors	Pays one rose to William [HR160]
1 mark rent from the house of the Archdeacon of Ely in Holy Trinity	John of Barton who gave it to his son John Porthors	Pays one rose to John of Barton [HR161]
18 acres of land in the fields of Cambridge in fief	John Porthors	Pays 1d to the Scholars of Merton by assignment of William [HR162]
3 acres of land in the fields of Cambridge	Agnes of Barton	Pays 1d to William [HR250]
4 acres of land in the fields of Cambridge	John of Aylsham	Pays 2d to the Scholars of Merton by assignment of William [HR291]
18 acres of land in the fields of Cambridge	Nicholas Morice	Pays 12d rent and 0.5 lb of ginger to the Scholars of Merton by assignment of William [HR364]
7 acres of land in the fields of Cambridge	John Porthors who sold them to Nicholas Morice	Pays John Porthors 1d rent [HR365]

Note: All properties were bought by William from Eustace Dunning, although this is not stated for HR158–9.

was simply to generate profits from agriculture in order to pay college officers and provide scholarships for students in Oxford.

Walter's success as a royal administrator was testament to his great ability. His success in building a property portfolio illustrates his command of the law of conveyancing. He also revealed financial acumen in obtaining many of his properties at bargain prices. He achieved this by identifying owners who had mortgaged their properties and were unable to repay. Such apparent ruthlessness seems at odds with his concern for his siblings, for the local poor and for young scholars financing their studies. In his will he made generous provision for the dependants of the owners from whom he bought, for example arranging good marriages for their daughters (an important consideration at the time). It is possible that he considered it good work to liberate people from debts to the Jews. It has been suggested that he disliked Jewish moneylenders, and possibly Jews in general, and that it was he who in 1268 persuaded the king to force the Oxford Jews, in response to various accusations against them, to erect at their own expense a memorial cross outside Merton College.[85] A mixture of motives seems to have driven him to rise in wealth and status and to leave behind such an impressive and tangible legacy.

6.7 Conclusion

This chapter has addressed the question of how Cambridge interacted with its hinterland. The short answer is that Cambridge dominated its hinterland. It occupied a favoured location in an area well suited to arable farming. It specialized in both wholesale and retail trade. Trade was drawn to Cambridge because the physical geography of the region destined the site of Cambridge to be the ideal transport and communications hub. The only other places to exert a similar degree of pull within the region seem to have been the coastal port of King's Lynn and the monastic towns of Norwich and Peterborough.

Cambridge was a relatively large town in the 13th century, but with large towns being concentrated in the south and east of England it had several potential rivals. Many of these towns did not, however, seriously compete in the corn trade, in which Cambridge specialized and in which it had a chartered monopoly. It was perceived at the time to be a highly successful town, and this may have deterred others from challenging it.

Transport infrastructure was crucial to realizing the potential of Cambridge as a road hub on a river system. The navigability of the Cam and the Ouse was critical to the export trade, while the maintenance of local roads was crucial to the retail trade. This could create conflict with the sheriff of the county. Although the condition of the Great Bridge was often a cause for concern, it seems that problems in Cambridge were no worse than in neighbouring towns.

As noted in earlier chapters, the town attracted a growing number of religious institutions, and their impact on the town was largely beneficial. They did not attempt to control the town or to interfere with its bailiffs or burgesses in matters affecting external trade, as happened elsewhere. The town was pious and devout, as noted earlier, but also tolerant, and generally welcomed the friars and their preaching. This toleration was not only good for trade but good for the development of the university too.

Because Cambridge was perceived as successful, it had a buoyant urban property market. Through the elite networks of its administrative class it attracted speculative investors from some considerable distance, especially for large well-situated properties that ordinary townspeople could not afford. Some property buyers were intermediaries, who bought and sold for short-term profit, while others were final buyers who were building up diversified portfolios to satisfy long-term ambitions.

Notes

[1] For work on London's wider market see James A. Galloway, 'One Market or Many? London and the Grain Trade of England', *Trade, Urban Hinterlands and Market Integration, c. 1300–1600: A Collection of Working Papers Given at a Conference Organised by the Centre for Metropolitan History and Supported by the Economic and Social Research Council, 7 July 1999 (Centre for Metropolitan History, Working Papers, 3)* ed. James A. Galloway (London, 2000), pp 23–42. For Cambridge's hinterland in subsequent centuries see Lee, *Cambridge*; Margaret Spufford, 'General View of the Rural Economy of the County of Cambridge', *Proceedings of the Cambridge Antiquarian Society* 89 (2000): 69–85.

[2] VCH 4 Cambs, pp 28–40.

[3] Edward Miller, *The Abbey and Bishopric of Ely: The Social History of the Ecclesiastical Estate from the Tenth Century* (Cambridge, 1951); Miller (trans), Willmoth and Oosthuizen (eds), *Ely Coucher Book*.

[4] VCH 2 Huntingdon, pp 210–23.

[5] VCH 2 Huntingdon, pp 121–39.

[6] VCH 2 Huntingdon, pp 121–39.

[7] Raftis, *Godmanchester*, pp 1–6; J. Ambrose Raftis, 'The land market at Godmanchester c.1300', *Medieval Studies* 50 (1988): 311–32.

[8] Samantha Letters, *Online Gazetteer of Markets and Fairs in England and Wales to 1516*, available at http://www.history.ac.uk/cmh/gaz/gazweb2.html (accessed 12 August 2016).

[9] Frank Meeres, *A History of Bury St Edmunds* (Chichester, 2002), pp 55–7.

[10] Letters, *Gazetteer*.

[11] Gottfried, *Bury St Edmunds*, p 220.

[12] David C. Douglas (ed.), *Feudal Documents from the Abbey of Bury St Edmunds* (London, 1932), p 62.

[13] Norfolk Heritage Explorer, 'Parish Summary: Thetford', available at http://www. heritage.norfolk.gov.uk/record-details?tnf2274 (accessed 21 February 2019).

[14] Letters, *Gazetteer.*

[15] Mark Bailey, *A Marginal Economy?: East Anglian Breckland in the Later Middle Ages* (Cambridge, 1989), p 149.

[16] Norfolk Heritage Explorer, 'Thetford'.

[17] Lee, *Cambridge*, pp 86–8.

[18] Beresford, *New Towns*, pp 14–15.

[19] John S. Lee, 'The Role of Fairs in Late Medieval England', *Town and Countryside in the Age of the Black Death: Essays in Honour of John Hatcher*, ed. Steve Rigby and Mark Bailey (Turnhout, 2012), pp 407–37.

[20] Britnell, *Commercialisation*; Jennifer Kermode, 'The Greater Towns 1300–1540', *The Cambridge Urban History of Britain, I: 600–1540*, ed. D. M. Palliser (3 vols) (Cambridge, 2000), pp 441–66; James Masschaele, 'Transport Costs in Medieval England', *Economic History Review* 2nd Series 46 (1993): 266–79.

[21] VCH 5 Cambs, pp 26–35; Letters, *Gazetteer.*

[22] VCH 4 Cambs, pp 28–33, Letters, *Gazetteer.*

[23] VCH 8 Cambs, pp 155–64; Letters, *Gazetteer.*

[24] VCH 5 Cambs, pp 68–87; Letters, *Gazetteer.*

[25] VCH 6 Cambs, pp 230–46; Letters, *Gazetteer.*

[26] VCH 6 Cambs, pp 80–105; Letters, *Gazetteer.*

[27] VCH 5 Cambs, pp 241–51; Letters, *Gazetteer.*

[28] VCH 9 Cambs, pp 374–81; Letters, *Gazetteer.*

[29] VCH 6 Cambs, pp 263–76; Letters, *Gazetteer.*

[30] VCH 4 Cambs, pp 239–43; Letters, *Gazetteer.*

[31] Letters, *Gazetteer.*

[32] VCH 8 Cambs, pp 248–67;

[33] *Rotuli Hundredorum*, pp 548–50; Cam, *Liberties and Communities*, pp 25–6, Tables I, II.

[34] Craig Cessford and Alison Dickens, 'The Origins and Early Development of Chesterton', *Proceedings of the Cambridge Antiquarian Society* 93 (2004): 125–42.

[35] Pipe Roll, 8 Henry III, 1224, p 80.

[36] VCH 9 Cambs, pp 5–13.

[37] The Barnwell Register is a leather-bound book with broken hinges and gold tooling of i + 309 leaves in Special Collections of The Bodleian Library (MS Gough Camb. 1). It is written in highly abbreviated medieval Latin. It was originally catalogued as 'Cambridgeshire 17751. A register of rents and fines payable to the priory of Barnwell near Cambridge from 1277 to 1377 year by year'. The manuscript itself is entitled 'Gersume (et fines) facte in curia de Cestreton (terrarum omnium tenencium Prioratus de Bernewell in Cestreton … extracto [sic] a rotuli curie)'. It is in one hand until the end of 1 Edw. 3 (1328) and then in contemporary hands until the end, but it is incomplete at beginning and end. See also the Gough catalogue of 1814, p 192.

The book comprises a formulaic listing of approximately 3,000 land transactions, is organised in yearly sequence and is well suited to spreadsheet analysis. It is one of two major sources used in Clarke, 'Peasant Society'. Supervised by Barbara Harvey, this thesis focuses on peasant land transactions during the agricultural crises 1314–25. The evidence is analysed using a card index system. The author's family reconstructions provide useful corroborating evidence on Cambridge families that held land in Chesterton. The thesis reveals strong connections between Cambridge and Chesterton, for example in landholding along the royal way from Cambridge castle to Chesterton church.

38 Newman, 'Medieval and Early Post-Modern Chesterton': 89–106.

39 Bernard W. Henderson, *Merton College* (London, 1899)

40 Geoffrey H. Martin, 'Merton, Walter of', *Oxford Dictionary of National Biography* ed. David Cannadine (Oxford, 2004).

41 James E. Thorold Rogers, *A History of Agriculture and Prices in England and Wales, II, 1259–1400* (7 vols) (Oxford, 1866).

42 B. M. S. Campbell, *English Seigniorial Agriculture 1250–1450* (Cambridge, 2000); Thorold Rogers, *Agriculture*.

43 Thorold Rogers, *Agriculture*, II, pp 1–5; Edith Clark Lowry, 'The Administration of the Estates of Merton College in the Fourteenth Century: With Special Reference to the Black Death and the Problems of Labour' (DPhil thesis, University of Oxford, 1933), Chapter 1.

44 George C. Brodrick, *Memorials of Merton College* (Oxford, 1885), p 11; Edmund [Hobhouse] Nelson, *Sketch of the Life of Walter de Merton Lord High Chancellor of England, and Bishop of Rochester, Founder of Merton College* (Oxford and London, 1859), p 14.

45 Geoffrey H. Martin and John L. R. Highfield, *A History of Merton College, Oxford* (Oxford, 1997), p 17.

46 Nelson, *Merton*, p 25.

47 Martin, 'Merton'; F. J. Baigent and J. E. Millard, *A History of the Ancient Town and Manor of Basingstoke* (Basingstoke, 1889), pp 593–658.

48 Baigent and Millard, *Basingstoke*; Michael Franks, *The Clerk of Basingstoke: A Life of Walter de Merton* (Oxford, 2003), p 44; Cecil A. F. Meekings and Philip Shearman, *Fitznells Cartulary: A Calendar of Bodleian Library MS. Rawlinson B430* (Guildford, 1968), pp lxiii–lxvi; M 890, 927/8, 1092/6.

49 Nicholas Farnham was a renowned Oxford scholar who was professor of medicine at the universities of Paris and Bologna. He returned to Oxford in 1229, where he taught logic and natural philosophy (Franks, *Merton*, p 55). After serving as royal physician he was appointed Bishop of Durham in 1241, retired in 1248 and died in 1257.

50 Philippa M. Hoskins (ed.), *English Episcopal Acta 29, Durham 1241–1283* (London, 2005), pp xxxv–xxxvii.

51 Hoskins, *Acta*, p xli.

52 Martin and Highfield, *Merton College*, p 5; M. L. Holford and K. J. Stringer, *Border Liberties and Loyalties* (Edinburgh, 2010); Geoffrey P. Stell, 'Balliol, Bernard de (d. 1154x62)', *Oxford Dictionary of National Biography* ed. David Cannadine (Oxford, 2004).

53 Franks, *Merton*, p 55.

54 Nicholas Karn (ed.), *English Episcopal Acta 42: Ely 1198–1256* (London, 2013), p lix.

55 Robert C. Stacey, 'Kilkenny, William of', *Oxford Dictionary of National Biography* ed. David Cannadine (Oxford, 2004).

56 Karn, *Acta*, p 293.

57 Stell, 'Balliol, Bernard de (d. 1154x62)'.

58 William witnessed six charters for the bishop. In all of these charters he is described as 'magister', suggesting an academic qualification. Hoskins, *Acta*, W5, 6, 10,15, 28–9, 41. All of these charters date from the period 1241–9 and all those that can be dated definitely date from 1247–9. One of these – a chirograph dated 17 July 1247 at Darlington – is particularly interesting as it was witnessed by both Walter

Merton and William of Manefield. Thus while there is no direct evidence that Walter Merton was an associate of Master Guy, there is a clear indication that he would have known Master William. William may have worked for the cathedral priory too; he received a pension of 10 marks from the Prior of Durham's chamber. As Hoskins observed, 'some men served more than one master in an attempt to gain ecclesiastical preferment or other benefits'. William married Margaret and had a son Andrew (Hoskins, *Acta*, p xli).

59 Karn, *Acta*, p lxxviii.
60 Karn, *Acta*, p 235.
61 Karn, *Acta*, p 245.
62 Nelson, *Merton*, p 31.
63 Henderson, *Merton*, pp 11–12.
64 S; SP.
65 MD 1545.
66 MD 1546.
67 MD 1548.
68 MD 1550.
69 MD 1549.
70 MD 1556
71 MD 1567
72 *Liber Ruber*: no number; SP, 39.
73 MD 1606.
74 MD 1568.
75 MD 1558.
76 MD 1561.
77 MD 1563.
78 MD 1564.
79 *Liber Ruber*, fol. 23d; wrongly identified by Gray as MD 1556.
80 MD 1565.
81 MD 1627.
82 MD 1627.
83 The role of Richard Dunning is discussed by Gray (SP, pp 9–11).
84 Nelson, *Merton*, pp 44–50.
85 Nelson, *Merton*, pp 33–4.

7

Legacy: Cambridge in the 14th and 15th Centuries

Introduction

This chapter explores the economy and society of Cambridge between the Hundred Rolls of 1279 and the midst of the great depression of the mid–15th century, c.1450. In doing so it connects the chronological coverage in this book to the literature on Cambridge from the period 1450 onwards and considers to what extent trends identified in the Hundred Rolls continued into the 14th century. The chapter focuses principally on the period after the Black Death of 1349 and considers its impact on Cambridge's property market and its wider economy.[1] This outbreak of plague probably halved both the population of the country as a whole and the population of Cambridge. Traditional interpretations have often described this as a bleak period of decline for the town: 'for Cambridge, as for most English towns, a period of retrogression and decay'.[2] Even the growth of the colleges and university do not appear to have benefited the wider economy of the town: 'For neither university town was the erection of growing centres of learning on the rubble of former streets an unmitigated blessing, let alone an immediate compensation for the loss of wealth-creating citizens.'[3] Indeed Cambridge's borough government made pleas for reductions to their tax quota and other payments to the Crown. On the other hand, some historians have seen the late 14th century more generally as a 'golden age' of new economic opportunities with rising living standards and the beginnings of a 'consumer economy'.[4] This chapter will reassess these views and suggest that a more nuanced picture is required, of both growth and decline in Cambridge.

The general consequences of the Black Death included reduced demand for urban property from a smaller population. The extent of this reduction varied between different towns, and within individual towns it varied over time and between different properties. In the property markets of some provincial towns and in London, for example, there appears to have been a phase of growth between about 1380 and 1420 in response to growing manufacturing, particularly within the cloth industry, and the rapid increase in the disposable income of wage earners. Even in these towns, though, the balance between the supply and demand for urban property appears to have been reached in c.1420, and thereafter there was a slow fall in urban land values.[5] Property became concentrated in fewer hands, and borough communities and urban guilds became important property owners.[6] In Cambridge, the corporation took ownership of waste spaces across the town, and the Cambridge guilds of Corpus Christi and the Blessed Virgin Mary founded an academic college that became a major property owner.

With a smaller population, though, and labour in short supply, wages grew, leading to the possibility of modest increases in living standards that might be reflected in the housing stock and the property market. Improvements in comfort for the wealthier in the later Middle Ages included the use of glazed tiles for floors, glass for windows, fireplaces and chimneys, and fixed beds. Wealthy urban residents, like their counterparts in the country, wanted greater privacy and comfort, and created more bedrooms, parlours and separate chambers. There was an expansion of low-end housing by landlords, such as rows of small dwellings or shops with solars above, often called 'rents', to meet the growing ability of wage earners to afford their own accommodation.[7] The increased bargaining power of wage earners also placed pressure on existing social ties. These tensions found expression in the Peasants' Revolt of 1381, when among the violent uprisings across many parts of south and east England were attacks on major Cambridge landowners, including Barnwell Priory and Corpus Christi College.

The growth of the university meant that Cambridge's population did not necessarily follow national trends by the 15th century. Given the new information from the Hundred Rolls, the estimated population of Cambridge in 1279 should be increased from the previous estimate of about 3,000 to 3,500 (based on the 17 per cent increase in the number of plots recorded). The population may have grown to about 5,800 by 1349, when it was probably halved by the Black Death. By 1377, the town's population may have recovered partially to around 3,600, but the university provided an additional 400 to 700 members, creating a total population of between 4,000 and 4,300.[8] The growth of the university generated important additional demand within the town's economy but also had major implications for the spatial layout of the town. Colleges developed in the west of the town in an area between the river and the main north/south thoroughfare known as the High Street. This process started in the 14th century with the foundation of several colleges, but the street plan was transformed radically by the royal foundation of King's College in the 1440s. Driven by the aspirations of Henry VI, this was one of several centrally imposed schemes by royal, aristocratic or civic authorities that redeveloped and renewed existing English townscapes in this period.[9] The university's demand for property must have helped to keep demand in Cambridge more buoyant than in many other towns.

7.1 The Black Death and its aftermath

The Black Death first entered England in the summer of 1348, and in little over a year between 40 and 50 per cent of the country's population died. Across the diocese of Ely, plague seems to have become virulent in March 1349, reaching its peak in May and June, and then falling away during the later summer months. Similar timescales are suggested by the evidence of manorial account from Downham-in-the-Isle and Wisbech in the Cambridgeshire fenland.[10] At King's Hall, almost half the scholars died from the mortality, although it is likely that some had already fled back to their homes before the plague hit the town.[11] Half the parish priests in Cambridge died and the Hospital of St John in Cambridge had four masters in the space of just over a year, with three dying during the peak months of the plague in May and June 1349. Ministering to and caring for the sick, they were particularly at risk during the plague. In the Cambridge parish of All Saints in the Jewry it was reported that the parishioners had 'suffered for so long from the pestilence, which is well known to be taking hold in this year, so that the oblations of those coming to the said church are by no means sufficient for the necessities', and the bishop granted the vicar his annual sustenance for two years in September 1349. A similar grant was made to the vicar of St John's in Mill Street, Cambridge.[12] The town's population may have been halved in less than three months, with maybe as many as 100 deaths each day at the height of the plague.[13]

7.2 Changing property ownership

Demand for urban property in most English towns generally reduced after the Black Death as a result of the smaller population. There was an overall reduction in the extent and density of settlement. Houses and lands became less subdivided, and gardens or waste ground appeared in most towns. Well-placed housing tended to maintain its value better than more marginal properties, which tended to fall in value. Tenants had greater choice and could relocate to better dwellings, while property owners collected less in rents.[14] The rentals of St John's Hospital in Cambridge show contraction between 1350 and 1356 in most town parishes. In the two parishes of All Saints' and St Botolph, for example, the hospital lost income from two out of its six tenements and from three out of seven tenements respectively. Later rentals between 1361 and 1371 show a sustained level of slightly lower rents compared with the 1350s. Parishes away from the centre of the town tended to see the most change.[15] The parish of All Saints by the Castle, one of the parishes with the lowest rents in the Hundred Rolls, and which had probably already stagnated economically in the 13th century as the importance of the castle declined, was so depopulated by 1365 that the Bishop of Ely united the parish with the neighbouring St Giles' parish, and the church fell into ruin.[16]

Similarly the bursars' rolls of Peterhouse for 1374–5, 1388–9 and 1396–7 reveal that the houses owned by the college around its site in the parish of St Mary the Less (formerly St Peter's without Trumpington Gate) were not always occupied, some were in a poor state of repair and the total rent drawn from them was relatively insignificant.[17] Much also depended on the amount of time and energy that landowners devoted to collecting their dues and chasing arrears. John Botwright, Master of Corpus Christi College between 1443 and 1474, appears to have taken a detailed interest in college administration and been zealous in defending the rights of his institution.[18] His collection of memoranda and accounts, known as the 'White Book', included a rental, notes of documentary records to the college's claims for certain property and a list of college property being improperly detained.[19] As one historian has noted 'quarrels with other Colleges were prosecuted with all the enthusiasm that later ages would give to inter-collegiate sport'.[20]

The growth of the borough corporation as a property holder

After the Black Death, borough communities took over some vacant urban properties. The number of people dying without heirs probably led to an exceptional amount of property falling into the possession of urban communities. Cambridge, like the boroughs of Colchester, Lincoln, Norwich and Grimsby, petitioned the king for permission to take over waste spaces, which would otherwise have gone to the Crown.[21] This development also reflected, though, the growing proprietary powers of medieval English towns and cities. Walls, ditches, streets and other spaces were increasingly seen as belonging to urban communities in their corporate capacities. The revenue from these lands became a very important addition to the city's rental income. Individuals who enclosed these common spaces were required to make appropriate financial contributions to the civic authorities.[22]

In 1330, the townspeople of Cambridge asked leave to 'approve' to make their profit of the small lanes and waste places of the town. Although there is no known record of the jury that the king permitted might be summoned to investigate this request, the corporation began to grant wasteland, such as the 'certain gutter or watercourse' leased to Trinity Hall in 1350. After Henry VI bought lanes and void places from the corporation for King's College and Edward IV asked the corporation to sell common land to Queens' College, this 'clinched the matter by sufficiently admitting that the corporation was owner of the intramural waste', although the matter was disputed in the early 19th century.[23]

Cambridge borough corporation began to charge rents for a whole series of small encroachments, including buttresses, chimneys, drains into the river or the King's Ditch, eavesdrops, footbridges across the King's Ditch, groundsells, projecting houses or sollars, porches, privies and water pipes from the river.[24] The first extant rental of the borough treasurers from 1422/3, for example, includes five payments from six people for parts of Alwyneslane that had been enclosed, as well as receipts for three buttresses under the tenement of Thomas Hert and 'one pair of beams raised on the king's highway'. Payments were also made for two tenter-yards on the common, where cloth would have been stretched and dried after fulling, and one chimney raised on the common, possibly for some form of industrial activity such as a forge. Rents were also collected from shops against Great St Mary's churchyard, towards the wall of the Augustinian friars, in front of King's Hall, and in *le Scaldyngled*.[25]

Even such small items of property could take considerable efforts and expense to obtain. King's Hall sought to obtain part of the lane that lay between the college and a garden belonging to the prior and canons of Chicksands, who had leased this green space to the college. The King's Hall accounts for 1431/2 contain the following entry: 'Item for remuneration made to the messenger of the duke of Gloucester sent to the community of Cambridge for a lane next to the college on the south part for him and his servants 15s.', as well as 2s in expenses for three days for the same. The corporation paid 13s 4d to the same messenger bearing letters to the mayor and burgesses for a certain lane next to the King's Hall. The corporation granted part of King's Hall Lane to the college on 8 April 1433. The intervention of the duke, perhaps on behalf of the king, may have ensured that the corporation only required the rent of a red rose at midsummer, if demanded, for the portion of the lane. Nonetheless, the college paid Richard Parys, the town clerk, 6s 4d for writing a deed of the grant.[26]

Through licensing these encroachments, the borough corporation was acquiring a longer rental of properties, which comprised 61 items in 1422/3 and 75 by 1435/6. Yet despite this growing property portfolio, the treasurers' accounts show a sharp decline in property income and average rents over the course of the 1420s and 1430s, as Table 7.1 shows. Accumulating arrears became a problem for many urban landlords. Great Hall in the University of Oxford, for example had arrears from rents and properties in Newcastle upon Tyne that totalled almost £50 in 1470–1.[27] The arrears recorded in the Cambridge treasurers' accounts, however, seem to have been small in this period, amounting generally to less than 3 per cent of gross income.

Table 7.1: Property income accounted for by the Cambridge borough treasurers, 1422/3–1435/6

	Total	Total	Average
	£	No	Shillings
1422/3	15.67	61	5.14
1423/4	17.83	68	5.24
1424/5	18.97	69	5.50
1425/6	16.31	67	4.87
1426/7	17.56	67	5.24
1427/8	15.94	67	4.76
1431/2	17.08	71	4.81
1433/4	11.70	71	3.30
1434/5	14.33	74	3.87
1435/6	14.18	75	3.78

Source: Cambridgeshire Archives, City/PB Box X/70/1–10

Private landowners

Despite the growth of institutional landowners, families continued to play an important part in the Cambridge property market. They adopted the same strategies for success as those identified in the 13th-century town: commercial profit, property finance and speculation, careers in the Church, education and the law, civic engagement and strategic marriage. They bought and sold land as a way of converting capital acquired elsewhere into income, which could be realized again if necessary. Geoffrey Seman, for example, from a local family (the Semans of Newnham), was trading property and cash loans in the early 14th century, including properties in Chesterton, the West fields of Cambridge and in the town.[28] A strategic marriage combined with property speculation and an extensive legal career aided Sir John Cambridge (d. 1335). A serjeant by 1309, a justice on eyre in 1329–30 and justice of the common pleas in 1331, John Cambridge was also made a knight in 1330. His marriage to Joan, daughter and heir of John Dunning, brought him substantial land in Cambridge. In 1311 he served as alderman of St Mary's Guild, and bequeathed his principal property, a stone hall in St Michael's parish, to the guild. After his son Thomas died in 1361, this and his other properties transferred to Corpus Christi College.[29]

Two particularly successful families in the 14th century were the Morys or Morices and the Harlestons. They held approximately 250 acres and 101 acres of land respectively in the West fields in the 14th century, compared with the Hospital of St John with 235 acres and Corpus Christi College with 177 acres.[30] Nicholas Morys had property in the parishes of St Michael and St Clement in 1279, including 58 acres of land in the latter parish. His son John I served as bailiff, Member of Parliament and mayor in Cambridge. Branches of the family continued to serve in office and hold land in the town over the course of the 14th century, but by 1454 a John Morys of Trumpington esquire controlled part of the holdings. The family's occupations are unclear, apart from one member described as a chandler.[31]

Roger Harleston was a wealthy lawyer, burgess and country squire. He consolidated urban properties between c.1360 and 1380 in St Clement's parish known as Harleston Place, which included a grange and dovecot, a messuage and part of a landing-stage. Roger also acquired lands and houses in villages in the country, at Chesterton, Fordham, Waterbeach, Denny, Haslingfield and Cottenham. He served as justice of the peace in the county and collector of poll tax in 1381. These offices, and also the possibility that he was an outsider, led to attacks on his houses at Harleston Place and at Cottenham during the Peasants' Revolt. Roger's son, Eudo, was given a godfather no less prestigious than Eudo de la Zouche, chancellor of the university. Eudo Harleston died in 1403 aged only 25, and his wife and infant son moved away from Cambridge. The early death of the father and the remarriage of the mother meant that this family's interests moved outside the town, and in 1466 Harleston Place was occupied as a university hostel; it was later acquired by St John's College.[32]

Development of religious institutions

There were continued gifts to the monasteries, friaries and St John's Hospital. 'Canons and nuns who promised prayers in return for acres' was how Frederic Maitland described the religious houses of Cambridge, who received gifts of land from the townspeople, mostly 'in small parcels from small people'. By the 14th century, the house of Augustinian canons at Barnwell Priory held around one third of the total land in the town's East fields and the other ecclesiastical and collegiate bodies held another third, leaving only a third to be held by townspeople.[33]

Chantries, in which endowments were left for one or more priests to celebrate daily or weekly masses for the donors and their relatives, became increasingly popular during the later Middle Ages in the wake of the increased mortality of the Black Death. Several chantries had already been established in Cambridge by 1279 through gifts of property to monasteries and parish churches. The Hundred Rolls record, for example, the messuage and piece of land in St Andrew's parish that the prioress and nuns of St Radegund's had by the gift of Robert Crocheman and Cassandria, his wife, and for which they paid 'to a certain chaplain in perpetuity for celebrating the divine mass in the aforesaid church of St Andrew's for the souls for the aforesaid Robert and Cassandria, and for the souls of all the deceased faithful'.[34] Similarly Radulph, chaplain of the parish of St Clement, had 5 marks paid annually from messuages and income in the same parish given by Master Robert Aunger, who gave the income 'for the celebration of mass of the Blessed Virgin Mary in the aforesaid church of St Clement's'.[35] Other grants of property to endow chantries are mentioned but not fully described in the Hundred Rolls, such as the messuage that Joanne de Benwick had given to St Michael's Church in pure and perpetual alms. This was on condition that mass should be celebrated there twice a year for the souls of herself and her relatives.[36] Such gifts continued to be made. In 1392, for instance, John Herries, John Thriplow, John Blankpayn and John Cotton founded a chantry in St Mary's Church, which they endowed by royal licence with five messuages, two gardens, 10 acres of land and £3 8s 8d rent in Cambridge and Chesterton.[37]

The range of religious institutions to which Cambridge citizens could make gifts and entrust their commemoration continued to expand during the 14th and 15th centuries with the establishment of religious guilds and academic colleges.[38] Among the earliest and most important Cambridge guild was that of St Mary, first mentioned in 1282–5, which attracted among its membership not only many leading townsmen but also Walter Reynolds, Archbishop of Canterbury, and Richard of Bury, Bishop of

Durham. It engaged in small-scale trading to boost its funds, and had five chaplains by 1337. This guild merged with the Corpus Christi Guild in 1352 to found an academic college, and Henry of Lancaster, the cousin of Edward III, became alderman of the joint guild.[39]

Expansion of the university and its colleges

Scholars needed to find lodgings and masters needed to hire schools at reasonable rents. This was a concern for the university from its infancy; indeed, one chapter of the earliest known compilation of statutes and ordinances, dating to c.1250, deals specifically with hostels and rents. This was discovered not in Cambridge but within a manuscript in the Angelica Library in Rome. This may represent the earliest official code of statutes for Cambridge University, as Father M. B. Hackett, who edited the text for publication, maintained, or perhaps it was merely a privately commissioned compilation containing both formal statutes and less official ordinances. Whatever its status, though, it clearly shows that within 40 years of its establishment the university had developed its own institutions and was having an impact on the property market within the town.[40] It should be noted that these rents were for short-term leases and were paid to the holders of property, unlike the rents recorded in the Hundred Rolls, which were perpetual rents paid by holders of property to previous holders of the property. Despite the regulation of lease rents, perpetual rents remained unregulated.

The text of the Angelica manuscript states that 'Two rectors appointed by the chancellor and masters, and two burgesses, bound by oath, are to make an equitable assessment of houses, which is to be entered by them in a document of a public nature'.[41] Unfortunately, none of these schedules is known to have survived.[42] The rectors, whose other duties included ensuring that bread, wine and other essential foods were sold at a fair price, and disciplining errant members of the university, soon became known as proctors.

One third of the rents of houses were to be paid on three fixed dates, namely All Saints' Day (1 November), the Purification of the Blessed Virgin Mary (2 February) and Ascension Day, which spread over the three terms of the academic year. No one, under pain of excommunication, was to leave the town, whether they had finished their studies or not, without first making proper payment for their rent and other debts contracted there. Creditors could distrain the pledge or security offered by a third party on behalf of scholars. If a scholar absconded without settling his accounts, the chancellor notified his bishop that the scholar was excommunicated. No one could rent a house as living quarters or put it to any other use if it had been used as a school for ten years or more, as long as a master required it for lectures, unless the owner himself had been living there.

Restraints were placed on both greedy landlords and on university members outbidding each other for premises. The owners of buildings were to receive nothing more, even by agreement, than the rent fixed under oath, and tenants were not to pay anything in excess of that. If a landlord was discovered to have raised the rent, the chancellor was empowered to debar scholars from lodging in his premises, and the amount paid in excess of the official rate was to be handed back and given to the tenant if he requested it. A scholar renting a house should have the sole right of living there the following year, provided he guaranteed to the landlord in advance the year's rent before the Nativity of the Blessed Virgin (8 September). Anyone who stayed in a rented house after this date was bound to pay the rent for the whole of the following year, unless the landlord had clearly granted him free lodging. A master or scholar who rented a house and shared it with other scholars was known as the principal, and he was answerable to the university for the conduct of his housemates, being responsible for damage caused to the property by himself or his fellow tenants. The text also states that feudal lords could lawfully distrain for their fees (known as rent charges), even if a master had lectured there or a student had occupied the premises. The rent paid to the landlord (known as the rent service) could in these circumstances be reduced by the chancellor.[43]

The Angelica manuscript shows a sophisticated system of checks and balances for both landlords and university members as tenants. Indeed, as early as 1231, when Henry III issued three writs to promote the security of scholars within the town, one provided the university with the legal right to fix the rents of houses for scholars in connection with representatives from the town. Alongside giving the sheriff the ability of arrest or expel, if the university thought fit, rebellious and troublesome scholars, and requiring clerks to register under an approved master within 15 days of coming to the university, the mayor and bailiffs were ordered to allow houses to be valued by two masters and two men of the town. The latter writ extolled the benefits of the nascent university and warned of the risks that if scholars were charged too much for their accommodation they would have to leave the town:

> You are aware that a multitude of scholars from divers parts,
> as well from this side the sea as from overseas, meets at our
> town of Cambridge for study, which we hold a very gratifying

and desirable thing, since no small benefit and glory accrues therefrom to our whole realm; and you, among whom these students personally live, ought especially to be pleased and delighted at it.

We have heard, however, that in letting your houses you make such heavy charges to the scholars living among you, that unless you conduct yourselves with more restrain and moderation towards them in this matter, they will be driven by your exactions to leave your town and, abandoning their studies, leave our country, which we by no means desire.[44]

A documentary example of the university exercising these powers survives in a deed of 1246 at St John's College in which the chancellor and regent masters of the university grant exemption from rent assessment to two hostels belonging to St John's Hospital.[45]

These interests were reconfirmed some time before 5 June 1255, when a writ was issued ordering the sheriff to see that effect was given to letters patent issued by the king in favour of the university regarding the renting of hostels, the imprisoning and delivery of scholars, the assize of bread and ale, and other liberties.[46] The oldest original royal charter now in the university archives is a writ of Henry III of 1266, ordering that the rents of houses were to be assessed every five years by two masters and two burgesses.[47] These four men were sworn in annually before the chancellor and mayor as taxors or rent-assessors of all the dwellings in the town. They promised to carry out a fair assessment of rents and enter them in a schedule that had to be produced for public inspection at request.

Despite this elaborate apparatus, disputes occurred. In 1290, the Prior of Barnwell declined to take the pledge offered by Ralph de Leycestria, doctor of law, to continue as tenant of a stone house owned by the priory in the parish of St Sepulchre. The regent master then took his caution to the university chancellor, who accepted it and installed him as chancellor. The prior then brought a suit of novel disseisin, the action used to attempt to recover lands of which the prior claimed he had been dispossessed. This protracted legal battle continued until April 1292, when the chancellor succeeded in withdrawing the case from the king's justices. The bishop's official arbitrated, and Leycestria agreed to waive his claim. He was granted an extension of 40 days as tenant of the house, and when the lease expired the keys were to be handed over, and Leycestria promised to pay the arrears of rent, which amounted to 40s. The bishop's official again intervened in another case brought by Barnwell Priory against a university member, Master Henry de Wysethe, in 1293, who had rented one of the priory's houses near St John's Hospital.[48] A more amicable agreement was reached in 1309 when Nicholas le Barber wanted to reoccupy a house that he owned called the *domus scolarum* opposite St Mary's, which housed three faculties, canon and civil law and theology. The university consented, and a deed of conveyance was signed in July 1309, but Barber allowed lectures to continue until July 1311.[49]

The statutes in the Angelica manuscript relating to property describe circumstances in which a master or scholar, known as a principal, rented a house, shared it with other scholars and was responsible to the landlord for the rent. As groups of academics began to build or hire larger premises for teaching and lodging, the hostels emerged. These had few endowments and many were later taken over by the colleges. By the end of the 14th century, for example, Michaelhouse had incorporated seven hostels: Garret Hostel, Oving's Inn, St Gregory's Hostel, St Margaret's Hostel, Physwick Hostel, St Katherine's Hostel and Tyler's (or Tyled) Hostel. These provided accommodation for fee-paying students known as pensioners, not necessarily members of Michaelhouse, and generated additional income for the college.[50]

The earliest Cambridge college, Peterhouse, was founded in 1284 by Hugh Balsham, Bishop of Ely. This followed an unsuccessful attempt in 1280 by the bishop to introduce scholars to the Hospital of St John in Cambridge, which had been approved by the king.[51] Bishop Hugh may, however, have been making earlier provisions for a separate institution for scholars. The Hundred Rolls refer to a Hospital of Balsham in 1279. They state that this hospital held three shops in St Edward's parish and two messuages in St Andrew's parish, all given by Bishop Hugh, and refer to Sir Alan of Little Bradley, chaplain, as its warden.[52] The Hospital of Balsham may be the name given to a shadow institution established by the bishop, as mentioned in a document of 1284.[53] It appears that when Peterhouse split from the hospital, the college received the church but the Hospital of St John received some properties from the Hospital of Balsham. All of the properties mentioned in the Hundred Rolls seem to have passed to the Hospital of St John, as the early deeds of Peterhouse make no mention of them.[54] The implication is that the bishop was possibly laying the ground for a separate college before the scholars moved into the Hospital of St John. The arrangement made in 1280 may have been planned as a temporary arrangement designed to reduce the living costs of the scholars until an independent college or hostel could be established for them.

Like the earlier Oxford colleges of Merton, University College and Balliol, Peterhouse was established for the support of graduate scholars, as well as to secure perpetual prayers for the founders and their families. Balsham's college of Peterhouse was modelled on Merton's foundation and was initially to be governed by the same statutes. The second collegiate foundation in Cambridge, King's Hall, was intended by its founder, Edward II, to provide recruits to the higher civil service. Six other colleges followed by the mid-14th century: Michaelhouse (1324), Clare (1326–46), Pembroke (1347), Gonville Hall (1347–9), Trinity Hall (1350) and Corpus Christi (1352).[55]

In founding Peterhouse in 1284, Bishop Hugh Balsham allocated assets for his scholars including the church of St Peter's without Trumpington Gate, and two hostels close by. The college slowly acquired other property in the vicinity, including a messuage formerly owned by Sabina, widow of John de Aylsham, who had been a significant property owner in the same parish in 1279, and the main house of the Friars of the Sack, who were dissolved in 1307.[56] King's Hall, founded by Edward II, acquired its first property in 1336 through the purchase of the house of Robert de Croyland, rector of Oundle, a large timber house, probably occupying three sides of a court, with the vacant side next to King's Hall Lane. Containing a hall and 13 chambers on two storeys, this grand house of a wealthy Cambridge resident was capable of accommodating the warden and the 32 scholars.[57] Further enlargement was necessary, however, and in 1339 the king empowered the Mayor of Cambridge and Thomas Powys, master of the college, to buy in the king's name any places and houses in Cambridge that might be for sale and suitable for the enlargement of the college. Within less than two years the site had extended northwards to a boundary with St John's Hospital. These encompassed five tenements at Dame Nichol's hythe, including 'le Cornhouse', and in 1351 the college acquired Cornhythe.[58] A former mercantile area was slowly being transformed into an academic quarter, and an important precedent had been set in using royal authority to transform part of the townscape for collegiate use, which would be repeated on an even larger scale just over a century later for the second site of King's College.

King's Hall also sought to tap into a conduit constructed to bring spring water from Madingley road to the Franciscan friary in 1325–7. This conduit crossed land that came into the ownership of King's Hall in 1433 after it had enclosed part of King's Childer Lane. King's Hall struggled, however, to obtain permission to draw water from this supply, requiring an inquisition in 1434 and letters patent from the king in 1441 before it was allowed to connect a 'qwil' (a quill or small pipe) to the friars' conduit.[59]

The main site of Michaelhouse was purchased by its founder, Hervey de Stanton, for 100 silver marks from Roger Botetourte, whose brother John had served with Stanton on *oyer* and *terminer* cases in East Anglia. This property had numerous buildings, a walled garden and a quay on the

King's Ditch.[60] Stanton purchased the church and living of St Michael's from Derota (or Dera) de Madingley, wife of Robert, a fellow judge who had worked with Stanton on cases in Suffolk, and probably a member of the Madingley family who held land in Cambridge in 1279.[61] The Madingleys remained closely involved in Stanton's foundation as their daughter, Alice de Heselarton, endowed the stipends of two chaplains at St Michael's, probably to create a chantry for her parents.[62] In 1329 the founder's executor, John de Illegh, purchased the college's first two hostels, together with another landing place called Flaxhythe and a group of small cottages, some occupied by fishermen, which had been bought up by William de Estdene, parson of Leverington church, and John de Ovyng, his nephew. Clergymen and fishermen seemed to be the main landowners in this part of the town at this time. De Illegh purchased from the daughter of a local fisherman the *hospicium angulare* (Corner Hostel), or 'Crouched Hall', adjacent to King's Hall, and in 1352–3 the college bought the former property of the Archdeacon of Norfolk, Adam de Ayrmynne, unsurprisingly known as the Archdeacon's Hostel.[63]

The colleges gradually obtained rights to the meadows adjoining the river to the west of the town. Parts of Garret Hostel Green were acquired by Michaelhouse, initially on leases from the borough corporation, comprising part of the town common in 1430 and a field called the Millestones in 1434. The borough had also permitted Michaelhouse in 1423 to have a ditch 'to have fuel and other goods brought in and taken out', on the condition that the ditch be common to all the burgesses of the town, and that the college create and maintain a footbridge and ford across the ditch. This reopened a disused ditch that had been formerly navigable to serve the landing places at Flaxhythe, a quay at Botetourte's place, Dame Nicol's hythe and Cornhythe.[64]

More new colleges followed in close succession. The foundation of an academic college, providing higher education and commemorative functions, had become fashionable in court circles. Mary de St Pol, Countess of Pembroke, founded Pembroke College; Elizabeth de Burgh, Countess of Clare, rescued and remodelled University Hall, which subsequently bore her name; William Bateman, Bishop of Norwich, established his own college of Trinity Hall in 1350 and also advised one of his wealthier clergy, Edmund Gonville, in establishing a college, which the bishop later placed on a stronger footing. Simon de Montacute, Bishop of Ely, revised the constitution and augmented the income of Peterhouse. The two Cambridge guilds of Corpus Christi and the Blessed Virgin Mary enlisted the patronage of Henry, Duke of Lancaster, who consented to become alderman of the united guild, and secured a royal licence for the foundation of a new college of Corpus Christi in 1352.[65]

These patrons secured property for each of their new colleges within the town. Richard de Badew, chancellor of the University of Cambridge, received licence in 1326 to establish a new college under the title of University Hall, using two houses, which probably served as a hostel for graduates and which had been acquired by the university in 1298. Unfortunately Badew's properties were dispersed over Essex, Huntingdonshire and Cambridgeshire, and between 1325 and 1343 he engaged in costly lawsuits for default of payments. He also got entangled in extensive litigation with university colleagues. University Hall faced an uncertain future until the master of the hall appealed to Lady Elizabeth de Clare for support, a granddaughter of King Edward I. She made an initial grant to the college in 1336, and major grants ten years later when she secured full rights of patronage, as well as providing the college with new statutes in 1359.[66] The first acquisition by Mary de St Pol, Countess of Pembroke, for her new college of Pembroke was a messuage of Hervey de Stanton, rector of Elm, probably the nephew of the founder of Michaelhouse. This was supplemented in 1351 by a hostel to the south, which had been given to the university before 1279 by Sir Roger de Heydon, and an acre of meadow, bought by the countess in 1363 and planted as an orchard. The college subsequently acquired St Thomas's Hostel from the Hospital of St John in 1451 on lease in perpetuity.[67]

Edmund Gonville was an ecclesiastic from a rising Norfolk gentry family who seems to have been a land agent, working for some of the leading men of East Anglia and even the king. In 1348 he obtained licence in mortmain allowing for the permanent endowment of his college, Gonville Hall in Cambridge, but he died in 1351 before this foundation was fully established and endowed. His bishop and executor, William Bateman, Bishop of Norwich (d. 1355), made proper provision for the endowment and moved the college from what is now part of Corpus Christi College to a more central site, adjacent to the university schools and to his own foundation of Trinity Hall.[68] This included the great stone house of Sir John de Cambridge, purchased by Bateman in 1311, and bequeathed by him to the Corpus Christi Guild. This had been the messuage and piece of vacant land in St Michael's parish, held in 1279 by Anglesey Priory from the gift of Robert son of Robert Hubert.[69] Gonville continued to pay an annual rent of 5s to the priory for this property.[70] Bateman issued Gonville Hall with new statutes, which included restricting the spending of the endowment to property-related expenses:

> It is further our will that the endowment of the college shall not be spent except on the building or repair of houses, walls

> or curtilage of the precincts or rectories of the college, or
> in the purchase of perpetual rents for the college, or in the
> defence of the legal rights of the college

and ordering that the immovable property of the college should never be alienated in any way or at any time.[71]

Bateman also founded his own college of Trinity Hall, whose deed of foundation was made in 1350. In November a hostel was purchased from Ely Priory, which Prior John de Crawden had bought for monks studying at the university, and the site was extended by further acquisitions in 1350 and 1354.[72] Simon Dalling, a fellow trained in civil and canon law, was appointed Master of Trinity Hall in 1443. In 1445 he was able to exchange low-lying land close to the river and St John Zachary's Church for land and adjoining property including the church and living of St Edward King and Martyr, close to the marketplace. This sustained the endowment and increased the number of fellows and scholars.[73]

According to the 16th-century writer John Josselin, Latin secretary to Archbishop Matthew Parker, when the royal licence was secured to found Corpus Christi College in 1352, the brethren of the guilds who had houses in Luthburne, now Free School Lane, pulled them down to clear a site for the new college. In March 1353, the two guilds conveyed to the new college a house next to St Bene't's churchyard together with the advowson of the church.[74] Trinity Hall and Corpus both owned and partly occupied a block of adjacent tenements on what is now known as Free School Lane, but had insufficient space to construct a satisfactory range of buildings. So an exchange of properties was negotiated during summer 1353 between Henry, Duke of Lancaster, as alderman of the united guilds, and Bishop William Bateman, as executor for Edmund Gonville deceased. Gonville Hall moved to a site near to Trinity Hall and Corpus received their site in Free School Lane, giving both foundations space to expand.[75]

Townsmen were behind the establishment of Queens' College in the 1440s. Andrew Dokett, vicar of St Botolph's Church and principal of St Bernard's Hostel in Cambridge, secured the patronage of Queen Margaret of Anjou and subsequently of Queen Elizabeth Woodville as well as providing an endowment. Several parishioners of Dokett's parish, St Botolph's, provided land, including Richard Andrew and John Morris. Dokett left the college further benefactions of money and property in his will in 1461.[76]

Henry VI founded his college of St Nicholas in 1441, which was changed two years later to 'the King's College of the Blessed St Mary and St Nicholas' when he provided that the scholars be recruited from those at Eton, the school that he had founded in 1440. The first buildings were erected on the site that now forms the west court of the Schools, to the north of the college chapel and adjoining the medieval Old Schools courtyard, with the gatehouse facing west towards Clare College across Trinity Lane. The greater part of this site, consisting of a garden of Trinity Hall, Crouched Hostel and the Grammar School, was acquired by the King's commissioners in autumn 1440, although a small portion to the north-east does not seem to have been completed until 1449. The university had purchased the Crouched Hostel from the Prior of the Hospital of St John of Jerusalem in 1432.[77] This was probably the messuage in the parish of St John, which the prior and brothers held in 1279.[78]

In summer 1443, the enlargement of the site began as Henry VI set about acquiring a block of property immediately to the south and six or seven times larger, extending from the river west to the High Street, now King's Parade. Requiring the demolition of houses and hostels, closing streets, relocating a college, and resiting and rebuilding a parish church, this transformed the townscape of the western part of the town: 'In all the recorded history of Cambridge, so drastic a clearance of buildings and closing of thoroughfares in the heart of the town has only one parallel: the clearing of the site for the Castle by William the Conqueror.'[79] The old parish church of St John Zachary was demolished and rebuilt on the northern boundary of the site, beside Gonville Hall Lane, but this soon became a ruin for lack of parishioners, and is last mentioned in 1488–9.[80]

Some compensation was offered but this was slow in being granted. In 1445 the Mayor and Corporation of Cambridge granted to the king all the streets within the site, and also the common land by the river and the quay called Salt Hithe. As this cut off a route along Piron Lane to the river for the townspeople, it was stipulated that another way should be obtained through ground north of Trinity Hall, called Henably. This was not granted until 1455, causing annoyance to the town and leading the borough council to send a memorandum in frustration to the college.[81] Some property owners, though, held out for advantageous terms. Draper Robert Lincoln owned two houses near the east end of the site chosen for the chapel and held out until 1452. Lincoln demanded a tenancy for the lives of himself and his wife, a payment of 100 marks, a yearly gowncloth during his lifetime from the provost and to dine in the college or the provost's place at Christmas, Easter, Whitsun and the Assumption of Our Lady.[82]

One casualty was the college of Godshouse on the east side of Milne Street, which was being established by William Bingham, a London parish priest concerned to remedy the country's 'great scarcity of masters of Grammar'. John Brokley, Mayor of London in 1433–4, was associated with Bingham in purchasing part of the original site in 1437. After Henry VI decided to incorporate the site of Godshouse into his new college of King's, it was only Bingham's energy and tenacity that prevented Godshouse from disappearing completely.[83] By summer 1446, Bingham had acquired a large alternative site in St Andrew's parish near Barnwell Gate with a property belonging to the Abbot of Tiltey, who had also been a Cambridge landowner at the time of the Hundred Rolls in St John's and St Edward's parishes.[84] Henry VI granted a foundation charter to Godshouse in 1448, which was to be refounded and renamed Christ's College by Lady Margaret Beaufort in 1505–6.

In 1446 the burgesses petitioned to have their subsidy assessment reduced, claiming that a number of houses were standing empty, and that many of the craftsmen in the borough were departing because sites acquired for King's College and for students' lodgings were exempted from taxation and the rest of the town was unduly burdened. The assessment was reduced from £46 12s 2½d to £20, and this concession was confirmed in 1465. [85] Such a reduction needs to be seen, however, as the culmination of repeated requests by the borough government to reduce the civic dues it paid to the Crown, including a request to reduce its fee farm in 1402, and a smaller reduction of 40s to its tax quota in 1433. It was also one of many requests for reduced taxation from English boroughs in this period accepted by the Crown, reflecting the desperate attempts by successive royal governments to buy political support from towns. In the same period, Oxford put forward a contrary argument to that advanced at Cambridge; that a decline in craftsmen had led to students withdrawing from the town.[86]

Peasants' Revolt

The Peasants' Revolt of 1381 saw long-term pressures merging with short-term protests over taxation and local grievances. The burgesses of Cambridge joined a group of county rebels to attack the manors of Thomas Haselden, 15 miles south-west of the town, on Saturday 15 June 1381. A series of disturbances followed within the town in which the burgesses paid off old grievances against the university and Barnwell Priory. The mayor and commonalty destroyed the house of William Bedell, a university official, in the town. The university's chancellor in 1381 was the hated John Cavendish, murdered in June 1381 at Lakenheath. The mayor and commonalty broke into the enclosure of Corpus Christi College and the dwellings of its scholars and carried off charters, writings, books and muniments. The masters and scholars of the university were compelled under pain of death and destruction of their houses to renounce all franchises and privileges granted to them by all kings and to submit to the governance of the burgesses. Charters and other documents of privileges were burned in the marketplace. Another group broke down a close of the Prior of Barnwell and carried off large trees growing there.[87] The attacks on Barnwell Priory and the university formed part of a general wave of contemporary anti-clerical opposition.

The rebels' motives for the attack on Corpus Christi College, however, seem to have been more complex. The college was ransacked of books, plate, muniments and furnishings, and in 1384 the Crown paid £80 towards the recovery of its losses, and permitted it to sell houses in Cambridge to raise further capital. No other Cambridge colleges are specifically mentioned as sustaining damage during the Peasants' Revolt. The sacking of Corpus has been attributed to the work of rival town guilds, or to townspeople's resentment of the college's widespread property ownership and the 'candle rents' that they were paying to maintain it.[88] It seems more likely, though, that Corpus was singled out by the rebels because it had received support from the unpopular John of Gaunt, Duke of Lancaster (1340–99), and his father in law, Henry of Grosmont, first Duke of Lancaster (c.1310–61). The two town gilds obtained the patronage of Henry of Grosmont, who secured the royal licence for the new foundation and negotiated an exchange of sites for the new college with Gonville Hall in 1353. His heir, John of Gaunt, successfully lobbied for the college to be granted permission to acquire additional lands and rents.[89] Indeed the rolls of parliament that detailed the rising in Cambridge referred to the college as 'the foundation of our most excellent lord of Lancaster'.[90] Gaunt was widely blamed by the rebels for the military failings and financial exactions of government. His name headed the list of traitors who the rebel army at Blackheath had demanded to be arrested and executed. Popular hostility towards the duke was also expressed in attacks on Lancastrian estates in East Anglia, and the destruction of his Savoy palace.[91] The attack on Corpus Christi College in 1381 should be viewed less as a demonstration of town/gown hatred and more as one of many examples of popular hostility towards John of Gaunt, whose patronage the college had enjoyed.

Leading Cambridge townsmen became caught up in the violent events of 1381 both as rebels and as victims. Rebels included wealthy burgesses such as Richard Martin, with two messuages, seven shops and a dovecot worth 60s per year, while the victims included Roger Harleston with his substantial town estate.[92] Several of these participants continued to play active parts in the affairs of the town. John Blankpayn of Cambridge, who had served as mayor in 1374–5 and 1379–80, had his house attacked by the rebels in 1381, probably owing to his roles as collector of the poll tax and as a Member of Parliament. A substantial property owner, he held at least two houses, one in the marketplace and one in Petty Cury. Blankpayn served as a Member of Parliament again in 1388 and as mayor in 1390–1. Robert Brigham, mayor in 1378–9 and Member of Parliament in 1377, was accused by the clerks of Corpus Christi of having led the rioters who attacked the college. The Crown confiscated his property, which comprised three messuages, eight shops and three cottages and had provided him with revenues of nearly £6 a year. After receiving royal pardons, however, he was able to recover his property, and served four further terms as mayor and Member of Parliament. Brigham and Blankpayn were two of the six burgesses who founded the Guild of the Purification in St Mary's Church in 1386.[93]

7.3 Conclusion

Despite the sweeping social and economic changes brought by the Black Death of 1349, the Cambridge property market in the later 14th and early 15th centuries reveals several continuities with trends identified in the pre-plague period. Centrally located properties within the town continued to be attractive, religious institutions continued to receive gifts of property and families continued to invest the profits of their trade or profession in land.

Nonetheless, there were important changes. A reduced population led to lower demand, particularly in more marginal areas. The amalgamating of the parish of All Saints by the Castle with St Giles' provides evidence of this. The borough corporation became a more significant landowner, taking derelict properties and empty spaces. Guilds and academic colleges provided new outlets for charitable gifts by the townspeople, and quickly became important urban landowners. With the foundations of the university colleges, the spatial layout of the town changed, slowly at first and then dramatically, with the clearance for the second site of King's College. Coinciding with a general economic slump of particularly severity, this was a period of dislocation both locally and nationally. The town's petition for the reduction of its subsidy in 1446 reflects this. Yet it was the increased royal patronage in the university from the mid-15th century that was to generate a cluster of major building projects in Cambridge by the early 16th century, dominated by the cathedral-like scale of King's College Chapel.

This was a period in which religious, academic and civic institutions played a larger role in the property market in Cambridge, as in other towns. This reflected the growth of these institutions as well as the general contraction in population and urban economies that were often relatively stagnant. We must be careful, though, about overstating this. There is no comprehensive snapshot of property ownership in Cambridge for this period similar to the Hundred Rolls. We rely on the piecemeal and often fragmentary evidence from surviving records, preserved predominantly by institutions, which therefore tells us much more about these organizations than about individual citizens. The careers of the Harlestons and the Morices in Cambridge show that families were still able to accumulate important landholdings, even if their property portfolios were more transitory than those of perpetual institutions, such as the colleges.

Notes

[1] For the economy and society of Cambridge after 1450, see Lee, *Cambridge*.

[2] VCH 3, pp 12–14.

[3] Charles Phythian-Adams, *Desolation of a City: Coventry and the Urban Crisis of the Late Middle Ages* (Cambridge, 1979), pp 17–18.

[4] Christopher Dyer, *An Age of Transition? Economy and Society in England in the Later Middle Ages* (Oxford, 2005), pp 126–57; Maryanne Kowaleski, 'A Consumer Economy', *A Social History of England 1200–1500* ed. R. Horrox and M. Ormrod (Oxford, 2004), pp 238–59.

[5] Keene, 'Property Market', pp 201–26. For the economic performance of cloth-making towns, see John S. Lee, *The Medieval Clothier* (Woodbridge, 2018), pp 115–56.

[6] Richard Britnell, 'The Black Death in English Towns', *Urban History* 21 (1994): 195–210, p 207.

[7] Dyer, *Age of Transition*, pp 52–3; Kowaleski, 'A Consumer Economy', pp 251–3.

[8] These estimates, which are very approximate, are taken from John Hatcher, 'Commemoration of Benefactors Address, 4 December 2009: "For the Souls of the Departed in the Mortality and after the year of the Lord 1349 and after"', *The Letter* (Corpus Christi College, Cambridge) 89 (2010): 14–23, pp 15, 17 (and increased by 17 per cent) and Lee, *Cambridge*, p 29.

[9] Lilley, 'Urban Planning': 22–42.

[10] John Aberth, 'The Black Death in the Diocese of Ely: The Evidence of the Bishop's Register', *Journal of Medieval History* 21 (1995): 275–87, pp 280–1; David Stone, 'The Black Death and its Immediate Aftermath: Crisis and Change in the Fenland Economy, 1346–1353', *Town and Countryside in the Age of the Black Death* ed. Mark Bailey and Stephen Rigby (Turnhout, 2012), pp 213–44, pp 224–5.

[11] A. B. Cobban, *The King's Hall Within the University of Cambridge in the Later Middle Ages* (Cambridge, 1969), p 221.

[12] Aberth, 'The Black Death': 286–7; Rubin, *Charity and Community*, pp 173, 302.

[13] Hatcher, '"For the Souls of the Departed"'.

[14] Britnell, 'The Black Death': 206–7; Alan Dyer, *Decline and Growth in English Towns 1400–1640* (Cambridge, 1995), pp 38–9.

15 Rubin, *Charity and Community*, pp 48–9.
16 Rubin, *Charity and Community*, pp 48–9; VCH 3, p 123.
17 Hall and Lovatt, 'The Site and Foundation of Peterhouse': 45.
18 E. C. Pearce, 'College Accounts of John Botwright, Master of Corpus Christi, 1443–74', *Proceedings of the Cambridge Antiquarian Society* 22 (1917–20): 76–90; P. Zutshi, 'John Botwright Master of the College, 1443–1474,' *Letter of the Corpus Association* 77 (1998): 13–19.
19 Corpus Christi College Cambridge Archives, CCCC02/M/7/1, 'Liber Albus', fols 6v–8, 74, 118–25.
20 Catherine Hall, 'Quit-rents', *Letter of the Corpus Association* 61 (1982): 49–54.
21 Britnell, 'The Black Death', p 207.
22 Christian D. Liddy, *Contesting the City: The Politics of Citizenship in English Towns, 1250–1530* (Oxford, 2007), pp 60–1.
23 M, pp 83–4, 187–8.
24 Palmer, *Borough Documents*, p xxxvii.
25 Cambridgeshire Archives, City/PB Box X/70/1.
26 City/PB Box X/70/7; Willis and Clark, *Architectural History*, II, pp 425–6.
27 Butcher, 'Newcastle': 70.
28 F, p 601; W, p 64.
29 Rosemary Horrox, 'Cambridge [Cantebrig], Sir John (d. 1335)', *ODNB*.
30 M, p 160.
31 F, pp 507–12; M. Underwood, 'The Impact of St John's College as Landowner in the West Fields of Cambridge in the Early Sixteenth Century', *Medieval Cambridge: Essays on the Pre-Reformation University* ed. P. Zutshi (Woodbridge, 1993), pp 167–88, p 172.
32 F, pp 387–95; Underwood, 'Impact of St John's College', pp 172–4.
33 M, pp 59–63, 129–33, 161–3.
34 HR A30.
35 HR R2.
36 HR 693; Willis and Clark, *Architectural History*, I, p 161.
37 CPR 1391–6, p 132.
38 John S. Lee, 'Monuments and Memory: A University Town in Late Medieval England', *Commemoration in Medieval Cambridge*, ed. John S. Lee and Christian Steer (Woodbridge, 2018), pp 10–33.
39 VCH 3, pp 133–5.
40 Hackett, *Original Statutes*; Leedham-Green, *A Concise History*, p 6; W. Ullman, 'Review of *The Original Statutes of Cambridge University* by M.B. Hackett', *Journal of Ecclesiastical History* 22 (1971): 134–9.
41 Hackett, *Original Statutes*, p 204.
42 Hackett, *Original Statutes*, p 155.
43 Hackett, *Original Statutes*, pp 169–74, 212–16.
44 *Close Rolls of the Reign of Henry III* (14 vols) I 1227-31 (London, 1908–38), pp 586–7; A. F. Leach, *Educational Charters and Documents, 598 to 1909* (Cambridge, 1911), pp 148–53 where printed with English translation.
45 St John's College Archives D3.58 reproduced in Mark Nicholls and Kathryn McKee (eds), *The Library Treasures of St John's College, Cambridge* (London, 2014), pp 32–3.
46 Hackett, *Original Statutes*, p 36. Hackett was unable to trace the original, an enrolment or a copy of these letters.

[47] Cambridge University Library, University Archives, Luard 1. The text is printed in G. Dyer, *The Privileges of the University of Cambridge* (2 vols) I (London, 1824), p 63.

[48] Hackett, *Original Statutes*, pp 172–3, 232.

[49] Hackett, *Original Statutes*, p 171; H. P. Stokes, 'Early University Property', *Proceedings of the Cambridge Antiquarian Society* 13 (2) (1909): 164–84, pp 183–4.

[50] Andreas Loewe, 'Michaelhouse: Hervey de Stanton's Cambridge Foundation', *Church History* 90 (4) (2010): 599–608, p 597.

[51] *Calendar of Patent Rolls 1272–1281*, pp 420–1.

[52] See below, HR 874–5.

[53] StJ D3.66, cited in StJ, p xvi, fn 17.

[54] Peterhouse, St Peter's College A1–3 and the Site of the College A1–29 (A23 is missing).

[55] Leedham-Green, *Concise History*, pp 21–3.

[56] HR 276–93; Willis and Clark, *Architectural History*, I, pp 1–8.

[57] Willis and Clark, *Architectural History*, II, pp 420–1, 430–2, 456.

[58] Willis and Clark, *Architectural History*, II, pp 421–4.

[59] John S. Lee, 'Piped Water Supplies Managed by Civic Bodies in Medieval English Towns', *Urban History* 41 (2014): 369–93.

[60] Loewe, 'Michaelhouse', pp 592–3.

[61] Loewe, 'Michaelhouse', pp 592–3.

[62] Loewe, 'Michaelhouse', pp 591–2.

[63] Loewe, 'Michaelhouse', pp 597–8; Willis and Clark, *Architectural History*, II, pp 396–7, 402–3.

[64] Willis and Clark, *Architectural History*, II, pp 405–6; Lee, 'Trinity and the Town'.

[65] Hall, 'Corpus Christi', pp 78–80.

[66] Alan B. Cobban, 'Badew, Richard (d. 1361)', *ODNB*; VCH 3, pp 340–1.

[67] Willis and Clark, *Architectural History*, I, pp 122–4.

[68] C. N. L. Brooke, 'Gonville [Gonvile], Edmund (d. 1351)', *ODNB*; Christopher Brooke, *A History of Gonville and Caius College* (Woodbridge, 1985), pp 1–15.

[69] HR P25.

[70] Willis and Clark, *Architectural History*, I, pp 158–9.

[71] Michael Prichard (ed.), *Gonville & Caius College: The Statutes of the Founders* (Woodbridge, 2017), pp 89, 91.

[72] Willis and Clark, *Architectural History*, I, pp 209–12.

[73] Claire Gobbi Daunton and Elizabeth A. New, 'The Masters of Trinity Hall in the Later Middle Ages', *Commemoration in Medieval Cambridge* ed. Lee and Steer: pp 61–89, 66–7.

[74] Willis and Clark, *Architectural History*, I, pp 242–3; VCH 3, p 371.

[75] Hall, 'Corpus Christi', p 84, n. 77.

[76] Malcolm G. Underwood, 'Dokett [Doket], Andrew (c. 1410–1484)', *ODNB*.

[77] KCA, KCAR/6/2/027/2/CAM6; Willis and Clark, *Architectural History*, III, p 8; VCH 3, pp 385–6.

[78] See HR P31.

[79] VCH 3, p 386.

[80] Willis and Clark, *Architectural History*, I, pp 548–51; VCH 3, p 129.

[81] King's College Archive, KCAR/6/2/027/2/CAM/18–19; Willis and Clark, *Architectural History*, I, pp 343–4.

[82] King's College Archive, KCAR/6/2/027/2/CAM/41; Willis and Clark, *Architectural History*, I, pp 336–7.

83 R. B. Dobson, 'Bingham [Byngham], William (d. 1451)', *ODNB*; Willis and Clark, *Architectural History*, I, pp 337–8, II, pp 188–9.

84 See HR 501, 528.

85 C, pp 197, 214; Maitland and Bateson, *Charters*, pp xxvi, 54–61.

86 Lee, *Cambridge*, pp 43–4; A. R. Bridbury, 'English Provincial Towns in the Later Middle Ages', *Economic History Review* 34 (1981): 1–24; Dyer, *Decline and Growth*, pp 39–41.

87 R. B. Dobson, *The Peasants' Revolt in 1381* (London, 1970), pp 239–42.

88 O. Rackham, 'Why Corpus Christi?', *Corpus within Living Memory: Life in a Cambridge College* ed. M. E. Bury and E. J. Winter (London, 2003), pp 9–17, 16; C, p 120, n 4.

89 TNA, C 143/367/3 Inquisitions taken as a result of applications to the Crown for licences to alienate land. John, Duke of Lancaster, to grant the manor of Landbeach, with the advowson of its church, and messuages and land in Cambridge, Barnwell, Grantchester and Coton, to the master and scholars of Corpus Christi College, 1369–70; Hall, 'Corpus Christi', pp 80–4; Christopher Brooke, Daniel Riehl Leader, Victor Morgan and Peter Searby, *A History of the University of Cambridge* (4 vols) 1 (Cambridge, 1988), pp 87–8.

90 Dobson, *Peasants' Revolt*, pp 240–1.

91 Simon Walker, 'John [John of Gaunt], Duke of Aquitaine and Duke of Lancaster, Styled King of Castile and León (1340–1399)', *ODNB*; Dobson, *Peasants' Revolt*, p 240.

92 Mingjie Xu, 'Disorder and Rebellion in Cambridgeshire in 1381' (PhD thesis, University of Cambridge, 2016), pp 165–6, 178, 198.

93 E. M. Wade, 'Blankpayn, John, of Cambridge', *History of Parliament, 1386–1421*; E. M. Wade, 'Brigham, Robert, of Cambridge', *History of Parliament, 1386–1421*.

8

Conclusions

Introduction

The cornerstone of this book is a set of three rolls in The National Archives that make up the Cambridge Hundred Rolls of 1279. The Hundred Rolls as a whole are important because they are the first royal survey that comprehensively and systematically itemized very small plots of land. Anglo-Saxon charters transferring land go back to the 9th century in several counties, but the lands to which they refer were typically large plots held by royalty, aristocrats or powerful religious institutions. The coverage in the Domesday Book in 1086 was superficial in comparison with the detail given in the Hundred Rolls. When investigating issues such as the incidence of hawgable, the Hundred Rolls provide some of the earliest written evidence.

The Hundred Rolls have long been recognized by historians as an important source. Raban noted that:

> The real afterlife of the 1279–80 inquiry began, not in the Middle Ages, but in the early nineteenth century, with the publication of the Record Commission edition. Since then the rolls have attracted the fitful but increasingly sophisticated attention of scholars ... The future is exciting, with the expectation of more results stimulated by the resources of modern technology.[1]

This book has aspired to fulfil these expectations. The Cambridge Rolls are a good starting point because, together with the Huntingdon Rolls, they provide the most detailed and comprehensive account of property holdings in any large town.

8.1 The importance of property transactions

The first question addressed in this book was whether the urban property market in late 13th-century Cambridge was a direct antecedent of property markets today. In particular, how common was the buying and selling of property? How were property rents determined? Were there professional speculators, and if so how did they operate?

The evidence shows that the property market was well developed by 1279, and indeed quite sophisticated. Demand for property was especially strong in elite residential areas, where the supply of property was limited and rents were consequently high. About half of all property transfers were effected through sale and purchase.

Properties were held by perpetual rents. Where properties increased in value additional rents could be added by vendors. Many properties carried multiple rents, suggesting that they had changed hands several times. Later rents represented increments in previous total rents, driven by increases in property values in the town. Rising property values were consistent with the expansion of the town, as described in previous chapters. If rents had been static or declining there would have been little incentive to build new property in the town.

Rents were fixed annually but were often paid on quarter days, and sometimes twice a year. Where multiple rents were owed, it appears that each rent was normally paid to the recipient directly by the owner of the property. This could create problems if the previous owner had left the town. The previous owner would need to appoint an agent to collect the rent on their behalf. Alternatively, the absentee could sell the rent to a local person for its capitalized value, which would be negotiated between the parties. The sale, or 'assignment', of rents was quite common according to the Hundred Rolls. In several cases, though, the assignment of rent appears to have involved a gift to a religious or charitable institution rather than a sale to another individual.

Property speculation was by no means unusual, although it was largely the prerogative of rich and well-connected people. Speculation was not confined to townspeople; outsiders were also involved, as illustrated by Walter Merton's acquisition of the Dunning estate. Speculative opportunities arose from a booming property market stimulated by the Commercial Revolution of the time. Some opportunities, however, arose from other people's misfortunes, such as indebtedness to moneylenders or expulsion from the town (as in the case of Jewish moneylenders and their associates).

Property holding fulfilled a number of roles. It was undoubtedly valued as a source of rental income. A property could also be a home, a place of business and a sign of status. Residence could be near a place of work, such as the quay or the market, or somewhere more congenial, in a quieter area close to the homes of other status-seeking families. Property could also be used as a substitute for holding cash. The profits from a successful venture could be invested in property until another business opportunity arose, and then sold to finance it. Given the shortage of coinage, and the risk of theft, investing profits in property could be safer than hoarding cash. Property could also be a useful speculation. In a property market with rising rents it offered the prospect of capital gains, which could be realized either from outright sales or through additional rent.

8.2 The significance of urban topography

The second finding concerns the economic topography of medieval Cambridge. What kinds of occupations were found in which parts of the town? How did the topography change as the town expanded? The new information employed in this study radically alters previous views of the town's topography. Residential development to the east occurred far earlier than previously believed. In particular, the arrival of the Dominicans in the 1230s had a significant impact on both the economy of the town and the development of the university.

By 1279 industrial activity was concentrated around the edge of the market, where the smiths were active, and towards the river, in the parishes of St John and St Michael. Towards the Great Bridge, and backing onto fields to the east, were the smart residences of St Clement's parish. Many professional people resided south of the market, near St Bene't's, St Andrew's and St Botolph's.

The Trumpington road seems to have been a prime location for residential development in the 13th century. Trumpington village was an elite residential area from the 12th century. The ground was high and well drained, with a fresh-water spring nearby. Access to the market down the Trumpington road was good, and houses along the road were some distance from the noise and smells of the market, the butchery and the quay. Land for development could also be acquired quite cheaply, at its previous rent (i.e. 'opportunity cost') in agricultural use.

The south-east of the town near the Barnwell Gate seems to have been initially less favoured, but once the Dominicans had settled there in the 1230s it developed quickly, as demonstrated by the evidence in the 'missing roll'. Old properties were demolished to make way for the friary, and new properties then sprung up around it. The new properties were probably more salubrious than the old ones and this may have encouraged rapid occupation of them.

Although there was some specialization of activity within the town, the degree of spatial segmentation should not be exaggerated. Most trades were not clustered entirely in a single parish.

8.3 The importance of the family

Where freeholders were concerned, the family was a key institution through which property was passed on through successive generations. There was no equivalent of the modern firm or business enterprise in medieval towns, and so the family was also an important unit of business organization. Cambridge had a Guild of Merchants, described in the Hundred Rolls, but it is unclear how far the guild organized trade. It appears to have been responsible for settling disputes between its members, but it is not recorded as holding any property in the town.

Evidence from the Hundred Rolls has been combined with evidence from deeds to reconstruct the family trees of leading Cambridge families. Previous attempts to construct such trees have been constrained by lack of evidence; not only the missing roll already referred to, but difficulties in accessing local deeds and relevant royal records.

The systematic synthesis of biographical information using modern information technology has made it possible to answer the following two questions raised at the outset: how important were the leading families in the urban economy, and what factors contributed to their survival and success? Did new wealth generated by business activity replace old wealth based on land as a source of status and influence in the town?

The evidence shows that many (though not all) successful Cambridge merchants were members of large families, or had relatives who married into such families. Small families could prosper too, but usually under the umbrella of a larger family to which members were related. Members of smaller families were often active in similar occupations. Large families, on the other hand, seem to have diversified their risks by different members taking employment in different fields, such as trade, administration and religious office.

The medieval Cambridge family was a unit of production as well as a unit of consumption, unlike the modern family. But they were not just family businesses; they were also engaged in the community. Their members served as bailiffs, they married into other families and other families married into them. Families whose success endured typically had at least one entrepreneurial family member in each generation. These entrepreneurs were not simple profit–maximizers in the modern sense. Wealth was merely a means to an end in many cases, rather than an end in itself. People sought reputation for themselves and their families, and perhaps especially for their children. As noted, they also sought spiritual security, through donations to local priories and friaries, as well as to local churches, where they often funded candles for specific altars.

Overall, the behaviour of successful Cambridge families, as recorded in the Hundred Rolls, suggests that they had dynastic objectives based on reputation-building. Profits from trade were just one source of income, and were supplemented to a significant degree by income derived from administration and royal service.

8.4 The importance of charitable giving to institutions

The fourth question addressed in this book concerns the importance of philanthropy. What proportion of income from property in Cambridge was used to support local charitable foundations? To what extent were profits from commerce recycled back into the local community?

Almost half of all rental income generated from local properties accrued to religious and charitable institutions. This appears to have resulted mainly from the accumulated gifts of townspeople. In many medieval towns, notably neighbouring Bury St Edmund's, the local abbey was a dominant landowner in the town from the outset, and in such cases a substantial proportion of rent accrued to the abbey simply because the townspeople had no option but to pay it. Barnwell was not a dominant landowner in Cambridge, however, and neither was St Radegund's, although between them they held significant property in the town. In neither case did the institution attempt to dominate or control urban life. Religious institutions in Cambridge prospered, and while both priories enjoyed some royal patronage, the majority of bequests and legacies came from the townspeople. Relationships between the townspeople and the religious houses were generally more positive that at Bury St Edmund's.

Cambridge had many churches, and there is evidence that church building, and perhaps more importantly, church rebuilding, was actively pursued throughout the 13th century on local initiative. Commercial prosperity seems to have gone hand in hand with local charity, enabling the town to expand its population without any serious erosion of the quality of life.

It is important not to exaggerate the point, however. The rents accruing to the religious institutions in 1279 represent the culmination of bequests going back to the 12th century; they were not all the consequence of gifts from those alive, or recently deceased, at the time of the Hundred Rolls. While some of these gifts were purely altruistic, self-interest undoubtedly played a part as well. Some donors may have received material benefits. Some gifts were certainly sales, in the sense that the donor received a rent from the institution, even though the rent may have been (in some cases at least) lower than a commercial level. Where major gifts were concerned, the purchase of a corrody was often involved. Details of some local corrodies have survived; typically the donor retired to the abbey with food and lodging provided until their death. Some corrodies read like business contracts in respect of the detail with which they specified the food and drink. The sale of corrodies was probably a significant aspect of the institutional business model, for in the absence of a substantial pilgrimage trade (owing to the lack of important relics), the sale of retirement packages could be an important source of income. Corrodies could be risky, however, as the donor might live long, possibly lingering on in poor health and therefore needing considerable care; furthermore, part of their gift might be committed to the finance of chaplaincies, creating additional costs for the institution. Overall, while some of the larger donations to religious and charitable institutions may have had mixed motives, most of the numerous small donations probably did not.

8.5 The significance of regional and national context

The final question addressed in this book relates to Cambridge's economic performance at the regional and national level.

Cambridge's success was closely connected to the locational advantage that it possessed as an inland port serving the corn trade. The logic of its growth was largely geographical. The River Great Ouse and its tributary the Cam provided a natural outlet for bulk commodities such as corn. Cambridge was situated on an outcrop of land suitable for arable farming. With fens to the north and extensive farmland to the south, Cambridge was the logical point at which to transship corn from road to water (in practice, cart to river boat). Because the corn was being loaded and unloaded, it was a convenient point at which to mill it and thereby reduce its bulk and improve its value/weight ratio. While wholesale trade was geared to the export of corn through King's Lynn, retail trade was geared to supplying a wide range of products, not only to the institutions and the residents of the town, but to a prosperous agricultural area within a 10-mile radius of the town centre, and probably even further afield.

Cambridge was suitable as an administrative centre because it had a defensible hill, once the site of a Roman camp, on which the Normans built a castle, which they kept in a reasonable state of repair. As the town developed across the river, however, its defence became more problematic. During the 13th century, the ditch that had been created proved unsatisfactory. But there were no further incursions after the 1260s, and so the town's role as the administrative centre of the shire was secure.

Cambridge dominated its hinterland. It occupied a favoured location in an area well suited to arable farming. It specialized in both wholesale and retail trade. Trade was drawn to Cambridge because the physical geography of the region destined the site of Cambridge to be the ideal transport and communications hub. The only other places to exert a similar degree of pull within the region seem to have been the coastal port of King's Lynn and the monastic towns of Norwich and Peterborough. However, unlike those towns, Cambridge specialized in the corn trade and had a chartered monopoly. The agricultural commodity market in Cambridge was integrated into the national market and followed similar trends, apart from wheat, where the influence of the export trade was strong.

Its administrative role as a county town, with a sheriff's court and as an administrative centre for the Bishop of Ely, attracted external investors to the town. The acquisition of the Dunning estates by Walter de Merton, founder of Merton College, Oxford, shows that social networks operating in the royal court and among administrators of the Bishop of Ely communicated information about opportunities in the Cambridge property market to external investors.

To sum up, there is no single answer to the question of why Cambridge was so successful in the late 13th century. A number of factors contributed to this. This book has identified these factors and shown how they interacted with each other. Cambridge was well positioned to serve its hinterland, and its hinterland was sufficiently well endowed with resources to facilitate the town's growth. Although the location of the town placed it off the major roads radiating from the capital, it was well integrated into the national economy. In particular, its long-distance social networks fostered both the growth of the urban economy and the growth of the university. The piety of the townspeople encouraged investment in social infrastructure, recycling profits from trade back into the community. Old wealth and new wealth coexisted and intermarried; social cohesion among property-owning families was a significant strength of the town. Cambridge's strength also lay, to some extent, in its freedom from weaknesses that afflicted other towns, in particular interference from local aristocrats, bishops and abbots. Its internal strengths, and freedom from external interventions, allowed Cambridge to share fully in the prosperity of the medieval Commercial Revolution.

8.6 Implications for future research

There are three main implications for future research; these concern sources, methods and themes in the history of medieval towns.

Every English town has its own individual strengths and weakness so far as sources are concerned. While the Hundred Rolls are a major strength of Cambridge, the town also has major weaknesses owing to missing early civic records. Future researchers may wish to identify more systematically the strengths and weaknesses of individual towns so far as their records are concerned. The Hundred Rolls can certainly be used to study other towns, notably Huntingdon, though in very large towns, such as London and Oxford, the coverage is incomplete. Many towns have early rentals, while surviving deeds provide detailed information on properties and their values. Smaller towns have good sources too, but their commercial activities tend to be on a smaller scale.[2]

This book has introduced new statistical methods into the study of medieval economic and urban history. They are, in fact, well-tried methods that have been used for many years in mainstream economic history. Thanks to modern software packages they are easy to implement. There is ample scope for extending these methods to other areas of research on the medieval economy.

Finally, there is an opportunity to develop some of the key themes that emerge from this book. These themes, concerned with property markets, urban topography, family and philanthropy are both distinct and related. They provide the basis for an integrated account of economic and social life in medieval towns. To develop these themes, greater use needs to be made of economic and sociological theories. For example, the economic theory of entrepreneurship sheds important light on the dynamics of the market economy, while the theory of social networks sheds light on the role of institutions, such as families and guilds, as channels of information flow. The recent growth of interest in the history of capitalism provides an opportunity to integrate the economic, social, technological and institutional aspects of economic evolution into studies of the development of medieval towns. Uniting primary source evidence with social science theory and statistical methods can help to fulfil the expectations set out by Raban, as summarized earlier. There is a wide range of sources waiting to be examined, and an unprecedented range of techniques available with which to analyse and interpret them.

Notes

1   Raban, *Second Domesday*, p 18.
2   Chris Dyer, 'Small Towns 1270–1540', *Cambridge Urban History* ed. D. M. Palliser (3 vols) I (Cambridge, 2000), pp 505–38.

References

Primary unpublished sources

Bodleian Library, Oxford

Bodleian MS Gough Cambridgeshire 1 General collections for the county and University of Cambridge with the Isle and Bishopric of Ely, extracted from the Charters, Registers, etc by Francis Blomefield, Clerk, late of Caius College and afterwards Rector of Fersfield in Norfolk: I Prior of Barnwell's Register (2 vols) I

Catalogue of the Books Relating to British Topography and Saxon and Norman Literature bequeathed to the Bodleian Library in the Year 1799 by Richard Gough Esquire (Oxford, 1814)

British Library

C.24.A.27(3) Oppidum Cantebrigiae, Richard Lyne's Map of Cambridge
MS Harley 5813, Excerpt Comprising Transcription of Corpus Christi Deeds
Cole MSS
Add. MS 5809, Friars of the Sack, fol. 85
Add. MS 5809, History of Barnwell Priory, fols 87–9
Add. MS 5810, Number of Houses and Inhabitants in Cambridge in 1728, fol. 190
Add. MS 5810, Index to Lyne's Map of Cambridge, 1574, fols 193–5
Add. MS 5813, History of St Clement's Church, fol. 38
Add. MS 5813, Various Deeds fols 32, 42, 43, 60–2
Add. MS 5813, Benefactors of the Guild of Our Lady (1315) fols 137–42
Add. MS 5821, History of Barton Manor and Deeds, fols 229–33
Add. MS 5821, Benjamin's House at the Tolbooth, fols 229–33

Add. MS 5826, Taxation and Advowsons Documents of 1291 from Bishop
 Grey's register, fols 171–88
Add. MS 5826, Account of the School of Pythagoras at Cambridge,
 fols 46–50
Add. MS 5832, Ancient Places in Cambridge, fols 214–15
Add. MS 5833, Mayors and Bailiffs of Cambridge to 1380

Cambridge University Library

University Archives, Luard 1 Letters patent of grant by Henry III to
 chancellor and masters allowing a five-yearly assessment of the rents of
 houses inhabited by scholars, 1266

Cambridgeshire Archives

City/PB Box X/70/1-10 Borough Treasurers' Accounts, 1422/3–1435/6
City/PB/Box 1/4 Cross Book fols 8a–9a

Cicely A. H. Howell Papers

Howell, Cicely A. H., 'Contrasting Communities: Arable and Marshland'
 (unpublished draft, 1979)

Corpus Christi College Archive, University of Cambridge

CCCC02/M/7/1 'Liber Albus'
CCCC/09 Deeds listed in online catalogue of Corpus Christi Deeds,
 available at https://janus.lib.cam.ac.uk/db/node.xsp?id=EAD%2FGBR
 %2F2938%2FCCCC09 (accessed 1 August 2017)

Harvard Library, Cambridge, Massachusetts

Harvard Map Collection, Oppidum Cantebrigiae, Richard Lyne's Map
 of Cambridge 1574

King's College Archive, University of Cambridge

KCAR/6/2/027/2/CAM/6 Grant from prior of the Hospital of St John of Jerusalem to the University of land in Cambridge, and subsequent grant, 1432–40

KCAR/6/027/2/CAM/18 Agreement between the provost of King's College and the mayor of Cambridge, 1445

KCAR/6/2/027/2/CAM/19 Feoffment of part of Mill Street by the mayor of Cambridge to Henry VI

KCAR/6/2/027/2/CAM/41 Sale of two tenements in St Mary's and St Edward's parishes

Merton College Archives, University of Oxford

Liber Ruber

Stevenson, W. H., *Calendar of Merton Deeds for Cambridgeshire* (n.d., Merton College Library)

Peterhouse Treasury, Peterhouse, University of Cambridge

Peterhouse, St Peter's College A1–3 and the Site of the College A1–29

The National Archives

C 143/367/3 Inquisitions taken as a result of applications to the Crown for licences to alienate land. John, duke of Lancaster, to grant the manor of Landbeach, with the advowson of its church, and messuages and land in Cambridge, Barnwell, Grantchester, and Coton, to the master and scholars of Corpus Christi College, 1369–70

E179 Database, available at http://www.nationalarchives.gov.uk/e179/default.asp (accessed 30 July 2017)

E 372/70 Tallage of 1225

JUST 1/81 Cambridgeshire Eyre of 1247 Foreign pleas roll, including essoins, 31 Henry III

JUST 1/82 Cambridgeshire Eyre of 1261, Roll of civil, foreign and crown pleas, jury calendar, essoins and attorneys 45 Henry III

JUST 1/83 Cambridgeshire Eyre of 1268 General oyer and terminer, lands given away as a result of the Barons' War, roll of pleas, presentments, amercements and jury calendar 53 Henry III

JUST 1/84 Cambridgeshire Eyre of 1272 Roll of civil and foreign pleas 56 Henry III

JUST 1/85 Cambridgeshire Eyre of 1272 Roll of crown pleas, 56 Henry III

JUST 1/86 Cambridgeshire Eyre of 1286 Rex roll of civil, foreign and crown pleas, gaol delivery, plaints, amercements and fines, jury calendar, essoins and attorneys, 14 Edward I

JUST 1/96 Cambridgeshire Eyre of 1299 Berwick's roll of civil, foreign, king's and crown pleas, gaol delivery, plaints, jury calendar, essoins and attorneys, 27 Edward I

SC5/CAMBRIDGE/TOWER/2 Barnwell Hundred Roll

SC5/CAMBS/TOWER/1/Parts1–3 Cambridge Borough Hundred Rolls

SC11/674 New Winchelsea, discussed at S. Alsford, *Florilegium Urbanum*, available at http://users.trytel.com/tristan/towns/florilegium/community/cmfabr28.html (accessed 23 April 2017)

Special Collections, 'Hundred Rolls and Eyre Veredicta', available at http://discovery.nationalarchives.gov.uk/details/r/C13523 (accessed 30 July 2017)

Primary published sources

Bateson, Mary (ed.), *Borough Customs* (2 vols) (London, 1904–6).

Bateson, Mary, *Cambridge Gild Records* (Cambridge, 1903)

Brand, P. (ed.), *Plea Rolls of the Exchequer of the Jews, VI: Edward I, 1279–81* (6 vols) (London, 2005)

Breay, Claire (ed.), *The Cartulary of Chatteris Abbey* (Woodbridge, 1999)

Close Rolls of the Reign of Henry III (14 vols) 1227–31 (London, 1908–1938)

Calendar of Close Rolls of Edward I (5 vols) 1272–1307 (London, 1970)

Calendar of Fine Rolls (22 vols), I–III 1272–1327 (London, 1911–62)

Calendar of Patent Rolls of Edward I (4 vols) 1272–1307 (London, 1893–1901)

Casson, Catherine, Mark Casson, John S. Lee and Katie Phillips, *Business and Community in Medieval England: The Cambridge Hundred Rolls Source Volume* (Bristol, 2020)

Cazel, Fred A. and Annarie P. Cazel (eds), *Rolls of the Fifteenth of the Ninth Year of the Reign of Henry III for Cambridgeshire, Lincolnshire and Wiltshire and Rolls of the Fortieth of the Seventeenth Year of the Reign of Henry III for Kent* (London, 1983)

Clark, John Willis (ed.), *Liber Memorandum Ecclesie de Bernewelle* (Cambridge, 1907)

Cohen, S. (ed.), *Plea Rolls of the Exchequer of the Jews, V: Edward I, 1277–9* (6 vols) (London, 1992)

Coss, P. R., *The Early Records of Medieval Coventry* (London, 1986)

Ekwall, Eilert (ed.), *Two Early London Subsidy Rolls* (London, 1951)

Emden, A. B., *Biographical Dictionary of the University of Cambridge to 1500* (Cambridge, 1963)

Evans, Nesta, *Cambridgeshire Hearth Tax Returns Michaelmas 1664*, British Records Society Hearth Tax Series, 1; Cambridgeshire Records Society, 15 (London, 2000)

Fairweather, Janet (ed.), *Liber Eliensis: A History of Isle of Ely from the Seventh Century to the Twelfth* (Woodbridge, 2005)

Feet of Fines of the Reign of Henry II and of the First Seven Years of the Reign of Richard I, AD 1182–96 (London, 1894)

Feet of Fines of the Tenth Year of the Reign of King Richard I, A. D. 1198 to A.D. 1199: Excepting those for the Counties of Bedford, Berkshire, Buckingham, Cambridge, Devon, and Dorset: Also a Roll of the King's Court in the Reign of King Richard (London, 1929)

Feltoe, C. L. and Ellis H. Minns (eds), *Vetus Liber Archidiaconi Eliensis* (Cambridge, 1917)

Fine Rolls, Henry III, 8/413, 1224, available at https://finerollshenry3.org.uk/home (accessed 17 October 2018)

Fine Rolls, C60/47, 7/299, 20 April 1250, available at https://finerollshenry3.org.uk/home (accessed 17 October 2018)

Flower, C. T., David Crook and Paul Brand (eds), *Rotuli Curiae Regis/Curia Regis Rolls* (10 vols) (London and Woodbridge, 1922–2006)

Fordham, Herbert George, 'Cambridgeshire Maps: An Annotated List of the Pre-Survey Maps of the County of Cambridge 1576–1800', *Proceedings of the Cambridge Antiquarian Society* 11 (1) (1905): 101–73

Foss, Edward, *Biographia Juridica: A Biographical Dictionary of the Judges of England from the Conquest* (9 vols) I (London, 1870)

Glasscock, R. E. (ed.), *The Lay Subsidy of 1334* (London, 1975)

Gray, J. Milner, *Biographical Notes on the Mayors of Cambridge* (Reprinted from *The Cambridge Chronicle*, 1922), pp. 1–11

Hackett, M. B., *The Original Statutes of Cambridge University: The Text and Its History* (Cambridge, 1970)

Hall, Catherine P. and J. R. Ravensdale (eds), *The West Fields of Cambridge* (Cambridge, 1976)

Harding, Vanessa and Laura Wright, (eds), *London Bridge: Selected Accounts and Rentals, 1381–1538* (London, 1995)

Hardy, Thomas (ed.), *Rotuli Litterarum Clausarum in Turri Londoniensi Asservati* (2 vols, 1833, 1844), I (London, 1833)

Harvey, P. D. A. (ed.), *Manorial Records of Cuxham, Oxfordshire, c.1200–1359* (Oxford and London, 1976)

Highfield, John R. L. (ed.), *The Early Rolls of Merton College: With an Appendix of Thirteenth-Century Oxford Charters* (Oxford, 1964)

Horrox, R. (ed.), *Selected Rentals and Accounts of Medieval Hull, 1293–1528* (York, 1983)

Hoskins, Philippa M. (ed.), *English Episcopal Acta 29, Durham 1241–83* (London, 2005)

Hunter, Joseph (ed.), *Fines, Sive, Pedes Finium: AD 1195–1214, I: Bedfordshire, Berkshire, Buckinghamshire, Cambridgeshire and Cornwall* (2 vols, 1835–44) (London, 1835)

Karn, Nicholas (ed.), *English Episcopal Acta 42: Ely 1198–1256* (London, 2013)

Leach, A. F., *Educational Charters and Documents, 598 to 1909* (Cambridge, 1911)

Letters, Samantha, *Online Gazetteer of Markets and Fairs in England and Wales to 1516*, available at http://www.history.ac.uk/cmh/gaz/gazweb2.html (accessed 12 August 2016)

Lunt, W. E., *The Valuation of Norwich* (Oxford, 1926)

Maitland, Frederic William and Mary Bateson (eds), *The Charters of the Borough of Cambridge* (Cambridge, 1901)

Maitland, Frederic William (ed.), *Three Rolls of the King's Court in the Reign of King Richard I, AD 1194–5* (London, 1891)

Maitland, F. W. (ed.), *Bracton's Note Book* (3 vols) (Cambridge, 1897)

Meekings, C. A. F., *Crown Pleas of the Wiltshire Eyre, 1249* (Devizes, 1961)

Meekings, Cecil A. F. and Philip Shearman, *Fitznells Cartulary: A Calendar of Bodleian Library MS. Rawlinson B430* (Guildford, 1968)

Miller, Edward (trans) and Frances Willmoth and Susan Oosthuizen (eds), *The Ely Coucher Book, 1249–50: The Bishop of Ely's Manors in the Cambridgeshire Fenland* (Cambridge, 2015)

Nelson, Alan H. (ed.), *Records of Early English Drama: Cambridge* (2 vols) (Toronto and London, 1989)

Nicholls, Mark and Kathryn McKee (eds), *The Library Treasures of St John's College, Cambridge* (London, 2014)

Palmer, William M., *Cambridgeshire Subsidy Rolls 1250–1695* (London, 1912)

Palmer, W. M. (ed.), *The Assizes held at Cambridge 1260: Being a Condensed Translation of Assize Roll 82 in the Public Record Office with an Introduction* (Linton, 1930)

Palmer, W. M. (ed.), *Cambridge Borough Documents* (Cambridge, 1931)

Jenkinson, H. (ed.), *Calendar of the Plea Rolls of the Exchequer of the Jews, III: Edward I, 1275–7* (6 vols) (London, 1925)

Pipe Rolls 98 vols (London, 1884–2016) especially the published rolls for the years 1130–1224, 1230 and 1242, vols 1–9, 11–19, 21–58, 50, 52–8, 60, 62, 64, 66, 68, 73, 75, 77, 80, 85, 86, 89, 91, 93, 94, 95, 98

Prichard, Michael (ed.), *Gonville & Caius College: The Statutes of the Founders* (Woodbridge, 2017)

Public Record Office, *Lists and Indexes: Lists of Sheriffs for England and Wales from the Earliest Times to AD 1831* (London, 1898)

Richardson, H. G. (ed.), *Calendar of the Plea Rolls of the Exchequer of the Jews, IV: Henry III, 1272; Edward I, 1275–1277* (6 vols) (London, 1972)

Rigg, J. M. (ed.), *Calendar of the Plea Rolls of the Exchequer of the Jews, I: Henry III, 1218–1272* (6 vols) (London, 1905)

Rigg, J. M. (ed.), *Calendar of the Plea Rolls of the Exchequer of the Jews, II: Edward I, 1273–5* (6 vols) (Edinburgh, 1910)

Rogers, Mary and May Wallace (eds), *Norwich Landgable Assessment, 1568–70* (Norfolk Record Society, 58) (Norwich, 1999)

Rotuli Hundredorum Temp. Henry III and Edward I., in Turr' Lond' et in Curia Receptæ Scaccarij Westm. Asservati (2 vols) (London, 1812 and 1818)

Rye, Walter, *Pedes Finium or Fines Relating to the County of Cambridge, Levied in the King's Court from the Seventh Year of the Reign of Richard I to the End of the Reign of Richard III* (Cambridge, 1891)

Sheffield Hundred Rolls Project, available at http://www.roffe.co.uk/shrp.htm (accessed 2 April 2017)

Sheriff of Cambridgeshire and Huntingdonshire, available at https://en.wikipedia.org/wiki/Sheriff_of_Cambridgeshire_and_Huntingdonshire (accessed 29 October 2018)

Stenton, Doris Mary (ed.), *Pleas before the King and His Justices 1198–1202 I: Introduction with Appendix Containing Essoins 1199–1201, A King's Roll of 1200 and Writs 1190–1200* (4 vols) (London, 1952–67)

Stenton, Doris Mary (ed.), *Pleas before the King and His Justices 1198–1202 II: Fragments of Rolls from the Years 1198, 1201 and 1202* (4 vols) (London, 1952–67)

Stenton, Doris Mary (ed.), *Pleas before the King and His Justices 1198–1202 III: Rolls or Fragments of Rolls from the Years 1199, 1201 and 1203–6* (4 vols) (London, 1952–67)

Stenton, Doris Mary (ed.), *Pleas before the King and His Justices 1198–1202 IV: Rolls or Fragments of Rolls from the Years 1207–12* (4 vols) (London, 1952–67)

Stevenson, W. H. (ed.), *Rental of the Houses in Gloucester AD 1455: From a Roll in the Possession of the Corporation of Gloucester* (Gloucester, 1890)

Turner, G. J., *A Calendar of the Feet of Fines Relating to the County of Huntingdon Levied in the King's Court from the Fifth Year of Richard I to the End of the Reign of Elizabeth, 1194–1603* (Cambridge, 1913)

Underwood, Malcolm (ed.), *Cartulary of the Hospital of St. John the Evangelist* (Cambridge, 2008)

Williams, Ann and G. H. Martin (eds), *Domesday Book: A Complete Translation* (London, 2002)

Willis Clark, John (ed.), *Liber Memorandum Ecclesie de Bernewelle* (Cambridge, 1907).

Secondary sources

Books and articles

Aberth, John, 'The Black Death in the Diocese of Ely: The Evidence of the Bishop's Register', *Journal of Medieval History* 21 (1995): 275–87

Addyman, P. V. and Martin Biddle (1965), 'Medieval Cambridge: Recent Finds and Excavations', *Proceedings of the Cambridge Antiquarian Society* 58 (1965): 74–137

Alfani, Guido and Roberta Frigeni, 'Inequality (Un)perceived: The Emergence of a Discourse on Economic Inequality from the Middle Ages to the Age of Revolution', *The Journal of European Economic History* 45 (1) (2016): 21–66

Anon, *The History and Antiquities of Barnwell Abbey and of Sturbridge Fair* (London, 1786)

Aston, T. H., G. D. Duncan and T. A. R. Evans, 'The Medieval Alumni of the University of Cambridge', *Past and Present* 86 (1980): 9–86

Atkins, Rob, 'Between River, Priory and Town: Excavations at the Former Cambridge Regional College Site, Brunswick, Cambridge', *Proceedings of the Cambridge Antiquarian Society* 101 (2012): 7–22

Atkinson, T. D., 'Old Cambridge Houses', *Proceedings of the Cambridge Antiquarian Society* 13 (1) (1909): 77–81

Baigent, F. J. and J. E. Millard, *A History of the Ancient Town and Manor of Basingstoke* (Basingstoke, 1889)

Bailey, Mark, *A Marginal Economy?: East Anglian Breckland in the Later Middle Ages* (Cambridge, 1989)

Baker, Nigel and Richard Holt, *Urban Growth and the Medieval Church: Gloucester and Worcester* (Aldershot, 2004)

Baker, N., J. Brett and R. Jones, *Bristol: A Worshipful Town and Famous City: An Archaeological Assessment* (Oxford, 2017)

Baker, N., P. Hughes and R. K. Morriss, *The Houses of Hereford 1200–1700* (Oxford, 2017)

Baker, Thomas and John. E. B. Mayor (eds), *History of the College of St. John the Evangelist, Cambridge* (2 vols) (Cambridge, 1869)

Ballard, Adolphus, *The Domesday Boroughs* (Oxford, 1904)

Ballard, Adolphus, *The English Borough in the Twelfth Century* (Cambridge, 1914)

Bentham, James, *The History and Antiquities of the Conventual and Cathedral Church of Ely* (Cambridge, 1771)

Beresford, Maurice, *New Towns of the Middle Ages: Town Plantation in England, Wales and Gascony* (Stroud, 1988)

Binns, John and Peter Meadows (eds), *Great St. Mary's: Cambridge's University Church* (Cambridge, 2000)

Blackfriars, Cambridge, available at http://www.blackfriarscambridge.org.uk/medieval-priory/ (accessed 9 January 2018)

Bonney, Margaret, *Lordship and the Urban Community: Durham and its Overlords, 1250–1540* (Cambridge, 1990)

Boyle, M. A. and K. A. Kiel, 'A Survey of House Price Hedonic Studies of the Impact of Environmental Externalities', *Journal of Real Estate Literature* 9 (2) (2009): 117–44

Brand, Paul, 'Henry II and the Creation of English Common Law', *Henry II: New Interpretations*, ed. Christopher Harper-Bill and Paul Brand (Woodbridge, 2007), pp 215–41

Braudel, Fernand, *Civilization and Capitalism, 15th–18th Century* (3 vols) (London, 2002)

Bridbury, A. R., 'English Provincial Towns in the Later Middle Ages', *Economic History Review* 34 (1981): 1–24

Briggs, Chris, 'Monitoring Demesne Managers through the Manor Court before and after the Black Death', *Survival and Discord in Medieval Society: Essays in Honour of Christopher Dyer* ed. Richard Goddard, John Langdon and Miriam Müller (Turnhout, 2010), pp 179–95

Briggs, Chris, 'Peasants, Lords, and Commerce: Market Regulation at Balsham, Cambridgeshire, in the Early Fourteenth Century', *Peasants and Lords in the Medieval English Economy: Essays in Honour of Bruce M. S. Campbell* ed. Maryanne Kowaleski, John Langdon and Phillipp R. Schofield (Turnhout, 2015), pp 247–96

Brink, Daphne H., *The Parish of St. Edward, King and Martyr, Cambridge: Survival of a Late Medieval Appropriation* (Cambridge, 1992)

Britnell, R. H., *The Commercialisation of English Society 1000–1500* (Cambridge, 1993)

Britnell, R., 'The Black Death in English Towns', *Urban History* 21 (1994): 195–210

Britnell, R., 'A History of Lavendon', available at https://nigelstickells.files.wordpress.com/2015/06/history-of-lavendon.pdf (accessed 20 February 2018)

Britnell, R. H., 'Specialisation of Work in England, 1100–1300', *Economic History Review* 54 (2001): 1–16

Britnell, R. H. and B. M. S. Campbell, *A Commercialising Economy: England 1086 to c. 1300* (Manchester, 1995)

Britnell, Richard, 'The Economy of British Towns 600–1300', in *Cambridge Urban History* ed. D. M. Palliser (3 vols) I (Cambridge, 2000), pp 105–26

Britnell, R. and J. Hatcher (eds), *Progress and Problems in Medieval England: Essays in Honour of Edward Miller* (Cambridge, 1996)

Brittain Bouchard, Constance, *Holy Entrepreneurs: Cistercians, Knights and Economic Exchange in Twelfth-Century Brittany* (Ithaca, NY, and London, 1991)

Brodrick, George C., *Memorials of Merton College* (Oxford, 1885)

Brooke, Christopher, *A History of Gonville and Caius College* (Woodbridge, 1985)

Brooke, Christopher, *Churches and Churchmen in Medieval Europe* (London, 1999)

Brooke, C. N. L., 'Gonville [Gonvile], Edmund (d. 1351)', *Oxford Dictionary of National Biography* ed. David Cannadine (Oxford, 2004)

Brooke, Christopher, Daniel Riehl Leader, Victor Morgan and Peter Searby, *A History of the University of Cambridge* (4 vols) 1 (Cambridge, 1988)

Brown, M. and K. Stevenson (eds), *Medieval St Andrews: Church, Cult, City* (Woodbridge, 2017)

Brundage, James A., 'The Cambridge Faculty of Canon Law and the Ecclesiastical Courts of Ely', *Medieval Cambridge: Essays on the Pre-Reformation University* ed. Patrick Zutshi (Woodbridge, 1993), pp 21–46

Bryan, Peter, *Cambridge: The Shaping of the City*, new ed. (Cambridge, 2008)

Bryan, Peter and Nick Wise, 'A Reconstruction of the Medieval Cambridge Market Place', *Proceedings of the Cambridge Antiquarian Society* 91 (2002): 73–87

Butcher, A. F., 'Rent, Population and Economic Change in Late-Medieval Newcastle', *Northern History* 14 (1978): 67–77

Butcher, A. F., 'Rent and the Urban Economy: Oxford and Canterbury in the Later Middle Ages', *Southern History* 1 (1979): 11–43

Butler, Lawrence, *Church of St Peter off Castle Street Cambridge* (London, 2007)

Cam, Helen M., 'Cambridgeshire Sheriffs in the Thirteenth Century', *Proceedings of the Cambridge Antiquarian Society* 25 (1924): 78–102

Cam, Helen M., 'The King's Government, as Administered by the Greater Abbots of East Anglia', *Proceedings of the Cambridge Antiquarian Society* 29 (1928): 25–49

Cam, Helen M., *The Hundred and the Hundred Rolls: An Outline of Local Government in Medieval England* (London, 1930)

Cam, Helen M., 'The Origin of the Borough of Cambridge: A Consideration of Prof. Carl Stephenson's Theories', *Proceedings of the Cambridge Antiquarian Society* 35 (1935): 33–53

Cam, Helen M., *Liberties and Communities in Medieval England* (Cambridge, 1944)

Cam, Helen M., 'The City of Cambridge', *A History of the County of Cambridge and the Isle of Ely, III: The City and University of Cambridge, Victoria History of the Counties of England* ed. J. P. C. Roach (10 vols) (London, 1959), pp 1–149

Campbell, B. M. S., *English Seigniorial Agriculture 1250–1450* (Cambridge, 2000)

Cantoni, Davide and Noam Yuchtman, 'Medieval Universities, Legal Institutions, and the Commercial Revolution', *The Quarterly Journal of Economics* 129 (2) (2014): 823–87

Cardale Babington, Charles, *History of the Infirmary and Chapel of the Hospital and College of St John the Evangelist at Cambridge* (Cambridge, 1874)

Casson, Catherine and Mark Casson, 'Location, Location, Location? Analysing Property Rents in Medieval Gloucester', *Economic History Review* 69 (2) (2016): 575–99

Casson, Catherine, Mark Casson, John S. Lee and Katie Phillips, 'Compassionate Capitalism in the Middle Ages: Profit and Philanthropy in Medieval Cambridge', http://voxeu.org/article/compassionate-capitalism-middle-ages (accessed 11 May 2017)

Casson, Catherine and Mark Casson, 'Property Rents in Medieval English Towns: Fourteenth-Century Hull', *Urban History* 46 (3) (2019): 374–97

Casson, Catherine and Mark Casson, '"To Dispose of Wealth in Works of Charity": Entrepreneurship and Philanthropy in Medieval England', *Business History Review* (forthcoming)

Casson, Catherine and Mark Casson, 'The Economy of Medieval English Towns: Property Values and Rents in Bristol, 1200–1500', working paper

Casson, Mark and Catherine Casson, *The Entrepreneur in History: From Medieval Merchant to Modern Business Leader* (Basingstoke, 2013)

Casson, Mark and Catherine Casson, 'The History of Entrepreneurship: Medieval Origins to a Modern Phenomenon?', *Business History* 56 (8) (2014): 1223–42

Cessford, Craig, 'The St. John's Hospital Cemetery and Environs, Cambridge: Contextualizing the Medieval Urban Dead', *Archaeological Journal* 172 (2015): 52–120

Cessford, Craig and Alison Dickens, 'The Origins and Early Development of Chesterton', *Proceedings of the Cambridge Antiquarian Society* 93 (2004): 125–42

Cessford, Craig and Alison Dickens, 'Castle Hill, Cambridge: Excavation of Saxon, Medieval and Post-medieval Deposits, Saxon Execution Site and a Medieval Coinhoard', *Proceedings of the Cambridge Antiquarian Society* 94 (2005): 73–102

Clark, G., 'Land Rental Values and the Agrarian Economy: England and Wales 1500–1914', *European Review of Economic History* 6 (3) (2002): 281–308

Clark, J. W. and J. E. Foster, 'History of a Site in Senate House Yard with Some Notes on Occupiers', *Proceedings of the Cambridge Antiquarian Society* 13 (1) (1909): 120–42

Clarke, H., S. Pearson, M. Mate and K. Parfitt, *Sandwich: The 'Completest Medieval Town in England': A Study of the Town and Port From its Origins to 1600* (Oxford, 2010)

Cobban, A. B., *The King's Hall Within the University of Cambridge in the Later Middle Ages* (Cambridge, 1969)

Cobban, Alan B., 'Badew, Richard (d. 1361)', *Oxford Dictionary of National Biography* ed. David Cannadine (Oxford, 2004)

Colson, Justin, 'Commerce, Clusters, and Community: A Re-Evaluation of the Occupational Geography of London, c. 1400–c. 1550', *Economic History Review* 69 (2016): 104–30

Cooper, Charles Henry, *Annals of Cambridge, I* (5 vols) (Cambridge, 1842)

Corley, T. A. B., 'Historical Biographies of Entrepreneurs', *Oxford Handbook of Entrepreneurship* ed. M. Casson, B. Yeung, A. Basu and N. Wadeson (Oxford, 2006), pp 138–60

Cranage, D. H. S. and H. P. Stokes, 'The Augustinian Friary in Cambridge and the History of its Site', *Proceedings of the Cambridge Antiquarian Society* 22 (1921): 53–75

Cullan, Patricia H., '"For Pore People Harberles": What Was the Function of the Maisonsdieu?', *Trade, Devotion and Governance: Papers in Later Medieval History* ed. Dorothy J. Clayton, Richard G. Davies and Peter McNiven (Stroud, 1994), pp 36–52

Cunningham, Archdeacon, 'The Problem as to the Changes in the Course of the Cam since Roman Times', *Proceedings of the Cambridge Antiquarian Society* 14 (1) (1909): 74–85

Darby, H. C., *The Domesday Geography of Cambridgeshire* (Cambridge, 1936)

Daunton, Claire Gobbi and Elizabeth A. New, 'The Masters of Trinity Hall in the Later Middle Ages', *Commemoration in Medieval Cambridge*, ed. John S. Lee and Christian Steer (Woodbridge, 2018), pp 61–89

Davis, James, *Medieval Market Morality: Life, Law and Ethics in the English Marketplace, 1200–1500* (Cambridge, 2012)

Davis, R. H. C., *The Early History of Coventry* (London, 1976)

Demidowicz, G., *Medieval Birmingham: The Borough Rentals of 1296 and 1344–5* (Stratford-upon-Avon, 2008)

Denton, J. H., 'The Valuation of the Ecclesiastical Benefices of England and Wales in 1291–2', *Historical Research* 66 (1993): 231–50

Denton, J. H., 'The 1291 Valuation of the Churches of the Ely Diocese', *Proceedings of the Cambridge Antiquarian Society* 90 (2001): 69–80

Dickens, Alison, 'A New Building at the Dominican Priory, Emmanuel College, Cambridge, and Associated Fourteenth Century Bawsey Floor Tiles', *Proceedings of the Cambridge Antiquarian Society* 87 (1998): 71–80

Dickens, Alison and Craig Cessford, 'Cambridge Historic City Centre Revealed', *Current Archaeology* 208 (March/April 2007): 22–31

Dobson, R. B., *The Peasants' Revolt in 1381* (London, 1970)

Dobson, R. B., 'The Jews of Medieval Cambridge', *Jewish Historical Studies* 32 (1990–2): 1–24

Dobson, R. B., 'Bingham [Byngham], William (d. 1451)', *Oxford Dictionary of National Biography* ed. David Cannadine (Oxford, 2004)

Dodwell, B., 'The Free Tenantry of the Hundred Rolls', *Economic History Review* 14 (2) (1944): 163–171

Douglas, David, *The Social Structure of Medieval East Anglia* (Oxford, 1927)

Douglas, David C. (ed.), *Feudal Documents from the Abbey of Bury St Edmunds* (London, 1932)

Dugdale, William, John Caley, Henry Ellis and Bulkeley Bandinel (eds), *Monasticon Anglicanum, II* (6 vols) (London, 1846)

Dunse, N. and C. Jones, 'A Hedonic Price Model of Office Rents', *Journal of Property Valuation and Investment* 16 (3) (1983): 297–312

Dyer, Alan, *Decline and Growth in English Towns 1400–1640* (Cambridge, 1995)

Dyer, Alan, 'Ranking Lists of English Medieval Towns', *Cambridge Urban History* ed. D. M. Palliser (3 vols) I (Cambridge, 2000), pp 755–7

Dyer, C., 'The Archaeology of Medieval Small Towns', *Medieval Archaeology* 47 (1) (2003): 85–114

Dyer, C., 'Small Towns 1270–1540', *Cambridge Urban History* ed. D. M. Palliser (3 vols) I (Cambridge, 2000), pp 505–38

Dyer, Christopher, *An Age of Transition? Economy and Society in England in the Later Middle Ages* (Oxford, 2005)

Dyer, Christopher, *A Country Merchant, 1495–1520: Trading and Farming at the End of the Middle Ages* (Oxford, 2011)

Dyer, G., *The Privileges of the University of Cambridge* (2 vols) I (London, 1824)

Edkins, Jo, *Walks around Cambridge*, available at http://gwydir.demon.co.uk/jo/walks/ (accessed 1 July 2017)

Ellis, Dorothy M. and L. F. Salzman, 'Religious Houses', *A History of the County of Cambridge and the Isle of Ely, II: Victoria History of the Counties of England* ed. L. F. Salzman (10 vols) III (Oxford, 1948), pp 197–319.

Evans, C., A. Dickens and D. A. H. Richmond, 'Cloister Communities: Archaeological and Architectural Investigations in Jesus College, Cambridge, 1988–97', *Proceedings of the Cambridge Antiquarian Society* 86 (1997): 91–144

Faber, T. E., *An Intimate History of the Parish of St Clement* (Cambridge, 2006)

Fanfani, Amintore, *Catholicism, Protestantism and Capitalism* (London, 1935)

Farrer, William, *Feudal Cambridgeshire* (Cambridge, 1920)

Fleming, Peter, *Time, Space and Power in Later Medieval Bristol*, available at https://eprints.uwe.ac.uk (2013) (accessed 26 February 2015)

Fowler, Joseph, *Medieval Sherborne* (Sherborne, 1951)

Franks, Michael, *The Clerk of Basingstoke: A Life of Walter de Merton* (Oxford, 2003)

Fuller, Thomas, ed. Marmaduke Prickett and Thomas Wright, *The History of the University from the Conquest to the Year 1634* (Cambridge, [1655] 1840)

Galloway, James A., 'One Market or Many? London and the Grain Trade of England', *Trade, Urban Hinterlands and Market Integration, c.1300–1600: A Collection of Working Papers Given at a Conference Organised by the Centre for Metropolitan History and Supported by the Economic and Social Research Council, 7 July 1999 (Centre for Metropolitan History, Working Papers, 3)* ed. James A. Galloway (London, 2000), pp 23–42

Goddard, Richard, *Lordship and Medieval Urbanisation: Coventry, 1043–1355* (Woodbridge, 2004)

Goddman, A. W., *A Little History of St. Botolph's, Cambridge* (Cambridge, 1922)

Goldberg, P. J. P., *Women, Work and Life Cycle in a Medieval Economy: Women in York and Yorkshire c.1300–1520* (Oxford, 1992)

Gottfried, Robert S., *Bury St Edmunds and the Urban Crisis: 1290–1539* (Princeton, NJ, 1982)

Gray, Arthur, *The Priory of St Radegund, Cambridge* (London, 1892)

Gray, Arthur, *The Dual Origin of the Town of Cambridge* (London, 1908)

Gray, Arthur, 'The Ford and Bridge of Cambridge', *Proceedings of the Cambridge Antiquarian Society* 14 (2) (1910): 126–39

Gray, Arthur, *Cambridge and its Story* (London, 1912)

Gray, Arthur and Frederick Brittain, *A History of Jesus College Cambridge* (London, 1979)

Gray, J. M., *The School of Pythagoras (Merton Hall)* (Cambridge, 1932)

Gray, J. M., 'The Barnwell Canons and the Papal Court at Avignon', *Proceedings of the Cambridge Antiquarian Society* 33 (1933): 98–107

Gray, Ronald and Peter Stubbings, *Cambridge Street Names: Their Origins and Associations* (Cambridge, 2000)

Greenway, Diana E., 'A Newly Discovered Fragment of the Hundred Rolls of 1279–80', *Journal of Society of Archivists* 7 (2) (1982): 73–7

Guerriero, Carmine, 'The Medieval Origins of a Culture of Corporation and Inclusive Political Institutions', Working Paper (ACLE University of Amsterdam, 2013), available at http://EconPapers.repec.org/RePEc:pra:mprapa:70879 (accessed 1 March 2017)

Hall, Catherine, 'Quit-rents', *Letter of the Corpus Association* 61 (1982): 49–54

Hall, Catherine P., 'In Search of Sabina: A Study in Cambridge Topography', *Proceedings of the Cambridge Antiquarian Society* 65 (1973–4): 60–78

Hall, Catherine P., 'The Gild of Corpus Christi and the Foundation of Corpus Christi College: An Investigation of the Documents', *Medieval Cambridge: Essays on the Pre-Reformation University* ed. Patrick Zutshi (Woodbridge, 1993), pp 65–91

Hall, Catherine P. and Roger Lovatt, 'The Site and Foundation of Peterhouse', *Proceedings of the Cambridge Antiquarian Society* 78 (1990): 5–46

Hall, Peter A. and David Soskice, 'Introduction', *Varieties of Capitalism: The Institutional Foundations of Comparative Advantage* ed. Peter A. Hall and David Soskice (Oxford, 2001), pp 1–91

Harvey, Barbara, *Westminster Abbey and Its Estates in the Middle Ages* (Oxford, 1977)

Harvey, P. D. A., *A Medieval Oxfordshire Village: Cuxham, 1240–1400* (London, 1965)

Hatcher, John, 'Commemoration of Benefactors Address, 4 December 2009: "For the Souls of the Departed in the Mortality and After the Year of the Lord 1349 and After"', *The Letter* (Corpus Christi College, Cambridge) 89 (2010): 14–23

Hemmeon, Morley de Wolf, *Burgage Tenure in Medieval England* (Cambridge, MA, 1914)

Henderson, Bernard W., *Merton College* (London, 1899)

Hesse, Mary, 'The East Fields of Cambridge', *Proceedings of the Cambridge Antiquarian Society* 96 (2007): 143–60

Hilton, R. H., 'Some Problems of Urban Real Property in the Middle Ages', *Socialism, Capitalism and Economic Growth: Essays Presented to Maurice Dobb* ed. C. H. Feinstein (Cambridge, 1967), pp 326–37

Hilton, Rodney H., *Medieval Peasant Movements and the English Rising of 1381* (2nd ed., Basingstoke, 2004)

Hilton, Rodney H., 'Towns in English Feudal Society', *Urban History Yearbook* (1982), pp 7–13, reprinted in Hilton, *Class Conflict and the Crisis of Feudalism* (London, 1985), pp 175–86

Hodgson, J. C., 'The "Domus Dei" of Newcastle Otherwise St Katherine's Hospital on the Sandhill', *Archaeologia Aeliana* 3rd series XIV (1917): 191–220

Holford, M. L. and K. J. Stringer, *Border Liberties and Loyalties* (Edinburgh, 2010)

Holt, Richard, 'Society and Population 600–1300', *The Cambridge Urban History of Britain, I: 600–1540* ed. D. M. Palliser (3 vols) (Cambridge, 2000), pp 79–104

Horrox, Rosemary, *The Changing Plan of Hull, 1290–1650* (Hull, 1978)

Horrox, Rosemary, 'Cambridge [Cantebrig], Sir John (d. 1335)', *Oxford Dictionary of National Biography* ed. David Cannadine (Oxford, 2004)

Howell, Cicely A. H., 'Stability and Change 1300–1700: The Socio-Economic Context of the Self-Perpetuating Family Farm in England', *Journal of Peasant Studies* 2 (4) (1975): 468–82

Howell, Cicely A. H, 'Peasant Inheritance Customs in the Midlands, 1280–1700', *Land and Inheritance: Rural Society in Western Europe, 1200–1800* ed. Jack Goody, Joan Thirsk and E. P. Thompson (Cambridge, 1978), pp 112–55

Howell, Cicely A. H., *Land, Family and Inheritance in Transition; Kibworth Harcourt 1280–1700* (Cambridge, 1983)

Howell, Martha C., *Commerce before Capitalism in Europe, 1300–1600* (Cambridge, 2010)

Hughes, H. C., 'Windmills in Cambridgeshire and the Isle of Ely', *Proceedings of the Cambridge Antiquarian Society* 31 (1931): 17–29

Hundley, Catherine E., 'Holy Sepulchre, Cambridge in the Twelfth Century' (unpublished paper presented at the British Archaeological Association Conference, Cambridge in 2018)

Jervis, B., 'Assessing Urban Fortunes in Six Late Medieval Ports: An Archaeological Application of Assemblage Theory', *Urban History* 44 (1) (2017): 2–26

Jewell, Helen M., *English Local Administration in the Middle Ages* (London, 1972)

Jones, Chester H., 'The Chapel of St Mary Magdalene at Sturbridge, Cambridge', *Proceedings of the Cambridge Antiquarian Society* 28 (1927): 126–50

Jordan, W. K., *Philanthropy in England 1480–1660: A Study of the Changing Pattern of English Social Aspirations* (London, 1959)

Jurkowski, Maureen, 'The History of Clerical Taxation in England and Wales, 1173–1663: The Findings of the E 179 Project', *Journal of Ecclesiastical History* 67 (2016): 53–81

Kanzaka, Junichi, 'Villein Rents in Thirteenth-Century England: An Analysis of the Hundred Rolls of 1279–1280', *Economic History Review* 55 (4) (2002): 593–619

Kaye, J. M., *Medieval English Conveyances* (Cambridge, 2009)

Keats-Rohan, K. S. B., *Domesday People, Domesday Descendants: A Prosopography of Persons Occurring in English Documents 1066–1166* (2 vols) (Woodbridge, 1999 and 2002)

Keene, Derek, 'The Property Market in English Towns AD 1100–1600', *D'Une Ville a L'Autre: Structures, Materielles et Organisati in de L'Espace dans les Villes Europeens, VIIIᵉ–XVIᵉ Siecle*, ed. J.-C. Maire Vigeur (Rome, 1989), pp 201–26

Keene, Derek, *Survey of Medieval Winchester, II Part I: Winchester in the Later Middle Ages* (2 vols) (Oxford, 1985)

Keene, Derek and Vanessa Harding, *A Survey of Sources for Property Holding in London before the Great Fire* (London, 1985)

Kermode, Jennifer, *Medieval Merchants; York, Beverley and Hull in the Later Middle Ages* (Cambridge, 1998)

Kermode, Jennifer, 'The Greater Towns 1300–1540', *The Cambridge Urban History of Britain, I: 600–1540*, ed. D. M. Palliser (3 vols) (Cambridge, 2000), pp 441–66

Kosminsky, E. 'The Hundred Rolls of 1279–80 as a Source for English Agrarian History', *Economic History Review* 3 (1) (1931): 16–44

Kowaleski, Maryanne, *Local Markets and Regional Trade in Medieval Exeter* (Cambridge, 1995)

Kowaleski, Maryanne, 'The History of Urban Families in Medieval England', *Journal of Medieval History* 14 (1) (1998): 47–63

Kowaleski, Maryanne, 'A Consumer Economy', *A Social History of England 1200–1500* ed. R. Horrox and M. Ormrod (Oxford, 2004), pp 238–59

Lancaster, J. C. and M. Tomlinson, 'Introduction', *The Victoria History of the County of Warwick, VIII: The City of Coventry and Borough of Warwick*, ed. W. B. Stephens (8 vols) (London, 1969)

Langdon, John and James Masschaele, 'Commercial Activity and Population Growth in Medieval England', *Past and Present* 190 (2006): 35–81

Langton, John, 'Late Medieval Gloucester: Some Data from a Rental of 1455', *Transactions of the Institute of British Geographers*, new series, 2 (1977): 259–77

Lee, John S. 'Tracing Regional and Local Changes in Population and Wealth during the Later Middle Ages using Taxation Records: Cambridgeshire, 1334–1563', *Local Population Studies* 69 (2002): 32–50

Lee, John S., *Cambridge and Its Economic Region* (Hatfield, 2005)

Lee, John S., 'The Role of Fairs in Late Medieval England', *Town and Countryside in the Age of the Black Death: Essays in Honour of John Hatcher*, ed. Steve Rigby and Mark Bailey (Turnhout, 2012), pp 407–37

Lee, John S., 'Piped Water Supplies Managed by Civic Bodies in Medieval English Towns', *Urban History*, 41 (2014): 369–93

Lee, John S., 'Decline and Growth in the Late Medieval Fenland: The Examples of Outwell and Upwell', *Proceedings of the Cambridge Antiquarian Society* 104 (2015): 137–47

Lee, John S., *The Medieval Clothier* (Woodbridge, 2018)

Lee, John S., 'Monuments and Memory: A University Town in Late Medieval England', *Commemoration in Medieval Cambridge* ed. John S. Lee and Christian Steer (Woodbridge, 2018), pp 10–33

Lee, John S., 'Trinity and the Town', *History of Trinity College, Cambridge* ed. E. Leedham-Green and A. Green, I: 1317–1742 (forthcoming)

Leedham-Green, E., *A Concise History of the University of Cambridge* (Cambridge, 1996)

Liddy, Christian D., *Contesting the City: The Politics of Citizenship in English Towns, 1250–1530* (Oxford, 2007)

Lilley, K. D., 'Urban Planning after the Black Death: Townscape Transformation in Later Medieval England (1350–1530)', *Urban History* 42 (1) (2015): 22–42

Lineham, P. (ed.), *St John's College Cambridge: A History* (Woodbridge, 2011)

Lloyd, A. H., 'The Parish Church of Madingley', *Proceedings of the Cambridge Antiquarian Society* 31 (1931): 105–23

Lobel, Mary D., *Historic Towns Atlas: Cambridge* (London, 1975)

Loewe, Andreas, 'Michaelhouse: Hervey de Stanton's Cambridge Foundation', *Church History* 90 (4) (2010): 599–608

Lord, E., *The Knights Templar in Britain* (Harlow, 2002)

Lovatt, Roger and Marie Lovatt, 'The Religious Life of the Townsmen of Medieval Cambridge', *Catholics in Cambridge* ed. Nicholas Rogers (Leominster, 2003), pp 4–21

Macfarlane, Alan, *The Making of the Modern World: Visions from the West and East* (Basingstoke, 2002)

Madox, Thomas, *Firma Burgi* (London, 1726)

Maitland, Frederic William, *Township and Borough* (Cambridge, 1898)

Martin, D. and B., *New Winchelsea, Sussex: A Medieval Port Town* (King's Lynn, 2004)

Martin, Geoffrey H., 'Merton, Walter of', *Oxford Dictionary of National Biography* ed. David Cannadine (Oxford, 2004)

Martin, Geoffrey H. and John L. R. Highfield, *A History of Merton College, Oxford* (Oxford, 1997)

Masschaele, James, 'Transport Costs in Medieval England', *Economic History Review,* 2nd Series 46 (1993): 266–79

Massing, J. M. and N. Zeeman (eds), *King's College Chapel 1515–2015: Art, Music and Religion in Cambridge* (London, 2014)

Mayer, Colin, *Prosperity: Better Business Makes the Greater Good* (Oxford, 2018)

McGrory, David, *A History of Coventry* (Chichester, 2003)

Medieval Prosopography: History and Collective Biography, 1–34 (1980–2019)

Meeres, Frank, *A History of Bury St Edmunds* (Chichester, 2002)

Merewether, Henry A. and Archibald J. Stephens, *The History of the Boroughs and Municipal Corporations of the United Kingdom* (3 vols) I (Brighton, 1835)

Midmer, Roy, *English Medieval Monasteries: A Summary (1066–1540)* (London, 1979)

Miller, Edward, 'Baldwin Blancgernun and His Family: Early Benefactors of the Hospital of St. John the Evangelist in Cambridge', *The Eagle* 53 (234) (1948): 73–9

Miller, Edward, *The Abbey and Bishopric of Ely: The Social History of the Ecclesiastical Estate from the Tenth Century* (Cambridge, 1951)

Miller, Edward and John Hatcher, *Medieval England: Towns, Commerce and Crafts 1086–1348* (London, 1995)

Mingay, G. E. (ed.), *The Agricultural Revolution: Changes in Agriculture, 1650–1880* (London, 1977)

Mokyr, Joel, *Economics of the Industrial Revolution* (London, 1985)

Mokyr, Joel, *A Culture of Growth: The Origins of the Modern Economy* (Princeton, NJ, 2018)

Murray, James M., 'Entrepreneurs and Entrepreneurship in Medieval Europe', *The Invention of Enterprise: Entrepreneurship from Ancient Mesopotamia to Modern Times* ed. David S. Landes, Joel Mokyr and William J. Baumol (Princeton, NJ, and Oxford, 2010), pp 88–106

Musson, Anthony and W. M. Ormrod, *The Evolution of English Justice: Law, Politics and Society in the Fourteenth Century* (Basingstoke, 1999)

Muth, Richard F. and Allen C. Goodman, *The Economics of Housing Markets* (London, 1989)

National Archives, 'Exchequer of the Jews Plea Rolls', available at http://discovery.nationalarchives.gov.uk/details/r/C6509 (accessed 9 January 2017).

National Archives, 'General Eyres', available at http://www.national archives.gov.uk/help-with-your-research/research-guides/general-eyres-1194-1348/#sevenpointthree (accessed 30 July 2017)

National Archives, 'Land Conveyances by Feet of Fines 1182–1833', available at http://www.nationalarchives.gov.uk/help-with-your-research/research-guides/land-conveyance-feet-of-fines-1182-1833/ (accessed 9 January 2017)

National Archives, 'Pipe Rolls', available at http://www.nationalarchives. gov.uk/help-with-your-research/research-guides/medieval-financial-records-pipe-rolls-1130-1300/ (accessed 30 July 2017)

National Archives, 'Taxation Before 1689', available at http://www. nationalarchives.gov.uk/help-with-your-research/research-guides/taxation-before-1689/ (accessed 30 July 2017)

Neilson, N. 'Customary Rents', *Oxford Studies in Social and Legal History, Vol II* ed. Paul Vinogradoff (ed.) (5 vols) (Oxford, 1910), pp 97–219

Nelson, Edmund [Hobhouse], *Sketch of the Life of Walter de Merton Lord High Chancellor of England, and Bishop of Rochester, Founder of Merton College* (Oxford and London, 1859)

Newman, Richard, 'Planned Redevelopments in Medieval and Early Post-Modern Chesterton', *Proceedings of the Cambridge Antiquarian Society* 104 (2015): 89–106

Newman, Richard and Christopher Evans, 'Archaeological Investigations at the Old Schools, University of Cambridge', *Proceedings of the Cambridge Antiquarian Society* 100 (2011): 185–96

Newman, Richard, Alison Dickens and Christopher Evans et al., 'Some Splendid Rooms: Further Archaeological and Architectural Investigations in Jesus College, Cambridge, 1998–2011', *Proceedings of the Cambridge Antiquarian Society* 102 (2013): 73–92

Nicholson, H. J., *The Knights Templar in Britain: The Trial of the Templars in the British Isles 1308–1311* (Stroud, 2009)

Norfolk Heritage Explorer, 'Parish Summary: Thetford', available at http://www.heritage.norfolk.gov.uk/record-details?tnf2274 (accessed 21 February 2019)

North, D. C., *Structure and Change in Economic History* (New York, 1981)

Orme, Nicholas, 'The Medieval Schools of Cambridge, 1200–1550', *Proceedings of the Cambridge Antiquarian Society* 104 (2015): 125–36

Ormrod, D., J. M. Gibson, J. Baker and O. D. Lyne, 'City and Region – Urban and Agricultural Rent in England, 1400–1914', available at https://kar.kent.ac.uk/29287/ (accessed 12 April 2017)

Palliser, David M., *Towns and Local Communities in Medieval and Early Modern England* (Aldershot, 2006)

Palmer, William Mortlock, *Cambridge Castle* (Cambridge, n.d.)

Palmer, William Mortlock, 'Cambridge Castle Building Accounts 1286–1299', *Proceedings of the Cambridge Antiquarian Society* 26 (1925): 66–89

Palmer, W. M., 'The Manor House of the Argentines at Melbourn, and their Farm Accounts for 1317–18', *Proceedings of the Cambridge Antiquarian Society* 27 (1926): 16–79

Palmer, W. M., 'The Benedictine Nunnery of Swaffham Bulbeck', *Proceedings of the Cambridge Antiquarian Society* 31 (1929): 30–65

Palmer, W. M., 'A History of Clopton, Cambridgeshire', *Proceedings of the Cambridge Antiquarian Society* 33 (1933): 3–60

Palmer, W. M., 'The Stokes and Hailstone MSS.', *Proceedings of the Cambridge Antiquarian Society* 33 (1933): 169–70

Pearce, E. C., 'College Accounts of John Botwright, Master of Corpus Christi, 1443–74', *Proceedings of the Cambridge Antiquarian Society* 22 (1917–20): 76–90

Phythian-Adams, Charles, *Desolation of a City: Coventry and the Urban Crisis of the Late Middle Ages* (Cambridge, 1979)

Piketty, Thomas, *Capital in the Twenty-First Century* (Cambridge, MA, 2014),

Platt, C., *Medieval Southampton: The Port and Trading Community, A. D. 1000–1600* (London and Boston, MA, 1973)

Pollock, Frederick and Frederic Maitland, *The History of English Law Before the Time of Edward I* (Cambridge, 1895)

Prickett, Marmaduke, *Some Account of Barnwell Priory in the Parish of St Andrew the Less, Cambridge* (Cambridge, 1837)

Raban, Sandra, 'Mortmain in Medieval England', *Past and Present* 62 (1974): 3–26

Raban, Sandra, *Mortmain Legislation and the English Church 1279–1500* (Cambridge, 1982)

Raban, Sandra, *A Second Domesday: The Hundred Rolls of 1279–80* (Oxford, 2004)

Rackham, O., 'Why Corpus Christi?', *Corpus within Living Memory: Life in a Cambridge College* ed. M. E. Bury and E. J. Winter (London, 2003), pp 9–17

Raftis, J. A., *A Small Town in Late Medieval England: Godmanchester, 1278–1400* (Toronto, 1982)

Raftis, J. Ambrose, 'The Land Market at Godmanchester c.1300', *Medieval Studies* 50 (1988): 311–32

Razi, Zvi, 'Family, Land and the Village Community in Later Medieval England', *Past and Present* 93 (1) (1981): 1–36

Rees Jones, Sarah, *York: The Making of a City 1068–1350* (Oxford, 2013)

Reynolds, D. (ed.), *Christ's: A Cambridge College over Five Centuries* (London, 2005)

Rigby, S. H., *Boston, 1086–1225 A Medieval Boom Town* (Lincoln, 2017)

Robson, Michael, 'The Commemoration of the Living and the Dead at the Friars Minor of Cambridge', *Commemoration in Medieval Cambridge* ed. John S. Lee and Christian Steer (Woodbridge, 2018)

Rosenwein, Barbara H., *To Be a Neighbour of St Peter: The Social Meaning of Cluny's Property, 909–1049* (Ithaca, NY, and London, 1989)

Rosenthal, Joel T., *The Purchase of Paradise: Gift Giving and the Aristocracy, 1307–1485* (London and Toronto, 1972)

Rosser, Gervase, *Medieval Westminster 1200–1540* (Oxford, 1989)

Rosser, Gervase, *The Art of Solidarity in the Middle Ages: Guilds in England 1250–1550* (Oxford, 2015)

Round, J. H., 'The Third Penny', *English Historical Review* 34 (1919): 62–4

Rousseau, Marie-Hélène, *Saving the Souls of Medieval London: Perpetual Chantries at St Paul's Cathedral c. 1200–1548* (Farnham, 2011)

Royal Commission on the Historical Monuments of England, *City of Cambridge* (2 vols) (London, 1959)

Rubin, Miri, *Charity and Community in Medieval Cambridge* (Cambridge, 1987)

Rushe, J. P., 'The Origin of St Mary's Guild', *Proceedings of the Cambridge Antiquarian Society* 16 (1) (1912): 20–52

Rutledge, Elizabeth, 'Landlords and Tenants: Housing and the Rented Property Market in Early Fourteenth-Century Norwich', *Urban History* 22 (1) (1995): 7–24

Rutledge, E. 'Economic Life', *Medieval Norwich* ed. Carole Rawcliffe and Richard Wilson (London, 2004), pp 157–88

Salter, H. E., *Oxford City Properties* (Oxford, 1929)

Salter, H. E., *Medieval Oxford* (Oxford, 1936)

Salzman, L. F. (ed.), *A History of the County of Cambridge and the Isle of Ely, II, Victoria History of the Counties of England* (10 vols) III (London, 1948)

Sapoznik, Alexandra, 'Resource Allocation and Peasant Decision-Making: Oakington, Cambridgeshire, 1361–1393', *Agricultural History Review* 61 (2) (2013): 187–205.

Scales, Leonard E., 'The Cambridgeshire Ragman Rolls', *English Historical Review* 113 (452) (1998): 553–7

Schofield, Phillipp R., 'Lordship and the Early History of Peasant Land Transfer on the Estates of the Abbey of Bury St Edmunds', *Peasants and Lords in the Medieval English Economy: Essays in Honour of Bruce M. S. Campbell* ed. Maryanne Kowaleski, John Langdon and Phillipp R. Schofield (Turnhout, 2015), pp 201–24

Schumpeter, J. A., trans. R. Opie, *The Theory of Economic Development* (Cambridge, MA, 1934)

Skeat, Walter W., *The Place-Names of Cambridgeshire* (Cambridge, 1901)

Skeat, W. W., 'Grantchester and Cambridge', *Proceedings of the Cambridge Antiquarian Society* 14 (1) (1909): 111–22

Spufford, Margaret, 'General View of the Rural Economy of the County of Cambridge', *Proceedings of the Cambridge Antiquarian Society* 89 (2000): 69–85

Stacey, Robert C., 'Kilkenny, William of', *Oxford Dictionary of National Biography* ed. David Cannadine (Oxford, 2004)

Stell, Geoffrey P., 'Balliol, Bernard de (d. 1154x62)', *Oxford Dictionary of National Biography* ed. David Cannadine (Oxford, 2004)

Stephenson, Carl, *Borough and Town: A Study of Urban Origins in England* (Cambridge, MA, 1933)

Stokes, H. P., *The Chaplains and the Chapel of the University of Cambridge (1256–1568)* (Cambridge, 1906)

Stokes, H. P., *Outside the Barnwell Gate* (Cambridge, 1908)

Stokes, H. P., 'Early University Property', *Proceedings of the Cambridge Antiquarian Society* 13 (2) (1909): 164–84

Stokes, H. P., *The Esquire Bedells of the University of Cambridge from the Thirteenth Century to the Twentieth Century* (Cambridge, 1911)

Stokes, H. P., *Studies in Anglo-Jewish History* (Edinburgh, 1913)

Stokes, H. P., *Outside the Trumpington Gates before Peterhouse Was Founded* (Cambridge, 1915)

Stokes, H. P., 'Cambridgeshire "Forests"', *Proceedings of the Cambridge Antiquarian Society* 23 (1922): 63–85

Stokes, H. P., *The Medieval Hostels of the University of Cambridge* (Cambridge, 1924)

Stone, David, 'The Black Death and its Immediate Aftermath: Crisis and Change in the Fenland Economy, 1346–1353', *Town and Countryside in the Age of the Black Death* ed. Mark Bailey and Stephen Rigby (Turnhout, 2012), pp 213–44

Stubbings, F. H., 'The Church of the Cambridge Dominicans', *Proceedings of the Cambridge Antiquarian Society* 62 (1969): 95–104

Swanson, H., *Medieval British Towns* (Basingstoke, 1999)

Tait, James, *The Medieval English Borough: Studies on Its Origins and Constitutional History* (Manchester, 1936)

Tawney, R. H., *The Agrarian Problem in the Sixteenth Century* (London, 1912)

Taylor, A., *Cambridge: The Hidden History* (Stroud, 1999)

Toynbee, Arnold, *The Industrial Revolution* (Boston, MA, 1956)

The British Academy, *Reforming Business for The Twenty-First Century: A Framework For the Future of The Corporation*, available at https://www.thebritishacademy.ac.uk/sites/default/files/Reforming-Business-for-21st-Century-British-Academy.pdf (accessed 1 March 2019)

The Gen Guide, Patent Rolls, available at https://www.genguide.co.uk/source/patent-rolls-medieval-courts/5/ (accessed 9 January 2018)

Thomas, Keith, *The Ends of Life: Roads to Fulfilment in Early Modern England* (Oxford, 2009)

Thorold Rogers, James E., *A History of Agriculture and Prices in England and Wales, II, 1259–1400* (7 vols) (Oxford, 1866)

Turner, M. E., J. V. Beckett and B. Afton, *Agricultural Rent in England, 1690–1914*, (Cambridge, 1997)

Turner, Ralph V., *The English Judiciary in the Age of Glanvill and Bracton, c.1176–1239* (Cambridge, 1985)

Ullman, W., 'Review of *The Original Statutes of Cambridge University* by M.B. Hackett', *Journal of Ecclesiastical History* 22 (1971): 134–9

Underwood, M., 'The Impact of St John's College as Landowner in the West Fields of Cambridge in the Early Sixteenth Century', *Medieval Cambridge: Essays on the Pre-Reformation University* ed. P. Zutshi, (Woodbridge, 1993), pp 167–88

Underwood, Malcolm G., 'Dokett [Doket], Andrew (c. 1410–1484)', *Oxford Dictionary of National Biography* ed. David Cannadine (Oxford, 2004)

University of Nottingham Manuscripts and Special Collections Guide, 'Letters Patent', available at https://www.nottingham.ac.uk/manuscriptsandspecialcollections/researchguidance/deedsindepth/freehold/letterspatent.aspx (accessed 9 January 2018)

Van Houts, Elizabeth, 'Nuns and Goldsmiths: The Foundation and Early Benefactors of St Radegund's Priory at Cambridge', *Church and City, 1000–1500: Essays in Honour of Christopher Brooke* ed. David Abulafia, Michael Franklin and Miri Rubin (Cambridge, 1992), pp 59–79

Wade, E. M., 'Blankpayn, John, of Cambridge', *History of Parliament, 1386–1421*, available at https://www.historyofparliamentonline.org/ (accessed 12 June 2018)

Wade, E. M., 'Brigham, Robert, of Cambridge', *History of Parliament, 1386–1421*, available at https://www.historyofparliamentonline.org/ (accessed 12 June 2018)

Walker, F. G., 'Roman Roads into Cambridge', *Proceedings of the Cambridge Antiquarian Society* 14 (2) (1910): 141–74

Walker, Simon, 'John [John of Gaunt], Duke of Aquitaine and Duke of Lancaster, Styled King of Castile and León (1340–1399)', *Oxford Dictionary of National Biography* ed. David Cannadine (Oxford, 2004)

Weber, Max, trans. Talcott Parsons, *The Protestant Ethic and the Spirit of Capitalism* (London, 1976)

Wherry, G. E., 'Rings under the Eves of Old Houses', *Proceedings of the Cambridge Antiquarian Society* 12 (3) (1908): 232–40

Willis, Robert and John Willis Clark, *The Architectural History of the University of Cambridge and the Colleges of Cambridge and Eton* (2 vols) I (Cambridge, 1886)

Wilson, J., *British Business History, 1720–1994* (Manchester, 1995)

Wood, Diana, *Medieval Economic Thought* (Cambridge, 2002)

Wooldridge, Jeffrey M., *Introductory Econometrics: A Modern Approach* 5th ed. (Mason, OH, 2013)

Yamamoto, Koji, *Taming Capitalism before Its Triumph: Public Service, Distrust, and 'Projecting' in Early Modern England* (Oxford, 2018)

Zutshi, P. (ed.), *Medieval Cambridge: Essays on the Pre-Reformation University* (Woodbridge, 1993)

Zutshi, P., 'John Botwright Master of the College, 1443–1474', *Letter of the Corpus Association,* 77 (1998): 13–19

Theses

Alsford, Stephen, 'The Men Behind the Masque: Office-Holding in East-Anglian Boroughs, 1272–1460' (MPhil thesis, University of Leicester, 1982), available at http://www.trytel.com/~tristan/towns/mcontent.html (accessed 7 February 2018)

Clarke, Carolyn A., 'Peasant Society and Land Transactions in Chesterton, Cambridgeshire 1277–1325' (DPhil thesis, University of Oxford, 1985)

Howell, Cicely A. H., 'The Economic and Social Condition of the Peasantry in South East Leicestershire, A.D. 1300–1700' (DPhil thesis, University of Oxford, 1974)

Lowry, Edith Clark, 'The Administration of the Estates of Merton College in the Fourteenth Century: With Special Reference to the Black Death and the Problems of Labour' (DPhil thesis, University of Oxford, 1933)

Xu, Mingjie, 'Disorder and Rebellion in Cambridgeshire in 1381' (PhD thesis, University of Cambridge, 2016)

Index